THE RISE OF MODERN EUROPE
Edited by William L. Langer

FROM DESPOTISM
TO REVOLUTION

1 7 6 3 - 1 7 8 9

BY
LEO GERSHOY
New York University

ILLUSTRATED

HARPER & ROW, PUBLISHERS
NEW YORK AND EVANSTON

FROM DESPOTISM TO REVOLUTION, 1763-1789

Copyright, 1944, by Harper & Brothers
Printed in the United States of America

G-M

To

IDA

TABLE OF CONTENTS

v

LIST OF ILLUSTRATIONS

The illustrations, grouped in a separate section, will be found following page 142.

Numbers 1, 3, 4, 7, 10, 17, 18, 34, 42 and 57 are reproduced by
The Metropolitan Museum of Art

PREFACE

THIS study is in many respects a pioneering work. It represents an effort to treat the movement known as enlightened despotism on a European basis, as an integral part of the historical evolution of the Continent during the latter part of the eighteenth century. This is, of course, not to deny the very considerable importance of the royal reforms as a phase of the internal history of the particular countries involved, even where those activities were least successful. But enlightened despotism, or benevolent despotism as it is also called, is even more significant as a moment in the evolution of Europe as a whole. Precisely because it was complex in its antecedents and contradictory in its goals, precisely because it was a product born in some instances of the harmony and in others of the clash between men and institutions, it was a bridge between the old world and the new. It led from the Europe that had evolved out of feudalism to the Europe that was to attain parliamentary democracy in the nineteenth century and revert to authoritarianism in the twentieth.

Many aspects of this transition, important in themselves, are not treated in detail. On so vast a canvas one may not hope to do more than sketch the main lines with reasonable accuracy and clarity. Moreover, certain developments are treated more allusively than would otherwise be desirable, because the preceding volume in this series, by W. L. Dorn, *Competition for Empire, 1740-1763*, has already examined them with care and distinction. Such is the case with the intellectual foundations and the methodology of the *philosophes*, and the structure and functioning of the state. Where necessary for the development of another point of view I have not hesitated, however, to go over at least part of the same ground. So, for instance, with the treatment of Rousseau and the physiocrats. Finally, since a companion volume in the series is to cover the economic and industrial developments of the period, I have made no attempt to deal systematically with science, invention, and technology, all of which could also fall within the scope of this volume.

The temptation always exists, when the historian examines the past, for him to allow himself to be more distressed by the limitations of contemporary vision than gratified by evidence of its foresight. I trust that I have not yielded to that temptation to the extent of arraigning the eighteenth century for not seeing with the eyes of the twentieth. For among other reasons, I am not convinced that the clarity of vision has increased in direct ratio to the passage of time. In any case, whatever the conclusions, they are inferences drawn from evidence that seemed to me most relevant and valid.

I am greatly indebted to many individuals and institutions for assistance granted in one stage or another of my work. My grateful acknowledgment is due to the John Simon Guggenheim Memorial Foundation—and in particular to its secretary, Mr. Henry Allen Moe— which on two separate occasions granted me fellowships; to the many librarians in this country and Europe who placed their collections at my disposal; to those graduate students who refused to accept my less tenable conclusions. My thanks also go to Professors Carl L. Becker and Louis Gottschalk, and Lieutenant Garrett Mattingly, U.S.N.R., who read the manuscript in part or *in toto* and offered critical suggestions which, with an author's perversity, I did not always accept. My old friend, Mr. Spencer Brodney, drew generously upon his vast editorial experience and his nice sense of style to spare me where he could from the more vulgar pitfalls of expression. To Dr. S. K. Padover I am grateful for his suggestion of the title. Dr. W. L. Langer has been from the start an understanding adviser, and has now found time, heaven alone knows how, from the heavy responsibilities of his war work for the necessary labor of editing the manuscript. For permission to reproduce a number of illustrations I am indebted to the galleries, museums, or individuals whose names are given alongside the relevant reproductions in the list of illustrations.

The greatest pleasure of all is to acknowledge the help of my wife, though that pleasure is mitigated by the fear that she experienced the making of this book more turbulently than anyone had the right to do except the author himself. Her services covered all phases of intellectual activity. If they included prosaic tasks, like gathering or recording material, they were not less often extended to proffering constructive criticism with an amiability that never disguised the acuteness of her observations. Merely dedicating the book to her is a grossly inadequate expression of my thanks.

LEO GERSHOY

January 24, 1944
Washington, D. C.

INTRODUCTION

Our age of specialization produces an almost incredible amount of monographic research in all fields of human knowledge. So great is the mass of this material that even the professional scholar cannot keep abreast of the contributions in anything but a restricted part of his general subject. In all branches of learning the need for intelligent synthesis is now more urgent than ever before, and this need is felt by the layman even more acutely than by the scholar. He cannot hope to read the products of microscopic research or to keep up with the changing interpretations of experts, unless new knowledge and new viewpoints are made accessible to him by those who make it their business to be informed and who are competent to speak with authority.

These volumes, published under the general title of "The Rise of Modern Europe," are designed primarily to give the general reader and student a reliable survey of European history written by experts in various branches of that vast subject. In consonance with the current broad conception of the scope of history, they attempt to go beyond a merely political-military narrative, and to lay stress upon social, economic, religious, scientific and artistic developments. The minutely detailed, chronological approach is to some extent sacrificed in the effort to emphasize the dominant factors and to set forth their inter-relationships. At the same time the division of European history into national histories has been abandoned and wherever possible attention has been focused upon larger forces common to the whole of European civilization. These are the broad lines on which this history as a whole has been laid out. The individual volumes are integral parts of the larger scheme, but they are intended also to stand as independent units, each the work of a scholar well qualified to treat the period covered by his book. Each volume contains about fifty illustrations selected from the mass of contemporary pictorial material. All non-contemporary illustrations have been excluded on principle. The bibliographical note appended to each volume is designed to facilitate further study of special aspects touched upon in the text. In general every effort has been made to give the reader a clear idea of the main movements in European history, to embody the monographic contributions of research workers, and to present the material in a forceful and vivid manner.

Some of the most renowned of modern historians have been fascinated by the period covered in this volume, and have written about it critically as well as brilliantly. But almost without exception they have approached it because of their interest in the great French Revolution and in the hope of uncovering the origins of that great upheaval. Such an approach is certainly legitimate, but it can hardly be said that it does justice to the period itself. For the later eighteenth century well deserves consideration in its own right, as an era of great progress and real achievement. It was the age of enlightened or benevolent despotism, during which, in many countries, the old political and social concepts and institutions were discarded and new, often revolutionary ideas freely accepted and put into practice. Professor Gershoy has examined his subject in this spirit. He has attempted to analyze the theory and practice of the new monarchism and the new bureaucracy. In this sense he has undertaken a pioneer work. This volume is a fine piece of dispassionate, well-balanced inquiry, and a very substantial contribution to our knowledge of the European past.

WILLIAM L. LANGER

FROM DESPOTISM TO REVOLUTION

1763-1789

Chapter One

THE RULERS AND THE GOVERNMENTS

I. THE PEACE TREATIES AND POST-WAR PROBLEMS

EUROPE sank into peace in 1763, a merciful peace following a murderous war. The great states of the western world had all participated in the naked inter-continental struggle for power; and all the issues and gains of state rivalry had been engaged in that long Seven Years' War: colonies, commerce, and markets overseas; strategic frontiers in Europe itself and control over its human and material resources. The actual fighting ceased almost a year before the signing of the peace treaties. On the Continent it ended in a military stalemate between the two great Germanic rivals; and on the seas and in the colonies Great Britain scored a resounding triumph over the French-Spanish allies.

Nevertheless, the Treaty of Paris (February 10, 1763) between victorious Britain and the two Bourbon states departed from the lines of the military decision.[1] Put in terms of policy, the peace treaty did not beat France to her knees. It did not sweep her from North America, the West Indies, or even ancient India; and it failed to maintain that effective partnership between Britain and Prussia on the Continent which Pitt had so skillfully utilized to distract Gallic energies from the maritime and colonial struggle. Put in terms of men, the peace was the handiwork of Lord Bute and the still lesser men who had forced Pitt from office. There were placemen and timeservers in the ranks of the new British ministers, ambitious men beguiled by hopes of political advancement into sacrificing their country's prestige and surrendering those paramount imperial interests which Pitt had so unreservedly pursued. Above all other considerations, Bute was concerned with turning the diplomatic negotiations to the account of his

[1] For a discussion of the peace negotiations, consult the final chapter of the preceding volume in this series, W. L. Dorn, *Competition for Empire, 1740-1763* (New York, 1940).

young royal master and linking the king's name with peace and economy, thus gaining for George III the prestige and popularity without which he could not hope to end the humiliating "elevated nullification of the Crown."

The tactics of the chief French negotiator, the Duke of Choiseul, were therefore to drive a wedge between the British peacemakers and exploit to the full their fear that Pitt might be returned to office. For Choiseul the peace was to be only a respite from actual fighting, an armistice which France would terminate when she was again prepared to reopen the duel for empire. Consequently, he bent all his efforts toward securing a treaty which would give his country the bases for the renewal of the struggle. He made bitter concessions to the victor, but he saved France from the status of a second-rate power that Pitt had in store for her.

In North America proud Albion became master of the vast Louisiana Territory east of the Mississippi, as well as "the frozen acres" of Canada. France was left the islands of St. Pierre and Miquelon and retained her fishing rights off the Newfoundland banks. Indignant English patriots angrily clamored that their country also retain the captured West Indian sugar islands, but despite the immense strategic naval importance of Guadeloupe and Martinique the sugar bloc in Parliament succeeded in having them returned to France. For English planters, bankers and allied interests, with an enormous capital stake in sugar plantations in Barbados, Jamaica, and the Leeward Islands, it was the essence of sound business practice to exclude enemy competitors with a superior sugar-planting economy from their own monopoly in the British imperial-colonial market. In this way they could maintain high prices at home and simultaneously cripple French competition by suppressing the illicit West Indies sugar trade which was making vast fortunes for the merchant capitalists of the North American colonies.[2] So Choiseul obtained the retrocession of the West Indian islands. His country kept also the island of Gorée, commanding the slave trade of Senegal, along with several trading stations on the eastern coast of India.

Spain too fared better by the peace terms than might have been

---

[2] Cf. L. M. Hacker, *The Triumph of American Capitalism* (New York, 1940), ch. ii; also J. C. Miller, *Origins of the American Revolution* (Boston, 1943), 69-74.

expected under the circumstances of her defeat. She lost Florida to England and abandoned her old claims to the Newfoundland fisheries. But she kept her South American colonies and islands in the West Indies. The victor restored conquered Cuba and the Philippines, while Choiseul, in order to place a lien upon his ally's good will, ceded to her that part of the French territory of Louisiana, including the port of New Orleans, west of the Mississippi.

Prussia also ended the war a victor, for the separate Peace of Hubertusburg (February 15, 1763) with Austria sealed the military failure of Maria Theresa to dislodge Frederick from Silesia. This formal recognition of the Hohenzollern monarchy as one of the great European powers was undoubtedly a glorious triumph for the heroic ruler whose small state had been ringed around with powerful enemies. The great triumph, this "miracle of the house of Brandenburg," was nevertheless seared by long trails of devastation. The lives of hundreds of thousands of his loyal subjects had been snuffed out. Thousands of families had been uprooted; scores of towns and villages had been burned to the ground. Ravaged and desolate fields stood untilled; epidemics raged, and hunger stalked the wilderness of what once had been flourishing scenes of peaceful toil. The formidable troops that had begun the war, so well equipped and supplied and so obediently responsive to an iron discipline, had degenerated during those terrible last years into shelterless and famished marauders, half-living and half-dying, and yearning for the peace that never came. For all of Frederick's brilliant strategy and his resounding victories, those years saw the Prussian ruler increasingly hard pressed. When he lost his British subsidy, the black abyss of extinction gaped before him. But the powerful anti-Hohenzollern coalition fashioned so tenderly by Kaunitz disintegrated; and after years of useless suffering, of futile expenditure of manpower and matériel, Maria Theresa was forced finally to admit that Silesia was lost. She sued for peace and Frederick was saved. Indeed he was victorious.[3]

The blessings of peace fell upon Europe. Until the armed doctrine of revolutionary France precipitated a new international conflict which

[3] *Mémoires de Frédéric II*, ed. by E. Boutaric and E. Compardon (Paris, 1866), II, 311-315, 388-389, 407-409, gives Frederick's own picture of the ruin and desolation. Cf. the vivid account in C. V. Easum's valuable biography, *Prince Henry of Prussia, Brother of Frederick the Great* (Madison, 1942), ch. xv.

was not to end until Waterloo, the Continent enjoyed a respite from major wars. Only a respite, however. The treaties of 1763 ushered in a peace without repose, a truce without tranquillity. Almost before the ink was dry on the agreements France and Spain were challenging the new equilibrium of empire. Triumphant Frederick yearned for peace and an opportunity for recuperation, but the restless territorial aggressions of Austria and the dynamic expansionist program of Russia made unflagging military preparation and tireless diplomatic vigilance the vital preoccupations of the Prussian state. No major war, then, but continuous tension magnified by the fiercer economic rivalries of commercial capitalism marked the relations of the powers for the next quarter of a century.

II. THE RULERS

Everywhere, in greater or lesser measure, the war had dislocated the normal economy. War finance had inflated prices, increased taxes, and swelled the public debt. When peace finally came and normal trade between Europe and the colonial world was resumed, accumulated stocks of goods were thrown on the market, prices collapsed, and merchants were swept to ruin. Peace also ended the ramified speculative transactions incidental to war finance. First in the great marts Amsterdam and Hamburg, then concurrently in Stockholm and Copenhagen, Berlin and Marseilles, wealthy banking houses crashed to the ground.[4]

The first years of peace found rulers straining all their resources to solve the immediate domestic problems of post-war adjustments. These problems were narrowly economic, but economic readjustment involved the play of political forces. And the monarch himself was a focal point in these political storms. No serious obstacle presented itself in the Germanies to the initiative of royal absolutism. Though worthy and even distinguished practitioners of enlightened rule, such as Charles William Ferdinand of Brunswick, Karl August of Weimar, and Karl Friedrich of Baden, graced the thrones of the larger secondary

---

[4] Cf. Tobias Smollett, *Travels through France and Italy* (London, 1766), II, 234-235, for the collapse of colonial prices; and P. J. Blok, *History of the People of the Netherlands*, V, 146-148, for northern Europe.

states of the Empire, it was the Austrian and the Prussian rulers who set the pace of reform. Above all others loomed the glamorous and heroic figure of Frederick II.

In 1763, Prussia was a bleeding stump, drained of vitality, and all the fortitude of the hatchet-faced and iron-willed ruler was tested in his long effort to bind up the mutilated end. He was only fifty-one years of age when the war ended, but in his own eyes as well as in those of his subjects, he was even then *der alte Fritz.* "It is a poor old man who is coming home," he said, "I'm returning to Potsdam where I won't find any of my old friends and where immense toil awaits me." The fighting had taken a heavy toll of this champion of rococo elegance and culture. It had hardened his heart, embittered his thoughts, and disciplined his once palpitating zest for life into the cold compulsion of duty. He, the man of the rococo, so typical of the best of his age in his clear and logical intelligence, his wit and grace, his love of books and music, his luxurious joy in sharp food and sharper conversation, he the triumphant commander, felt himself alone among the shadows of his dead generals and his old companions. He had become moody and irascible, fleeing the inanity of courtly existence, discouraging visitors, relaxing from his heavy duties in solitary promenades, in the melancholy pleasures of his music and his writing, and in the occasional treat of discussion with a few confidants. Excepting only his youngest sister Amelia, his relations with his own flesh and blood were never intimate and rarely friendly. His beloved sister Wilhelmina had died; his brother Prince Henry he had never won. To his wife he was unspeakably distant and chilly. He had married her against his will, and from her he demanded only the indifference that he so plentifully bestowed. The society of women was felicity that nature had not designed for him.

Indifferent to ceremony and attire, even to cleanliness, he drove himself hard, arising with the dawn and jealously allocating every hour of his long day to the consuming needs of the state. Simplicity reigned in the charming New Palace at Potsdam. Neither the gilded extravaganza of Versailles nor the calisthenics of courtesy which made the French court the European model of formal elegance obtruded on this replica of Gallic artistic and cultural genius. One sees Frederick best at his most informal, as his few friends and associates knew him, head cocked to one side, broad hat shadowing his forehead and penetrating eyes, in his patched blue suit lined and faced with red, snuff-stained yellow waistcoat and breeches, and heavy boots. On rare festive occasions he would deck himself out in a silver-embroidered, blue velvet company suit. At the dinner table the stooped figure would straighten itself, the thin sarcastic mouth soften, and the piercing blue eyes flash as animation returned to the weary features. And what a flood of witty and brilliant conversation rolled forth from the tired cynic! The Prince de Ligne, who paid compliments with difficulty, wrote, "His conversation was encyclopedic! The fine arts, medicine, literature and religion, philosophy, morality, history and legislation passed, each in turn, in review."[5]

Heavy, too, were the post-war problems of the widespread Hapsburg monarchy, the mighty heir of the Caesars. Its newly installed civil administration had broken down, the military machine had crumbled, and the loss of Silesia had disorganized economic life. For Maria Theresa herself the rose had already lost its bloom when the sudden death of her husband—that otherwise forgotten man of the century—plunged her into the black sorrow of widowhood. The death of Francis of Lorraine in 1765 was a terrible blow to this *gemütliche* matriarch, this statuesque pink and white Brünnehilde of lively blue eyes and delicate features, who had ripened into lissom grace and flowing curves in the Danubian sun. In her early years, as a young bride, she had been the life of the stiff, ceremonious court. Despite the exuberant and monumental baroque which commemorated Hapsburg victory over the Turks, despite the profuse expenditures of a seemingly limitless wealth, the Austrian aristocracy had successsfully reduced court life to an almost institutionalized inanity. As a young empress Maria Theresa had breathed a fresh and charming spirit into the gloom. Whether at her favorite residence at the delightful chateau of Schönbrunn just outside of Vienna, or in her winter residence at the cold and cheerless Hofburg, planned by the great Fischer von Erlach, card playing and dancing, amateur musicales and theatricals, rounds of parties and merry excursions, riding and sleighing gave a

---

[5] Dr. John Moore, *A View of Society and Manners in France, Switzerland, and Germany,* 2 vols. (London, 1780), II, 244-256 (ed. of 1783); P. Gaxotte, *Frederick the Great* (New Haven, 1942), chs. xi-xii; and G. B. Volz, *Friedrich der Grosse im Spiegel seiner Zeit,* 3 vols. (Berlin, 1926-1927), II and III.

spurious gaiety to a court existence that had attained a portentous pitch of dullness and stupidity. These innocent enjoyments, shared only by the 2,400 permanent members of her magnificent retinue, devoured even her great income, and she barely managed to make both ends meet on 6,000,000 florins per annum.

As time went on, as the heavy cares of motherhood—and her still heavier responsibilities as mother of her people—weighed upon her, Maria Theresa's gaiety waned and her devotions were multiplied. Amiable and kindhearted the empress was, and liberally endowed both with courage and with tact. But her intelligence was limited and rigid, and her piety coalesced with her royalist and aristocratic convictions, coloring her outlook and stamping it with an acute abhorrence for the innovations of the *"Aufklärungspartei"* to which the intractable Joseph belonged. Between mother and son lay an unbridgeable gap, for nothing could bring together her baroque conservatism and his zealous humanitarian fervor. Grief-stricken after the death of Francis, she turned for solace to the austere beauties of religion; and for the inescapable and secular tasks of reconstruction she leaned heavily upon the indispensable Kaunitz, trusting that the old reliable servant would hold her domineering son in leash.[6]

Apart from the Hohenzollern, the Hapsburg, and the large secondary states, there were the duodecimo princelets of the Holy Roman Empire, who were unimportant politically even when enlightened. In the Italian peninsula Lombard and Tuscan patrician intellectuals, ably seconded by liberal bourgeois entrepreneurs, had early in the century set into motion a train of reforms, while a new spirit of inquiry arose also in the retrograde Kingdom of the Two Sicilies. The dour fanatical premier, the Marquis of Pombal, was giving enlightened despotism its bloody certificate of credit in Portugal; and the Spanish throne was graced by Charles III, eldest son of Philip V and Elizabeth Farnese, enthroned in 1759 after his reforming efforts in the Two Sicilies. He was no intellectual giant, this squat, brick-faced, hawk-nosed enthusiast of the chase. But he was one of the major rulers of the century and one of Spain's greatest. Though his stock of ideas

6 Moore, *op. cit.*, II, 300 ff., 335, 382, 394; M. von Boehm, *Deutschland im achtzehnten Jahrhundert* (Berlin, 1921), 238 ff.; H. Kretschmayr, *Maria Theresia*, new ed. (Leipzig, 1938), 147-208.

was sparse, they were for the most part of his age at its most progressive and he clung to them with invincible tenacity. Admirable too was the methodical devotion with which he plied his royal profession. His court was free from even the suspicion of petticoat influence. Gravely, as became a Spanish grandee, and with regal dignity, he governed his land with a systematic absence of imagination that gave ponderous reassurance to his fortunate subjects. He gave full constitutional authority to his remarkable reforming ministers and supported them unswervingly against their critics in their far-reaching program of national regeneration and social welfare.[7]

Far east in Europe, in Russia, a political struggle loomed, a conflict over the issue whether Catherine II would actually rule or merely reign. Beautiful in the accepted sense the German-born usurper was not, but of her attractiveness there can be no two opinions. She was of medium height, possessing in 1763 a good figure that had not yet broadened into the ampler proportions of her later years. She had an open forehead and a slightly aquiline nose. Her vivacious blue eyes were shielded by thick black eyebrows and set off by a fine head of chestnut hair. The long, unhappy years preceding her elevation to the throne had fashioned her character and molded her views. They had taught her prudence and caution—indeed, the need for dissimulation: to mask her turbulent emotions and veil her resolution. Aware of the popular patriotic hostility, she, the foreigner, had ingratiated herself, strategically building up her own coterie at the court and among the Palace Guard. Audacity, a bold gamble, if not homicide itself, had won her the throne. Henceforth she had to draw upon all her courage and charm, as well as her intelligence and patience, to make her power secure. In the early years of imposed leisure, when she was still only a grand duchess, she had read extensively in the French philosophers. From their works she had mined a rich store of serviceable information. Most important, perhaps, she had found a learned corroboration for her own deep and intuitive conviction that the most rational art of government lay in following the practices of enlightened absolutism. However inconsistent she may have been in her emotional

---

[7] Henry Swinburne, *Travels . . . through Spain in the Years 1775 and 1776* (London, 1778), 334-336; Desdevises du Dézert, "L'Espagne de l'ancien régime," in *Revue hispanique*, LXX (1927), 16 ff.

life—and of her mutability some evidence exists—her political career as empress proceeded faithfully down the line of that single con-viction.[8]

III. GOVERNMENTS AND THEIR POLICIES

Rulers also had their troubles at home. The emergencies of post-war recuperation and stabilization were perplexing enough, but the normal growing pains of institutionalized absolutism were not less acute. Problems, implicit in the very development of royal absolutism, pressed for solution—problems of social relations, of the full utilization of the national economic resources, and of the place of the individual in governmental relations. By the mid-century Prussia had emerged as a dominant power in central Europe, the great vitalizing nucleus of that conglomeration of territories which was neither Holy, nor Roman, nor an Empire. From the days of the Great Elector the rulers of Brandenburg-Prussia had subordinated all other considerations to the fundamental task of fashioning a united and centralized state out of the scattered dynastic provinces which were separated from one an-other by geography and by persistent and intangible particularist traditions. In 1740 the true architect of the Prussian system, the bull-headed, irascible, and unbending martinet, Frederick William I, be-queathed to his frivolous, flute-playing son Frederick the newly rooted ways of an absolutist monarchy.[9] His subjects were united in com-pulsory obligations to the state, and the state itself was served by an inordinately large but peerless army and a disciplined and loyal bureaucracy of civil servants. Compared to its neighbors, Austria, France, and Russia, Prussia was only a tiny country of 4,500,000 sub-jects with an annual revenue of only 7,000,000 thalers, plus a metallic reserve of 8,000,000 more. But it was, in terms of power and prestige, already great, a model for other and larger states.

The institutional core of the governmental system was the old Gen-

---

[8] V. O. Kluchevsky, *A History of Russia*, 5 vols. (London, 1911-1931), V, ch. i; G. Sacke, "Katharina II. von Russland im Kampf um Thron und Selbstherrschaft," in *Archiv für Kulturgeschichte*, XXIII (1932), 191-216.

[9] S. B. Fay, *The Rise of Brandenburg-Prussia, to 1786* (in the *Berkshire Studies in European History*, New York, 1937), chs. ii and iii, gives a succinct account of the origins of the Prussian Kingdom; also M. Braubach, *Der Aufstieg Brandenburg-Preussens, 1640 bis 1815* (Freiburg, 1933), ch. iii; and the valuable study of Frederick's father, R. E. Ergang, *The Potsdam Fuehrer* (New York, 1941).

eral-Supreme-War-Finance-Domains Directory that Frederick William I had established in 1723. At the beginning of Frederick's reign it was still divided into its original four departments, each of which had its own presiding minister and its staff of trained specialists. There was, however, no prime minister to provide continuous direction of policy or to give quick impetus to deliberations. Despite those specialized and in many respects autonomous ministries, the collegiate principle of collective responsibility still prevailed; and as the decisions had to be signed by all four ministers, the plenary session of the Directory only too often provided an opportunity for lengthy debate over departmental disputes. Other specialized services were handled by such boards as the State Conference for Foreign Affairs (*Cabinetsministerium*), the High Court of Appeals (*Oberappelationsgericht*), and the various civil and military treasuries that had budded off from the original Privy Council. From the point of view of modern governmental efficiency the structure of the central administration was annoyingly cumbersome. But it discharged its obligations, and more than adequately. The officials of the central and provincial administration, whether bourgeois or noble, were the best trained in all Europe, having obtained their positions through professional merit. Moreover, for almost half a century Frederick was in direct personal control, literally personal, of the central administration. By disregarding the formal mechanism, ignoring protocol, cutting through bureaucratic red tape, establishing new specialized departments, and working directly with special commissions and the invaluable secretaries who constituted his unofficial "Cabinet" at Potsdam, he gave the cumbersome machine a flexibility such as it never had had before or ever was to have again.

Frederick's personal intervention in provincial administration was equally decisive, especially after 1748. By going over the heads of recognized ministers, he established direct and regular and confidential contacts with the president of each provincial board (*Kammer*) and did much to overcome the blight of collective responsibility which prolonged discussions, compounded confusion, and generated sharp personal rivalries and jealousies. Once determined, the resolutions were implemented by the various executive officials of the provincial board, subject to the check of the secret central agents called "fiscals."

Of these provincial officials the first in importance was the *Landrat*. He was a paid official, usually appointed by the king from a panel of local noblemen, with jurisdiction over the rural area within each of the Districts (*Kreise*) into which the province was subdivided. His colleague, the local commissary (*Steuerrat*), had full jurisdiction over the urban communities of his particular *Kreis*. The authority of these officials was as final as their competence was broad, for there was little indeed of public and individual activity that did not come within the flexible rubric of the "*Polizei*," which defined the scope of their authority. The local bailiff (*Amtmann*) represented the crown in the leased royal domain.

The private patrimonial estate was the most numerous unit and the ultimate base of the local administrative system. For obvious reasons such estates required little supervision and less regulation on the part of the royal bureaucratic officials. It was not to the interests of the patrimonial proprietor to challenge the all-embracing authority of the *Polizeistaat*. To serve the state was the career par excellence of the Junker, whether he served it in the military branch which was almost his monopoly or as an unpaid civil servant on his lands. He lost nothing by his loyalty, for in addition to many personal privileges he was given virtually a free hand over the peasantry on his estate. For them he was indeed the state: police official, justice of the peace, tax collector, and recruiting officer, all rolled into one.[10]

While the moribund Holy Roman Empire staggered fitfully toward its final extinction, the dynastic Hapsburg realm, which was the vital core of that "chaos upheld by providence," vigorously secured itself against disaster. When Joseph became emperor and co-regent with his mother Maria Theresa, in 1765, the miracle of administrative reorganization had already been accomplished. The hereditary possessions of the House of Austria (excluding the distant possession of the Netherlands, the transalpine Duchy of Milan, and the still nominally autonomous lands of the Hungarian crown) had been consolidated into a unitary political state. In 1763, when the great war was over, Vienna had the necessary administrative equipment at hand: a United

10 Cf. the admirable articles of W. L. Dorn, "The Prussian Bureaucracy in the Eighteenth Century," in *Political Science Quarterly*, XLVI (1931), 403-423; XLVII (1932), 75-94; 259-273.

Bohemian-Austrian Chancery to handle domestic civil and fiscal affairs, a centralized War Office, a Foreign Office (headed from 1753 by Kaunitz), a Ministry of Commerce, a High Court of Justice, and a unified Treasury, together with a number of temporary commissions for special purposes.

In reorganizing the provincial administration the royal reformers effected an administrative revolution which lasted with only minor modifications until the middle of the nineteenth century. In essence, it was the destruction of the governmental autonomy of the provinces comprising the lands of the Bohemian crown (Bohemia, Moravia, and Austrian Silesia) and their reduction to the status of the already non-autonomous provinces of the lands of the Austrian crown (the Austrian duchies proper, Tyrol, Styria, Carinthia, and Carniola). Racial and religious diversity still obtained, but administrative unity was in the making. Early in Maria Theresa's reign the Viennese bureaucrats coerced the provincial diets (*Landtage*) of the Austrian and Bohemian crown lands into sacrificing the complete fiscal immunity of the aristocracy with respect to the basic land tax and into having Viennese officials supervise the new tax arrangements. Hapsburg absolutism was becoming a reality. The provincial *Landtage* continued to hold their periodical assemblies after the first of the ten-year agreements (*Dezenniale Recesse*), but their power had been taken from them: the presiding officer in time came to be a state official, the Governor, who headed a newly created provincial administrative unit (the *Gubernia*).

As in Prussia, which furnished the model for many of the changes, the Hapsburg provincial unit was divided into districts (*Kreise*), each of which had its collegiate board of civil servants (*Kreisamt*). Yet for a variety of reasons the temper of the Hapsburg officials, particularly of the executive head of the district, the *Kreishauptmann*, was distinctly more anti-provincial and anti-feudal than in the Hohenzollern realm. Bohemia was thoroughly co-ordinated, but Hungary still enjoyed a degree of self-rule in 1763 that was entirely anachronistic in that heyday of centralized absolutism. The establishment of the new Council of State (*Staatsrat*) in 1761 foreboded the end of Maria Theresa's policy of more or less delicate handling and insidious corruption of the magnates (her famous "*douce violence*") and marked the beginning of a sharper drive to bring the Hungarian crown lands into the unified Austrian-Bohemian system. For such an intransigent policy the young Joseph was ready, prepared by temperament and fortified by his training at the sessions of the Council of State.[11]

In Russia, too, the crown was theoretically supreme, organized according to Peter the Great's intent "after the model of a merchant's counting house." The state was secular, and absolutist, too, in the sense that it was secure against any formidable military threat to its authority. But the absolutism of the crown veiled the effective power of the landowning nobility (the *dvorianstvo*). The old aristocracy of blood had been numerically swamped by the new service nobility first created by Peter, the new army of vested interests where the position of the official determined his rank in the table of the nobility. The four decades between the death of the first great Russian "Westerner" and the accession of Catherine II had, however, played havoc with his intention of making the nobility the instrument of monarchical rule. Profiting by the recurring disorders between 1726 and 1762, the landed and service nobility had gained a large degree of control over the direction of state activities. When Catherine ascended the throne, they monopolized the positions in the central ministries and councils and the all-important Senate; and in their praetorian shock troops, the Palace Guard, they had the power to make and unmake monarchs—as Catherine knew only too well. The monarchy had also delegated or sacrificed all rights of effective surveillance to the gentry in local administration. The subordinate officials of the province who stemmed from and were (from 1761) elected by the petty landed proprietors were only nominally under the jurisdiction of the royal governor. In Russia even as in Prussia the bedrock of public administration was the patrimonial estate, with the private proprietor exercising the duties and holding the powers both of feudal lord and of governmental servant over his peasantry.

Whatever the appearance, the actual governmental structure of Russia rested upon shifting and outmoded foundations that could not bear the stress of new needs. In addition, the administration of justice

---

11 I. Beidtel, *Geschichte der oesterreichischen Staatsverwaltung, 1740-1792* (Innsbruck, 1896); also H. Marczali, *Hungary in the Eighteenth Century* (Cambridge, 1910); and R. J. Kerner, *Bohemia in the Eighteenth Century* (New York, 1932).

was not yet separated from political administration; an organic law code and uniform legal procedure were both conspicuously absent; and the civil servants were corrupt, ill trained, and grossly inadequate in number for the vast stretches of the country.[12]

Pre-partition Poland was an anarchy tempered by civil war. It was a feudal congeries of provinces dominated centrally by the great magnates and locally by the gentry. It lived by the sufferance of its powerful neighbors. Stubbornly jealous of their "golden liberties," and spurred by racial and religious hatreds, the Polish landed aristocracy had seemingly hypnotized themselves into crusading for self-extinction. The king, whom they elected, was little more than a presiding officer of the diet (*sejm*), narrowly restricted in the scope of his power by the *pacta conventa* which he signed with his electors. Each royal election, since the extinction of the Jagellon dynasty, furnished the occasion for violence at home and for intrigue, bribery, or interference from abroad. The effective control of the diet and with it of the country rested with the gentry. They sat—there were two houses—not as representatives of the public but as quasi-plenipotentiaries from the local assemblies (dietines) of the provinces and were bound by instructions to vote for family or corporate interests, even against the national interest. By a flexible interpretation of the famous *liberum veto*, which called for a unanimous vote, they could hamstring proceedings in any given assembly, force its dissolution, and even nullify previous decisions. In such a case the dissidents formed either armed "confederations," on a county basis, or a general confederation, on a national basis, which according to constitutional theory could pass binding resolutions by a majority vote. If the king joined such a confederation, he made it legal; if he indicted its members as rebels, a period of civil strife ensued. With a tiny army far inferior in strength to that of one of the great magnates; with a small privy purse and a state income perhaps one-fiftieth that of the current revenue of the French crown; without the numerical, technical, or financial support of a middle class; and with hungry neighbors surrounding it, the Polish republic was slated for early death.[13]

[12] V. O. Kluchevsky, *op. cit.*, IV, chs. xii-xvi; and S. F. Platonov, *Histoire de la Russie* (Paris, 1929), 703-754.

[13] See the lucid chapter iii of P. Skwarczynski, "The Constitution of Poland before the

The general trend in the Scandinavian states during this period favored the landed aristocracy at the expense of the crown, while in the United Provinces it was the municipal oligarchies that held the royal executive in leading strings. In the Italian peninsula conditions varied enormously, ranging from the comparative governmental efficiency of Piedmont and real enlightenment of the Hapsburg-ruled duchies of Tuscany and Lombardy to the almost legendary maladministration of the Papal States and the Kingdom of the Two Sicilies. In Portugal Pombal was ruthlessly extirpating the forces opposing institutional absolutism. At Madrid absolutism also made headway. A multiplicity of councils, boards, and commissions may have ". . . divided up the powers of the crown the way an executioner quarters a condemned man." The new provincial administrators, the intendants and the *corregidores*, may have been checked by old provincial and ecclesiastical barriers stemming from the feudal and mediaeval past. The subordinate officials may have been imperfectly trained, something less than honest, and not entirely disinclined to evading responsibility. Doubtlessly the fiscal administration was both corrupt and inefficient, the crown's revenue meager, and the public expenditures disproportionately high. Yet slowly and surely the royalist reformers hacked away at the vestiges of the past. The resourceful new state officials undermined old institutional arrangements and triumphed over man's hostility. The incomplete and roughly hewn framework of a bureaucratic system already existed when Charles III began that astounding chapter of Spain's regeneration which almost invested loyalty to the crown with the sanctity and intensity of religious belief.[14]

Absolutism in central and eastern Europe had manifestly come to a turning point. Paced by Richelieu and Mazarin and the *grand monarque* himself in the seventeenth century and by Prussia a century later, the makers of modern Europe had advanced a long way toward institutionalizing government in the name of the absolute monarch. They had set up on the firm foundation of law and order an intricate network of public obligations linking the individual subject

---

Partitions," in *The Cambridge History of Poland, 1697-1935* (Cambridge, 1941), ed. by W. F. Reddaway and others.
14 A. Ballesteros y Beretta, *Historia de España y de su influencia en la historia universal,* 6 vols. (Barcelona, 1918-1932), VI, ch. i; G. Desdevises du Dézert, *loc. cit.,* 56 ff.

to royal authorities. They had made memorable progress toward the ideal of public administration by trained officials, skilled in their specialized functions, professionally impersonal in their code of conduct, and accepting responsibility to the monarch for their acts. While the princes had no choice but to avow their own responsibility as the first servants of the state, the range of governmental activity itself had broadened enormously.

Yet never before had monarchical absolutism stood in such need of inspired guidance. At the moment of its great triumph in making princely rule the uncontested norm of political relations, an old perplexing problem obtruded itself, the problem of determining anew for whose benefit the prince should exercise the rule that no one contested at home. In Prussia and Russia royal absolutism was largely a façade for the effective rule of the aristocracy of birth who employed their broad powers to retard the advance of enlightened absolutism or put absolutist means to their own personal, family, and corporate ends. Whatever the personal inclination of Frederick II or Catherine II may have been, or the desires of an influential minority of supporters, the disposition of social forces in each of these *Herrenstaaten* gave a strong backward tug to Prussian and Russian living, pulling it back to the regime of caste, provincial autonomies, corporate privileges, and patrimonial and feudal relations.

Conversely, in the Hapsburg state, Spain, and most of the Italian peninsula, strategically important groups or individuals in the administration demanded that the control devices of absolutism be loosened. They looked forward to a relaxation of the rules and regulations that still hampered and hemmed in the free play of individual initiative. Urging them forward were wealthy commoners and progressive patricians, comparatively few in number, not strong enough to assume direction of governmental policy and aghast at the very thought of toppling princes from their thrones, yet exceedingly eager to restrict the scope of governmental activity. Above all they wanted to direct state activity along lines best calculated to serve the public welfare by simultaneously serving the private good of the moneyed classes whose cause they represented. If indifference to their trading and manufacturing interests was the least defect of the new aristocracy of wealth, not the least of their virtues was their stand in the van of the European movement for a more enterprising and imaginative use of human and material resources. Joined in spirit with the French *philosophes* and identified in material interests with the bourgeoisie of western Europe, these progressives of central, eastern, and southern Europe reconciled themselves to their contemporary prosperity but also formulated the prints of a superior economy of abundance for the future. Whether the orientation looked forward to the modern regime of contract and the pattern of political democracy or back toward the regime of status, in all these continental states it was still the crown that initiated and directed public policies. Their common model was England, but an England admired far more for her achievements than for her administrative practices and constitutional theory.

IV. ENGLAND

An extraordinary spurt of economic production had brought prosperity to England's possessing classes during the years of strife, though the immediate post-war deflation loomed disastrously for the entire nation. The public debt had risen from slightly over £72,000,000 to £132,000,000; and the annual carrying charges from just under £3,-000,000 to more than £5,000,000. Unemployment kindled the fires of mass discontent, and economic stress soon coalesced with political grievances. George III had ascended the throne in 1760 on the crest of victory, indeed, of high popular enthusiasm, for the young ruler who brought triumph to England was British born, unlike his two Hanoverian predecessors. Bute's peace cast a first shadow over his popularity; and soon the fatal flaws in the king's political plans, reinforced by his defects of character, precipitated a grim and violent political conflict.

The king's project, far from being the infamous Lord Bute-George III plot against a hallowed, albeit non-existent, English constitution, rested on at least a superficially plausible constitutional theory of its own.[15] Ideally speaking, George III aimed to restore an independent sovereign in the very pattern of Bolingbroke's "Patriot King," who,

15 For the scholarly *coup de grâce* to the Whig version of the king's intentions, consult the two works of L. B. Namier, *The Structure of Politics at the Accession of George III*, 2 vols. (London, 1929); and *England in the Age of the American Revolution* (London, 1930).

while mindful of the constitutional restrictions set upon his office, would initiate his own policy and choose his ministers for their fitness alone, irrespective of their party affiliations. By breaking the power of the Whig oligarchy and destroying ministerial corruption at its source, the royal reformer would effectively re-establish the independence of the legislature and also become empowered to rule in fact and not rest condemned merely to reign in name.

The royal intent unquestionably synchronized with existing public discontent. It was more than a protest against the Newcastle system of parliamentary corruption and apparent debasement of royal influence. It rested on a broadening interpretation of kingship, on an anglicized version of the continental idea of the state as trustee, of a refurbished monarchy using its constitutional authority to further the realization of evolving national needs. Regrettably, it had the rather important demerit of violating the constitutional compromise of 1688, for which the English people had already staged a sanguinary struggle that with characteristic understatement they preferred to call the "bloodless revolution." Though the king made no direct attempt to extend the prerogative, the consequences of his intent to constitute himself "a crowned Duke of Newcastle" could only be the reduction of Parliament to a mere agency of the royal administration. Perhaps the advisers of the king as much as George III himself made the "king's system" as odious as Newcastle's; but the king's character also proved a majestic disqualification.

There was in fact strikingly little in the king's personality to hold the admiration of his contemporaries and gain him the kindness of posterity. Ancestry and education had endowed him with the major domestic virtues. He was simple in manner and physically brave. His moral rectitude was invincible and his piety was impregnably secure against latitudinarian probings. His stubbornness and his arbitrary will could be forgiven him, indeed his conceit and vindictive temper, for he suffered from the disadvantage of having been born to the purple. But he had no inkling of the new mood that was dawning. He never broadened in sympathy toward the new demands that came with the slow unraveling of the familiar pattern of social relations. Surrounded by petty politicians who used his impatience with Parliament for their own interests, he was pushed back into the grooves of the past, grad-

ually becoming identified in the popular mind with a policy of vindictive reaction.

The silver sea in which the precious stone of England was set served
it in an office never described by Shakespeare, for one of the greatest
benefits that the Channel conferred was to keep England secure from
the administrative absolutism of the Continent. England knew no
droit administratif; and her officials could invoke no *raison d'état* to
override the common law, the irremovable judges, and the jury of
commoners that protected the rights of the free-born individual. The
standing army was always regarded with suspicion and its strength was
kept down by a jealous Parliament to the lowest point consistent with
national safety; and even a paid constabulary awakened fears of royal
outrage. Admiring foreigners dutifully genuflected before the visible
glories of the parliamentary system. There is no question that parliamentarism was a buffer of the strongest sort against despotism; but it
had the defects of its qualities. The famed checks and balances were
more apparent than real; the two-party system was only nascent; and
ministerial responsibility to a Parliament supposedly representative of
the sovereign people was largely a myth. Land was king in England,
land and all other forms of property; and the Parliament, composed
of squires, lawyers, and placemen, legislated in the interests of the
great proprietors. The new aristocracy was entrenched at every strategic
point in the governing system: in Parliament, the church, the military,
the law, the universities, and, not least, the local administration.
Property and liberty were veritably one in the minds of most Englishmen. Individual ownership was the greatest single shield against
despotism. The home of the individual Englishman was his castle, and
his private life was "sweet majesty."

The unpaid worthies in charge of local government could not compare with the trained and efficient civil servants on the Continent.
Lacking professional training, they had only the faintest conception
of the high bureaucratic standards that prevailed elsewhere. Perhaps
their administration was both mild and beneficent, and gratefully
accepted by their public wards. Such a relationship is not inconceivable,
but there is adequate evidence that their rough sense of justice was
often tinctured with brutality and their conception of liberty was
ignorant and anti-social. From the point of view of English develop-

ments the reform movement which helped to install a growing minority of superior personnel among the justices of the peace, selectmen, and lesser parish officials was of highest significance. From the point of view of constitutional orientation the consolidation of the administrative powers of the local squirearchy (rather than the extension of the agencies of the central authority), together with the steady growth of a true parliamentary system, was not less important. Under such circumstances it is idle to speak of enlightened despotism in England. The rule and reality was a kind of political neo-feudalism under a constitutional gloss.[16]

V. FRANCE

Between England and the "policed states" of the Continent lay France; and the France of Louis XV and Louis XVI was a bridge between two contrasting types of political institutions. Here too a political storm was raging. With a sharpness of vision that his contempt for France doubtlessly pointed, Tobias Smollett made an extraordinarily acute appraisal of the situation in 1765:

There are, undoubtedly, many marks of relaxation in the reins of the French government, and, in all probability, the subjects of France will be the first to take advantage of it. There is at present a violent fermentation of *different* principles among them, which under the reign of a very weak king, or during a long minority, may produce a great change in the constitution. . . . Many of the commons, enriched by commerce and manufacture, grow impatient of those odious distinctions, which exclude them from the honours and privileges due to their importance in the common wealth; and all the parlements, or tribunals of justice in the kingdom, seem bent upon asserting their rights and independence, in the face of the king's prerogative, and even at the expense of his power and authority.[17]

The defeated country could ill afford the luxury of internal strife. Her empire was lost and her colonial trade cut in half. The navy and the merchant marine were decimated. A passionate religious controversy rocked the land, and a plague of vagrants and beggars defied the police. Meantime the government teetered on the edge of bank-

16 S. and B. Webb, *The Parish and the County* (London, 1906) and *The Manor and the Borough*, 2 vols. (London, 1908), forming volumes I-III of the series *English Local Government*, 9 vols. (London, 1906-1929).
17 Tobias Smollett, *op. cit.*, II, 202.

ruptcy. The aged voluptuary Louis XV still reigned, beginning the fifth decade of a calamitous rule. He remained handsome in the heavy sensual manner of the predatory male, elegant in demeanor, and dignified in his majesty, as befitted the sunglass of royal decorum. Maturity had long since overcome his native shyness, and experience had sharpened his intelligence and swelled his knowledge of affairs. But his excesses had robbed him of not a little of his once tireless energy and soon the death of his gracious and intelligent *belle amie*, Madame de Pompadour (1764), was to plunge him into modified grief and invincible boredom. From this ennui he sought consolation in his ill-famed bachelor's retreat at the Parc aux Cerfs and in the mysterious fascination of secret diplomacy. He was cut off from his people, discredited by his personal vices and public reverses. In the fierce whirlpools of political, religious, and economic discontent he was helpless, buffeted by currents that he could not control. The deluge came after him, for he had indeed opened the dikes.

The monarchy in the generation immediately preceding the Revolution was far less absolute in fact than one would gather from the writings of present-day liberal historians, or from the contemporary liberal English tourist who discovered that "Roi is a word which conveys to the mind of the Frenchman the ideas of benevolence, gratitude, and love; as well as those of power, grandeur, happiness. . . ."[18] Loyalty remained, but the "grandeur" certainly had faded and the "power" was subject to many restrictions. There were many cracks in the magnificent centralized system that a century earlier had welded a congeries of semi-autonomous provinces into a unified monarchy. A clear demarcation of jurisdiction was lacking between the different divisions of the royal council. The basis for allocating work was not clearly determined, in some instances remaining geographical and in others becoming functional. Political administration was still tangled with the administration of justice, to the detriment of both. The ministers (usually six in number) not only vied with the councilors but through the "ministerial letter," which did not require registration by the Parlement of Paris, tended to reduce the royal council to a decorative and needless appendage. In the absence of a leading minister to

[18] John Andrews, *A Comparative View of the English and French Nations* . . . (London, 1785), 409.

co-ordinate all activities and provide for long-range government, there remained only the king; and Louis XV roused himself from his royal indifference only to intervene with sporadic and costly inefficiency.[19]

The provincial intendants were the great stabilizing flywheel of the administrative machine, but there is little in sober fact to commend Tocqueville's memorable characterization of them as "thirty tyrants." His picture was drawn, it is interesting to note, by a nineteenth-century liberal who feared and condemned state action. Assuredly they displayed a ceaseless activity, taking virtually every aspect of public and not a few of private relations for their province. Trained civil servants recruited from the judicial and administrative officialdom and generally wealthy in their own right, they were neither tyrants nor narrow-minded bureaucratic functionaries. They were the most "enlightened" and enterprising public servants of the realm, communicating suggestions to Versailles almost as often as they received instructions from the council of state, and serving their country's—and very often their community's—welfare not in the interests of but against capricious and arbitrary despotism. Modern understanding has at last caught up with their contemporary popularity, appreciating their benevolent efficiency. But their eulogists have not sufficiently emphasized the limits of their power. "They have failed to draw a distinction," writes a recent student, "between their ceaseless activity in attacking a multiplicity of abuses singly and their constant frustration when more comprehensive and more drastic measures were attempted."[20] A Turgot at Limoges, a Tourny at Bordeaux, and the Brissacs at Poitiers could achieve marvels in secondary reforms, but the odds were too heavy against any attempt on their part to make a major frontal attack upon the institutional foundations of the *ancien régime*. The area under administration was most often too large; their associates and assistants, even when technically trained, too few; and the sniping obstructionism of local oligarchs too injurious.

The most effective check of all upon monarchical absolutism was the powerfully organized aristocracy of lawyers. The *noblesse de la robe*, which was at the head of the hierarchical legal profession that ranged

19 The best account is in G. Pagès, *La monarchie d'ancien régime en France* (Paris, 1928).
20 D. Dakin, *Turgot and the Ancien Régime in France* (London, 1939), 27.

from the arrogant magistrates of the thirteen sovereign courts (*parlements*) at the top through the petty judges to the advocates and notaries at the bottom, was a professional and social complex of imposing strength. Related by marriage ties to the older military aristocracy (*noblesse de l'épée*) the *parlementaires* had thousands of clients in the country. Like the administrative nobility (*noblesse de la cloche*) and the high financial officials of the new oligarchy, with whom they were also closely affiliated through marriage and interests, these magistrates owned their public offices in exactly the same way as they owned other property. Even when the crown could present a legal case for the dismissal of one of their number, it would still need the funds that it rarely possessed to buy back the office from the ousted official. Moreover, while from the point of view of absolutist theory the Parlement of Paris and the twelve provincial parlements dispensed high and appellate justice only in the name of the king, from the point of view of real practice the Parlement of Paris had effectively gained its long-standing claim to serve as the accredited depository and the legal custodian of the many statutes and practices that comprised "the fundamental laws of the realm." And it exercised its right of review over royal edicts always to restrain and frequently to nullify the executive authority of the king. France lacked a parliament in the English sense, but the unwritten English constitution was never guarded with more jealous care than the Parlement of Paris defended the fundamental laws.[21]

More was obviously at stake in the century-long contest between the monarchy and the parlements than the narrow issue of conformity to the letter of the unwritten French constitution. The constitution was only the frame for the decisive struggle for power. The stakes involved everything vital in living relations: social status, tax relations, religious arrangements, political control. The Jansenists were behind the *parlementaires* and often enough it was their arguments that carried decisive weight with the peasantry and urban workers. No one has ever more succinctly summarized the tactics of the magistrates than their shrewd eighteenth-century contemporary, Friar Véri, who recorded in his diary:

21 J. Flammermont, *Remonstrances du Parlement de Paris au XVIIIe siècle*, 3 vols. (Paris, 1888-1898), II and III.

They know how to employ the name of the public weal in all their acts of obstruction. . . . There was never a conflict in which the magistrates did not base their arguments upon the sanctity of fundamental laws, upon their zeal for the good of the people, upon the sacred duties of the magistrature, upon their loyalty to the King, their disinterested service and continual sacrifice—even at the times when their actions travestied all these good principles.[22]

In all controversies their weight was on the side of the past against the present. Rationalizing their opposition, they put forth the constitutional theory that the king obligated himself by his coronation oath to maintain the fundamental laws, and that these laws postulated a France organized into "estates" or classes, each of which was "privileged," though in a different way. Hence the function of the monarch was to keep the balance between them. Translated into practical terms this meant that he was not to curb the provincial estates (the French equivalent of *Landtage*), nor destroy the historic privilege of the *pays d'états*, nor in any way modify the *status quo* against the vested aristocratic interests that were its chief beneficiaries.[23]

During the fifties and the entire course of the Seven Years' War the magistrates steadily obstructed the crown officials, but after the war ended, Louis XV vigorously reaffirmed the theory of royal absolutism. In the memorable declaration on the "Day of Flagellation" (1766), he rejected a pending remonstrance of the Parlement of Paris, reiterating: "It is in my person alone that the sovereign power resides . . . and the rights and interests of the nation . . . are necessarily joined with mine and rest only in my hands."[24] Five years later he put sharp teeth into his declaration by confiscating the offices of the magistrates and "exiling" their exalted persons to their estates. So sunken was the crown or perhaps only Louis XV in prestige, and so strong the hold of the *parlementaires* over public opinion, that the populace hailed the heroic "conscript fathers" who had dared to brave "ministerial despotism"; and when the new king reinstated them in 1774, the populace went wild with joy.

22 Abbé de Véri, *Journal*, 2 vols. (Paris, 1928), I, 64-65, quoted in Dakin, *op. cit.*, 25.
23 The most comprehensive attempt to make this corporative theory presentable is in François Olivier-Martin's *L'organisation corporative de l'ancien régime* (Paris, 1938); cf. also H. Hintze, *Staatseinheit und Föderalismus im alten Frankreich* . . . (Stuttgart, 1928).
24 J. Flammermont, *op. cit.*, II, 556-560.

Summing up, a conservative opposition constantly hampered the crown, whose ablest and most loyal executive officials sought to redistribute social benefits in the interests of the propertied middle classes and peasantry. This opposition was able to defeat the efforts of the intendants and reforming ministers which would have established precedents for enlightened despotism. Strong enough to badger the crown, the magistracy lacked the force to assume power itself and re-create a pre-Richelieu state; and whatever theoretical possibility existed for a strong ruler to become the real master of the state, Louis XVI's failure to support Turgot clearly sounded the knell of enlightened despotism in France. In fact, the failure of the *expérience Turgot* also sealed the doom of the monarchy itself. Under normal circumstances the restive bourgeoisie would have been delighted to support enlightened despotism, for such a dispensation promised well for them. When, however, the king showed his unwillingness or, what was worse, his inability to change from inefficient absolutism to efficient despotism, the leaders of the middle classes turned to other solutions for their grievances than princely rule. The last fifteen years of the *ancien régime* were to witness a marked revulsion of feeling from faith in royal reform to a significant trend toward the belief that the initiative had to come from the bourgeoisie itself. The exigent pressure of business needs came together with the idealization of republican democrats—of the quick in the thirteen colonies and the hallowed dead in Greece and Rome—to give rise to the doctrine of bourgeois nationalism. And in its cultural and economic aspects this doctrine vigorously prepared the minds of men for the revolution that they soon translated into disruptive reality.

Chapter Two

STATE AND SOCIETY

I. THE ARISTOCRACY AND THE SQUIREARCHY

EACH state was a social pyramid, the base resting upon the peasantry, the aristocracy constituting the apex, and the urban bourgeoisie between them. The status of the titled aristocracy gave them in law or custom advantages not possessed by groups otherwise privileged. On the Continent their almost exclusive ownership of land endowed them with many pleasing symbolical marks of distinction. It gave them patrimonial rights entitling them to labor services and dues from their peasantry. They were entrenched in the high posts of the civil and diplomatic administration, in ecclesiastical and educational offices, with exclusive control over the ranking positions in the military. They were often legally exempt from compulsory military obligations and entirely exempt from public taxes, or else they enjoyed a preferred rate when they did pay.

An international solidarity obtained in noble Europe, grounded on landed estates and cemented by marriage alliances. Education as well as attire, the snobbery of language, and the familiar pattern of elevated social behavior reinforced their wealth and confirmed the scions of the aristocracy in their exclusiveness. The baroque magnificence of Maria Theresa's Vienna worthily expressed the venerable Caesarian claims of the Hapsburgs, but it was the resplendent Versailles, fashioned by the "Sun King," that still remained the aesthetic shrine for all Europe's court aristocracy. From that sacred fount flowed the streams of fashion, taste, manners, and morals to Schönbrunn, to the residence seats of the many princelets of the Holy Roman Empire, to the semi-Asiatic, barbaric splendor of Russia, and to the Moorish citadels of Spain. The great aristocrats, who were so intensely proud and often so ludicrous in their meticulous observance of their "honor," hedged themselves round in elaborate ceremonials. At profane theaters and concerts and at sacred churches they held themselves grandly aloof from commoners. Their sons enjoyed the superiority of segregation at the universities—when they attended them—eating and sleeping in separate quarters, sitting apart in lecture halls, and studying apart on occasions that were doubtlessly rare.

Their pretensions reached prodigal heights of magnificence in the Danubian and Rhine courts where the aristocracy of imperial Germany surpassed themselves in absurd extravaganza. But the court nobility everywhere, with a studied determination and a nice sense of discrimination that merited a worthier concern, insisted upon the observance of such consecrated and conspicuous honorific distinctions as carrying swords, wearing plumed hats, and powdering their hair. They also insisted upon genealogical qualifications, upon the requisite number of quarterings, either to exclude parvenu noblemen entirely or to keep the petty nobility, particularly the impoverished country cousins, at elbow's distance. The court was a powerful magnet for these poor country noblemen—for all, indeed, who were ambitious or weighed down with debt. Even the puffy little residence seat of a petty Germanic prince was an open-sesame to advancement, showering gifts, favors, social esteem, refined pleasures, and positions upon the needy and the greedy—or at least holding forth the promise of such blessings.

The building mania of the century paid monumental tribute to their wealth and glory, as well as to the skill of the architects and craftsmen. Comfort, combined with opulence, was the ideal, from England to the Muscovite outposts of European civilization: a country house or a town dwelling built of enduring stone and brick, with spacious rooms, generously high ceilings and many windows within, and with walks and gardens, shrubs and flower beds surrounding the mansion without. Vanished now from these homes of the wealthy aristocracy was the somber, rectilinear furniture of an earlier day, ousted after the mid-century by the strong yet delicately fashioned mahogany of Thomas Chippendale. All was carved now, doors, windows, cupboards, and cabinets. Beautifully colored tapestries and in increasing measure decorative prints half-concealed the gracefully carved woodwork. Heavy chandeliers glittered overhead; and porcelain and lacquer *objets d'art* everywhere delighted the eye, or were designed to do so. Across the drawing room, over waxed parquet floors, moved bewigged powdered gentlemen, vivid in braided and embroidered velvet coats, gaily colored waistcoats and knee breeches, and lace-bordered sleeves and necks. As the music struck the strains of the stately minuet, jeweled ladies moved smilingly to its measures—heavily rouged, with towering coiffures, and dressed in shimmering silk or satin gowns that drew long trains in the wake of their hooped skirts.[1]

It is not unlikely that an excess of moral zeal on the part of historians has exaggerated the corruption, economic parasitism, and cultural decadence of the high aristocracy, in all European states as well as in the France of the *ancien régime*.[2] Despite the formalism and the ceremonial of their living many of them were exquisite connoisseurs and some discriminating patrons of and contributors to the arts and sciences. This is not too surprising, for the continental nobility constantly revitalized itself by taking in dynamic recruits from the successful bourgeoisie on the lower rung of the social ladder. The ornamental and decorative qualities of the aristocracy are matters of aesthetic, not sociological, judgment. Whether noblemen were absolutely devoid of creativeness or only half culturally sterile is actually unimportant. If not so degenerate as their contemporary chroniclers or later bourgeois historians painted them, they were still considerably more ornamental than culturally creative and more distinguished by conspicuous waste than by conspicuous intelligence.

The educational ideals and practices of the richer nobility, their continued emphasis upon class distinctions, the stress that they placed upon court conduct as a model and upon courtly and military life as careers illustrate their decline. Lesser continental courts displayed something almost akin to imagination in emulating the worst faults of Versailles: copying the elaborate ceremonial which minutely prescribed the etiquette of behavior or misbehavior; adopting the undeviating protocol of formal conduct which condemned rulers rarely to have a moment's privacy and most courtiers always to act alike; and taking over all the hothouse cultivation of the arts of luxurious living which were devised to provide pleasure and cheat boredom. With all due

[1] M. von Boehn, *Modes and Manners. The Eighteenth Century*, tr. from the German (London, 1935); also F. M. Kelly and R. Schwabe, *Historic Costumes, A Chronicle of Fashion in Western Europe, 1490-1790* (New York, 1925), ch. vi.

[2] Cf. Crane Brinton's sprightly observations on that score in *The Lives of Talleyrand* (New York, 1936), 44 ff.

deference to the cultural galaxies at Carlsruhe, Gotha, and even Weimar; to the dilettante patricians of arcadian Italy; to the Pompadour culture of France and the aristocracy of Augustan England, their role as cultural leaders of Europe was far inferior to that of the middle-class thinkers and artists. Goethe's sneer in *Goetz*: "As learned as a German squire" ("*So Gelehrt wie ein Deutscher von Adel*") brooked no retort as a substantially accurate if ungenerous characterization. Least of all could one discover cultural superiority in the bigoted and dull Viennese nobility or the tens and hundreds of thousands of Spanish and Italian, Polish and Russian squires who differed from one another mainly in degree of religious superstition, fanaticism, and the brutality and violence of their daily living.

These exquisite pleasures of the court or the capital were not for the squirearchy. The country gentlemen were widely diversified. In the lower depths there were impoverished descendants of old, proud families whose fixed income from feudal dues and services never sufficed to balance rising prices. Such were the many thousands of wretched and poverty-stricken *hidalgos* in Spain, the miserable yet arrogant alms-begging *hobereaux* of France, and the pitiful retainers of Polish magnates. A fortunate minority supplemented or supported their agrarian incomes with revenue from offices and investments. By and large the country nobility lived simply on their estates, complacently barricaded against change and patiently practicing the traditional husbandry of breeding their stock, tending their land, planting their gardens, marrying off their daughters, and rearing their sons in the mysterious ways of horses and dogs. The German country gentleman "took no more notice of the great world than was necessary, mixed without ceremony at great family parties with the whole nobility of the country, allowed himself an occasional carousal, bred his foal, sold his wool, and disputed with his parson. If he was not too strict, he maintained tolerably good relations with his subjects."[3] Such too was the Compleat English Gentleman of Defoe's acidulous pages, who improved his estate and neglected nothing but his heir, on the assumption that the estate had to be improved but not the head of his son. Such was Fielding's Squire Western who showered Tom

---

[3] G. Freytag, *Bilder aus der deutschen Vergangenheit*, III, ch. ix, quoted in Bruford, *Germany in the Eighteenth Century* (Cambridge, Eng., 1935), 125-126.

Jones with favors so that "everything which the squire held most dear, to wit, his guns, dogs, and horses, were now as much at the command of Jones as if they had been his own."[4]

II. AGRARIAN RELATIONS AND THE PEASANTRY

Europe was still overwhelmingly a continent of peasant farmers, and in all countries without exception the peasantry constituted four-fifths or more of the total population. England too was preponderantly agricultural despite its great commercial advance. The legal structure of agrarian society had scarcely been modified since the turmoil of the enclosure movement under the Tudors centuries earlier. All cultivators, irrespective of their social status and their economic position, were free men, for serfdom had long since disappeared. Feudal dues of course were of the past, and commoners and noblemen alike paid taxes to the state. Much of the land remained uncultivated; and of the total arable land of over nine million acres half was put to pasturage. Production remained low, hampered by the mediaeval open-field system of village units and strip farming. But it was stimulated by a growing domestic demand and partly subsidized by the Corn Law of 1689, which provided a bounty on the export of surplus produce. Political circumstances also favored greater production. Parliament was "a landlord's club," passing many private agricultural acts of local application which gave the squirearchy a comparatively free hand to manage their estates, unimpeded by government supervision or regulation.

Changes in production began early in the century and the attack upon paleolithic-technical survivals of mediaeval production was led by men with eyes quick to see the possibilities of gain, and with capital wealth great enough to finance the purchase and installation of the improved equipment, the superior stock and seed, and, ultimately, the machinery that was required. Many of the progressive landlords were only gifted amateurs, "dabblers and adventurers in cultivation, brilliant speculators in stocks and crops"; and in the main the innovations were not revolutionary. They were part of a long-continuing process of capitalist improvement which attacked the open-field system,

---

4 To avoid repetitious references, the writer refers to his detailed bibliography of descriptive works on Europe during the second half of the century, *infra*, pp. 327-328.

encroached upon the commons, and sought to improve methods of tillage, pasturage, and animal breeding. Among the first deities of the agricultural pantheon were men like Jethro Tull, theorist, scientific investigator, and pioneer inventor, and Viscount ("Turnip") Townshend, spectacularly successful in rotating wheat, turnips, barley, and clover crops. Later came the internationally famous breeder, Robert Bakewell, whose scientifically bred sheep and cattle swelled his country's supply of fresh meat precisely when the increasing population required it most during the wars with France. Alongside him was Arthur Young, a curious combination of knight errant, traveling salesman, and publicity director for the new agriculture, and lastly the sensationally successful Thomas Coke, Coke of Holkham.

In the last three decades the tempo of change was enormously accelerated. Landed heirs and younger sons, country parsons, returned nabobs, the king himself—"Farmer George"—all turned to farming. The needs of industry supplied new markets; a growing population, new demands; and thousands of miles of canals and improved roads furnished new means of transportation. Patriotism blended with the desire for profit; and enlightened public opinion as well as the law were all on the side of progress, endorsing the agricultural revolution and the rigors of the enclosure movement now about to set in in full earnest.[5]

Continental reformers waxed enthusiastic over English rural relations and agricultural progress, none more so than the French. France's own system was unique: as in other European states the crown, the church, and the aristocracy were the great landlords, but they were not the exclusive owners. A small fraction of the urban commoners owned landed property. Far more important, the great majority of the peasants themselves were proprietors, and fewer than 20 per cent of the rural population were entirely landless. These peasant proprietors worked somewhere between one-third and two-fifths of all the tillable land of the country. From a strictly legal point of view they were not true proprietors, for they were only the possessors of hereditary and inalienable leaseholds. But they were

---

[5] Lord Ernle (R. E. Prothero), *English Farming, Past and Present*, 4th ed. (London, 1927), chs. vii-xiv; and J. L. and B. Hammond, *The Village Labourer, 1760-1832*, 4th ed. (London, 1927), chs. i-iv.

proprietors *de facto* if not *de jure*, and it was the sense of ownership that counted.

This state of affairs was unique, but less than ideal for most of the cultivators. A great deal of sentimental nonsense has been written about the crippling obligations that they owed to several masters. These obligations were real enough and heavy, but they were not primarily responsible for the hardship and sordidness of peasant life. The recurrent epidemics of smallpox and typhus, the unending privations, and the lawlessness and violence are not to be explained in terms of fiscal extortions by the state or labor exactions on the part of the lord's bailiff. Not individual malevolence from a story-book Simon Legree but a complex of institutional burdens provides the explanation. Labor obligations and fiscal charges interacted with a relentless pressure of population growth which raised the French population from 22 million to approximately 26 million in the single generation after 1763. An inequitable system of inheritance, scarcity of working capital, inadequate transportation and marketing facilities, manifold restrictions on internal trade, ignorance and technical backwardness—all these factors combined to make the lot of the peasant extremely hard. It was the gnawing land hunger that drove peasants into mutual competition for short-term tenancies, for land to work on shares, for positions as millers and innkeepers, and for work in rural spinning and weaving. The inevitable shortage of production, indeed, the very fear of shortage, resulting from these circumstances, forced the government to practice continual supervision and maintain a variety of controls, such as licensing grain merchants, storing food reserves and making requisitions, fixing prices, and arranging hours of sale. But it was the peasants' land hunger that made them resist the innovations and improvements of capitalist farming *à l'anglaise* and cling stubbornly to a collectivism of rights and practices.[6]

Nevertheless, French peasants lived far better than the Spanish. The careful English observer, Henry Swinburne, who jeopardized his comfort to tour Spain, was shocked by the contrast between the natural fertility of the land and the havoc and ruin to which man's wastefulness had reduced it. Before paying a tribute to the kindness, the

[6] H. Sée, *Esquisse d'une histoire du régime agraire en Europe au 18e et 19e siècles* (Paris, 1921), ch. xii.

patience, and the dauntless spirit of the peasants, he analyzed their attitude in a passage that deserves quotation for its sympathetic understanding:

> Listless indolence . . . is nowhere more indulged in than in Spain; thousands of men in all parts of the realm are seen to pass their whole day, wrapped up in a cloak, standing in rows against a wall, or dozing under a tree. . . . They feel little or no concern for the welfare or glory of a country, where the surface of the earth is engrossed by a few overgrown families, who seldom bestow a thought on the conditions of their vassals. The poor Spaniard does not work, unless urged by irresistible want, because he perceives no advantage accrue from their [*sic*] industry.[7]

Elsewhere peasant conditions were less terrible than in the terrestrial paradises of the south, where the military conquistadores had ousted the Moors, annihilated their rich culture, and destroyed their admirable system of reservoirs and canals. For intensive farming as practiced by the Moors they had substituted sprawling latifundia worked by landless farmhands whose common fare was bread steeped in oil, occasionally seasoned with vinegar. In the squalid central provinces, the Mesta of ranchers populated the land with cattle and stripped it of human beings, and absentee owners held their peasants down to precarious tenancies. In the more thickly populated northern and northeastern regions the peasants were hereditary leaseholders, but they suffered from more numerous burdens than fell upon the French copyholder. Even the interference of nature frustrated good husbandry, for devastating storms and floods periodically ravaged a land whose inhabitants were unable to give it their care.[8]

Some of the Italian peasants were now enjoying more than the dubious consolation of memories of agricultural prosperity. After generations of evil times recovery was setting in on the rich alluvial plains of the north. Once more the fields of Lombardy grew bumper crops of rice, wheat, and corn, bringing prosperity unparalleled in years to proprietors, while a well-balanced governmental program, based on a system of public works, eased the hardships of tenants and the landless croppers. In Tuscany private physiocratic reformers, the

---

[7] Henry Swinburne, *op. cit.*, 368.
[8] Ballesteros y Beretta, *op. cit.*, VI, ch. ii; Desdevises du Dézert, *op. cit.*, in *Revue hispanique*, LXXIII (1928), 18 ff.

geografili, took the lead in agrarian reform, attenuating feudal exactions and trying to attract capital to agriculture. Neighboring Piedmont abolished personal and real serfdom, but widespread brigandage and begging, as well as servile labor on large cattle ranches, still prevailed in the Papal States and in the Kingdom of the Two Sicilies.[9]

The structure of agrarian society in southwestern Rhenish Germany also resembled the French model. Serfdom was virtually unknown except in the tiny handkerchief patches of the imperial knights and the larger estates of the Bavarian nobility. The majority of the peasants were personally free and hereditary leaseholders, as they were also in the Austrian Netherlands. In northwestern Germany short-term tenure was normal. Along the Rhineland, and generally speaking in the western part of the Germanic land, a mild variant of feudal tenancy prevailed whereby the bulk of the landlord's revenue came from money rent and dues in kind, while the peasant gave only his stipulated labor services and relied upon his village organization to safeguard him against encroachments by the lord.

Peasant-lord relations in the large estates and endless stretches of Brandenburg, Pomerania, East Prussia, and Silesia were quite otherwise. The trend in those regions was toward destroying what remained of peasant tenancy and transforming feudal tenancy (*Grundherrschaft*) into estate ownership (*Gutsherrschaft*). While the free peasant sank into serfdom, the plot from which he was ousted was incorporated with the lord's own domain land, especially along the Baltic, to form large estates, which were then worked by servile labor for the enormously profitable export trade in rye and wheat. Only by way of exception did advanced English methods establish themselves on these East Prussian latifundia. The social dislocation that attended capitalist economic progress was never more cruel for the propertyless than in Prussia, where it accentuated the existing hardships of patrimonial relations. Few real checks existed to keep the Junker proprietor from supplementing his already vast prerogatives and imposing new labor services upon the adults or forcing compulsory labor obligations upon the minors (*Gesindedienst*).[10]

9 Of the many travel accounts, cf. John Moore, *A View of Society and Manners in Italy*, 2 vols. (London, 1781); also G. Renard and G. Weulersse's *Life and Work in Modern Europe* (London, 1926), ch. v.

10 For Germany as a whole, the brief summary by W. Wittich, "Epochen der deutschen

Juridically and economically, the Bohemian peasant was perhaps no worse off than the serf of East Prussia or the Austrian duchies. Actually, he was the victim of a military conqueror and the pawn of a self-styled superior race that sought to impose its German speech and ways, its Roman law, and its Roman Catholic faith on him. The history of the conquered Bohemian peasantry, up to the accession of Maria Theresa in 1740, was blackened with their fierce *jacqueries*. They rebelled against the alien landlord who added new weight to their corvée (*robot*), restricted their freedom of movement, and controlled their right to marry whom they willed or to seek the occupation they desired. They protested against the church that harried them for their Lutheran faith and levied its tithe upon them; and they rose up against an unfeeling state that saddled them with taxation exceptionally heavy even for those days.[11]

The native Austrian serf fared no better than the alien Bohemian, except for the absence of religious and cultural persecution. Most of the Hungarian peasants too were serfs, burdened with heavy obligations. The Magyar gentry may have exercised patriarchal benevolence toward their own people and kept their ancient folkways unsullied by the Hapsburg conquerors, but despite such services the frequency and violence of rural uprisings argue that there was still considerable room for improvement of peasant conditions.[12]

In Russia, too, the age of the enlightenment was for the peasantry "a century of abysmal darkness and depression." "When even in Junker-ridden Prussia," writes Kluchevsky, "the Crown was trying to defend the serf, Russia divorced herself anew, in respect then of its social foundations from the course of continental European developments."[13] Russia had already become a slave-owning state when Catherine ascended the throne. The nobleman had been transformed into a full proprietor, with his estate rights legally recognized, while the peasant, whether erstwhile chattel slave or free cultivator, had fallen under the yoke of serfdom. These serfs of the private noble

---

Agrargeschichte," in *Grundriss der Sozialökonomik*, VII. Abteilung (Tübingen, 1922); and G. S. Ford, *Stein and the Era of Reforms in Prussia, 1807-1815* (Princeton, 1922), ch. vi, for the Prussian peasantry.

[11] R. J. Kerner, *op. cit.*, 22-30; 272-278.
[12] H. Marczali, *op. cit.*, 170-190.
[13] V. O. Kluchevsky, *op. cit.*, IV, 344.

landlords, most of whom owned between 100 and 200 "souls," greatly outnumbered both those owned by the crown and the free or semi-free peasants (*odnovortsi* and *polovniki*).

The serf paid a high poll tax and owed heavy military service to the state. In legal theory he was entitled to the master's good offices in periods of famine or illness, and he could also appeal in law to the tsar's representative for state protection against his private master. Practically, however, he was defenseless against both. The nobleman (*dvorianan*) was legally exempted both from military service and from the payment of the tax. Like the Prussian Junker he served as unpaid tax collector and recruiting agent for the state. As in Prussia he intervened more and more in "peasant affairs." He regulated the allotment of land to the individual household, interfered more frequently in the debates, and guided the decisions of the village community (*mir*). By the sixties he had acquired the right to settle all criminal cases involving his serfs, impose corporal punishment on them, select them for military service, exile them to hard labor in Siberia, and even to sell them apart from the land to which they were attached. As the crown became a kind of executive agent for the *dvorianstvo*, it was coerced by the nobility into lowering the peasant's poll tax, which permitted the landowners forthwith to increase the serf's labor dues (*barshchina*). Since this development decreased the crown's revenues, the latter had recourse to various time-honored expedients, such as debasing the coinage and establishing salt and vodka monopolies, to meet its expenses. These abuses enormously swelled rural discontent. The peasant was ground between two crushing millstones. Difficult as it was for the *moujik* to cope with his taxes and services in good times, it was impossible for him to meet his obligations when harvests failed or epidemics raged. Many of the peasantry were already in arms when Catherine ascended her blood-stained throne, fighting legal violence with illegal terror, and hundreds of thousands of them were in flight, tracked like animals by the military.[14]

Though Poland had a sprinkling of free peasants, most of whom

---

[14] The best account in English is in G. T. Robinson, *Rural Russia under the Old Regime* (New York, 1932), chs. ii-iv; a longer account, somewhat confusing for its details, is in J. Mavor, *An Economic History of Russia*, 2 vols., 2nd ed. (New York, 1925), I, Bk. 2, chs. i-vi.

were landless, the great majority of Polish cultivators were serfs, the most benighted and degraded in Europe. From the state they received no aid, and to the government they neither paid direct taxes nor gave military service. They were bound hand and foot—as nowhere else on the Continent—to the patrimonial landlord. Sunk in blackest poverty and abysmally ignorant, huddled with their cattle in clusters of ramshackle wooden villages along miserable muddy roads that were practically impassable save in summer, "the natives," wrote the ubiquitous Archdeacon Coxe, "were poorer, humbler, and more miserable than any people we had yet observed in the course of our travels."[15] The clans of the Radziwills, the Potockis, and the Czartoryskis, were great capitalist landlords. Producing for the export markets of Riga and Danzig, they derived fabulous incomes from the servile labor on their own estates as well as from the royal fiefs which they possessed as life annuities. The middle nobility, living comfortably on 2,000 to 4,000 florins per annum, were more numerous than the great magnates, and most numerous of all were the titled gentry. There were over a million of these proud John Lacklands, who attached themselves like leeches to the great magnates, but for whose patriarchal benevolence famines would have been endemic in the unhappy land.[16]

Absentee landlords and enterprising noblemen who bought up large estates for large-scale farming transformed Denmark, for a moment in the eighteenth century, into one of the great exporting states of Europe, but the worst rigors of feudal restraints held persistent sway in the kingdom. Except in Norway, which had for centuries resolutely safeguarded its heritage of rural democracy, the bulk of the Danish peasants were either serfs or free cultivators subjected to servile disabilities and obligations as well as to economic oppression. Sweden, on the other hand, offered a welcome relief from the depressing tableau of peasant subjection. The country knew neither serfdom nor political feudalism. But it was exceptionally backward in production technique. Only 12 per cent of the soil was under cultivation, for forestry, fisheries, and mining took precedence over agri-

15 Rev. Wm. Coxe, *Travels into Poland, Russia, Sweden and Denmark*, 3 vols. (London, 1784), I, 169.
16 J. Rutkowski, *Le régime agraire en Pologne au XVIIIe siècle* (Paris, 1928).

culture. Large landowners were few, their lands being worked either by tenant farmers or on the crofter system, whereby laborers were hired to cultivate a specified portion of the main estate on the equivalent of shares. With that exception, the land was divided among many small proprietors whose average holding, taking the relatively small total population into account, compared favorably with that elsewhere in Europe.[17]

The variety of living conditions in Europe defies easy generalization. Well-to-do peasants lived in solidly built homes with wooden floors and glass windows. They owned sturdy wooden chairs and tables, and stout beds. Their substantial cupboards were stocked with linens, and copper or pewter utensils hung in the brick fireplace. The men wore strong homespuns and leather shoes. The women tended to wear calicoes and striped cottons instead of heavy woolens. All, the rich along with the less prosperous, relied upon the common lands. Village wastelands and woods supplied the wood for fuel and repairs, and furnished acorn for the pigs. The poorest dwellings, by way of contrast, were cheerless and smoky thatched-roof hovels without windows and wooden flooring. Dank and dark, they were devoid of all but the roughest tools and the most necessary utensils and furniture, together with one or two coffers, benches, and a kneading trough. The peasants hardly ever ate meat. They used the wheat and rye crop to pay their dues, and they ate bread made of a combination of barley, maize, and chestnut. Isolated in their village communities and too poor to buy the wares of the nearest town, they used the local facilities and relied upon self-help. Each village had its local mill and smithy. As much as possible they were their own craftsmen, doing their tailoring, tanning, and carpentry. In the long winter evenings the men repaired their tools and plied the old household craft of wood carving; the women wove and plaited, and the spinning wheel and distaff and sewing needle were always busy. Feast days, fortunately numerous in the Catholic countries, brought a round of visits and the relaxation of dancing and singing and drinking. The itinerant pedlar too, and the periodic fair, gave thrills and excitement to the drab monotony of existence.

17 Renard and Weulersse, *op. cit.*, ch. viii.

The villager would scarcely have recognized his idealized self in the rapturous pictures drawn by the Rousseauists. He was not *le bon villageois*, tender and gentle as in the prints of Chardin and Greuze, but rather *der dumme Bauer* of the Germans. Mercier and Rétif de la Bretonne knew him well: coarse and cunning, stupid and quarrelsome, occasionally dishonest and often alcoholic. Indigence, ignorance, and backbreaking labor under almost primitive conditions, and an unchanging cycle of service dues and money obligations, were not calculated to fashion Lord Chesterfields. So long as the crops were harvested, they at least kept the body together. But no individual peasant, however resolute and capable, could singlehanded break through the cruel ring of marginal farming, overcome the superstitions of his fellows, and satisfy the demands of his masters. To console him for his weariness or despair he had the man of God in his parish, but when harvests failed or the deadly epidemics recurred, the man of secular science was rarely at hand to aid him. Only too frequently was the local healer a blind man leading the blind, and the village teacher, as in Prussia, a discharged veteran returned from the wars and rewarded for his scars and his years of service with a schoolhouse and a beggarly pittance. Vagrancy and beggary, brigandage on the king's highway and pillaging in the towns, were alternatives to starvation and death—even in law-abiding England. Private charity and medical aid could not cope with the needs of the rural disinherited when the great dislocations of capitalist agriculture hit them. Ecclesiastical assistance was inadequate. The monarch alone on the Continent had it in his power, whether out of humanitarian promptings or under the spur of calculation, to succor the needy villagers.

III. MERCHANT CAPITALISM AND THE MIDDLE CLASSES

The outlook of the middle classes was manifestly different. England comes first to mind when one thinks of the urban middle classes and economic advance, for it was already capitalist in spirit well before the coming of machinery.[18] The country possessed a large supply of capital and made advanced use of credit. It had an elaborate system for

[18] See E. Lipson, "England in the Age of Mercantilism," in *Journal of Business History*, IV (1932), 691-707, for a stimulating essay.

supplying raw materials and disposing of finished goods, while in a growing population, dislocated by the agricultural revolution, it had a cheap and plentiful labor supply. Private merchant capitalism had already financed and organized large enterprises in shipbuilding, mining, and metallurgy, sugar refining and distilling, and in the production of woolens and fustians. But large-scale production was still in the offing, and even the putting-out system was the exception rather than the rule. The characteristic producers were the small householder working for his own use and the master urban craftsman, selling his wares either directly to the local inhabitant or, in the expanding woolen and worsted trade, to a near-by merchant entrepreneur.

Of the total labor force that worked for the market, exclusive of agricultural and pastoral workers, only a minority were unskilled workers. The majority were still the well-trained artisans, skilled in the older crafts: in cutlery as at Sheffield; in small metal wares of every conceivable kind as at Birmingham; in watchmaking, carpentry, tanning, pottery, tailoring elsewhere. Unskilled workers were in the minority even in the rapidly growing woolen industries, which were soon to suck in thousands of the untrained. The cotton industry was in its infancy, requiring comparatively few operatives. Iron mining remained handicapped by its bondage to charcoal, and coal mining waited upon still greater technical improvements. Yet the day of the entrepreneur and the capitalistic industrialist was soon to come, to weaken the independence and nullify the influence of petty master craftsmen and domestic producers and introduce large-scale production.

The accumulations of merchant capital meantime effected a profound revolution in English life. The improvement of river and coastal facilities had stimulated internal trade, and England and Scotland, functioning as a single economic unit, formed the largest customs-free trading area in Europe. The older metropolitan economy with London as its focal point had been replaced by a more extensive and lucrative imperial-colonial exchange, almost world-wide in range. British exports doubled in value between 1720 and 1760, increasing from £6,999,000 to £14,500,000, while imports went up from £6,000,000 to £9,750,000. By 1774 the American colonial trade alone made up one-third of the total British overseas trade. The great international merchants, the shipping magnates, and the fabulously wealthy "nabobs" were the commanding figures in the business world. Wealth from overseas commerce and investment flowed through the arteries of English life: the wealth stored in the hundreds of ships which crowded the Pool of London and linked the old world with the new, the countryside with the capital, and the farmer with the capitalist merchant and manufacturer.

Colossal were the profits from that trade and investment: in spices and sugar, rum, slaves and tobacco, furs and fish, indigo and drugs, naval stores and notions; above all, from the huge capital investments in the East India Company, the fifty millions of dollars in the northern American colonies, and the three hundred million in the southern colonies and the West Indies. This wealth brought undreamed-of luxury to the fortunate few, while on the many it bestowed comfort far beyond comparison with continental living. The hope of gain was a magnet that drew votaries from all walks of life. It enlisted among its followers the disgruntled and the restless, the ambitious and the greedy. Wealth leveled social distinctions, stirring the ranks of the old landed aristocracy and fashioning a new plutocracy, hard and brutally courageous, endowed with immense vitality and imbued with a deep sense that in this competition rewards went to the enterprising, the imaginative, and those not scrupulous to excess. Georgian England was a creation of their own initiative. They created it without requiring the stimulus of inter-state competitive militarism to spur English economic activity. Nor did the crown count for much in this magnificent flowering. It neither provided subsidies nor imposed the supervisory hand of regulation. The powerful mercantile oligarchy and the landed aristocracy, joined with the new capitalists, conducted their business affairs as they did the political administration, with a minimum of interference by the king.[19]

Similar changes were transforming Bourbon France. Wholesale trade within the country and almost all its immensely lucrative international trade were controlled by the great bourgeois families and

[19] The most useful works are J. B. Botsford, *English Society in the Eighteenth Century as Influenced from Oversea* (New York, 1924); Witt Bowden, *Industrial Society in England toward the End of the Eighteenth Century* (New York, 1925); E. Lipson, *Economic History of England* (London, 1931), III; and the excellent brief account in H. Heaton, *Economic History of Europe* (New York, 1936), ch. xiv.

their associates (and in-laws) among the blue-blooded landed aristocracy.[20] Careful contemporary statistics reveal the sweep of that commercial revolution. From 1723 to the eve of war in 1756 the value of
foreign trade went up from 215,000,000 francs to 600,000,000, mainly in
the Levant and the West Indies islands. Bourgeois wealth also multiplied from financial speculations and fiscal operations. Court bankers,
such as the Crozat and the Pâris families, were occult powers behind
the throne, reaping stupendous fortunes from their loans and the
myriad business enterprises in which they invested their capital. They
were linked in many ways to the opulent farmers-general, now risen
both in merit and public esteem since the day early in the century
when Lesage mercilessly ridiculed the race of Turcarets. Hosts of secondary fiscal officials—receivers, inspectors, directors—impartially
defrauded both state and taxpayers. All of them, from millionaires
down, invested and reinvested their wealth in these lush years of
prosperity in banking and brokerage, insurance, and large-scale industry.

Extensive industrial enterprises were founded at and about the
foreign trade centers on the Atlantic seaboard: distilleries and refineries,
shipbuilding plants and factories for the manufacture of sailcloth and
the processing of colonial wares. Merchant capitalists were organizing
rural cotton textile production on the putting-out system long before
the royal decree of 1762 legally permitted non-guild members to
manufacture cotton cloth. As early as the forties capitalist producers
gained control in the famous old silk center of Lyons and degraded
the once prosperous guild masters to wage earners dependent on the
entrepreneur. Urban woolen production also required that capital,
workers, and materials be brought together. Only mining and metallurgy, however, were predominantly modern in their organization as
large-scale industries.

Petty industry, organized by the old craft-guild unit, prevailed in
the basic feeding, housing, and clothing trades. Many of the newer
industrial ventures outside the craft guild, in printed cloths, calicoes,
cottons, glass blowing, papermaking, and dyeing, were still modest
enterprises that required comparatively slight concentration of workers

20 H. Lévy-Bruhl, "La noblesse commerçante de France et le commerce à la fin de
l'Ancien Régime," in *Revue d'histoire moderne* (1933), 209-235.

and little capital investment. Seen in retrospect, the stringent governmental regulations and supervision over the guilds and even over the new enterprises outside the guild system were illusory. Royal statutes notwithstanding, free industrial production and distribution were making headway. Despite mercantilist controls and regulation, free trade at home and abroad was increasing. The economic framework of corporative France was beginning to crack.

The French bourgeoisie were no more homogeneous than the titled aristocracy. In the legal sense all were bourgeois: craftsmen and petty tradespeople; lesser officials and members of the liberal professions; wealthy wholesalers, merchant princes, industrialists, and holders of public offices that carried ennoblement with them. But carefully structured gradations, perpetuated with the loving attention to detail that only intense rivalry and envy can give, also separated the ranks. A shower of jealousies rippled nicely over the social scale. Incongruously diversified in material status, the French middle class had certain common characteristics: the vivifying traits of physical energy and tenacity, ambition, faith in the liberating power of education, and, above all, confidence in themselves. Like the English middle classes, which had already carried through their correlated revolutions in thought and institutions, the French bourgeoisie were now on the eve of making their own. They demanded *laissez faire* in industry and trade. Their sense of what was rational and natural made them tolerant and enlightened. And the implications of their political speculation compelled them to turn against political absolutism as well, but only after enlightened despotism in France had played out its unsuccessful and unhappy hour.[21]

Economic progress, as evidenced by steady population growth and increased agricultural yield, was equally rapid in the Austrian Netherlands. Craft-guild organization obtained, but merchant capitalism was advancing, and while internal trade improved only slightly, foreign trade shot up. Despite the enforced liquidation of the Ostend Company, Belgian ships plied the seas, if only under the flags of Poland, Holland, and Portugal. The newly established Trieste and

---

21 The works of Henri Sée are invaluable guides: in English, *Economic and Social Conditions in France During the Eighteenth Century* (New York, 1927); and in French the fuller *L'évolution commerciale et industrielle de la France sous l'ancien régime* (Paris, 1925).

Fiume Company (1750), which profitably exploited the sugar refineries, shipyards, and coal mines of the Upper Adriatic, was financed and directed by Austrian-Belgian capital, a signal illustration of how once again Antwerp was resuming its place as the nerve center of a highly ramified international network of banking operations that linked Belgium with all the great financing operations of Europe.[22]

The United Provinces was a land of well-fed, amiable, and unexciting citizenry, "A land," sneered a foreign visitor, "where the demon of gold, crowned with tobacco, sat on a throne of cheese." So long as Amsterdam remained a world focus for stock-market speculations, moneylending, and investment in governmental securities, the Dutch burghers lived serenely, enjoying their ease and turning their thoughts away from such disturbing realities as a neglected fleet, languishing manufactures, declining commercial monopolies, and dwindling profits from the East Indies and West Indies Companies. But the deflation after the Seven Years' War aggravated the evils; and out of the tardy realization that only sweeping reforms and reorganization could stem the decline arose a new set of aspirations that clashed violently with the more conservative middle classes.[23]

Any sweeping generalization concerning the Holy Roman Empire as a whole must inevitably result in inaccuracy concerning any one of the many hundreds of autonomous units into which it was divided. The economic development of the particular states was bound to differ enormously, given the wide variations in strength, area, and population. Not only did the growth suffer from the absence of political unity, but it reflected also the absence of internal economic unity. There was nothing comparable to England, nor even anything remotely resembling the incomplete internal unification of neighboring France. No wealth from the profits of colonial trade poured into the life stream of the Germanies, for there were no colonies to exploit. There was no stimulus from new demands and tastes from overseas, nor of new ideas. The whole vast area of central Europe was divided by many internal customs boundaries. The roads remained

22 A valuable digest of the conclusions based on the most recent researches is to be found in A. Puttemans' bibliographical article, "L'histoire de la Belgique de 1715 à 1789," in *Revue d'histoire moderne* (jan.-mai, 1940), 105-156, which modifies and corrects the interpretations in Pirenne, Van Houtte, and Tassier.

23 P. J. Blok, *op. cit.*, V, chs. x-xiv; and H. W. Van Loon, *The Fall of the Dutch Republic* (New York, 1913), ch. ii.

miserable. Neither a uniform system of weights and measures, nor one of coinage, nor one of commercial practices existed. Many of the older trade routes of early modern times that had once linked the cities along the Rhine and the Danube to southern and northern Europe had lost their importance. The newer routes were hampered by manifold restrictions, not the least of which were the tariffs which the states imposed to exclude the competing products of neighbors. Consequently, large-scale production had progressed far less than in the countries of the west; and the capital investment was considerably lower. Production for family use prevailed, together with craft-guild production for the local market, both supplemented by the familiar figure of the itinerant pedlar as well as the periodic regional fair.

Yet the larger secondary states of Germany, such as Prussia, Saxony, Silesia, and the Austrian duchies, necessarily tended to recapitulate the economic development of England and France. In the absence of the stimulus of overseas markets and growing consumer demand at home, large-scale economic production depended upon the state itself to provide the necessary fillips of demand and capital investment. The needs of competitive state militarism, set in the frame of a mercantilist rivalry and objectives, supplied the initiative for the establishment of the textile mills, the metal factories, the mines, and the foundries in the larger states. The main benefits perforce redounded to the state, with only incidental gains for the small minority of the population that constituted the wealthy middle class.

The stolidity of the petty German bourgeoisie was at no time an exhilarating phenomenon. It is impossible to conceive the doughty Dr. Johnson making about them the grudgingly admiring observation that he did of his own people: "Subordination is sadly broken down in this age [1778]. No man, now, has the same authority which his father had except a gaoler." When pressed by Boswell as to the cause, he answered, "Why, sir, there are many causes, the chief of which is, I think, the great increase of money. . . . But, besides, there is a general relaxation of reverence. No son now depends upon his father as in former times."[24] This general relaxation of "reverence" and "the great increase of money," this consciousness of a new world in birth,

---

24 J. Boswell, *Life of Johnson*, 2 vols. (Oxford, 1927 ed.) II, 199.

had not deeply penetrated the tidy little world of the orderly German bourgeoisie. With irritated indignation liberal reformers satirized the burghers' respectful resignation to authority; their rigid prescriptions governing rights and prerogatives; their regulations concerning correct dress, and the proper address, among the different legal classes as well as within their own hierarchically structured group; their untiring cultivation of frugality, piety, honesty, and sobriety; their seemly deference toward their superiors and their compensatory scorn for those beneath them; and above all, their disheartening unawareness that free inquiry and critical imagination, enterprise, audacity were also bourgeois virtues—and not the least valuable![25]

In neighboring Russia Peter the Great's efforts to renovate his country's economic foundations collapsed in the misrule following his death. For several decades Russia gradually subsided into older ways, her economy moving in the narrow ambit of local and regional production and exchange. The population grew with extraordinary rapidity, rising from 14 million in the thirties to 19 or 20 million in 1762, but towns were still few and the urban population was less than 3 per cent of the total. The bracing tonic of bourgeois enterprise was even more wanting than in the Germanies. The bustling figure of the promoter and the more leisurely and contemplative figures of the scientist and the inventor, his associates in progress, rarely obtruded themselves on the Slavic horizon. But Peter's conquest of the Baltic coast had permanently revolutionized Russia's foreign-trade relations. St. Petersburg became the greatest single point for the Baltic trade, though the profits were shared by the famous old trading cities of Riga, Reval, Narva, and Viborg. Nor did English producers and the many resident English merchants lose in exchanging their cutlery, textiles, hardware, base metal, and ale against Russian flax, hemp, tallow, timber, turpentine, and pitch.[26] In the forties and fifties, under Elizabeth, domestic trade increased rapidly, thanks to easier credit facilities for merchants and the abolition of many internal customs dues. Elizabeth's reign also saw a renewed effort at industrialization. Noble landowners, well supplied with capital, put their serfs to rural

25 For Germany in general, see Bruford, *op. cit.*, Part 3, ch. ii; for Prussia, R. Koser, *Geschichte Friedrichs des Grossen,* 4 vols., 7th ed. (Berlin, 1921-1925), II, 173-196; for Bohemia, Kerner, *op. cit.*, 197-272; and for Hungary, Marczali, *op. cit.*, 61-99.
26 D. Gerhard, *England und der Aufstieg Russlands* (Munich, 1933), ch. i; and D. Redding, *The Anglo-Russian Commercial Treaty of 1734* (New Haven, 1938); Rev. W. Coxe, *op. cit.*, Bk. VI, chs. iii and v.

textile production on the increasingly familiar "putting-out" basis, or sent them during the off season to work in the few medium-sized glass and porcelain factories and iron mills and refineries that were established in the Moscow area. In the southern Urals the state itself was the greatest capitalist, putting its crown peasants to work in its huge iron and gold mines and foundries. Needless to say, such ventures were not characteristic, indeed, only accentuated the prevailing backwardness.[27]

Elsewhere the middle classes were not numerous enough to be of moment in European developments. Incessant wars and invasion, changes in trade routes, the closing of outlets to the Black Sea and the Mediterranean, the enactment of punitive commercial legislation by the gentry, and the exclusion of the bourgeoisie from political life had sealed the decline of the Polish middle classes. By the eighteenth century, when most of Europe was leaping into new life, economic activities in the "Most Serene Republic" had lapsed almost entirely into household and local production and exchange, relying upon the native Jewish traders and the immigrant German residents even for that slight activity. Sweden made a breathless effort in the second third of the century to snatch economic modernity out of inadequate resources, and her artificial expansion collapsed in a storm of bankruptcies and cruel deflation. Danish merchants profited by the sinking of thousands of tons of foreign ships in the great international wars to revive their own prosperous carrying trade; while hardy Norse sailors blessed with a large merchant marine and a plentiful supply of fish, timber, and copper ore for export enjoyed uninterrupted commercial prosperity. But neither the Danes nor the Norwegians were in the main stream of continental development. In southern Europe the Italian states showed wide variations, and only Tuscany and Lombardy had a mercantile bourgeoisie of any importance. Only 3 per cent of the total Spanish population lived in cities and towns, and only in rare instances, as in textile production at Barcelona, were manufactures other than on a craft-guild or domestic basis. The entire value of Spanish industrial production was a scant one-sixth of that of agriculture.[28]

[27] J. Castéra, *Histoire de Cathérine II, impératrice de Russie* (Paris, an viii), III, 272 ff., of the modern studies D. S. Mirsky, *Russia, a Social History* (New York, 1934), ch. v, is stimulating; and J. Mavor, *op. cit.*, I, Bk. 3, chs. i-ii, is detailed.

[28] For the less important states, see Renard and Weulersse, *op. cit.*, chs. v-ix.

Chapter Three

THE MANDATES OF SECURITY AND POWER

"I sell here what all the world desires, power."
Matthew Boulton at his Soho factory, 1776.

I. THE HERITAGE OF ABSOLUTISM

FOR all the problems besetting rulers and statesmen in the era following the Seven Years' War, it was an epoch made illustrious by the reforms of the enlightened despots. It was an age of peaceful renovation and, in the main, of recuperation from war. It was also an age of transition, an intensely confused period, during which European life experienced the embarrassment of repudiating its own past. Thoughtful men were dismantling governmental control and ending ecclesiastical constraints; and they were ratifying in liberal theory the large measure of individual liberty that western Europe had already gained in practice. Seen in retrospect, the western world was advancing, slowly and falteringly, toward democracy.

However, one must distinguish the enlightenment as tradition and renovation from the age of reason as repudiation and innovation. The bourgeois liberals of France had, by mid-century, unraveled in thought the tight web of prescription that enmeshed the individual with corporate groups and the crown. The arguments for greater individual liberties had rooted themselves deeply between the mid-century and the outbreak of the Revolution in the speculation of all European thinkers. In many instances the defenders of the old order were forced to employ the language of the critics. Nevertheless, the prodigious influence of a persistent tradition to the contrary cannot be underestimated, particularly in its hold on the reforming monarchs themselves. It must not be underestimated, even if it has been overshadowed by the intellectual brilliance and literary charm of the literary spokesmen. It must not be ignored even if the Revolution repudiated it, and its tenets have been pushed into the background by the nineteenth-century triumphs of bourgeois democracy and by the writing of history that reflects the victory of liberalism.

In those very theories that denied the right of any state and challenged the competence of the existing state to direct the thinking and control the activities of the individual, a surprisingly large margin of necessary work was earmarked for the government itself. Ruggedly individualist as were the eighteenth-century humanists, and sterling in their self-reliance on vital matters like thought and speech, almost to the very eve of the revolutionary disturbances in 1789 they too saw nothing unnatural in having the fiat of the prince usher in civil and political liberties. However one interprets that anomaly, the optimism that made Turgot yearn for five years of despotism to set men free or the hopefulness that made men expect the Leviathan state to become the architect of its own extinction, there it was, the tenacious faith that only the absolutism of the prince's authority could guarantee the efficacy of his governing power. Such reservations obtained even in France and they prevailed almost uncontested everywhere in Europe. No insistent tug came from subjects in central and eastern Europe to tear down state superintendence over their lives. The ancient traditions of royal absolutism held firm. At no time was there any intimation that the monarchical system was facing its end. The individualism of the west could have little dissolvent force in countries where centralized absolutism had not fully established itself. Indeed, the lessons drawn from the troubled past argued that the existing and successfully applied controls be strengthened rather than relaxed in order to allow the state to bear the heavier strains of more extensive activities and support the sharper tensions of post-war recovery. The very law of nature, interpreted as Hobbes had read it and Sonnenfels was reading it, if not as Rousseau was about to scan it, confirmed statesmen in the belief that only through the unmitigated authority of the prince could present problems be solved and the still unresolved perplexities dating from the mediaeval past be laid to rest.

The enlightened ruler was bringing to full maturity governmental procedures that arose out of the revolutionary upheavals of the sixteenth century which first shattered the bases of mediaevalism. Slowly, with blood and bitterness, and always with guile and cunning, the prince of early modern times had created his new little world of set relationships. In the disorders, even anarchy, that accompanied the birth of modern European society, it was the prince who had undertaken the ungrateful task of imposing obedience upon recalcitrant subjects, of making religion a handmaiden of good government, and of establishing a system of public law capable of protecting life and private property and enforcing social peace. These responsibilities he had discharged well, if not always equitably. Meantime the individual had laid many liberties, not yet construed as inalienable and imprescriptible, upon the altar of state security. In order to gain the blessings of tolerable tranquillity in a social order that remained unreasonably violent he had perforce to move together with other individuals. He responded, because there was nothing else for him to do, to mass stimuli which arose from the collective wants of the group with which he lived and moved and truly had his being.

In time the subjects of the prince began to question the wisdom and even the necessity of royal prescriptions. They raised such ungrateful doubts after the passage of several centuries of relatively stable living; but they raised them almost exclusively in western Europe. In central and eastern Europe men still took the bad with the good. They protested against abuses, but they neither indulged in serious criticism of the procedures nor questioned the premises of state activity in the militarized *Polizeistaat* that governed their living. The reforming ruler therefore carefully trimmed his sails to the wind, going as far as the circumstances required. He went as far as dissident social groups pushed him and the group whose interests he represented permitted him to go toward eliminating social friction and improving governmental efficiency. He had long since given up almost all pretense of divine justification and had resigned himself to having only secular sanctions for his full power. The confessional absolutism of a Philip II and the court absolutism of a Louis XIV were things of the past. The enlightened monarch of the eighteenth century did indeed see his quest for power in the light of its ideal purposes of broader duties toward his subjects and wider social obligations. But a fundamental rearrangement of existing social relations he would not promote, when exacerbated international relations alone seemed to demand that the utmost tranquillity be maintained at home against the dangers from rival states abroad.

The decision not to depart from customary practices was substantiated in the minds of monarchs by the principles of their mercantilist belief. Mercantilism, both as a system of thought and as a pattern of behavior, referred all trends and activities to the centralized absolute state as the norm. Its postulates were purely pragmatic. Starting from entirely practical considerations of security, mercantilism had in the course of generations developed into a distinct body of economic ideas and practices which were applied by statesmen to obtain certain clearly designated political objectives.[1] Broadly stated, these aims were to achieve the economic unification of the territory of the state by systematically utilizing all its resources in the sole interests of the government and thus to gain for the unified state the maximum of power over and against all similarly organized rival countries.[2] State activity had long since achieved the desired goal in England. It had never operated in Holland; and it was now both irksome as a concept and wholly cumbersome and unnecessary in practice in the merchant capitalist economy of France. For more than two centuries mercantilism had had the consensus of public opinion behind it, but it had now outlived its usefulness in western Europe, retaining a ghostly existence as a false doctrine still believed in by the very old.[3]

On the ebb tide in France, it was only beginning to flow with full force in the Germanies and Russia, in Spain and the still disunited Italian states. Practices elsewhere outmoded and arguments elsewhere obsolete remained here remarkably apposite; and reality had no rejoinder to the mercantilist claim that "no reason can be given why men should always be let alone in their folly, when they may easily be made wise for themselves and their country." The very prosperity and power of England and France supported the argument that state regulation and control were imperative, at least until the state had sunk its foundations deep into the soil. From that conviction stemmed the acts of mercantilist policy in central and eastern Europe: the tireless

[1] P. W. Buck, *The Politics of Mercantilism* (New York, 1932), especially chs. iii and v.
[2] For a succinct interpretation, see E. Heckscher, "Mercantilism," in No. 5 of "Revisions in Economic History" in *Economic History Review*, VII (1936), 44-54; and for a detailed elaboration, the same author's *Mercantilism*, 2 vols. (New York, 1935), II.
[3] Cf. *infra*, ch. xi, p. 312 ff.

governmental efforts to set up diversified industries; the fostering of a favorable foreign trade; the disposal of surplus products abroad and the increase of the store of precious metals at home with which the expanded activities could be financed; the establishment, in short, of an integrated national economy as nearly self-sufficient as possible.

Reasoning from the same historical experiences, the eighteenth-century mercantilists accepted the need of secularizing social life and liberating it from ecclesiastical controls. But it was no part of the thinking of the state's rights apologists to dispense with faith in divine governance in order to establish in its place belief in a secular scheme of things whereby social equilibrium was automatically established without any checks or supervision from the state. They did not deny that there were unalterable natural laws governing human relations, for mercantilists were themselves among the foremost formulators of natural laws. Only through the "dextrous management of a skillful politician," they argued, could those laws be put to the service of humanity and avert either grave disorders or perhaps even a relapse into the Hobbesian phantasmagoria of war of all against all. They conceived the state as a trustee, a surrogate for its subjects, saving the community from the unrestrained greed and innate predacity of individuals, while by a wise and tempered system of controls it corrected the evils due to natural inequality. Hence, the unquestioning political loyalty of subjects to the king was the first line of state defense. This premise was the inner core of a political mythology which, by uniting subjects with their rulers in a benevolently coercive pattern of regulation, sanctified the acceptance of heavy obligations that seemed otherwise intolerable in the stark light of individual wants and aspirations. Not "Freedom," but "Order" was the slogan of statesmen; and there was no feeling that the two were incompatible.[4]

II. CAMERALISM IN CENTRAL AND SOUTHERN EUROPE

Mercantilism also had a long life in central, southern, and eastern Europe under the name of cameralism. Properly speaking, cameralism was a changing complex of ideals and practices which accompanied

---

[4] Apart from the orderly academic treatment, spiced with tart observations, in H. Finer, *The Theory and Practice of Modern Government*, 2 vols. (London. 1932), I, Part 2, ch. iii,

the historical evolution of the larger German states, and modified itself according to developing needs. Like the English mercantilists the German cameralists were the several generations of theorists who speculated on the nature of political sovereignty. They were also practical, everyday administrators who devised appropriately effective administrative procedure to make sure of the subjects' loyal obedience. Their outstanding figures in the age of enlightenment were J. H. G. Justi (1717-1771), scholar and teacher at various German universities, and J. von Sonnenfels (1732-1817), the adviser of three successive Hapsburg rulers and a tower of influence in shaping Austrian state policy.

With Hobbes and Pufendorff as their sources they readily proved by their own interpretation of the original social compact that state security demanded the surrender of individual rights into the repository of the monarch. Such was the argument in Sonnenfels' widely read textbook, *Grundsätze der Polizei, Handlung und Finanz-Wissenschaft.* Flexibly adjusting the doctrine to the altered circumstances of their day, Justi and Sonnenfels distinguished themselves in enfolding the understandably greater contemporary need for social justice in an elaborate economic argument replete with impressive repetition of such terms as "marginal," "aggregate demands," and "surplus." When one penetrates to the core of the disputation, it seems that they desired the prince to apply the state's surplus revenue for public welfare. As Justi put it with the characteristically light touch of legal phraseology:

The substance of all the duties of the ruler is accordingly to make his people happy, or to unite the happiness of each several citizen with the general good. All the duties of people and subjects may be reduced to the formula: to promote all the ways and means adopted by the ruler for their happiness, by their obedience, fidelity and diligence.[5]

These great eighteenth-century cameralists were also distinguished by their precepts for attaining administrative efficiency. They were

there are the two magnificent monographs, Fr. Meinecke, *Die Idee der Staatsräson in der neueren Geschichte* (Munich, 1924), and K. Wolzendorff, *Der Polizeigedanke des modernen Staats* (Breslau, (1918), chs. i and ii.

5 A. W. Small, *The Cameralists* (Chicago, 1909), 413, from Justi's *Die Natur und das Wesen der Staaten* (1760).

unyielding in their insistence that the existing administrative forms be modified and adapted to newer governmental services and that state officials receive a rigorously systematic and precise training in civil service. In that way educational selection would serve to buttress the social structure. Without other careers to attract the enterprising youth or opposing theoretical concepts to excite their emotions, it is easy to understand why cameralism enlisted the services and kept the intellectual approval of the most active and most capable of middle-class talents.[6]

Political speculators, apart from professionals like the cameralists, were on the whole a rarity in Germany. One could ill expect that curious mediaeval ghost, that historical anachronism called the Holy Roman Empire, to enlist the political loyalties of active Germans. Powerless to end the most flagrantly outrageous deeds of its member states, it lacked vitality even for its own affairs. It was an unburied corpse and an object of derision and shame for intelligent Germans, who wondered with the young Goethe how it contrived to stay together. The reforming princes, and they alone, captured the fancy and enlisted the allegiance of contemporaries. Yet the effete Holy Roman Empire successfully achieved by masterly ineptitude, and the smaller states through obscurantist misrule, what the larger showpiece states like Prussia, Austria, Weimar, and Brunswick accomplished by an excess of competence and coercive efficiency: they rendered individual political action supererogatory.

In the realm of political speculation no social group presumed to challenge the existing views. The German middle classes were far removed in spirit from that bourgeois nationalism which inspired the French alternately to robust criticism and high expectations. They had no burning interest in uniting the Germanies and establishing their control over it, because they still thought in local and regional terms. They were personally unknown to each other. By tradition, and also by economic interest, they left the initiative with their ruler and accepted his leadership. The German peasantry were also forced by circumstances to look to the prince for *panem et circenses*. The latter

6 The standard treatment in English is A. W. Small, *op. cit.*, chs. xiii-xxi; in German, the authoritative study of Louise Sommer, *Die Osterreichischen Kameralisten in Dogmen geschichtlicher Darstellung*, 2 vols. (Vienna, 1921-1925), II, 170-318; 319-444.

they rarely got, and the former only with sporadic sufficiency. And the aristocracy took political absolutism for granted and ate the king's bread.

Hence political thinking existed almost by default, impinging only upon the tranquil lives of that tiny fraction of the middle classes which by a determined stretch of interpretation could be called the intelligentsia: the professors, preachers, and civil servants. Since they all had a vested interest—their economic security and their spiritual peace—in maintaining the authority of the prince, there could be no question of faltering in loyalty. As men of ethical rectitude, they protested occasionally against the abuses of princely authority, but they couched their protests *sub specie aeternitatis*. This approach did not enhance the efficacy of their intervention against present evils. There were also unruly youthful spirits, loving liberty with only the vaguest ideas of what liberty was, who braved the princely lightning. But they were not numerous, these proto-Shelleys of the old regime, and most of them speedily acquired tact in rendering unto Caesar what was Caesar's.

There was another minority of well-to-do, educated, and serious-minded Germans whose protest against absolutism and coercion took a more poignant form. Refugees from the forbidding present, they found solace in the occult and the psychic, and in the esoteric rites of the more imaginative secret societies. United in spirit with the high priests of pure mumbo-jumbery, such as Knigge, Hamann and Cagliostro, they expressed their faith in liberty, equality, and benevolence in ways that pass the rational understanding of the uninitiate. These deviations were interesting but not significant, and the verdict that "the [serious] political thinkers in Germany in the eighteenth century until the time of the French Revolution were unanimous in their belief that enlightened despotism was the quintessence of political wisdom,"[7] can not be challenged.

The men of letters—the great Augustans, Lessing, Wieland, Goethe, and Schiller—were unimportant in the development of political speculation. Lessing may indeed have been "the champion destroyer of despotism and the master-builder of lawful freedom," as an admirer

7 R. Aris, *History of Political Thought in Germany, 1789-1815* (London, 1936), 65.

calls him, but for all the virility of his writing and thinking, his political speculation ranged far above the existing social world. He was truly above the battle, working for perfection and therefore not provoked into irritated impatience by the slowness of man's progress. Wieland, too, made his peace with princely absolutism, even less turbulently. Though he rarely hesitated to suggest improvements, he never went beyond the golden and peaceful mean of advocating the education of mankind as a remedy. He admired the French Revolution, when it came, at a safe distance, even as he admired the enlightenment of Frederick and Joseph and in his political novel, *Der Goldene Spiegel*, had set up a literary monument to these rulers. At first sight the immensely popular social novel, *Der Herr und der Diener* of Friedrich Karl von Moser (1759), which sold the unprecedented number of 10,000 copies, may have seemed like a challenge to princely authority. Actually, it was only a criticism of the inefficiency of government, and it had no substitute for the principle of government by enlightened absolutism. In the youthful Schiller, Germany had at least a rhetorical revolutionary, but the Olympian seer and patrician Goethe never allowed social problems seriously to disturb his magisterial serenity. "It is simply in my nature that I shall rather commit an injustice than suffer disorder." Even in his youthful Werther period it was not sociology but physiology that upset him. His highest ambition was to shape his life by the compulsion of his own superior inner being. This drain upon his energies disqualified him for an imaginative or sympathetic understanding of similar endeavors on the part of the less gifted. A royalist to the core, the faithful servant of Karl August of Weimar accepted the *status quo*. What is more, he thoroughly believed in it.[8]

The Spanish counterpart of the German cameralists were the *regalistas*, or the king's party. In Spain, as also throughout the Italian peninsula, the point of departure for the militant eighteenth-century champions of the royal prerogative had been the renewal of the ancient struggle between church and state. The original conflict

8 The most graphic and perhaps Germanic way of indicating the indifference of this urbane and typical representative of German middle-class intelligence to matters political is to cite statistics: During the fifty-four years (1778-1832) that he used the Weimar library, Goethe borrowed 2,276 books from it; of these only 29 had a political content, most of them dealing with the French Revolution. Cf. *ibid.*, 179, footnote 2.

deepened into a struggle involving all feudal and mediaeval restraints upon state activity. The great Spanish administrators were also men of thought: the intractable nobleman Count Aranda, foe of the Jesuits; the ennobled diplomat and economic reformer, Count Floridablanca, like Aranda an enthusiastic disciple of the French philosophers, and like Aranda too an uncompromising supporter of royal authority; the statesman, economist, and educator, Gaspar Jovellanos, one of the luminaries of the Spanish enlightenment and a tireless advocate of state initiative in the furtherance of popular education; and looming above all others, Count Campomanes, encyclopedic in his learning and his interests, jurist, classicist, historian, and economist, and of extraordinary influence as a practical administrator and reformer.[9]

Italian speculation bore a particularist rather than national impress. For sound historical reasons the intellectual spokesmen of southern Italy were strangely predisposed in favor of the doctrines of enlightened absolutism. Neapolitan thought was particularly conditioned in that respect because of the long conflict that the state had waged since the middle ages against the temporal claims of the papacy. The cogent arguments of the Neapolitan jurist and philosopher, P. Giannone, against the political claims of the curia and his plea for democratic government within the church itself were echoed by a long line of writers throughout the century.[10] A generation later, the writings of the Neapolitan economist, the Abbé Galiani (1728-1787), wit and darling of the Paris salons, took up Giannone's views. Arguing more from the point of view of the economist than from that of the statesman, he too stressed the inescapable necessity in a well-ordered state of having only one authority and one law. His contemporary, Antonio Genovesi, professor of commerce at the University of Naples, inclined somewhat more sympathetically to physiocracy, but he was also essentially a proponent of state action against the centrifugal forces of feudalism and economic urbanism. It was in that spirit that Tanucci, the great statesman of Charles III's Neapolitan days, effected his reforms, and that the pro-Rousseauist Gaetano Filangieri wrote his

9 Desdevises du Dézert, *op. cit.*, LXX (1927), 30 ff.
10 Cf. his *The Civil History of the Kingdom of Naples* (in English translation, 1729-1731).

hopeful treatise for the guidance of man, *La Scienza della Legislazione* (1787).[11]

III. THE TRANSIT OF LIBERALISM TO THE CONTINENT

While state's rights theorists enlarged the scope of princely duties and justified absolutism to itself, restive men elsewhere, more eager to put curbs on princes and priests, renewed the search for sanctions that would confirm the right of resistance. Logical justifications to combat royal oppression they had at hand in the political theories both of Jesuits and of Calvinists. But apart from the incongruity of having Jansenist-minded French Catholics accept Jesuit papal arguments against absolutism, the very cast of thought of the French critics compelled them to look for secular rather than theological arguments against royal absolutism. Such an argument, indeed a polity resting upon the cardinal proposition that a government derives its just powers from the consent of the governed, existed for all to admire in England.

The English had torn down the structure of dynastic relations which demanded prescriptive obedience from the subjects. They had fashioned the new conception of a community of ungraded citizens pursuing their joint and mutual interests independently of the fiat of their royal master. Freeing themselves first from the supervision of Rome, they rejected both the fiscal demands of the papacy and the argument for the ecclesiastical superintendence of economic activities. By the eighteenth century the older religious controversies between Anglicans and Dissenters had passed into memory, and orthodox theology itself had become a prudential compromise between the claims of God and mammon. The Protestant ethic meantime had blandly accommodated itself to the robust spirit of capitalist gain. The revolution in thought was correlative with the bloodless political revolution and the religious transformations. It dated back to and reflected the stupendous material changes effected from the seventeenth century on, by the constant and uninterrupted play of overseas endeavor.

---

11 The most useful treatments in English are G. Ruggiero, *A History of European Liberalism* (London, 1927), 275 ff., and F. De Sanctis, *A History of Italian Literature*, 2 vols. (New York, 1931), II, 275 ff.; in Italian, the brief volume of A. M. Ghisalberti, *Gli albori del risorgimento italiano* (Rome, 1931), is a valuable introduction, and G. Ruggiero's detailed study, *Il Pensiero politico meridionale nei secoli 18 e 19* (Bari, 1922), is fundamental.

As adventurers and merchant capitalists moved away in their practice from mediaeval collectivism into the orbit of private gain, and as the mediaeval ideal of mutual obligation weakened under the impact of innumerable projects that fired the imagination of men and enterprise, as "human knowledge and human powers met in one," the thinking of man was profoundly altered. With Locke's seminal *Essay on the Human Understanding* as his gospel, the eighteenth-century Englishman made the senses the basis of a new ethic divorced from Christian theology. For those who gave thought, Locke sealed the legitimacy of man's right to change his institutions by making that right derive from man's rational nature. He formulated a new metaphysic by postulating a new psychology which reintegrated man into the universal order of nature, that nature from which man had so long been excluded by the long-faced theology of original sin.

In doing so he only gave intellectual certification to the faith that successful men had obtained from experience itself. Life was already convincing them that by taking thought and profiting by their mistakes, they could improve themselves and rise to a higher station in life. This they could do, Locke thought, not only without flouting God's will, but also without recourse to the formal, exclusive guidance of Christian leaders. Indeed, by taking thought for themselves they would on the contrary most efficaciously and most reverently fulfill His will and bring themselves and their institutions into harmony with the divine plan. This same human reason and experience, when applied to the world of political relations, also demonstrated that only one type of government would correspond with the natural harmony of God's universe. Such a government would manifestly derive its powers from and rest upon the individual's consent and would be jealously protective of his life, liberty, and possessions.[12]

After the final stilling of political convulsions, when the Pretender's reckless Highlanders were routed at Culloden in 1746, the prosperous English oligarchy could rightly reckon that liberty repaid in blessings what it had cost in sacrifice, particularly since the blessings were largely theirs and the sacrifices those of other social groups. Almost

12 In addition to Locke's own writings and the formal histories of political thought, there is the illuminating second chapter of Carl Becker's *Declaration of Independence* (New York, 1922).

as much as Englishmen themselves, the discerning *cognoscenti* of the Continent extolled the advantages of constitutionalism. They gloried in the supremacy of the civil law over military arrogance. They vaunted a judiciary that was independent of the executive and they swelled with pride over a press that appeared free and uncensored. They pointed admiringly to the Commons' control of the public purse, to the orderliness of parliamentary government, and to its resolute check against irresponsible executive initiative. Embittered by their own grievances and only casually acquainted with the English system, its admirers failed to note that all those great constitutional achievements were relatively true, and they had no eyes to see the squalor and disease, the cruelty, the violence, the misery, and the suffering, that also characterized the lives of the admired free-born Englishmen.

To a Europe held fast in the meshes of bureaucratic and absolutist restraints the example of England was therefore both a challenge and an inspiration. With her constitutional government and her doctrine of political liberty, with her resplendent prosperity, with her powerful navy and her empire, and with resounding victories in war, England seemed to proclaim that order followed not from despotism but from freedom; that liberty, not restraint, was the seal of national unity; that individual enterprise, not monarchical regulation, was the golden road to wealth and plenty. By adapting the needs of the state to the claims of the individual and by extending the idea of national interest to include, if not to rest upon, the sense of private property and the right of free enterprise, the English revolutionaries had given a decisive orientation to man's thinking. Gibbon was guilty only of a lesser rhetorical flourish when he noted, shortly after the close of the Seven Years' war, that "Our ways, our fashions, even our games were adopted in France; a ray of national glory illuminated each individual and every Englishman was supposed to be born a patriot and a philosopher." And a decade and a half later the perfect figure of a liberal, Dr. Moore, discovered in the *grand tour* a supreme opportunity for the fuller appreciation of the advantages of being born an Englishman:

Lastly, by visiting other countries, a subject of Great Britain, will acquire a greater esteem than ever for the constitution of his own. Freed from vulgar prejudices, he will perceive that the blessings and advantages which his countrymen enjoy do not flow from their superiority in wisdom, courage or virtue over the other nations of the world, but in some degree from the peculiarity of their situation in an island; and, above all, from those just and equitable laws which secure property, that mild free government which abhors tyranny, protects the meanest subjects and leaves the mind of man to its own exertion, unrestrained by those arbitrary, capricious, impolitic shackles, which confine and weaken its noblest endeavors in almost every other country of the world.[13]

Early in the century the spirit of inquiry crossed the Channel. English ideas infiltrated into France through travelers and merchants and through the private correspondence of those unhappy Huguenot exiles who had fled abroad to escape the plague of persecution. So long as the Sun King still reigned, his critics were isolated figures. *Jacqueries* there were, and curses to speed the monarch to his grave, but no more. In the period of post-war recuperation and new expansion, in the generation from 1713-1740, fissures first showed themselves in the governmental structure, and an anonymous generation of literary levelers broached most of the ideas associated with the later *philosophes*. Copied in longhand by tireless scribes, their treatises, more than a hundred in number, circulated *sub rosa* but widely among the Parisian intellectuals and the liberal aristocratic opposition.[14]

The major and familiar works of the great *philosophes* were all published during the decades of the fifties and the sixties. The censorship still existed and its penalties were still ferocious, but with the assistance of such strategically situated sympathizers in the administration as Machault, Malesherbes, and the cultivated Madame de Pompadour, the "armed doctrine" of liberalism overcame the malevolence of the "devout faction" at the court and the opposition of "the arrogant magistracy and a persecuting clergy." By a multitude of devices, some almost frivolously gay and others recklessly dangerous, the liberals who professed to speak for humanity triumphed over the opposition and radiated their propaganda all over France. Not only over France, however. For in the salons, where they so finely tempered their literary expression, foregathered the élite of

13 J. Moore, *op. cit.*, 567-568.
14 O. Wade, *The Clandestine Organization and Diffusion of Philosophic Ideas in France from 1700 to 1750* (Princeton, 1928).

the European intellectual aristocracy. Through the undisputed sway which French culture still held over European thought, in that prevailing cosmopolitan freemasonry of the spirit, they found an opportunity as had never before presented itself to disseminate their views and collaborate with the cultural leaders of all Europe in the glorious task of regenerating humanity.

The French *philosophes* were no formal academic philosophers. True philosophers there were indeed among them, and psychologists of acute critical discernment. They counted in their ranks scientists, geographers, historians, and economists, novelists, poets, and essayists of unquestioned technical proficiency and unparalleled literary persuasiveness. Many were men of enormous talent. A few of them, like Diderot, were men of genius. They had also a normal quota of hacks, perhaps even an abnormal quota. But they were no secret conspirators plotting the violent overthrow of society. They mingled easily and openly in the best and highest circles and they desired nothing so much as wide publicity for their works and plaudits from their readers. They were no schemers, working each in obedience to instructions, according to his special capacity for subversive mischief. There was in fact much to keep them apart in personal antipathies and in more impersonal differences of opinion. United the *philosophes* were, however, in their single earnestness to rid the world of monkishness, superstition, hypocrisy and hocus-pocus, injustice, and cruelty. They were knights of the pen, fired by a truly religious fervor to deserve well of mankind in all posterity—and yet not do too badly for themselves in the present. "It gives me pleasure to note," wrote the jubilant Grimm late in 1767, "that an immense republic of cultivated spirits is being formed in Europe; enlightenment is spreading on all sides."[15] Joined in a compulsion to annihilate what was evil, and confident that, if not they, surely their children would use as a gauge for human betterment the standards they discovered in reason and science, the *philosophes* stood at the very threshold of modernity.

Social Newtonism was their gospel during most of the century, however much they broadened the range of their scientific interest from mathematics and physics to anatomy, chemistry, and natural

15 Grimm, *Correspondance littéraire*, VII (Sept. 15, 1767), 420.

history. Nature to them was the great whole, an assemblage presenting only matter and motion, an immense, uninterrupted succession of causes and effects, all orderly, all harmonious, all established and directed by a master mechanic for the edification and the guidance of thinking man. So orderly and rational did the great system of nature appear that the natural became identified with the rational; and by an easy extension, that which was reasonable in *human* society perforce was also natural, rooted in the very nature of things. Nature was sovereign of all things; virtue, reason, and truth were her "adorable daughters." As the century advanced, the meaning of natural and rational received other shadings; and natural, for a handful of intransigent materialists, became identified with the blind and irrational. Yet somehow the schematic simplicity and grandeur of the orderly Newtonian universe remained as an after-image in the thinking of the *philosophes* about the social universe.

Many a hostile critic has subsequently denied their conclusions and condemned the character of their speculation. But almost two centuries ago Grimm had already scored the abstract quality of their thought:

All our knowledge consists in generalizing our ideas, in imagining relations which exist only in our head which, while they honor our imagination or our wisdom, are none the less chimerical; in formulating, in a word, on the basis of a few particular facts, inductions from which we establish so-called eternal and invariable laws that nature has never known.[16]

Time has not withered the justice of his observation, but the *philosophes'* comprehension of social reality more than atones for the deficiencies of their formal logic. Voltaire got at the hard common sense of the matter when he wrote that God had endowed man with reason in order to live well and not to penetrate into the essence of His being. What was involved was not an issue of pure reason, but the problem of applying reason to provide solutions for pressing human problems. The *philosophes* who blew up the once solid bases of mediaeval speculation and created the social sciences compelled the modern world to judge political relations in terms of human dignity here and now, and to evaluate their worth by norms of social reason and in the light of human experiment. For that service alone

16 *Ibid.*, VI (July 1, 1764), 26.

humanity is still in their debt. Their own individual reasoning was no doubt still shortsighted, but in the realm of the socially blind even a one-eyed scientist was king.

Much remained to be written, and indeed much was written in the last two decades of the old regime. But even in the France of the old regime which is traditionally associated with the emerging slogans of Liberty and Equality, the dominant trend of political speculation endorsed the rule of the enlightened and benevolent prince. At least it did so until the concomitant failure of the Turgot-Necker reform program and the victory of the thirteen American colonies inflicted a violent shock alike to the traditional system and to the champions of enlightened absolutism.

Voltaire and Diderot were not unrepresentative of the older generation of *philosophes*, who in the main helped to gain the advantages of constitutional rule but vaguely expected to attain them by following the road of enlightened monarchical rule. Bourgeois by birth, aristocratic humanist by training and inclination, but *grand seigneur* by social acclimatization, Voltaire was a complete worldling, loving his ease and reveling in the luxury of tasteful adornments. "Every *honnête homme*," he wrote, "has those views." Confident in man's progress, he was enormously practical and incapable of abandoning a cautious reserve in social matters. He was certainly no radical, not even a democrat. More than once he referred to the masses as *canaille*, certainly without any ill intent but, what is worse, without true consciousness of his prejudice. He had, too, very little specific interest in the details of political theories, and his tireless pen never wrote a systematic treatise on political relations. He was by conviction and temperament an enthusiast of enlightened despotism. His *Age of Louis XIV* can hardly be considered a hostile treatment of the *grand monarque*. His praise of Frederick and his well-rewarded admiration for Catherine were notorious. If he was excited to enthusiasm over the government of China and its civilization, it was because he was convinced that the greatness of that country stemmed from the practical application that the responsible classes of the state made of the teaching of its sages, such as Confucius. If he set great store by the English constitutional arrangement, it was for the benefit of the French middle classes that he courageously extolled the conquests won by their English compeers. With these liberties he remained content in deed and in thought. Even as the deist in him built God a temple, preferring to invent a God even if He did not exist, so the landed proprietor who attacked the cruel absurdities of serfdom shrank from the idea of economic equality. It was a property-conscious liberal who wrote, "We are all equals as men but not equal in society." Manifestly, there was nothing reprehensible in his doing so, but the fact is worth recording. To put the authority of the enlightened prince behind the accomplishment of Voltairian reforms was the real essence of his political credo.[17]

The generous and warmhearted Diderot was torn between two contradictory passions. The moralist and sentimentalist in him propelled him forward to think in egalitarian terms that could be called Rousseauist had they not appeared a full decade before the *Social Contract* saw the light of day. His hatred of privilege and his humanitarian benevolence made him advocate sweeping measures to remedy the existing social inequalities. But there was a Diderot who looked for short cuts to Utopia, who enthusiastically admired Le Mercier's "legal despotism." The Diderot who was the beneficiary of Catherine the Great's largesse drew back from the implications of his sentimental radicalism. In substance he too placed his faith in progress from above. "We will preach against insensate laws until they are reformed," he said, "and meantime we will submit to them." Though he limited the authority of the prince to executing the laws of nature, he made active membership in the state a function of property. "It is property that makes the citizen: every man who has possessions in the state is interested in the state; and . . . it is by reason of his possessions that he ought to speak, and that he acquires the right of having himself represented."[18]

IV. "LEGAL DESPOTISM"

Voltaire and Diderot threw out suggestions, but the three volumes of Holbach's *Système sociale ou principes naturelles de la morale et de*

17 In many respects, H. N. Brailsford's small volume, *Voltaire* (London, 1935), is the most useful introduction to this aspect of Voltaire's career.
18 From his article "Représentants" in the *Encyclopédie*, quoted in J. H. Randall, *The Making of the Modern Mind* (New York, 1926), 337.

la politique (1772-1773) was a true code of enlightened despotism.[19] Rejecting all recourse to supernatural sanctions, Holbach made universal necessity, the complete determinism prevailing in nature and in human nature, the motive force of human conduct. Out of self-love man is fated to seek pleasure and avoid pain. But men differ among themselves, and in their diversity resides inequality. This inequality is the basis of society. While men are different and unequal by nature—differences of environment, food, and clothing enhancing biologic differences—they are not good or bad by nature. Such distinctions do not arise out of human conventions. Even less do they derive from divine law. Goodness and badness correspond to eternal and invariable relations between human beings living in society. A social compact therefore exists, but it is a natural, not man-made, pact which binds men together. According to these necessary relations "virtue" resolves itself into a descriptive term for those actions which are constantly useful to society.

Thus Holbach secularized ethics, cutting the umbilical cord which tied morality to religion. Morality becomes the necessity of employing the proper means ("fulfilling one's duties") of making happy those with whom we have to live, so that they in turn may make us happy. Were we living in a properly organized society, we would recognize that it is to our own interest to be virtuous, and that self-interest alone is the basis of morality. But experience has shown that the individual is neither always quick enough nor always able to act according to his own interests. Hence he must be aided by more enlightened minds, and "politics ought to be the art of regulating the passions of men, and directing them towards the good of society.[20] By that aphorism Holbach means that the obligations inherent in the natural social pact must be effectively enforced by the sanctions of the law. He is a libertarian for whom true liberty lies in obeying "the laws which remedy the natural inequality of men." Law is equally binding on all members of the state. As the expression of the general will, it ought to restrain the sovereign as well as the people, to define and limit

---

[19] An illuminating and discriminating treatment of French political ideas is the old work of H. Michel, *L'idée de l'état* (Paris, 1896).
[20] From Holbach's *Système de la nature* (1780 ed.), I, 141, quoted in B. Willey, *The Eighteenth Century Background* (New York, 1940), 159.

his powers and give the people the right not to obey him when the prince fails "to assure to the greatest number of citizens the advantages for which they are leagued together. These advantages are liberty, property, and security."

Like Rousseau before him, Holbach was manifestly prescribing for the ideal state. His reiterated use of "ought" alone made that clear. The spirit of his thought was democratic; but the letter prescribed enlightened absolutism. While awaiting that happy era when all subjects of the prince would reach the requisite intellectual maturity to share in legislation, the philosopher-king, supported by the intellectual élite, would take a short cut toward Utopia. For all his enticing suggestions concerning the future, Holbach entrusted man's fate in the present to the prince. Ultimately the prince would become supererogatory, but not until he had dispelled the ignorance that made the people a prey to demagogues and cruel fanatics and achieved his destiny of educating his subjects into the responsibilities of citizenship. Stimulated by hopefulness in his own picture of the rule of morality, Holbach was inspired, when Louis XVI and Turgot collaborated for a moment in their reform program, to dedicate a little book to them. He called it *Ethocracy*, the rule of virtue. The political thinking of his fellow Encyclopedist, the great Alembert, followed similar lines. Even after one discounts his conventionally trite compliments, more than a modicum of sincerity remains in his Discourse to the Academy of Science in 1768, when, calling upon the French king to protect philosophy, that "timid and modest truth," he declared that the "greatest happiness of a nation is to have those who govern it be in accord with those who instruct it."[21]

The position of the physiocrats is more difficult of analysis. Experienced and progressive business men and trained, many of them, in government administration, they were also theorists who wove their keen observations about capitalist economics into the pattern of a broad social philosophy. Upon the bases of their utilitarian philosophy of social relations they set a theory of political relations which was symbolized in their own catch phrase of "Legal Despotism." All of them from their revered leader, the court physician Dr. Quesnay,

21 Grimm, *op. cit.*, VIII. 216-218.

whom they styled the "Confucius of the West," to the humblest of
his disciples concerned themselves primarily with the economic renovation of France. From firsthand business experience they drew the
conclusion that the basic structural flaw was the unjustly conceived
and wretchedly administered system of taxation. The first endeavor,
accordingly, of these keen capitalist economists was to lay the foundations of a solid fiscal administration. Their views on taxation were
therefore no appendix tagged on, as it were, to their discussion of
economic problems. These views were the very core of their credo.[22]
One-third of Le Mercier de la Rivière's once famous study *L'ordre
naturel et essentiel des sociétés politiques* (1767) deals with the theory
of taxation and almost another third compiles data on the wealth of
nations. This is a work which Adam Smith is known to have read
with much profit and of which another physiocrat, Dupont de
Nemours, stated with truly modest candor: "Here is a summary of
that teaching which in accordance with the nature of man, reveals the
laws essential to government made for man and proper to all climates
and to all lands."[23]

The fundamental basis of the natural order according to Le Mercier
was the right of property. Without it society could have no meaning.
All governmental activity should "trend toward the greatest possible
increase of production and population and assure the greatest possible
happiness to those living in society." But less pontifically, it was the
duty of the state, through the person of the "legal despot," to guarantee
the rights of property, security, and that free competition which they
deemed the mainspring of human perfectibility. The most vital link
between the "legal despot" and his subjects being the system of
taxation, "therefore," argued Le Mercier, "by reason of the fact that
this public revenue for annual expenditures can be maintained only
by annual replenishing, it is evident that this public revenue can be
nothing else but a portion of the value of production which the soil
gives every year.[24] Here was the great panacea for the fiscal ills of

22 The best brief treatment is G. Weulersse, *Les physiocrates* (Paris, 1932), which is a
condensed restatement of his earlier and fuller work, *Le mouvement physiocratique en
France depuis 1756 à 1770*, 2 vols. (Paris, 1910); in English cf. H. Higgs, *The Physiocrats*
(London, 1897).
23 Lotte Silberstein, *Lemercier de la Rivière und seine politischen Ideen* (Berlin, 1928).
24 Le Mercier de la Rivière, *L'ordre naturel et essentiel des sociétés politiques* (Paris,
1767), 459.

society, and for the evils that swept in the train of inequitable taxation: the single tax upon the land, their famous *impôt unique*. However, this single tax could not be equitably assessed until the monarchy had first set up a *cadastre*, or public registration, giving a catalogued statement of the location, extent, and value of the landed property in the realm. Once instituted, the single tax brought it within the realm of possibility to rationalize the whole of agricultural life. The augmented revenues of the state would be more than ample to finance the necessary economic improvements: abolition of the vexatious survivals of feudalism in the hunting and fishing rights, the grant of advances and subsidies to progressive proprietors, the improvement of means of transportation, and introduction of the absolute freedom of grain trade throughout the length and breadth of the kingdom.

Fiscal reforms and the increase of agricultural production would be incomplete without a similar guarantee of individual rights in other fields of economic endeavor. To assure the individual his full rights to possess property, to work, buy, and sell in perfect freedom, it was also necessary to abolish corporate guilds and introduce a free internal transit in human and intellectual resources as well as in goods and money. Money, men, and materials had to be brought together when and where they were most needed with the minimum of regulation and red tape. Their "natural and essential order" connoted peace in international relations as well as tranquillity within each country. It implied a federation of nations, a kind of holy alliance of proprietors, bound to one another by self-interest to end the scourge of ruinous war and, through free trade for all, gain security for each. Finally, all this program of material advance would remain otiose unless the citizen were concurrently protected in his less material interests, in his right to speak and write freely and believe as his conscience impelled him to believe; above all, his right to receive that public instruction which would some day make him too like unto a king.

The detailed blueprints for governmental action in Le Mercier's book tremendously impressed his contemporaries. The ebullient Diderot wrote in characteristic, unmeasured enthusiasm: "When the Empress [Catherine] will have that man, what good to her will be the Quesnay, the Mirabeau, the Voltaire, the D'Alembert, the Diderot? None, my good friend, none. It is he who has discovered the secret, the real secret, the eternal and unchanging secret of the security, the duration, and the happiness of states."[25] By their stress upon man's liberties, and his capacity along with his right to be responsible for his destiny, the physiocrats seemed to take an unequivocal stand with the champions of individualism. They appeared thus at the antipodes of the cameralists who would attain order through "the dextrous manipulations of a skillful politician." Nevertheless, this stand was more apparent than real. The heart of their political doctrine was the way in which the legal despot fulfilled what Le Mercier called "the obligations laid upon sovereigns to promulgate by positive ordinances the natural and essential laws of the social order." Again and again they made clear that state activity had to continue and that these liberties could not be secured save by the singleness of political authority. "It is the essence of authority," intoned by Le Mercier, "that to separate it and divide it, is to render it incapable of action and in consequence to nullify it."

Their legal despotism was in fact a gigantic effort at compromise between monarchical and individual rights. In a way it was also a threat that amounted to saying to rulers that this was how monarchs should govern, if their propertied subjects would allow them to govern at all. Each contemporary prince, sitting on his throne, could satisfy their requirements, provided that he, "the single force and single unity," agreed to chart his policy under the guidance of the laws which their wisdom had discovered. Their doctrine thus transformed the absolute prince into the "legal despot." It left him with all the trappings of power, but it gave him little more actual authority than a supreme gendarme patrolling the area of bourgeois enterprise. As in their greatly admired China, the enlightened prince would give peace and bring happiness to all because, while following the laws of nature himself, he would be guiding all his subjects toward an understanding of the eternal principles presently grasped by only the élite. For the moment he was to accept the counsel of a quasi-senate of landed proprietors. When, however, in the fullness of philosophical time, all his subjects were sufficiently educated, he would have to rely upon a broader enlightened public opinion.[26]

All that these warmhearted reformers, these foes of clerical asceticism and enemies of aristocratic and monarchical absurdities, could do was to bring themselves to a sort of negative, restricted individualism. The absolute monarch was their foe, the enemy of the upper middle classes whom they represented, but they would not have the property-less as their associates in the struggle for power. The ruler they would tame, bloodlessly, without violence, binding him by the restraints of the law. To the masses, whom their doctrine also endowed with rights, they counseled patience. They were agreed to unravel the web of governmental regulations, but slowly and with discretion. They left much for the state to perform in maintaining law and order, in public administration, in education and social welfare. They permitted themselves the exercise of their natural right to negotiate as equals with the monarch, but they hesitated to place the burden of such heavy responsibilities upon the untutored and the unpropertied.

It is not too difficult to follow them in their reservations concerning the wisdom of permitting all individuals alike to participate in government. Rigidly determinist in their utilitarian explanations concerning the vagaries of human behavior, they had convinced themselves that only the peaceful intervention of the naturally superior could rescue the naturally inferior from the disadvantages of their position. That conclusion was an abstraction which rationalized their social snobbery. It articulated with their intellectualist scorn for "vulgar enthusiasm," as for example, the untempered piety of crude Methodist evangelicals. It reflected their fear of the turbulent populace. The sharp tensions created by the shift from a dying mediaeval and feudal society to a nascent capitalist world of free enterprise provoked recurring outbreaks of popular violence. It is scarcely surprising that leading capitalist theorists failed to approve of attacks upon law and order.[27]

---

[26] For an interesting discussion of the influence of China upon the physiocrats and especially upon Dr. Quesnay, cf. A. Reichwein, *China and Europe* (New York, 1925), 102 ff., and L. A. Maverick, "Chinese Influences upon the Physiocrats," in *Economic History* (1938), 54-68.

[27] For the attitude of the French liberals toward the English experiment in self-government, cf. E. Bonno, *La constitution britannique devant l'opinion française de Montesquieu à Bonaparte* (Paris, 1932); consult also H. Holldeck, "Der Physiokratismus und die Absolute Monarchie," in *Historische Zeitschrift*, Bd. CXLV (1931), 517-549; and A. Mathiez, "Les doctrines politiques des physiocrates," in *Annales historiques de la Révolution française* (mai-juin, 1936).

These champions of enlightened despotism dwelt in a strange political no-man's-land, a border country still reminiscent of the familiar topography of old regime absolutism, but verging upon the new terrain of parliamentary constitutionalism. When rulers stood on the defensive, calling themselves the first servants of the state, writing political "testaments" for the edification of their successors, and doing vicarious penance through their own heightened welfare activities for their predecessors' sins of omission, the intellectual élite also grasped at the opportunity to make princes useful to society. The more conservative frankly defended monarchical institutions on historical grounds, adapting and extending state activity to newer needs. The more liberal of the liberal-conservatives narrowed the range of state action without daring to eliminate it entirely. Resigning their children and grandchildren to the seemly tranquillity of a world without princes, they made the best of the present world by keeping the prince on his throne, but in leading strings of purple. The only remedy against the complexity of modern life and ever-threatening anarchy, wrote Grimm, lay in the genius and in the heart of him who acquired the right to rule by birth. Hence a catechism, composed by sages like Grimm himself for the guidance of princes, "would stifle in his heart the germs of all teachings contrary to justice, goodness and humanity."[28]

28 The catechism that Grimm helpfully drew up after this introduction is a classic statement of the position of the conservative intellectual reformer. Cf. Grimm, *op. cit.*, III (May 1, 1756), 217-220.

Chapter Four

THE SEARCH FOR SECURITY: THE GERMAN MODEL

I. THE TAP ROOTS OF PRUSSIANISM

FREDERICK II was the royal frontispiece of the century and his Prussia was the model *par excellence* for all other practitioners of enlightened despotism. He was, said Goethe, recalling his own youthful admiration: "The polar star, who seemed to turn about himself, Germany, Europe, nay the whole world." The three Silesian wars subjected his resources, the very existence of his heritage, to a terrific strain. From these wars he emerged victorious, but Prussia was exhausted, drained of her strength. No one realized better that only by a long period of peaceful recuperation could the ravages of the past two decades be repaired and the rich resources of the dearly won Silesia be exploited. It was in that second half of his long reign, from 1763 to 1786, when his statesmanship was put to the supreme test, that he showed himself according to his many admirers the "personification of creative action" whose "will exploited the shrewdness of his country, broke through the narrow-mindedness of his subjects . . . [and] completely transformed the modest and inferior milieu which he had inherited. . . ."[1]

Certainly, his views had not altered during the terrible years of war. After the peace he strove with patience and infinite resourcefulness to realize the domestic policies whose fulfillment long years of fighting had thwarted. He remained wedded to the cameralist precepts which he had penned in the *Considérations sur l'état présent du corps politique de l'Europe* (1738) and in the *Réfutation du prince Machiavel* (1739) when he was still only the heir to the throne. In the two *Political Testaments* of 1752 and 1768, in private correspondence, and in his *Essai sur les formes de gouvernement* (1777) he reiterated his

[1] Veit Valentin, "Some Interpretations of Frederick the Great," in *History* (1934), 115-123.

conception of the sovereign as the first servant of the state: "The prince is to the society that he governs what the head is to the body."[2] To a considerable extent he kept intact the form of the administrative system as he inherited it. In practice he violated the famed and admired principle of anonymous, impersonal, and collegiate responsibility of the civil servants—even as his father had occasionally done in the very process of creating the Prussian bureaucracy. From the very outset of his reign he began to give up the geographical location of the provinces as an efficient basis for the distribution of work among the departments of the General Directory. He set up new specialized departments—Commerce and Industry in 1741, War Supplies in 1746, Excise and Tolls in 1766, Mines in 1768, and Forestry in 1770—to whose ministerial heads he gave a far greater measure of initiative than the old department chiefs of the Directory had ever enjoyed. In withdrawing these functions from the jurisdiction of the Directory Frederick did not give up his intention of supervising and co-ordinating and supplying the indispensable unity of planning to all aspects of public policy. This intention was not always realized. The key administrators did not readily resign themselves to the role of superior clerks. He continued to the end the procedure of communicating directly with the leading provincial officials and of initiating as many measures as his tireless energy and the weakness or affability of individual administrators permitted. Katt and Boden were efficient administrators, Heinitz and Zedlitz, loyal ministers, and Podewils, Finckenstein, and Hertzberg, able officials. But the impulse came from the ruler himself. Conquered Silesia was not incorporated into the general system but was governed by a resident official directly responsible to the king.

Frederick worked, silent and alone, in his Potsdam fastness, toiling like no other ruler of his day for almost half a century. A splenetic type, alternately gay and irascible, he was a hard taskmaster and unloved. But he drove himself as hard as any of his subordinates. The ruler who swore that he would not "enjoy happiness while everybody suffers" died a sordid death, unworthy of such selfless devotion

2 O. Hintze, "Friedrich der Grosse nach dem Siebenjährigen Kriege und das Politische Testament von 1768," in *Forschungen zur Brandenburgischen und Preussischen Geschichte*, hereafter cited as F. B. P. G., XXXII (1920), 1-56, for the continuity of Frederick's political views.

to duty. For days at the end he suffered dreadfully, and when he failed to meet his secretaries by midday on August 16, 1786, it was presumed that he was dying. So sneered Mirabeau, who has recorded the relief of the Berlin populace at the monarch's passing. He died before the following dawn in the arms of his orderly with no one from his family present.

The Prussian argus impaired the principle of collegiate bureaucratic solidarity built up by his forebears, but he remained faithful to his inherited social outlook. His views received their final incorporation in the famous law code which was promulgated after his death in 1794, after being elaborated in intermittent bursts of legal energy by his jurists over a span of several decades. First, however, they effected that far-reaching reformation of civil procedure which was to make Prussian justice the most honest and efficient in Europe. While the major credit for the changes goes to the veteran jurist Samuel von Cocceji, it was the king who supported him unswervingly and, with a conscientiousness unique among rulers, refrained from interfering with due process of law. In 1781 Chancellor von Carmer and the great Silesian jurist K. G. Svarez completed the earlier work of Cocceji by instituting a uniform civil procedure for the entire country, a reform which permitted the average well-trained, honest, and well-paid magistrate to rule "like an earthly providence."

To Cocceji also belongs credit for the first draft of a civil code for Prussia. His project, while abortive, was enormously admired at home and abroad by a generation sympathetically inclined to believe that all problems involving the law and possibly life itself could be solved if only jurists had a neat and rationally synthesized code to light the road to their decisions. "If laws are simple and clear," said the Abbé Mably reflecting that belief, "there is no need for much study to make good men."[3] Voltaire burst into rapturous verse over Cocceji's astounding patchwork of Roman, feudal, and ecclesiastical legal procedures. He surpassed even his own lofty standards of fulsome praise for monarchs and hailed Frederick, the inspiration of that draft, as *"grand juge, grand faiseur de vers, conquérant législateur."* Though Frederick loaded Cocceji with honors, the old man soon died, as old men do. Fortunately his draft was buried with him.

[3] Quoted in W. Seagle, *The Quest for Law* (New York, 1941), 279.

A generation later Svarez and Carmer utilized what they could of his conceptions and, adding their own and Frederick's views, drew up that famous Prussian code of 1794 which was to remain in force until 1900. Its preamble promised well: "The welfare of the state and its inhabitants is the object of society and the limiting condition of legislation. Laws must limit the liberty and the rights of the citizen only in the interest of the general good." But the promise was largely illusory. The concern for social welfare, real as it undoubtedly was, remained an empty phrase so long as it was joined to a conception of a state in which the individuals of each class performed duties and had rights inherent in their membership in a particular legal group, and so long as it rested upon the monarch's blind faith in the surpassing if not exclusive courage, loyalty, and moral supremacy of the landowning nobility. The legal ratification of the predominant position of the landed aristocracy consequently far outweighed in social significance the recognition that the code paid to liberty of conscience, the civil rights of the individual (provided he were not a serf), and the sanctity of private property. To say with Schmoller of Frederick that "under him the Prussian state was based as much on legal security and on freedom of thought and individual opinion as upon discipline, obedience and subordination" is to possess a singularly starved conception of security and freedom and evince an awe-inspiring predisposition for obedience and subordination.[4]

II. AGRICULTURAL POLICY

During the so-called "halcyon years" between 1746 and 1756, when Frederick's troops were not campaigning in the field, he launched the agricultural schemes that were only to see full realization many years later. Here too he followed his father's lines. The greatest single achievement was the draining and the recovery for cultivation of the swampy area along the lower Oder River, and its settlement by more than 50,000 colonists drawn from neighboring states by easy terms and

4 G. Schmoller, *The Mercantile System and its Historical Significance* (printing of 1931), 90. Apart from the excellent brief account in O. Hintze, *Die Hohenzollern und ihr Werk*, 7th ed. (Berlin, 1916), 395 ff., see the longer account in H. Tuttle's older and more severe *History of Prussia Under Frederick the Great*, 3 vols. (Boston, 1884-1896), III, 107-132. The most detailed study of Cocceji is in M. Springer, *Die Coccejische Justizreform* (Berlin, 1914).

promises easier still. The catastrophic war undid much of his early work but, undaunted, Frederick devised his famous *"Rétablissements"* program of post-war recovery. Drawing upon his dwindled (and debased) metallic reserve, he disbursed millions of thalers to succor the devastated areas, giving the peasants free grain for consumption and sowing, fodder together with cattle and draft animals themselves, and timber to rebuild the thousands of destroyed dwellings and farms. To his hard-hit nobility alone he gave 3,000,000 thalers in free gifts or loans and arranged for a two-year moratorium on their debts.

Beginning with the first year of peace he made annual visits to his lands, devoting himself with physiocratic zeal to the many aspects of agricultural improvement. It is characteristic of his real interest that in his correspondence with Voltaire he, the enlightened prince *par excellence*, should argue the merits of different broods of laying hens and fertilizers with the prince of European intellectuals. With the acquisition of the "piece of anarchy," as Frederick called West Prussia, he gained control of the Warthe and the Netze as well as a considerable section of the lower Vistula. This territory was soon linked by the Bromberg Canal to the Oder, thus bringing the still politically independent Danzig—unhappy shuttlecock of the Germanic and Slavic powers—via this all-water east-west system of transportation into the economic orbit of Prussia. With Poland's chief outlet effectively his, Prussia was reasonably safe against the pinch of famine, for it was through this great port of Danzig that Poland exported her surplus grain. The increased productivity of the new territory soon made its acquisition as valuable for agriculture as Silesia's had been for manufacture. Fifty new villages sprang up, settled by German peasants recruited from the Empire. Ending the sway of the Polish *starosti*, Frederick instituted the Prussian administrative system. The crown itself took over considerable territory as royal domain, vastly improving the living conditions of its own serfs. Even where private noblemen took landed possession, Frederick made them liable to taxation as in East Prussia and Silesia.[5]

All told, the ruler settled some 57,475 families, or roughly 300,000 individuals on Prussian territory. From Frankfurt and from Hamburg,

[5] M. Bär, *Westpreussen unter Friedrich dem Grossen,* 2 vols. (Leipzig, 1909), I, in the *Publikationen aus der Königlichen Staatsarchiv* series.

the two centers for incoming settlers, they streamed, or frequently were forcibly carried, to Pomerania, the Altmark of Brandenburg, Ostfriedland in East Prussia, and Silesia. Counting them along with the foreigners who had entered the country before his reign, 20 per cent of the total population of the country was non-German in its origin. This racial pollution seemingly did not disturb Frederick's repose. He was concerned with seeing that their manpower was put to profitable military and agricultural purposes. Rivers were dredged and widened, dams built and swamps drained, dead forests cleared and young firs and pines planted. The agricultural reformers, such as the famous agronomist, J. C. Schubart, redoubled their efforts during the last two decades of the reign to introduce fodder crops and institute scientific rotation in the English way. Much was accomplished, for potatoes and turnips came into general use as food, the breed of cattle was improved by experimentation, and the export of wool proved profitable. While there is scant evidence to warrant belief that the improvements corresponded to the highest expectations of the reformers, undoubtedly they greatly strengthened the agricultural position of the state.[6]

The living conditions of the peasantry, however, did not change for the better. On the royal domain Frederick was able to put limits on the onerous labor dues of his own serfs, many of whom obtained hereditary rights of possession. On several occasions he also made strong efforts to restrict the compulsory domestic service (Gesindedienst) to which minors were obligated. He also remained the thrifty squire, anxious to have his land yield a profit. For all his detestation of serfdom, which he called an abomination, he shrank from the radical legal remedy of liberating even his own serfs. His efforts to help private serfs were in the main still more unavailing. He failed utterly to win hereditary possessional rights for the peasantry in Pomerania and Upper Silesia. Though he planned also to improve their condition without changing their legal status, that problem was equally baffling. Innumerable royal edicts indicate that his humanitarian compassion was fortified by more sober considerations. "We

6 The sources are in G. Schmoller, G. Naudé, and A. Skalweit, eds., Getreidehandelspolitik, III (1910) of Acta Borussica series; and R. Stadelmann, ed., in II of Preussens Könige in ihrer Thätigkeit für die Landeskultur (Leipzig, 1902), in the Publikationen series; brief accounts in R. Koser, op. cit., III, 260-267; and O. Hintze, op. cit., 380-387.

must try to keep the peasants from buying 'noble lands,'" he wrote in his *Testament* of 1752, ". . . and noblemen from buying peasant lands, because the peasants could not serve as officers in the army; and noblemen, by converting peasants' lands into farms [i.e., ousting the peasants from their holdings], would thus decrease the number of inhabitants and cultivators," i.e., the number of soldiers for the army.[7] His personal efforts were unavailing, because impersonal circumstances worked against him. Prussia had no agricultural revolution comparable to England's, but there was a pronounced trend toward large-scale capitalist farming on the large estates of the Junkers for the market and the army needs. Peasant cultivators were forced out to less fertile areas or squeezed out entirely from their small parcels. They were forbidden to migrate to the towns or engage in competitive rural industry with the lord. As free peasants sank into real economic serfdom, feudal and hereditary tenures (*Grundherrschaften*) were also slowly transformed into estate ownership (*Gutsherrschaft*). Small farms were joined together into vast estates, bringing about an appreciation in rentals which put them beyond the reach of the peasant tenants. The lord or his resident steward generally shirked the responsibilities to the state for the relief and well-being of the men, while Frederick himself was often ignorant of real conditions and unaware of the grievances.[8]

Not only was the monarchy powerless to stop this capitalistic development and only halfhearted in endeavoring to temper the abuses, but it was practically compelled by its own fast-growing grain requirements to aid and encourage it and to insure the Junkers an exclusive labor monopoly while maintaining them in their feudal privileges. For the benefit of these noble capitalists it established credit facilities, without which they could not survive disaster in bad years or expand in good. First in Silesia in 1770, and then in Pomerania and Brandenburg, Frederick organized Land Mortgage Credit Associations (*Landschaften*), whose activities the government supervised and whose initial expenses it defrayed. These credit associations were co-

---

[7] Volz, *op. cit.*, 31; his attitude in the *Political Testament of 1768* was unchanged.
[8] G. S. Ford, *Stein and the Era of Reforms in Prussia, 1807-1815* (Princeton, 1922), ch. vi, is excellent. Cf. the old classic G. F. Knapp, *Die Bauernbefreiung und der Ursprung der Landarbeiter in den älteren Teilen Preussens*, ed. by C. J. Fuchs (Berlin, 1927) for the fullest account.

operatives of all the estates of nobility in a given district. They issued interest-paying securities which, secured by the total property of their members and therefore regarded as gilt-edged, sold with comparative ease. From the credit thus raised, the co-operative made loans on easy terms up to two-thirds of the assessed value of the borrower's estate. At the same time the government forbade the sale of portions of landed estates for the purpose of paying off debts, a step which helped to prevent the breakup of the large estates of the aristocracy. More-over, by allowing specified estates, *Fideikommisse*, to be bequeathed in entail, it supplied legal protection against their sale outside the family. In this fashion, while immediately protecting his indispensable servitors from the usury which was the common fate elsewhere of the debt-ridden aristocracy, Frederick more lastingly consolidated the economic privileges of his landed aristocracy on whose support his state leaned so heavily.[9]

III. COMMERCE, MANUFACTURE, AND FINANCE

The core of Frederick's economic policy was the old mercantilist preoccupation with state building. He rightly gauged his task at home as the problem of bringing to completion that transformation of social institutions which his ancestors had begun. It was the heavy task of subordinating sectional and private interests to the needs of the state as a whole. A national policy was to supersede regional and private policies so that the state itself would be made secure both in peace and in war. Until the goal of state self-sufficiency was reached, it was to continue to stimulate and support and most important of all to super-vise productive enterprise, whether private or state-controlled. Once self-sufficiency was reached, so ran the calculations, the revenues from taxation on domestic products and customs fees on foreign goods would yield the treasury enough for its normal needs together with a comfortable reserve for emergencies. In this conception of public policy the state and industry entered upon a close partnership in which each had rights and assumed grave obligations toward the other. Actually

9 M. Tcherkinsky, *Les Landschaften et leurs opérations de crédit hypothécaire en Alle-magne, 1770-1920* (Paris, 1922); A. Skalweit, "Getreidenhandelspolitik und Kriegsmaga-zinverwaltung Friedrichs des Grossen," in *Schmollers Jahrbuch* (1932), Heft I; G. Dauphin-Meunier, *Mirabeau et l'économie prussienne de son temps* (Paris, 1933), 67-75.

it was inevitable that the real rights of industry should prove slight compared to its obligations.[10]

The Political Testament of 1752 permits us to follow Frederick's initial efforts to realize this ideal of industrial relations. He disbursed large sums of money to attract immigrant spinners, set up rural schools for the training of both spinners and weavers, and established cotton mills. He granted bounties to silk growers and the planters of mulberry trees, while the government built large warehouses that were used both to store the raw silk, which it sold on cheap terms to producers, and to purchase the finished silk, velvet, or cotton products from them. The conquest of Silesia brought a veritable treasure to the impoverished Hohenzollern land. The new province, his "Peru" as Frederick lovingly called it, was not only the most advanced of the Hapsburg possessions in textile production but extraordinarily rich in mineral resources of iron, lead, and coal.

During these halcyon years Prussian trading relations kept pace with industrial progress. Internal trade profited by the abolition of internal tolls, the widening of the harbor of Stettin in Pomerania, and the building of a canal link between the North and Baltic seas. Foreign trade flourished. A ten-year agreement with France gave Prussia a most-favored-nation status with her Gallic neighbor. The joining of Breslau on the southeast to Berlin and Berlin to Hamburg on the northwest in an all-water route gave the needed western outlet to the manufactured products of Silesia. Goods could now be shipped from the Silesian center via the Oder and the Friedrich-Wilhelm Canal to Berlin, and thence by lake and the new Plauer Canal down the Elbe to Hamburg. Returning traffic brought colonial wares, fruits, and wines to Breslau for redistribution to the Hapsburg territory, Poland, and Russia. The important eastern outlet was the widened Stettin harbor. Also linked in the all-water network to Berlin and subsidiary points, it competed successfully with Hamburg as the chief Silesian export center. Such were the main arteries of international

---

10 G. Schmoller, *op. cit.*, gives the classic exposition of the mercantilist ideal, to which both Koser and Hintze adhere with only varying degrees of deviation. F. Wolff, *Grundriss der preussisch-deutschen Sozial-politischen und Volkswirtschaftlichen Geschichte*, 3rd ed. (Berlin, 1909), 76-95, is a handy manual which also follows Schmoller, while A. Zottman's *Die Wirtschaftspolitik Friedrichs des Grossen* (Leipzig, 1937), although very valuable for its figures, unsuccessfully covers its essential similarity to Schmoller with intellectual paradoxes borrowed from O. Spann.

exchange until ruinous tariff wars beginning in 1753 and the more ruinous military strife of the Seven Years' War effectively choked these channels of trade.

With the end of the war Frederick had his opportunity to integrate the whole of Prussian economic life by co-ordinating capital, men, and resources. After stimulating recovery—his famous program of *"Rétablissements"*—by public spending, he would maintain and increase national prosperity by continuing to supply the same stimulus of state aid. With millions of thalers from the state treasury at his disposition Frederick left little undone for the next quarter of a century to transform his essentially agricultural country into a major industrial power.

An idea of the vast scale of governmental operations can be gleaned from the fact that Frederick expended some 60,000,000 thalers, or almost 3,000,000 per annum in the heroic undertaking to stimulate the progress of private enterprise under direct or indirect control of the state. Ably served and seconded by administrators von Heinitz, von Hagen, and the Italian Calzabigi, he persevered in his very ambitious undertaking. The record shows the setting up of many factories, not a few to be turned over to private entrepreneurs if they could make the venture profitable, but meantime supported with government funds and equipment, materials and monopoly rights. The monopolies and semi-governmental trusts ran into the hundreds: for iron production in Westphalia; metallurgical and mining companies in Upper Silesia; insurance companies and trading monopolies like the Levant Company and the Russian Company; most numerous of all, textile and silk ventures. The state itself had a very lucrative monopoly in salt, sugar, porcelain production, and, after 1781, in coffee. In 1766 the monarch had accepted Calzabigi's proposal for the establishment of a state bank in order to widen credit facilities. The bank was set up with main offices in Berlin and Breslau and branches in the leading trading cities. But the venture was less than successful, for business men especially in Silesia were loath to pay the high service fees for using facilities supposedly made available for their benefit but which actually served to yield additional revenue to the treasury.

The official statistics of 1783 indicate that the annual value of industrial production, everything included, had risen to 32,000,000 thalers.

Silesian production alone amounted to 11,000,000. According to von Heinitz's report mining production of all types employed 88,000 men in 1786, with a value of 5,000,000 thalers. When Frederick ascended the throne in 1740, Prussia had only three main products for export: wool, linens, and timber. At the close of his reign every conceivable type of manufacture had found a home in his state: sugar refineries, porcelain works, embroideries, iron and steel mills, glass and copper enterprises, cotton, silk, woolen and linen factories, paper and leather plants, and manufactories of gold and silver braid. Poverty-ridden Prussia had assumed her place as one of the great European producers, exporting roughly one-third of her manufactured products abroad.

While the course of internal trade was smooth, international trade lagged behind industrial production. The lag was absolute and not relative. In sharp contrast to the situation in 1752 on the eve of the trade wars, when there were 22,000,000 thalers of exports and 17,000,000 of imports, the trade figures for 1781-1782 showed only 14,800,000 thalers of exports and 11,800,000 of imports. From the decade of the fifties Prussia was linked at different times in a mutualism of mercantilist hostility with Austria, Electoral Saxony, Poland, and Sweden. Considering that it pursued a ruthlessly protectionist policy with no fewer than 490 articles on the prohibited export list (in 1766) and severe ultra-modern travel restrictions and money limitations, it is somewhat difficult to accept the conclusion of Frederick's admirers that ungrateful freetraders, dishonest officials, and Jews were responsible for the decline.[11]

Until the reorganization of the taxation system in 1776, a move which was an essential part of the broader industrial program, the burden of taxation fell with crushing weight upon the peasantry. After that reorganization, designed in part to ease their lot by decreasing the rates on necessities and increasing them on luxuries, the burden was still carried by the countryman. Except in East Prussia and Silesia (also in West Prussia after its acquisition), the peasant alone paid the land tax, which constituted the largest single direct tax levied by the government. In the towns the excise was the chief governmental

11 Zottman, *op. cit.*, *passim*, argues to that effect; M. Herzfeld, "Der polnische Handelverträg von 1775" in *F.B.P.G.*, XXXII (1920), 57-107, illustrates how Prussia used her military force to impose disadvantageous trading terms on her weaker neighbors.

source of revenue, a combined consumer tax on all goods brought to or produced in the towns and a sales tax on wholesale transactions. These two taxes, amounting to 3,600,000 thalers in 1740, yielded between 10,000,000 and 11,000,000 in 1786. From the rentals on the leased royal domain, dues on the royal forests, posts, profits of coinage, customs, and government monopolies the state collected 3,300,000 in 1740 versus a total of between 6,000,000 and 7,000,000 in 1786. The balance of the 22,000,000 or 23,000,000 thalers of revenue at that later date came from Silesia, which paid its own special quota from the outset. After 1763 the stored reserve (*Staatsschatz*) which remained in various treasuries after current expenditures had been met formed the nucleus of a new treasury, the *Dispositionskasse*. As the name implied, the king was free to dispose of its fund without giving an accounting to the regular financial authorities. He drew from it to finance his economic ventures, but even with his stupendous expenditures, the metal store still rose from 14,500,000 thalers (of the debased 1763 coinage) to 23,500,000 thalers in 1776 and 52,500,000 thalers ten years later, mostly gold and silver.

The reorganization of all indirect taxes, including customs, transit, and excise, which was effected in 1776, encompassed a simultaneous rearrangement of rates and the establishment of a *régie* or state control. The model for the latter was the French system, and the head and the staff of the new administration which largely superseded the *Steuerräte* and the other provincial collectors and administrators were mainly French. Estimates of the net revenue that the state obtained from the supposedly more efficient and more honest system vary in well-nigh fantastic manner, but the failure of the venture to bring about the alleviation of popular hardship was pronounced. The reductions were largely on paper, and the rates on the indispensable state-controlled monopolies of beer, salt, tobacco, and coffee went up rather than down. While Frederick blustered his way out of the public indignation and his apologists have subsequently devised explanations, the last word still remained with the English envoy, Sir Andrew Mitchell, who wrote to his government: "The new projects of excise have really alienated the affections of the people from their sovereign to a degree hardly to be described."[12]

[12] For Sir Andrew, cf. A. Bissett, ed., *Memoirs and Papers of Sir Andrew Mitchell*, 2 vols. (London, 1850); F. F. von Schrötter, *Das preussische Münzwesen im achtzehnten*

IV. THE PRICE OF GLORY

No other ruler in that age of royal luminaries so aroused the admiration of his contemporaries as Frederick the Great. Posterity remains dazzled, too, by the magnitude of his achievements, and an outstanding liberal among American scholars of our own day could write: "And in everything but his militarism he was the most enlightened ruler of his time; his government was the most economical, the most efficient, the most tolerant, and the most progressive then known . . . he made Prussia the most enlightened country in the world."[13]

A decent respect toward his claims to greatness does not preclude an examination of the price of glory, nor does it forbid raising the question of how much he sacrificed of the aggregate good in this attainment of prestige, power, and security for the state. Frederick himself grew old before his time in his struggle with the bureaucracy. Opposing tugs and pulls joined him to the chariot of officialdom, not a oneness of will and direction. The silent obstruction of his functionaries sapped his tough vitality. Even his extraordinary vigilance proved unavailing against intrigues and cabals. Prussian tradition makes the disciplined civil bureaucracy the true builders of the country's unity. These administrators and officers, runs the official version, were the fountainhead of the state's power, paragons of disinterestedness, efficiency, honesty, and obedience. These virtues they possessed at least in part, but Frederick's reign also reveals them in a harsher light. They emerge from the recesses of almost mythological greatness as long-suffering, long-complaining, and embittered scribes, secretaries, and secret agents, overworked and underpaid functionaries struggling with voluminous reports and batches of memoranda.

To correct their low efficiency, which infuriated him when it did not fill him with dismay, Frederick introduced, as has been seen, a considerable measure of personal supervision. Neither his personality nor his outlook favored the success of his command over subordinate officials. He was incurably, almost pathologically, misanthropic, regarding

Jahrhundert, IV, in the *Acta Borussica* series, is an invaluable collection of source material. A. F. Riedel, *Der brandenburgische-preussische Staatshaushalt* (Berlin, 1866); R. Grabower, *Preussens Steuern vor und nach den Befreiungskriegen* (Berlin, 1932), I, ch. ii; and R. Koser, "Die preussische Finanzen von 1763-1786," in *F.B.P.G.*, XVI (1903), 445-476, are indispensable.
13 Preserved Smith, *A History of Modern Culture: The Enlightenment, 1687-1776* (New York, 1934), 387-388.

the bulk of humanity as foolish at best and ferocious at worst. Men were governed, he insisted, by two principal motives: fear of punishment and hope of reward. "The enlightenment," he said, "is a light from heaven for those who stand on the heights, and a destructive firebrand for the masses."[14] Of his own countrymen he wrote doubtlessly with justice but in any case with step-fatherly contempt that they were Brandenburgers and not Englishmen.

As he grew older, his worst qualities came to the fore in the morose and royal neurotic. He chivied and harassed his officials, making his own tours of inspection and relying upon the reports of his secret inspectors, the dreaded fiscals. For a model of administrative efficiency Prussian officialdom presented an astonishingly high total of purges. Toward his associates he was without thanks, gratitude being reserved—as Voltaire once acidly observed—for the horse that carried him away from his first encounter on the battlefield. To his subordinates he was coarse of speech and penurious of purse. He endeavored to improve the efficiency of his officials by the singular expedient of stifling their initiative. But by ruthlessly imposing his own *"Kabinets-Ordres"* upon them he largely impaired their usefulness for tasks other than of his own invention.[15]

The cost to society of this curious blend of personal despotism and institutionalized absolutism was equally high. The officials could not tap a potentially rich vein of individual talent in the local area, for the mass of the population was disbarred from participating and denied a responsibility in the conduct of local affairs. The townspeople and the villagers detested the royal agents for a dullish fidelity to a state that was remote from them, alien to their expectations, and aloof and unheeding to their wants. It seemed remote and unheeding to them, because the supreme ruler could not minister to their needs. The great increase in agricultural productivity brought no gain to the peasantry. The harsh juridical relations between Junker and peasant were not relaxed. The stupendous expansion of industrial and commercial enterprise under the aegis of a state working largely for the

14 Quoted in K. T. Heigel, *Deutsche Geschichte vom Tode Friedrichs des Grossen bis zur Auflösung des alten Reiches*, 2 vols. (Berlin, 1911), I, 6.
15 The admirable articles of W. L. Dorn, "The Prussian Bureaucracy in the Eighteenth Century," in *Political Science Quarterly*, XLVI (1931), 403-423; XLVII (1932), 75-94; 259-273, reveal both sides of the story.

needs of its military machine unquestionably gave a vitalizing shock to the more alert villagers and quickened the capitalist zeal of the urban enterpreneur. By destroying the old mediaeval and communal torpor Frederick's Prussia opened the vistas of boundless opportunities of free enterprise for the resourceful and ambitious. But Frederick thwarted the hopes that he awakened in the capitalist producer. Though the economic changes cleared the way for the disciplined labor force of a later day and prepared the way for the transformation of social power relationship, it was in Frederick's own day, as Treitschke candidly noted, "an unnoticed and an undesired transformation." Whatever the future relations were to be, for the present the state hemmed producer and production in the strait jacket of regulation and control.

The fiscal arrangements fell heavily upon both producers and consumers. Military needs came first in public finances, for war was indeed the national industry of Prussia. Out of the 22,000,000 or 23,000,000 thalers of governmental revenue in 1786, between 12,000,000 and 13,000,000 alone were expended directly to support the huge army of 195,000 men. Even after 60,000,000 thalers had been disbursed between 1763 and 1786 to encourage economic growth, the *Dispositions-kasse* still contained a metallic hoard of 52,500,000 thalers when Frederick died. Of the 100,000,000 or more thalers that were minted during the second half of his reign, only 66,000,000 were in circulation.[16] It is absurd to deny that he began the transformation of Prussia into a modern industrialized state; and it would be equally absurd to deny that the policy of sterilizing money and hoarding specie—which was of a piece with his general mercantilist outlook—seriously retarded a potentially still more rapid extension than took place. He could not raise capital from the public because there were no accumulated savings to be absorbed; and he would not do so because he treated public finance in the manner that a householder considered a family budget, regarding public debt as a liability instead of the obverse of national investment. There was no great capacity to consume finished products at home, because there was no widely distributed purchasing power. The inherited practice of total or partial tax exemption for the old privileged social groups put the weight of tax liability upon those

16 Schrötter, *op. cit.*, IV, 28 ff.

least qualified to bear it and simultaneously depressed the living standards of the many. Government savings, expenditures on agriculture and
industry, and the upkeep of the enormous military establishment all
came from the taxes that were efficiently exacted, mainly from the
poor. The free-born and free-trading English envoy, Sir James Harris
(Lord Malmesbury), got at the root of the matter when he reported in
1776:

> The King of Prussia never can be taught to believe that a large treasure
> laying [sic] dormant in his coffers impoverishes his kingdom; that riches
> increase by circulation; that trade cannot subsist without reciprocal profit;
> that monopolies and exclusive grants put a stop to emulation and, of
> course, to industry; and, in short, that the real wealth of a sovereign
> consists in the ease and affluence of his subjects. These errors, however
> capital they are, have rather served to augment the misery of these subjects
> than impede the progress of his own grandeur. . . .[17]

Seen in retrospect the imposing might of militarized Prussia was
already hollow when Frederick died. Frederick's Prussia, a military
superstructure set upon crumbling foundations, faced the new world
that was dawning. It collapsed dramatically during the stress of the
Napoleonic wars, because in a world increasingly based upon individual
contact, in a world that was already revolutionary before the upheaval
in France, the great Prussian ruler kept its bases unchanged and the
ends and purposes of state policy unaltered. An artist like Winckelmann shuddered when he thought of his native "Prussian despotism
. . . that scourge of nations," and the cultured Lessing wrote (in a
private letter): "Let somebody raise his voice for the rights of subjects or against exploitation and despotism, and you will soon see
which is the most slavish land in Europe."[18] In a world moving toward
the liberating play of bourgeois enterprise and free international exchange, Prussian purposes and ends remained, theory notwithstanding,
outmoded and reactionary in practice. To see, as Spengler in an uninspired moment saw, the systematized and militarized statism of
Prussia as the point of departure for modern socialism is to twist the
meaning of socialism out of all semblance to the original. The great
renovation that Frederick quickened could not release the humanist

---

17 Quoted in Norwood Young, *Life of Frederick the Great* (London, 1919), 364.
18 Quoted in G. P. Gooch, *Germany Before the French Revolution* (London, 1920), 15.

values at the core of the eighteenth-century enlightenment, because he himself was enlightened but not liberal. The Gallic and rococo veneer of his personal surroundings was a thin gloss over a great body of barrack brutality. A wit and a cynic, and at heart a true son of his martinet father, he wove more tightly the pattern of a society that was dying and ably reinforced a structure that required razing. The dynamic ruler was in short a reforming reactionary who propounded solutions for the dilemmas of a new age in terms of remedies that were already outmoded for his own.[19]

V. ENLIGHTENED ABSOLUTISM IN AUSTRIA: THE CO-REGENCY, 1765-1780

An administrative revolution, supported by Maria Theresa, had transformed the central hereditary possessions of the "House of Austria" into a compact and effective military-bureaucratic state. The empress herself was neither an acolyte of "right-Reason" nor a partisan of human perfectibility. Instinctively, this pious champion of the baroque, who forbade the teaching of English at the universities "because of the dangerous character of this language in respect of its corrupting religious and ethical principles,"[20] sensed that the doctrinal winds blowing from the west were baleful. The absolutism of the early anti-feudal measures and the restrictions upon the temporal powers of the church were hers; the sharper overtones of the enlightenment came from her advisers. To her mentor, the rare Prince Kaunitz, to her personal physician, the Dutchman Gerhard van Swieten, and to the great administrator, Count Haugwitz, belong the credit for the anti-Jesuit decrees and for filling the key positions in the civil service with younger men steeped in more advanced views. For indoctrinating these lesser officials and the jurists who rose to prominence in public affairs after 1763, indeed, for the intellectual formation of the new generation which called itself the *Aufklärungspartei*, much of the credit goes to the professors at the state University

---

[19] An excellent critical evaluation of Frederick may be found in F. Hartung, "Die geschichtliche Bedeutung des aufgeklärten Despotismus in Preussen und in den deutschen Kleinstaaten," in *B.I.C.H.S.*, IX (1937), 3-22. C. C. Brinton's work in this series, *A Decade of Revolution* (New York, 1934), 73-77, takes up the anticlimax of enlightened despotism in Prussia, 1786-1789.

[20] Quoted in P. Muller, "Der aufgeklärte Absolutismus in Österreich," in *B.I.C.H.S.*, IX (1937), 23.

of Vienna. Fresh from the lecture halls where Joseph von Sonnenfels expounded liberal neo-cameralism and Anton Martini and Paul Riegger imbued them with the concepts of natural law, these fledglings were pressed into state service. It was not alone in the Law School that out of the disparate and cosmopolitan elements the formula of the Austrian enlightenment was blended. The Benedictine Abbot Franz Rautenstrauch did likewise at the Theological Faculty, while thanks to van Swieten's earlier reforms the high schools had already become centers of enlightenment.[21]

When, in 1765, Joseph became emperor and co-regent with his mother, the Austrian *Aufklärung* was already passing into its more militant phase. For a full decade Maria Theresa succeeded in checking her son, with whom her relations were often strained to the breaking point. Time and again storms blew up, and unseemly family recriminations rent the imperial air of the court. But the masterly hand of Chancellor Kaunitz was always at the helm to bring things back to a steady keel. Kaunitz's idiosyncrasies were fabulous, and his garrulous self-esteem ridiculous even in a *grand seigneur*.[22] He had only one asset to balance these oddities: he was indispensable to mother and son alike. Nominally the director of Austrian foreign policy from 1753 to 1792, actually he was a *deus ex machina* behind the entire course of domestic developments. For two decades he displayed his encyclopedic knowledge and his rare talent for persuasive exposition in the immensely important *Staatsrat* (Council of State) which the empress established in 1762.[23] Upon the specialists who made up the *Staatsrat*, Prince Kaunitz and Baron Borie, Counts Chotek and Hatzfeldt, Blumeggen and Kollowrat—upon these gifted and experienced administrators and the young Joseph who audited the sessions fell the great

21 Cf. the two old but still valuable bibliographical studies of Wilibold Müller: *Gerhard van Swieten; biographischer Beitrag zur Geschichte der Aufklärung in Oesterreich, 1770-1772* (Wien, 1883); and *Joseph von Sonnenfels; biographische Studie aus dem Zeitalter der Aufklärung in Oesterreich* (Wien, 1882).

22 Frederick II described him as "a solemn, arrogant, mouthing, brow-beating kind of man, with a clear intellect twisted by perversities of temper, especially by a self-conceit and arrogance which are boundless." Kaunitz not less impartially analyzed himself as follows: "Heaven is a hundred years in forming a great mind for the restoration of an Empire, and then it rests another hundred years; in this event I tremble for the fate which awaits this monarchy." Lord Eversley, *The Partitions of Poland* (London, 1915), 48-49.

23 F. Walter, "Der letzte grosse Versuch einer Verwaltungsreform unter Maria Theresa, 1764-1765," in *Mitteilungen des Oesterreichischen Instituts für Geschichtsforschungen*, vol. 47, no. 4, analyzes the differences between Kaunitz and Haugwitz over its establishment.

responsibilities of civil government. Upon the *Staatsrat*, too, fell the first great task, strongly advocated by Kaunitz, of incorporating Hungary into the unified administration governing the lands of the Austrian and Bohemian crowns.[24]

Maria Theresa defeated an open drive on Hungarian autonomy, still relying upon her own indirect tactics of *"douce violence."* Beyond abolishing the Palatinate and installing her son-in-law, Albert, Duke of Teschen, as governor, she would not go. In this dispute, as in all her controversies, the younger bureaucrats rallied around Joseph and seconded him against the aging empress. Events and new aspirations swept past her so rapidly that she seemed riveted to her tracks. With a discriminating caution she had limited Joseph's competence as co-regent to affairs of the royal household, public finance, and the military, but his energy and ambition overflowed these dikes.[25] Restlessly inquisitive, he plied his royal trade, attending board meetings, traveling through his realm, conscientiously storing away detailed information to serve him in his reforming crusade. While the civil administrators labored to establish a triune Austrian, Bohemian, and Hungarian Kingdom of the Danube, further progress was made in the reform of judicial affairs. The appellate and supreme divisions were separated from the civil administration and the number of provincial and corporate law codes was reduced. With respect to codifying all the civil laws, a royal commission gathered evidence for more than a decade and then reported not unreasonably in 1767 that to scrap the legal heritage of the past and promulgate a new comprehensive code of civil law all in one stroke would only result in monumental confusion. Less reasonably, it failed to suggest even nominal changes in the existing situation. A new criminal code, the *Nemesis Theresiana*, went into effect in 1770. While an improvement over the existing cruelties and anachronisms of criminal law and procedure, it was neither an organic text nor even tinctured with the humanitarian spirit of the lawyers trained in the school of Riegger and Martini.[26]

24 "If the great and rich Kingdom of Hungary would only get the right constitution," he said, "the strength of the illustrious Hereditary House would be doubled and the greatest resources and benefits of a wise administration could be drawn upon." Quoted in T. Barath, "L'absolutisme éclairé en Hongrie (1761-1795)," in *B.I.C.H.S.*, IX (1937), 69.
25 H. Kretschmayr, *op. cit.*, 161 ff., gives a sympathetic account favoring Maria Theresa.
26 Beidtel, *op. cit.*, 149-154; P. Mitrofanov, *Joseph II. Seine politische und kulturelle Tätigkeit*, tr. from the Russian (Wien, 1910), 502-514.

This trend toward centralizing judicial procedure, together with the new administrative practices and constitutional relations, greatly augmented the authority of state officials (*Politische Behörde*) over the feudal lords. It was never part of the empress's intentions, however, to deprive the squirearchy of their legal rights over the peasantry. Her philanthropy was nicely articulated with reasons of state. She must not be credited either with real anti-feudal indignation or with exclusive humanitarian fervor in advocating such measures as extending the right of the peasant to marry without the permission of his lord, facilitating his purchase of the plot of land that he worked, and granting him the right to appeal to crown officials in criminal cases. It was an essential part of her somewhat diffuse physiocratic views to build up a large group of peasant proprietors who would be served by state-supported agricultural societies. In return for governmental distribution of seed and suggestions, control of waterways, reclamation of uncultivated land, and the general financing of rural improvements, the state would gain spiritual rewards in the peasant's gratitude and material gain in his capacity to pay greater taxes.[27]

Under the influence of state councilor Von Raab, the crown set an example of reform on its own extensive domain land in Bohemia. Von Raab abolished the *robot* and, after breaking up the leased land into small parcels, sold much of it on easy and individual terms to the serfs. This reform was a great step forward, Simultaneously, while cautioning the peasantry against entertaining false hopes of liberation from service obligations, the government created fact-finding commissions for the Austrian and Bohemian provinces, whose task was to record in written protocols (*Urbarien*) an exact statement of the nature and extent of these obligations (*robot*). Inspired by the best of intentions it went so far as to enact the theoretical legal conditions on which serfs could become proprietors. But peasant uprisings in the Bohemian and Moravian territories also revealed the weakness and the almost criminal frivolity of such a temporizing and tempting policy. The despairing serfs, who had greeted the first promises with unrestrained enthusiasm, were speedily disabused in their expectations of relief from intolerable conditions. Angered by the evasive tactics

---

[27] F. Valsecchi, *L'Assolutismo illuminato in Austria e in Lombardia*, I (Bologna, 1934), Pt. II, ch. iv, has the most penetrating treatment of Maria Theresa's agrarian policy.

of the Bohemian landowners and decimated by famine, they broke out in a fierce rebellion against a state that seemingly had tricked them and against landlords who remained oppressively harsh. These mass uprisings, which came hard on the heels of the Pugachev rebellion in Russia, swelled into wild pillage when Protestant Dissenters from near-by Prussian Silesia slipped across the border to join forces with the thousands of secret Bohemian Hussites who were coerced by the religious intolerance of the empress.

Joseph, still the junior partner of the co-regency, was plunged in despair. His pleas and his threats were unavailing. At last the absolutist asserted his authority. Going over the heads of the landowners in the Bohemian estates, he decreed the immediate application of the new *Urbarien*, the electrifying Patent of 1775 which opened another era in the history of Bohemian serfdom. This law, which marked the end of the limitless exploitation of the peasants' labor and broke up the time-consecrated agreement of public and private authorities to mulct the Bohemian serfs, rigorously restricted the feudal lord to the letter of his recorded rights. For the moment, however, the Patent was a useless document, for nothing but counter-violence could end the violence of the fiercely raging social war. Reluctantly the young emperor gave his assent to the government's decision to turn the military against the peasant rebels. The uprising was crushed in blood. This tragic finale only confirmed the outraged empress in her belief that gratitude was not to be had from benighted serfs, but upon Joseph the sanguinary dénouement had the contrary effect of strengthening his resolution to go beyond palliatives.[28]

Two decades earlier the mercantilist Count Chotek had begun to marshal Austrian resources in order to establish a balanced, planned, and unified economy in the heart of the hereditary possessions. The almost irreparable loss of Silesia, following the terrible losses of war, forced the economic advisers of the crown to redouble their efforts. During the co-regency the tide ran hard against mercantilist views and controls. In both the central and local administration civil officials loyal to physiocratic and free-trade conceptions gained increasing

[28] Kerner, op. cit., ch. ix, while critical of Maria Theresa, is less sympathetic to Joseph's generous aspirations than S. K. Padover, *The Revolutionary Emperor, Joseph II* (New York, 1934), Pt. II.

authority. Following an almost classical pattern of transition from mercantilism to economic liberalism, the very beneficiaries of the earlier
aids and restraints now clamored for a free hand and were almost
prepared to renounce state aid. This native impulse, which was
strengthened by Joseph's personal admiration for Turgot, then at the
helm in France, resulted in a marked relaxation of governmental industrial regulation and a tapering off of its financial subsidies. Anonymous pamphlets, memoranda, and reports from responsible officials,
such as Zinzendorff and Weinbrenner, discussions in the *Staatsrat*,
and a circular issued over Maria Theresa's own name in 1776, all
attested this waning of the mercantilist-cameralist ideology and practices.[29]

Corporative regulations and state control were also curtailed in
trading regulations. With the textiles, pottery, and metalware of the
small independent craftsman selling far more rapidly than the more
expensive but still inferior products of the newer large-scale enterprises, a unified home market liberated from inter-provincial tolls came
into being. The outlying possessions of Lombardy and Belgium, the
province of Tyrol, the free port of Trieste, and Hungary remained
excluded from this Austrian-Bohemian *Zollverein*. Since Prussia
blocked the routes to the north and west, Austria had no choice in the
direction of its foreign trade, and an economic *Drang nach Osten*
followed in the wake of the eastward military and cultural expansion.
The "colonization" of Hungary proceeded rapidly, and a long stretch
of German villages was founded on the right bank of the Danube
and the left bank of the Tisza. In order to tap the Balkan markets the
government improved the Danubian river service, hastened the completion of the Via Carolina linking Hungary by land with the
coastal towns of the Adriatic, and improved the harbor facilities of
Trieste. After Fiume and the territory of Bukovina were acquired, the
Hapsburg state increased its trading relations with the satellite states
in Italy, drafted commercial treaties with Poland (1775) and Russia
(1783), and sought to revive the old imperial project of direct trading
relations with the Far East. These efforts met with only moderate success, mostly with respect to Hungarian trade with Italy and the Levant,

29 Valsecchi, *op. cit.*, I, Pt. I, chs. ii-v.

and were to eventuate during Joseph's rule in sheer catastrophe for
Bohemian and Hungarian merchants.

VI. JOSEPH AS SOLE RULER, 1780-1790: CIVIL AND JUDICIAL ADMINISTRATION

The decade of the emperor's sole rule began in 1780, when he was
not yet forty years of age. Peasant legends commemorate him as the
"good emperor," a ubiquitous and generous Harun-al-Raschid of the
Danube. He was in real life a bitter and disappointed man, undermined in health and sadly alone after the death of his adored first
wife, Isabella of Parma. Contemporary chroniclers speak of his posing
for the eye of posterity, but he was modest and unaffected in manner
and simple in his tastes, affable and courteous, and readily available to
his subjects. Hailed by the devotees of reason, the supreme absolutist
wasted little time in completing the concentration of governmental
authority at Vienna. Dispensing with the once powerful Council of
State, Joseph relied increasingly upon individual statesmen for counsel
and suggestions. Among them were younger men like Tobias von
Gebler and Count Franz Kessel, as well as the veteran Zinzendorff
and Kollowrat for economics and finance; Sonnenfels, as ever, for general policy; and the aging Kaunitz, the two Cobenzls, and Count
Hrczan-Harras for foreign affairs.

There was first the unfinished business of making Hungary progressive by forcibly incorporating its administration into the central system.
Maria Theresa had lured the great Magyar magnates to Vienna, de-
nationalizing them as it were by kindness. Joseph, who had old scores
to settle with "*Messieurs les Hongrois,*" renounced her subtler tactics
of patronage and perquisites in favor of a frontal assault on their
"liberties." As an earnest of his newer ways he omitted the traditional
coronation ceremonies, lest he be forced by oath to observe Hungary's
autonomy; and to the indignation of Magyar patriots he transferred
the sacred crown of Saint Stephen from Budapest to Vienna. He made
German the official language in Hungary. While the hitherto separated
Hungarian and Transylvanian chancelleries in Vienna were being
united into one, the Hungarian diet was stripped of its authority and
the whole structure of administrative existence was altered. He destroyed the historic county assemblies of the gentry, whose elected local

officials had executed imperial laws, and he established one separate *gubernium* for Hungary and another for Transylvania, each of course under a Viennese governor. For the old feudal *comitati* he substituted the new Austrian-staffed district units (*Kreisämter*). By way of completing the holocaust of the aristocracy's and gentry's power, he forbade feudal military levies and introduced the conscription system in its stead. It is not strange that his administrative reign of terror provoked a nationalist rebellion which turned starkly anti-liberal as well as anti-Austrian under the fears awakened by the French Revolution.[30]

There was no need after a full century's endeavors for any further co-ordination of Bohemia. It was already little more than a dependent province with historic Prague reduced to the status of a secondary provincial capital. The process of political centralization and cultural Germanization was also extended to Belgium and Lombardy. Lombardy resisted these inroads by bending before the storm, and Belgium revolted even more violently than did Hungary. When the last reorganization was completed, the empire was divided into thirteen *gubernia,* and each of these large units was subdivided into *Kreise* staffed by an Austrian captain of the district and Viennese subordinates. Having totally eliminated provincial autonomy, at least on paper, the emperor could put the finishing touch upon his centralized structure by effacing the last vestiges of municipal self-rule. In some instances the semblance of town government was kept, but royal officials were as omnipresent as in Prussia, directing tax-collecting, supervising schools and religious activity, and attending with meticulous care to all the countless other details of private and public life which fell under the elastic heading of *Polizei.*

On the other hand, Joseph's nationalization of the judicial system was one of his most admirable and lasting achievements. In civil cases of primary instance town courts and the nobleman's patrimonial court were left untouched, though the new royal officials narrowly supervised them and the new anti-feudal legislation decreased the scope of their jurisdiction. The courts of second and third instances were new, corresponding exactly to the political divisions of the *Kreis* and the *gubernium.* All their procedure was carefully regulated from the

[30] Marczali, *op. cit.,* 127-148.

Supreme Court which Maria Theresa had established at Vienna early in her reign. The high professional standards of the judicial bureaucracy were also maintained. Magistrates were appointed on the basis of prior exact training in the principles of "natural law" and only after passing difficult examinations. This reorganization hit Hungarian autonomy more heavily than it did the Austrian and Bohemian provinces, because in Hungary judicial reform was also colored by the political consideration of crushing the national spirit. The long-existing patrimonial courts were abolished, and the newly established state courts of the first instance administered justice according to the principles of imperial law. Each district had an appellate court which in similar fashion nullified the authority of the once-influential county court judge (*tablabiró*), while the erstwhile autonomous high court (the *Septemviratafel*) was metamorphosed into the supreme royal court in Hungary.[31]

The changes in judicial procedure and structure were more lasting than the revolutionary changes in the law, because much of the legislation was either modified or entirely rescinded after the emperor's death. Only the first part of a projected civil code, the part concerning the law of persons and their property, was promulgated in his lifetime (1786). Together with his laws on marriage and the status of the serfs, it was the high-water mark of the Josephian legal revolution. Joseph's brother and successor, Leopold II, fought to save the best of those measures in the reaction that had set in after the former's death. The Civil Code (which lasted until 1918) was completed and promulgated in 1811 under Francis, Leopold's son. It was a compromise between Joseph's humanitarian egalitarianism and the reaction that Leopold had stemmed. The Penal Code of 1787 and the Code of Criminal Procedure of 1788 were equally abrupt departures from old Hapsburg practice and experience. They abolished class distinctions before the law, provided generous legal protection to the accused and wide opportunities for appeal to higher courts. In most instances the death penalty was abolished. Many religious courts were abolished, and marriages between Christians and non-Christians were no longer treated as

31 For the Bohemian and Austrian crown lands, cf. Kerner's excellent treatment, 169-197; and Marczali, *op. cit.*, 127-148; for Hungary, 327-347; and the detailed account in Mitrofanov, *op. cit.*, 514-579.

"religious crimes." Conversely, there was a sharp increase in the number of "crimes against the state," and the new law did little to mitigate the brutal, often ferocious, treatment of prisoners.[32]

VII. THE PEASANTRY AND THE LAND QUESTION

Meantime the impatient ruler had become convinced that the only solution of the peasant question was the radical cure of abolishing serfdom. Acting on his convictions, he issued three basic decrees concerning the peasantry in the second year of his reign. By the preliminary *Unterthanspatent* of September, 1781, and the accompanying *Strafpatent* of the same date, the overlord practically lost the slight discretionary authority that had been left him in criminal justice by the reforms of the co-regency; and the serf obtained facilities for legal appeal in civil and criminal cases from the lord to the district council authorities through a royal advocate whom he could freely consult in the capital city of each province.[33] These two decrees cut right through the chains of feudalism by snapping the legal link binding peasant to lord. By endowing the serf with civil rights they transformed him from a creature depending on his lord into a subject and ward of the state. Two months later, on November 1, 1781, the epochal Patent on Serfdom conferred legal freedom upon all serfs in the lands of the Austrian and Bohemian crowns with respect to conditions of marriage and choice of work. Transylvania in 1783 and Hungary in 1785 received similar decrees. Henceforth the peasant could move about freely wherever he willed, without requiring the permission of the lord; he could marry without permission and without paying a fee to his master; and he could choose any vocation he wished for himself and train his children in any trade he deemed best.

These emancipating decrees dramatically altered relations that had centuries of injustice behind them. They were soon supplemented by fiscal measures that broke with equal abruptness from traditional relations. The peasantry, though now endowed with legal personality,

---

32 The classic treatment is S. Adler, *Das Adelige Landrecht . . . und die Gerichts-Reform des xviii. Jahrhunderts* (Vienna, 1912); ch. vi in Kerner, *op. cit.*, is an excellent brief account.

33 Despite the efforts of the landlords to have the *Strafpatent* revoked, Leopold II ruled in 1791 that it should be maintained.

found that freedom had not ended their various fiscal obligations to either the state, the church, or the landlord. Without having real property rights over the lands which they and their ancestors had held in virtual perpetuity they still lacked sufficient land for their own needs. Joseph quite readily perceived that there was an inescapable necessity to complete their legal emancipation by affording economic and tax relief to the peasant cultivators. He therefore set into motion a broadly conceived program of land transfer which was intended to remove legal restrictions upon peasant acquistion of landed property by breaking up the large noble estates; to extend facilities to the villagers for installment buying; and to guarantee them rights of ownership, sale, and exchange.

The physiocratic ruler needed no one to tell him that the mere acquisition of property by the peasants would be only a hollow advance unless they were also emancipated from their labor services to the lord and their crushing tax obligations to church and state. Holding that "the soil alone should support the state . . . that there should be complete equality between noble and peasant and between crown and church lands, and each should be proportionately classified according to surface, fertility, and location," Joseph ordered a land survey of all the territory of the "House of Austria" to be taken. This initial move toward drawing up the *cadastre* so dear to all physiocrats was supplemented in the following year (1783) by a still clearer indication that Joseph was moving in rapid stages toward the institution of the single land tax. The principle was enunciated that all lands, irrespective of the social status of the possessor, were identically liable to the government with respect to state taxation. This was tantamount to declaring that in the eyes of the government the peasant cultivator was as much a true proprietor of the land that he cultivated as the lord who held the title.

When the survey was completed in 1789, the royal radical by a single stroke of the pen ended the existing tax system and service obligations of the former serfs and established his cherished single land tax. In the first place this memorable Urbarial Patent completely abolished the tithe without indemnification to the church on the ground that ecclesiastics were already salaried civil servants who needed no special support. More significantly, it ended the onerous labor obligation (*robot*) for all private peasants who were then paying 2 florins or more in land taxes to the crown. Under the new dispensation no longer would approximately 34 out of 100 florins of the peasant's income go to the state, 10 to the church, and 29 to the lord of the estate. He would now keep 70 for himself. Of the remaining 30 the lord would receive a little more than half in settlement for the *robot* and other obligations and the state would receive the balance as a land tax—the only tax that all proprietors henceforth would pay.

Joseph died before this most sweeping edict of his reign became effective, but the mounting opposition of the nobility had forced him to suspend its execution while the ink was almost literally not yet dry on the terms. Leopold revoked the reform of the land tax shortly after he ascended the throne in 1790.[34] Hard pressed by the feudal estates, Joseph's brother also restored the abolished *robot* but held out strongly against the landlords' claims that his Patents of May, 1790, had re-established the older practice of allowing them free bargaining with the individual serf whereby they could abolish the *robot* on their own terms unhampered by the government. When the definitive law was finally promulgated in 1798 the landlords won a complete victory; and the bonds of serfdom remained until the revolution of 1848.

The very threat, however, of the new taxation, coming together with all the preceding economic decrees, had provoked a crisis in agrarian relations. The sullen Hungarian nobility, already otherwise menaced, faced ruin. In Bohemia and only slightly less in the Austrian provinces, the hard-pressed noble proprietors stood on the brink of disaster, for their incomes declined catastrophically and their labor costs soared. As Kerner says, "One could not suddenly change a dilettante farmer-landowner who lived off his *robot* and the dues of his serf, into a real farmer who, if the 17 florins 46 2/3 kreuzer of every 100 florins of the serf's income did not suffice, would find it necessary to hire labor and cultivate his own lands."[35] On the other hand the bewildered and frustrated peasantry, refusing to believe that the tax law was actually

---

34 By the Patent of 1792 the Theresian bases were re-established in calculating the land tax. The lord once again made his own evaluation and collected the land tax from the serf for the state, though the rates were modified somewhat to his disadvantage and for the benefit of the serf. The standard works on the peasantry are K. Grünberg's *Studien zur Oesterreichischen Agrargeschichte und Agrarpolitik* (Berlin, 1896) and *Die Bauern-befreiung und die Auflösung des gutsherrlich-bäuerlichen Verhältnisses in Böhmen, Möhren, und Schlesien,* 2 vols. (Leipzig, 1894).

35 Kerner, *op. cit.,* 242.

suspended, stopped giving their labor services and paying their dues. Their indignation and their confusion were doubled, for the great majority of peasants had not even been included in the measure concerning the *robot*, since they paid less than the minimum 2 florins per annum in land taxes. With peasant disorder raging again on all sides as in 1775, the dying emancipator again, in 1790, called out the soldiery to teach his beloved peasantry to honor their obligations.

VIII. COMMERCE AND INDUSTRY

The reforming emperor was equally determined to liberate the economic man by fiat and to set him on the open road of free enterprise. Joseph was at once a cameralist, faithful to the precepts of Sonnenfels, and a physiocratic enthusiast on terms of personal friendship with Turgot. His policy had been laid down in the last years of the co-regency. It involved emancipating manufacture and trade from the old Theresian control, abolishing craft guilds, curtailing the privileges still possessed by the state-controlled guilds, and decreasing state subsidies to large-scale non-guild enterprises. But it concurrently entailed the maintenance and if necessary the stiffening of customs tariffs to protect native products.

Arguing that "nothing is more necessary than liberty for commerce and industry; nothing is more harmful than exclusive rights and monopolies," he dismantled the greater part of the control apparatus. The most humble itinerant pedlar could now sell his wares without let or hindrance. Out of sheer necessity the emperor was forced to restore a measure of governmental financial support to the newer metallurgical and textile industries, but the total financial subsidy remained only a fraction of former expenditures. Many factors furthered rapid economic expansion. The population rose from 18,700,000 in 1780 in the hereditary lands (exclusive of Belgium and Lombardy but inclusive of Hungary) to more than 21,000,000 a decade later. While consumer demands increased, the producers' overhead continued low, for almost all new manufacturers enjoyed a remission of taxes for the first few years and not a few had purchased their establishments at a ridiculously low price from the confiscated monastic institutions.

The statistics of governmental revenues indirectly bespeak the great advances made toward a modern economy. While the total government revenue in 1753 from agricultural and industrial activities was only 45,000,000 florins, it rose to 53,800,000 florins in 1777 and appreciated still more sharply to 92,500,000 florins in 1787. This fiscal paradise was never to be regained. The 55,000,000 florins of expenditure of 1774 swelled to 85,300,000 florins in 1787; and in the year of Joseph's death the budget was unbalanced to the extent of 22,000,000 florins. Several items explain the mounting governmental expenditures: tariff wars with the Hapsburg neighbors, unremitting preparations for war, and finally the costly military campaign against the Turks. Even for an expanding economy the public debt of almost 400,000,000 florins was disproportionately high under the circumstances.

The military budget was a heavy drain upon the coffers of the state, for the great rationalist was also a great militarist. All his personal enthusiasm and all the impersonal resources of officialdom were pressed into service to propagandize for a large army. Convinced, perhaps too easily, that his vast and scattered dominions of 250,000 square miles with their diversified races were unsafe against attack, he lent himself violently to maintaining the military revival begun a generation earlier by Marshals Daun and Lacy. On this score, too, as in his tariff policy, he was challenged by Kaunitz, who rightly pointed out the high costs in diplomatic anxiety abroad and lessened prosperity at home involved in the policy of reinforcing the military machine. Joseph was not deterred. Fired, though more modestly than his critics give him credit for, by the Prussian example, he made plans for an army of 108,000 men. He would have "an army as large as our needs demand," he wrote to Leopold, "a well-trained and disciplined army, ever ready and fit to act vigorously if the necessity should arise; and at the same time [he would] lessen its expenses for the state as much as possible."[36]

Conscription was introduced in the Austrian-Bohemian lands in 1771, but the burden of service fell as usual upon the poorest peasants, leaving the nobility and the richer urban dwellers virtually exempt. Following the general pattern of continental militarism, vagrants and criminals were forcibly impressed into the armed services. It is a curious

[36] Quoted in Valsecchi, *op. cit.*, I, 101.

commentary that the disaffected Hungarian contingent remained to the close of his reign the best trained and most valuable of all the troops.

The formation of the economic union comprising Austria and Bohemia, along with the new economic freedom of production within it, greatly increased the state exchequer. But Joseph's tariff policy, an exact economic counterpart of his aggressive military preparation, cast a blight upon foreign trade. With Prussia, Saxony, and the Ottoman Porte, Austria was linked in reciprocally injurious tariff relations. In the end, the three great river outlets of central Europe, the Elbe, the Oder, and the Danube, were barred to Hapsburg goods. A Chinese wall of tariffs cut off the diversified and superior wares of Bohemia whose production Joseph's liberal-economic policy had so greatly furthered. The conjunction of a threefold emergency in the last years of his reign—the radical agricultural and taxation reforms, the sequestration of monastic lands, and war—brought untold hardships to his industrious subjects. Particularly in Bohemia prices collapsed in the glutted market, unemployment hit the workers, and a train of bankruptcies ruined the producers. The less highly industrialized Hungary hardly fared better. While producers in the Austrian-Bohemian crown lands complained of exorbitant prices for Hungarian cattle, grain, and dairy products, the Hungarian consumers were bitter over the prohibitive tariff imposed on the import of manufactured goods from the central provinces. The ambitious economic drive to the east broke against Turkish reprisals, and in any case the alien resident in Hungary rather than the native Magyar benefited from such curtailed trade as existed.[37]

IX. BALANCE SHEETS OF THE DESPOTISM OF VIRTUE

Joseph's reign came to a close with the marks of failure confronting him on all sides. A rebellion had broken out in Belgium. Violent disorders raged in Hungary. The peasants were in insurrection, the ecclesiastics and the landlords embittered, and the intellectuals indignant over his cultural coercion. The imperial arms had suffered sharp

---

[37] A. Beer, "Studien zur Geschichte der österreichischen Volks-Wirtschaft unter Maria Theresia. I. Die österreichische Industriepolitik," in *Archiv für österreichische Geschichte*, LXXXI (1895), 1-135.

reverses on the field of battle in the Balkans. As if to taunt him, a bourgeois revolution exploded in France, identical in program with many of his measures but antipodal in its procedure to the tactics of enlightened despotism. Most of his great reforms, together with his hopes and his spleen, were buried with him in January, 1790. Biographers have made much of his defects: his dogmatic impatience, his inflexibility and his rigid, fanatical idealism, his unrestrained ambition and his want of tact. They have lamented the harm that such attributes imposed upon a man whose honesty and sincerity they are at one in recognizing, whose compassion for the downtrodden they admire, whose loftiness of intentions they extol.

Joseph was indeed a soul in conflict, as these accounts indicate, but not with himself. About the wisdom and the rightness of what he was doing he himself never entertained the slightest doubt. He saw himself in mortal conflict with "Evil," with the evil deeds and cruel institutions and debased thoughts of men, with the evil that seeped into all foundations and corrupted all men, even his most trusted associates, an evil against which eternal vigilance had to be exercised lest "Virtue" be destroyed. Hence the enemy was to get no breathing spell. There was a sense of desperate urgency in his acts, as though he knew that time was running out. Too rigid and too honest to cultivate political tact and insinuate reforms by indirection, he ruled by fiat, infuriating all his enemies, and occasionally his own supporters, by his high-pitched ardor. The unity of Joseph's career rests in that compulsion neurosis to establish the despotism of "Virtue." He was the royal egalitarian *par excellence*. His doctrinaire inflexibility and his almost maniacal suspicion that he was being deceived were not at odds with his yearning to serve humanity. They were joined to his benevolence, because Joseph was passionately aware that his plans raised fundamental issues which could not be favorably resolved unless he unremittingly employed every resource of his absolute power to insure the triumph of his cause. He made open war upon all the intermediate loyalties of class, territorial, guild, feudal, and religious bonds that intervened between his subjects and the supreme cause incorporate in his enlightened despotism. "The service of God," he once declared, "is inseparable from that of the state."

He was an absolutist and a martinet, a gendarme of the mind and a drillmaster of the body. The legions of Count Pergen's secret police were a plague upon society. Nothing so clearly revealed his despotic attitude as the countless instructions he gave in writing to his officials, the innumerable marginal annotations on official documents, and his confidential files, the dreaded *Conduitlisten*, on important functionaries. To Leopold he kept writing complaining letters, all in the same vein: "I do what I can and no one can reproach me with neglecting anything; but no one aids me either in management or in details." An authoritarian by temperament, he was doubly an absolutist by reason of his training. He had no sense of the political liberty of the individual, because Austrian history had not passed through the experience that honored such a concept. The soil of Austrian speculation was not yet prepared for the flowering of any other political philosophy than that enlightened despotism which Joseph had imbibed from the most progressive and most illustrious of his teachers. It would strain historical impartiality to condemn him for being of his age.

Nor can he be condemned merely for possessing a plenitude of power. Life has grimly revealed the shallowness of the Victorian aphorism that all power corrupts. The only relevant inquiries of the historian concern the use to which he put his power and the costs of his reign. Joseph was a self-conscious royal revolutionary, the herald of the ideas of the revolutionary French bourgeoisie. That is what he had in mind when he wrote to his confidant Leopold: "I have weakened deep-rooted traditions by the introduction of enlightened principles." His projected reforms pointed toward a fundamental rearrangement of human relations and they reflected that invincible hopefulness which gave high luster to the best of eighteenth-century thinking. He was the advocate of the civil and religious liberties of the individual. He reduced religion to a function of the state. He strove to destroy serfdom, abolish the guilds, and liberate economic enterprise. He championed tax equality. No ruler of the entire century was his peer in the intensity and sincerity of his conviction that the health, wealth, and happiness of its individuals were the paramount concerns of the state.

Even his shattering defeats were not without the compensation of partial victory. The serf was not emancipated, and the *robot* was restored. The single land tax was defeated and the large landed estates were not broken up to insure their use by independent peasant proprietors. But Leopold's firmness saved most of the judicial rights that Joseph had won for the peasantry. The feudal lord never regained his legal right to exact unlimited labor service from his serf. The Leopoldian compromise gave up the single land tax, but by the terms of the new taxation law the serf was still better off than he had been before Joseph's legislation. The costs of the emperor's commercial and industrial policy also came high, but it furthered population growth, swelled state revenues, and established the nucleus of a Danubian *Zollverein*. As much as possible it broke corporative and state controls, brushed away the cobwebs of old habits, released new energy, stimulated the acquisition of new skills and techniques, and began that slow annihilation of the regime of status which the bourgeois individualism of the nineteenth century triumphantly completed.

Undeniably, his bludgeon blows freed the individual from the tyranny of revelation and outworn authority to put him securely under the yoke of the omnipotent secular state. Joseph sought in his way, in the way of his country and in the way of his century, through a trained bureaucracy rather than through representative institutions, to bring heaven down to earth. His abrupt break with the past terrified his opponents and was too revolutionary even for most of his supporters. He ran ahead of enlightened public opinion, which was still too immature for his program. He lacked the aid of a powerful and strategically located middle class. If the experience of the eighteenth century proved anything at all, it was that royal liberalism, liberalism by fiat, could not alone solve the problems of a society waging war upon its own past.

Perhaps his tragic career did vindicate the cynical apothegm that virtue is more dangerous than vice because its despotism is not subject to the restraints of conscience. The price that the new subjection entailed was high, grievous, and even odious. But one must balance the costs by the gains: by the widened horizons, the revelation of new worlds of endeavor and happiness, the vision of security and independence for the lowly that his violence won for his subjects. It was in the train of his innovations if not of his methods that all liberals and progressives were to tread in the generations which followed.

Chapter Five

THE FOUNDATIONS OF POWER IN EASTERN EUROPE

I. THE ACCESSION OF CATHERINE II

CATHERINE was in her thirty-fourth year when the beneficent workings of the palace revolution of 1762 deposed her husband and set her upon the Russian throne. Peter III contributed generously to his own downfall. Highly unbalanced, he required a mere half-year to gain enormous unpopularity with all classes. His decree exempting the nobility from military service should have made him an ideal puppet for the grandees of the realm, but his aberrations decided otherwise. He shocked patriotic feeling by making peace with his idolized Frederick II and returning all the territory which the Russian troops had conquered from their "bitterest enemy." He estranged the Palace Guard by substituting the Prussian drill and the Prussian type of uniform for the Russian. To the colonelcy of the Guard, the rank traditionally held by the tsar, he appointed his uncle, like himself a Holsteiner by birth. Then he announced plans for a campaign to recover a patch of disputed territory in Schleswig. To withdraw cavalierly from the major European war against Frederick in order to embark on a campaign against Denmark was an artless combination of the stupid with the ignominious. By secularizing the church lands but failing to satisfy smoldering peasant grievances he successfully crystallized both religious and popular feeling against him.

His dissolute life had long been notorious and his hatred for Catherine an open secret. But his unconcealed intention to divorce her, drive her to a nunnery, and then marry his mistress, Vorontsova, brought home to his wife the acuteness of her danger. In the dénouement of the several plots that were simultaneously hatched, the decisive role belonged to her and to the Palace Guard, where her current lover, Gregory Orlov, and his brothers had built up support in her behalf. Her seizure of power was bloodless, for Peter was helpless against the military revolt. He accepted his deposition without a struggle—"like a child being sent to sleep," sneered Frederick II. But within a fortnight the imprisoned ex-ruler died under mysterious circumstances. While Catherine was not directly responsible for his murder, the actual murderer, Alexis Orlov, was not punished, nor was any official investigation ever instituted. Beyond concealing an incriminating letter from Alexis Orlov and issuing a statement that Peter had died of "hemorrhoidal colic"—which prompted Alembert, from a safe distance, to indulge in the pertinent observation that hemorrhoids were terribly dangerous in Russia—the empress took refuge in silence.[1]

For years, however, she felt insecure, fearing lest violence topple her from power as violence had elevated her. The Prussian ambassador expressed the prevailing conviction when he wrote to Frederick shortly after her accession: "It is certain that the reign of the Empress Catherine is not to be more than a brief episode in the history of the world."[2] Even a Prussian agent could err, as Catherine's maneuvering to entrench herself was to reveal. Her first proclamation denounced her late husband's treaty of eternal peace with Prussia and played up to patriotic feelings by stigmatizing Frederick as "a disturber of the peace." Nevertheless she maintained externally amicable relations with him. Indeed, the needs and the fears provoked by the Polish question forced her to elaborate the understanding into an alliance which constituted the diplomatic cornerstone of the "System of the North" (1764). With similar attention to popular feeling she deferred applying her husband's law which had secularized the ecclesiastical foundations. She was fully aware of the fact that to the masses she was still only a foreigner and a cursed Lutheran heretic by birth. Once the immediate crisis was passed, she resumed Peter III's course. The church was made subordinate to the state, which retained its lands, while almost two million former church peasants fell under the control of the government. An "economical commission" was set up to administer the sequestered property and take over the collection of church revenues. Part of these monies was applied to indemnify the

---

[1] R. N. Bain, *Peter III, Emperor of Russia* (Westminster, 1902), discusses the assassination in great detail; and V. O. Kluchevsky, *op. cit.*, IV, ch. xvi, absolves Catherine of the actual murder.

[2] Quoted in K. Waliszewski, *Le roman d'une impératrice, Cathérine II* (Paris, 1894), 303.

monasteries while the rest, at least in intent, went either to support or to endow ecclesiastical schools, hospitals, and asylums for the invalid and the aged. Disaffected ecclesiastics continued to stir up sporadic opposition, but governmental force ultimately deprived threats from that quarter of all but a nuisance value.

Unfailing in her sense of public relations, Catherine also planned an elaborate coronation to dazzle her new subjects. The ceremony took place in Moscow with the customary religious consecration which graces such occasions and amidst spontaneous rejoicing whose expression unstinted royal largess of food and liquor among the populace did not impede. If she had once entertained dreams of marrying the handsome Gregory Orlov, a delicate sounding of opinion dissuaded her, and she resigned herself to the politically more engaging venture of wedding herself to all her subjects. Drawing upon the resources of a realistic intelligence as well as on a fund of feminine sensitivity, she made several trips through the country with the laudable intent of establishing the fact that she was as Orthodox as the Procurator of the Holy Synod and as authentically Russian as any ignorant *moujik*. She temporized with that faction of the Guard which was not averse to another *Putsch* because it had neither participated in nor profited by the deposition of Peter III. But she fought and defeated the court group headed by Nikita Panin which desired to thwart her absolutist conceptions and reap for itself the benefits of Peter's deposition.

II. THE SOCIAL BASES OF THE ADMINISTRATIVE SYSTEM

In many significant respects Catherine was a true tsarina of the landed aristocracy (*dvorianstvo*). As grand duchess she bathed in the atmosphere of the court; to the élite of the aristocracy in the Palace Guard she owed her throne; and as empress she selected all her leading helpers from that group. In the early years the influence of the Orlovs was predominant: Gregory, the favorite, was the grand master of artillery; Alexis was an admiral of the fleet; and Theodore at one time filled the highly important post of procurator-general. Later, it was another lover, Potemkin, the creator of "New Russia" and the organizer of the Crimea, who gained ascendancy, especially in foreign relations. The scions of the old nobility were entrenched in the diplomatic service: Repnin in Poland; Semen Vorontsov in London; Dmitri Galitsin in Paris. The commanding officers in the army and navy bore the old and distinguished names of Dolgorouki, Roumantsov, Galitsin, Chitchagov, Spiridov. Unconscious class prejudice naturally impelled the empress to favor their interests, while many considerations of policy and all those of personal security confirmed the arrangement. Her reign was therefore to see the completion of the orientation in favor of the nobility begun under Peter the Great's successors: their monopoly of key positions in the administration; the legalization of their status as unpaid governmental agents in the local administration; the extension of their serf rights and the juridic recognition of their privileged position as hereditary serf proprietors exempted from military obligations.

Yet she was more than the tsarina of the *dvorianstvo*. She was an absolutist to the core, a farsighted and capitalist-minded absolutist who worked for the greater glory of the Russian crown. As much as she dared she reverted from the outset to Peter's anti-noble policy and endeavored to make and keep the service nobility in a subordinate position as the civil arm of her authoritarian state. Like the great Peter she was a modern-minded dynast; and she succeeded better because she harnessed the power of large-scale individual enterprise to the chariot of the state. She was more effective too. Peter I had worked almost exclusively through violence and terror, but she divided the opposition and attached her adherents to her cause by the golden chains of self-interest. It was part of her deliberate policy to accelerate capitalist development by associating the rich bourgeois merchants with the great landed aristocrats in a movement that would liberate production and exchange from their old fetters. Grandees like the Orlovs, Viazemski, Potemkin, and Bezborodko not only pressed for free capitalist enterprise but were the partners and associates in the business ventures of such notable bourgeois entrepreneurs as Schemiakin, Batashev, Vladimirov, Faleev, Jakovlev, and Lazarev. Both groups alike were the sponsors of the aggressive expansionist program which swept Russian arms, prestige, and authority into the Ukraine and the harbors of the Black Sea and ultimately brought their country into military conflict with the Porte.[3]

3 Cf. the reinterpretation of Catherine's role by Georg Sacke, in his "Adel und Bürgertum in der Regierungszeit Katharinas II. von Russland," in *Revue belge de*

The empress's tactics against the court groups during the first decade of her rule were primarily a struggle for political control. But they were also the initial phase of a broader effort to win for the crown the direction of Russia's social and economic policy. They reached an early climax in the proceedings of the highly publicized Legislative Commission of 1767-1768. According to conventional interpretations Catherine was at her most liberal in these years, retreating into conservatism after the defeat of her efforts in this assembly. Such interpretations strain reality. The political and so-called constitutional measures that she introduced immediately after her seizure of power bore the germs of the non-liberal and authoritarian administrative changes of 1775 and 1785, even as her social policy in those early years adumbrated what followed in subsequent days. The elaborate paraphernalia of hocus-pocus which deceived so many of the liberals in the west was a classical illustration of Catherine's talent for political maneuvering and her flair for favorable publicity. She was the first Russian ruler fully to appreciate the value of a good press abroad and at home. In Russia she paraded her liberalism in order to upset the plans of the feudal-minded aristocracy. Abroad her paid and unpaid propagandists among the *philosophes* bought her the plaudits of the European intelligentsia. Without being insincere in her admiration for such giants of the French enlightenment as Voltaire and Diderot, Grimm and Alembert, she also had a very nice sense of what they were worth to her. Voltaire, now the venerable Patriarch of Ferney, was a sort of commander in chief of the literary brigade which, for a few "*douceurs*" that the Russian treasury easily spared, wrote commendatory articles concerning her accession, placed inspired stories in the newspapers and periodicals about her devotion to their doctrines, and reinterpreted her Polish and Turkish policy to make good reading in western Europe.[4]

According to her publicity agents, in whose ranks Catherine herself held a high position, her plan was to redraft in a single organic code the bewildering variety of imperial and local legislation which had

philologie et d'histoire, XVII (1938), 815-852; cf. also Kizevetter's account in Milioukov, Seignobos, *et al.*, *Histoire de Russie*, 3 vols. (Paris, 1932-1933), II.

[4] Cf. W. F. Reddaway, *Documents of Catherine the Great* (Cambridge, 1931), which includes the text of 159 letters of her correspondence with Voltaire; G. Sacke, "Die Pressepolitik Katharinas II. von Russland," in *Zeitungswissenschaft*, Heft 9 (1938), 570-579; and by the same author "Die Kaiserin Katharina II., Voltaire, und die Gazette de Berne," in *Zeitschrift für Schweizerische Geschichte*, XVIII (1938), 305-314.

remained uncodified since 1649. Unlike Justinian she was to accomplish this worthy deed through the medium of a deliberative assembly representative of all the social classes. She issued a *Nakaz* or *Instruction*, supposedly to guide the deputies, and advertised her indebtedness to Montesquieu and Beccaria for the draft of the broad general principles of the proposed code. Liberal Europe melted in admiration over this widely heralded endeavor to legislate parliamentarism into being by one stroke of the pen. But analysis of the various drafts of the *Nakaz* indicates very clearly that Catherine pillaged only what she wanted from Montesquieu. She took over almost nothing of his anti-absolutist political doctrine and little enough of his general social philosophy. Indeed, the very idea of a *Nakaz* was orginally conceived as a move to defeat Nikita Panin's project of establishing a small Imperial Council composed of competent advisers from the ranks of the court aristocracy. The earliest draft of the *Nakaz* in 1763 was a counter-thrust to Panin's project, which would have effectively limited her real political authority. When she submitted the original version to a small group of advisers, Panin was reported to have exclaimed in horror that it contained "axioms which would batter down walls." What shocked him was not its liberalism, as has been falsely assumed. He was aghast over its absolutism, which thwarted his own design and that of the grandees of keeping the empress in check.

Moreover, the *Nakaz* and the Legislative Commission were not originally joined in her thinking. The idea of convoking that assembly was not fully formulated until 1766, three years after the publication of the first draft of the *Nakaz*. Like the *Instruction*, which had served its purpose at least in part, the supplementary plan was a move in a cunningly conceived campaign. In the words of the French diplomatic agent the plan

. . . concealed more elaborate views. This princess realizes only too well her utter dependence upon the grandees. . . . The opinion obtains that in order to shake off the yoke the Empress has assembled the estates so that she may sound out public opinion. In the event that it is favorable to her, she will enact *constitutional* laws which will assure her position and that of her [and Orlov's] son. If not, if public opinion is ill-disposed, she will be satisfied with enacting *civil* legislation from which she will still derive the advantage of being able to subordinate the grandees and their subjects . . . without appearing to subject them.[5]

Hence it mattered little to her that the Commission was poorly organized to fulfill its functions as a lawgiving body. Catherine had stated explicitly in the electoral decree that the deputies were only to provide her with specific information. She never intended and never allowed their suggestions to alter her predetermined ideas. Procurator-General Viazemski rigged the elections in accordance with her views and made the urban deputation, whose loyalty she could count on, the single largest bloc in the assembly. This group consisted of 207 deputies, while the gentry, whose opposition was even more certain than the good will of the town representatives, had only 160. The private serfs, who probably would have opposed her and in any case were uncertain, were not represented by their own delegates. The remaining deputies represented the administration and the other safe social groups.[6]

The sessions were held from midsummer, 1767, to December, 1768, at first in Moscow and later in St. Petersburg. As most of the conscientious but inexperienced deputies were intent upon making themselves heard, the two hundred meetings of the assembly resolved themselves into lengthy and eloquent debates over trivia. The English envoy called them "a farce." When the deputies were not "blinded by outer appearances," they served their own interests "by strewing incense before the idol of the vanity of their Empress."[7] When the outbreak of the war against the Ottoman Empire gave the empress the opportunity to suspend the hearings, the draft of a new law code had not been advanced even by a single paragraph. The task of the Commission was subsequently turned over to subcommittees, some of which held sessions up to 1775.

Catherine's benefits from this "ethnographical rally" cannot be evaluated in terms of its failure to draft a law code. The mandates of

---

[5] For a searching examination of the empress's calculations as revealed in the drafts of the *Nakaz* and her private correspondence, see G. Sacke, "Katharina II. im Kampf um Thron und Selbstherrschaft," in *Archiv für Kulturgeschichte*, XXIII (1932), 191-216; and "Zur Charakteristik der gesetzgebenden Kommission Katharinas II. von Russland," *ibid.*, XXI (1931), 166-191.

[6] G. Sacke, "Adel und Bürgertum in der gesetzgebenden Kommission Katharinas II. von Russland," in *Jahrbücher für Geschichte Osteuropas*, III (1938), 408-417.

[7] *Sbornik Imperatorskavo Obschestva*, XII, 304 ff.

the deputies and the rhetorical debates provided her with invaluable information on the state of her realm. Above all, she obtained the sense of security that she wanted and needed. From abroad she received unparalleled acclaim. The measure of her success at home was the assembly's proffer of such appellations as "Great" and "Wise" and her final acceptance of an equally unpretentious title, "Mother of the Country." Her expectations had not been defeated. "By these and other measures," wrote the English envoy, "glittering enough to dazzle the eyes of the Russians, the power of Her Imperial Majesty increases every day, and is already arrived to such a degree that this prudent Princess thinks herself strong enough to humble the Guards, who placed her upon the throne."[8]

The "prudent Princess" proceeded cautiously along the road she had chosen "to humble the Guards, who placed her upon the throne." It is always essential to remember that her admiration for the "*despotisme légal*" of Le Mercier was a much clearer gauge of her constitutional views than her supposed enthusiasm for Montesquieu. She effected no formal reorganization of the central administrative system, but she established her personal rule in the place of the old bureaucratic apparatus. Several of the collegiate boards were abolished, the title of chancellor was allowed to lapse, and the senate, revived in importance by Elizabeth, once again sank into insignificance. Of the officials whose counsel she relied upon, Prince Viazemski, procurator-general from 1764, was one of the most influential. On the other hand, she turned to a comprehensive reform of the provincial administration in the very year of the suppression of the Pugachev rebellion, aghast at the revelation of its disorder and inefficiency.[9]

The basic ordinance concerning the provincial *gubernias* was issued in 1775, and it remained in force for almost a century. The recently issued *Commentaries* of Blackstone may have served Catherine in good stead, as she alleged, but it is more likely that the real model for the reorganization came from the example of her own Baltic provinces. The twenty huge and unwieldy *gubernia* units set up by Peter I and his successors were abolished and, under the supervision

---

[8] Sacke, "Zur Charakteristik der gesetzgebenden Kommission," already cited, p. 191; also V. O. Kluchevsky, *op. cit.*, V, ch. v.
[9] For the Pugachev rebellion, *infra*, pp. 117-119.

of the Balt nobleman, Count Sievers, fifty new *gubernias* were created, each with approximately 300,000 to 400,000 inhabitants. Each new unit, furthermore, was divided into districts (*uyezdi*) so as to give each smaller unit an approximate population of 20,000 to 30,000. In the *gubernia* the presiding official was the governor, a royal appointee endowed with broad discretionary authority. Three collegiate boards were set up to assist him, composed of officials nominated by the central administration: administration and police; finance; and justice. In addition there was an Office of Public Welfare, headed by the governor, to superintend sanitation and hygiene, education and poor relief. Similar boards, except the last, were created in the district administration. There, the personnel was elected locally, save for the presiding officer, who was also an appointee of the state. The reorganized judicial system provided for the separation of civil cases from criminal. Cases of the first instance were excluded from the new provisions, the needs of law and order being upheld in the towns by the district police tribunal under the headship of a local nobleman, the *ispravnik*, and on the manorial estate by the landowner or his bailiff. Each of the three social groups of the nobility, the urban inhabitants, and the crown peasants came under the jurisdiction of its own hierarchy of courts.

Liberal Europe intoned Catherine's praises. The experienced traveler Archdeacon Coxe gave the reform his blessings: "By the new code this enormous power of the lords is reduced to restrictions more consonant to the humane principles which distinguish all the regulations of the present empress. . . ."[10] Closer scrutiny shows that "self-government" in Russia was still largely an empty phrase. Only the local gentry were permitted to form assemblies for electoral purposes, so that in the new local boards their representatives were greatly in the majority and exercised preponderant influence. The administrative changes did not in the slightest weaken their control over their serfs, for serf-lord relations were left untouched on the manorial estate. The innovations, which gave the shadow of authority to the gentry, gave the substance to the crown. Unable to deprive them of their formal exemption from state service, Catherine transformed the

10 Wm. Coxe, *op. cit.*, II, 114.

squirearchy into administrative agents as Peter I had wished to do. The specialized functions once executed by the abolished collegiate boards of St. Petersburg were now to be carried out locally, where in fact they belonged. But by one device or another the royal officials of the *Tchin*, who defended their own vested interests in the administrative system, restricted the role of the local officials to carrying out policies that were initiated centrally. The reform, in brief, was excellent and long overdue, but neither the improvements of decentralization nor those of specialization of services seriously interfered with the progress of Catherine's absolutist rule.

A decade later two edicts, issued simultaneously, gave legal recognition to the corporative existence and organization of the nobility and the town citizens. The "Letters of Grace to the Nobility" of 1785 largely ratified an already existing state of affairs. This charter expressly reaffirmed the manifesto of 1762, which exempted noblemen from military service. They retained their exemption from personal taxation, corporal punishment, and the billeting of troops. They could be tried only before their peers. Their peers alone, subject to royal ratification, could deprive them either of their possessions or of their position in the Table of Ranks. It gave them what their spokesmen had asked for in the Commission: the legal recognition that "the estate of the nobility be separated by its rights and privileges from the rest of the people of other ranks and status."

The economic privileges threw a significant light upon Catherine's conception of the new role that the great landowning aristocracy, together with the merchant capitalists, could play in developing industrial enterprise. They could own real estate in towns and cities, dispose freely of the land which they possessed, and exploit the subsoil. They were also given the exclusive right to set up factories and sink mines, but shared the privilege of engaging in wholesale trade with the urban bourgeoisie. In addition to reaffirming their privileges, the charter also enumerated their responsibilities: to have their serfs discharge obligatory military service and pay the poll tax. Retention of hereditary nobility and the privileges appertaining to it was made contingent upon the loyal fulfillment of these auxiliary duties. Exactly like the Prussian Junkers, the Russian gentry had become unpaid civil agents of the crown on the manorial estate, rich in prerogatives and privileges and devoid of power to challenge the monarchy. Yet the arrangement was mutually satisfactory.

In the charter for the towns Catherine incorporated as much as she safely could afford of her views concerning the bourgeoisie without unduly antagonizing the gentry. She incorporated town inhabitants possessing the requisite minimum of real, commercial, or industrial property into a separate estate. They were exempted from military service, and they compounded for the poll tax by paying a small percentage of the capital invested in their business. They too obtained an illusory measure of self-government, but it was even less real than that held by the gentry, for the town council to which the propertied citizens elected representatives was narrowly hemmed in by the royal *gubernia* officials in financial matters and by the *ispravnik* in police affairs. By itself the town charter is unimpressive as an earnest of Catherine's policy of organizing and pitting the power of the bourgeoisie against the gentry. Together with measures more purely economic, however, it confirms the impression that she was relying increasingly upon merchant capitalists.[11]

III. THE PEASANTRY AND THE LAND QUESTION

The peasant problem was particularly tense during Catherine's first decade, when the wildest of rumors found credence among the ignorant, superstitious, and sorely oppressed peasantry. Even the rumor of emancipation was not too wild to find *moujiks* to believe it. In the ranks of the lowly and discontented there were vagabonds of all types and kinds: military deserters, unfrocked priests, runaway serfs, ruined noblemen, bandits, and river pirates. The Cossacks of the Jaik (Ural) and the Don and the Zaporogue Cossacks of the Dnieper, too, were restless under the new authority of Russia. The lawless Cossack tribes along the Volga needed only a pretext to fight for the lands which the Russian colonists had taken from them. Many of the malcontents were secret *Raskolniks* (religious dissidents) or else deeply sympathetic with the curious blend of ethical asceticism and economic

---

11 The most elaborate account of the changes is in Kluchevsky, *op. cit.*, V, chs. vi and vii; Kizevetter, *op. cit.*, 586 ff. gives them in a briefer and more readily understandable form; while Hoetzsch's account in the *Cambridge Modern History*, VI, 682 ff., is still very useful.

collectivism that constituted the heresy of these "Old Believers." Peasant resistance was stirring in the early years of the succession, but the ferment deepened with the excitement attending the electoral preparations for the Legislative Commission, with the years of warfare against the Turks, and the cruel outbreak of a plague in Moscow that snuffed out the lives of thousands of its inhabitants. This smoldering crater of peasant unrest burst forth in destructive fury in 1773.

The immediate occasion was the refusal of the government to satisfy the complaints of the starving Cossack fishermen of the Urals. At the height of their recriminations the Don Cossack, Emilian Pugachev, appeared in the troubled district. Pugachev was a daring soldier who had seen service in the Seven Years' War. A clever and daring agitator and a man of commanding ability, he announced himself to the superstitious serfs as the real Peter III, miraculously alive and now returned to succor his people. Backed by the Old Believers, this runaway convict from the prison of Kazan speedily enlisted the support of all the disaffected: aggrieved Cossacks, state serfs ascribed to the mines and foundries of the lower Urals, and the various tribal non-Russians in the no-man's-land between Russia and Asia. From the Bashkir herdsmen he obtained a fast-riding cavalry and from the factory workers he received supplies of much-needed cannon and shot. His bands of workers, Bashkirs, and peasants enjoyed technical superiority over the governmental forces that were first sent out against him, and won disquieting victories late in 1773. They suffered some reverses, too, but Pugachev withdrew into the secure Bashkir country, and when he returned in the spring of 1774 he spread new terror in his path. He routed the army forces and captured the strategic city of Kazan on the Volga, destroying most of it. The peasantry flocked enthusiastically to his banner and welcomed him as their liberator. For the better part of a year he was the master of the Volga valley. Moving northward, he captured Nizhni Novgorod and threatened the capital itself, whose terrified inhabitants prepared for a siege. In his new role as the rightful tsar he issued a manifesto to the serfs, bidding them to rise in their might, refuse military service and the payment of taxes, and "seize, execute, and hang all the landlords." His ruthless advice was superfluous. The rebels required no other encouragement than victory to even up old scores with their oppressors. An orgy of robbery, rapine, and murder attended this most terrifying of Russian peasant uprisings. The landlords fell back in panic before the devastating hordes, and Moscow, a city with a servile population of 100,000, girded itself for his attack.

Gradually his motley array fell back from central Russia. Disciplined army troops, released for service against him by the ending of the Turkish war, methodically attacked, giving him no respite. As Pugachev retreated down the Volga, sacking village after village in his course, his followers melted away with the matchless cavalry of Suvorov hot on his tracks. The end was in sight. Before the year was out, the false Peter was a prisoner, betrayed by his own lieutenants. An iron cage, built for the occasion, transported him to Moscow. There, Catherine brought him to reason by having him drawn and quartered. This severe penalty, which was prescribed by law, also helped to make his erstwhile followers more accommodating. When the systematic whirlwind of punishment had spent itself, the bases of Russian serfdom remained intact. Never again, until the overthrow of the monarchy, were peasants and Cossacks to stand together against the crown.[12]

Henceforth, Catherine had no choice but to renounce such notions as she may have once harbored of emancipating the serfs. It is difficult to write with any certainty of her ideas on peasant reform. An immense gap lay between her professed ideal intentions and the reality of her peasant policy. It is less difficult to reach the conclusion that she discharged most of her benevolent intentions with fine-sounding words. Apart from giving personal freedom to peasants settled in new towns and favoring the German colonists in the Volga area whom her agents had coaxed into the country, she completely sacrificed the peasantry to the *dvorianstvo*. To the landowners she gave as gifts immense sweeps of royal domain and some 800,000 crown peasants, who sank to the status of private serfs. The suppression of the independence of the Hetmanate of Little Russia in 1764 was a first step toward introducing the Catherine system into the southern

12 The documents are in M. Martinov, *Vostanie Emiliana Pugacheva. Sbornik dokumentov* (Leningrad, 1935); cf. also B. H. Sumner, "New Material on the Revolt of Pugachev," in *Slavonic Review*, VII (1926), 113-127 and 338-348; and the treatment in M. N. Pokrovsky, *A Brief History of Russia*, 2 vols. (New York, 1933), I, 145-149.

steppes, while the destruction of the republic of the Zaporogue Cossacks in 1775 along the great bend of the Dnieper speeded the Russification of Little Russia. When Prince Potemkin occupied the reservation (*syetch*) of these warlike tribes, who insured the safety of communications with the recently acquired Black Sea littoral, the civil administration also passed into the hands of St. Petersburg. Some of the Cossacks fled defiantly to the territory of the Ottoman Porte, but the rest proved more docile and were organized to defend the shores of the Azov, the Terek, and the Kuban. The exploitation of the Ukraine was rapid. New cities were founded and the vast steppes were transformed into fertile cultivated fields. Catherine carefully courted the support of the gentry and gradually curtailed the rights of the once free peasantry. In 1783 the Great Russian type of serfdom was introduced.[13] Serfdom also made inroads into the White Russian and Little Russian territory that Catherine acquired from the Polish partitions.

Irrespective of what she said, Catherine was thoroughly consistent during all of her reign in strengthening the landlord's rights over his serfs. Even before the Pugachev rebellion she had already permitted the public sale of serfs and their transfer from the land they cultivated, a practice that was to make sad headway later in her reign. As early as 1767 she had deprived them of their ancient right to appeal to the state authorities against their masters. During the entire long rule of this princess, who flaunted her admiration for Beccaria's *Crimes and Punishments*, there were only twenty recorded instances in which the government intervened to punish the abuse of the lord's penal authority over his serfs. The allotments of the individual serfs were steadily cut down by applying a new method of conducting the periodical surveys, but their obligations grew heavier. In the black-soil provinces, where *barshchina* (i.e., *corvée*) was the rule, the number of days' service per week increased from an average of three to four or five. During the harvest it was not uncommon to have the serf give all his days to work in the lord's fields. In the majority of cases the peasant cultivated his master's land with his own tools and draft animals, exactly as did his fellow serf in East Prussia and Poland.

13 V. Miakotin, "La fixation des paysans ukrainiens à la glèbe," in *Le Monde slave* (1932), 31-58; 182-207.

Where the peasant was an *obrochny* serf, his money dues rose catastrophically from an average of two rubles per annum in 1760 to five rubles in the nineties.

These increases in labor and money obligations came together with an attack upon the collectivism of the *mir*; and in these correlated developments one can see the first inroads of capitalist production for the market upon the old subsistence economy of the manor. To rescue debt-ridden landlords Catherine extended the operations of the State Land Bank (established in 1754) and provided for the loan of government funds at 6 per cent interest on the security of the borrower's property. For their benefit also she maintained their monopoly of liquor production and gave them the exclusive right to establish factories and mills and mines. She ascribed her own crown peasants to their factories as well as to state and semi-public establishments. Her expansionist foreign policy involved increasing domestic production both for a larger home market and for export abroad; and exactly like Frederick, she was compelled by her policy to buy the good will of the gentry and sacrifice the peasantry to them.[14]

IV. TRADE AND INDUSTRY

Meantime the volume of internal trade grew appreciably greater. This increase was due in part to natural causes, such as population growth and police security. But it was also aided by Catherine's policy of economic liberalism. Within a fortnight of her accession she abolished most of the state sales monopolies (which Elizabeth had farmed out to private individuals). She continued the earlier efforts of Peter Shuvalov to establish internal free trade in the empire and extend easier credit facilities to merchants. Though much of this trade was either local or regional, the improved canal service swelled the volume of river traffic; and in the last years of her reign a reliable foreign observer noted, perhaps with some exaggeration, that no state in Europe was so free of restrictions upon trade as Russia.

The growth of the export trade was more spectacular. Much of the increased internal trade represented either goods that were destined

[14] G. T. Robinson, *op. cit.*, ch. ii, is a succinct and illuminating account; J. Mavor, *op. cit.*, I, Bk. II, chs. i-vi, is far more elaborate, while Kluchevsky, *op. cit.*, V, ch. ix, is excellent but makes hard reading.

for shipment abroad or else imports redistributed from one or another of the terminal points for foreign trade. Peter I's conquest of the Baltic ports had given a revolutionary orientation to Russia's foreign trade. All the principal products of the north and the northwest (and from the Upper Volga as well through canal and river connections) gravitated towards St. Petersburg and the Baltic ports of Riga, Narva, and Reval, where immense stockpiles were accumulated in the warehouses. The reacquisition of the Duchy of Courland shortly after Catherine's accession added the ice-free port of Libau to these bustling commercial centers. The ships of all Europe plied in Baltic waters. In addition to Russian grain, now more or less freely exported, they carried away from the country flax and hemp, furs and skins, iron, and the indispensable naval stores of timber, copper, tar, pitch, and turpentine. England was still Russia's best customer (even as resident Englishmen in St. Petersburg were the greatest individual beneficiaries of the capital's trade) and sent in exchange for these imports her own manufactured textiles, colonial wares, cutlery, and ales. By the second half of the century the once excellent trading relations grew strained with the trade treaty itself lapsing in 1786. But the contact had served its purpose of giving a remarkable fillip to Russian commercial life.

The commercial links with the east were next in importance to this Baltic trade. They were strengthened by imperial conquests to the south, rapid colonization in newly acquired lands, and the establishment of secure military frontiers on the southeast. The balance of trade with Asia was unfavorable, for Russia lacked manufactured products to send in exchange for the imports of spices, fruits, precious stones, tea, rhubarb, raw silk, and cotton. The China trade was a government monopoly. The commercial axis to China was the new, protected military highway that ran from Kazan on the Volga, along the Kama to the Urals, and, from the other side of the mountains, by water and land via Tomsk and Irkutsk to Kyakhta on the Chinese border, just south of Lake Baikal. From Persia traffic crossed the Caspian to Astrakhan, going up the Volga and by a short land carriage to the great bend of the Don River.

The treaty of Küchük Kainarja (1774) with the Porte gave Russia her first opportunity to gain an important share of the Black Sea trade. It not only threw the Black Sea open to Russian ships, but it also gave them passage through the Bosporus and the Dardanelles into the Mediterranean. The acquisition of Azov and Taganrog and three fortresses between the Sea of Azov and the Black Sea, along with the whole steppe between the Bug and the Dnieper, secured the western and northern shore. The acquisition of the Kuban and Terek districts gave Russia a footing on the eastern shore and the Caucasus. On the lower Dnieper, now freed of the menace of the Zaporogue Cossacks, the empress founded the city of Kherson, which was made secure by the fortress of the Ochakov opposite the river's mouth. In 1783 the Crimea itself, for the past decade nominally independent of Turkey, was occupied by Russian troops.

The trade potential with southern and western Europe via the new water highways was enormous, and for its sake the Russian expansionists had risked a dangerously aggressive foreign policy. To a great extent the risk was successful, for with goods moving freely down the Don and the Dnieper, the vast stored and unexploited wealth of Russia's rich southern provinces was at last tapped. Measured by the far more spectacular nineteenth-century trade developments Catherine's and Potemkin's interest in the southern trade route bore only scanty results. But the burst of commercial activity was none the less extraordinary. With many of the European states Russia entered upon new commercial relations and signed treaties, e.g., with Poland in 1775; Denmark in 1782; Turkey in 1783; Austria in 1785; and Naples, Portugal, and France, all in 1787. After one discounts the depreciated currency, an increase in the value of foreign trade from 21 million rubles in 1762 to an annual average of 96 million rubles between 1794 and 1798 still indicated a change of immense scope. The same observer who had admired the growth of internal trade observed that Russia's foreign trade reached a level "that would have been considered as chimerical thirty years earlier."[15]

Manufactures occupied only an insignificant place in this spectacular growth of merchant capitalism. The people engaged in large-scale production remained startlingly few compared to the total population or

[15] Mirksky, *op. cit.*, ch. vi, has a good territorial survey of the empire; while the works of the travelers Coxe, *op. cit.*, II, and Castéra, *op. cit.*, III, *Appendix*, are useful for the trade routes, the nature, and the statistics of trade.

even to the workers engaged in agriculture and pasturage. For many years to come peasant craftwork (*kustar*) both in the household and on the estate remained dominant in Russian economy, each region producing its own famed specialties. The factories and mills, mines and foundries, may have numbered several thousand, but they bore little resemblance to factories in the modern sense. Machinery was rare; human and animal power were more frequent than water; and steam power was unheard of. The great majority of the so-called factories were exceedingly modest in size. Only very rarely were workers assembled in any great numbers. Such was the case, for instance, in the cloth factory of Potemkin which employed a total of 9,000 men.

Many of Peter the Great's original foundations survived as "possessional factories," or semi-public establishments under governmental supervision and regulation. Whether textile factories for the making of soldiers' uniforms or sailcloth for the navy, arms foundries and ammunition factories, mines and metallurgical enterprises, these enterprises were operated by noblemen with ascribed state serf labor. Without doing anything to improve the labor conditions the state ascribed more and more laborers to these factories, the number rising from 142,000 in 1762 to 312,000 in 1794. Noble entrepreneurs also operated the "manorial factories." Some of these had survived from the days when Peter the Great set up bourgeois merchant capitalists in industry, and others were run from the outset by noblemen. In any case, they all employed the labor of the private manorial serfs and were engaged mainly in cloth or iron production for the market. Since government policy strongly favored them and they could exploit their untrained labor force under conditions which came close to chattel slavery, it is not surprising that many of them reaped vast fortunes.

Meantime, the urban merchants who had lost the right to compete with the nobility in factory production turned to entrepreneur activities on the English model. Together with occasional rich serfs who had commuted their labor obligations into *obrok*, they established themselves as promoters on the classic "putting-out" system in those towns which were adjacent to available serf labor. The greatest success of this domestic or putting-out system was naturally in rural spinning and weaving, but rural industry along these lines made slight progress on the whole until the next century. The bourgeois merchant promoter lacked the governmental patronage and encouragement that were extended to the noblemen in industry. He had to compete for manpower with the *kustar* crafts. The manorial restrictions upon a flexible labor supply also greatly hindered the development of free enterprise on the model of western Europe. Nevertheless, the age witnessed a great growth in the numbers of the urban dwellers, who increased from 328,000 in 1724 to 1,300,000 in 1796. They were still only about 4 per cent of the total population of European Russia, but they were slowly acquiring a corporate sense. Though Catherine discriminated against them in industry, the richest of the bourgeois merchants were associated with the aristocracy in commercial enterprises. In many ways—by their memorials against the serf system which cut off their labor supply for industrial production; by their support of the empress's expansionist policies; by their attempts to obtain a corporative organization and the privileges connected therewith—they showed that Catherine's policy of building up the town middle classes was bringing results.

The increase in national wealth was reflected in higher state revenues, which rose from under 17 million rubles at the beginning of Catherine's reign to a nominal 78 million rubles (in depreciated currency) in 1796. They were derived, in order of importance, from the poll tax, customs dues, contributions from the conquered territory, government salt and liquor monopolies, stamp duties, and regalian rights from the mines, the mint, and the church lands. The embezzlement of the collectors was colossal, for an amount more considerable than the government received was collected at the source. The knavery of tax collectors paled before the wastefulness of the crown itself. Expenses ran far ahead of income. The support of the huge army of theoretically over 200,000 men was a terrible drain upon the exchequer. Lavish court expenditures completed what corruption, inefficiency, and the heavy burden of militarism had begun. Consequently, Catherine floated loans amounting to 130,000,000 rubles, both at home and abroad, through the intermediary of Dutch and Italian bankers. She also issued paper money, more or less supported by gold collateral. At home the paper ruble circulated at par, for the empress used her full power to induce confidence in fiat money. Abroad, the paper ruble was quoted almost 50 per cent off.

After a stormy and turbulent reign Catherine died peacefully in 1796. Her violent, hysterical outburst against the French Revolution was not the measure of her capacity. Her real greatness consisted in flouting the logic that she admired in the *philosophes*, in combining opposites and uniting contradictions. She concealed her courage transparently under her feminine guile. Her patience was not inferior to her sense of publicity. She did not indiscriminately make her lovers generals or ministers of state. The difficult situation that she inherited, she handled with the realistic flexibility of a masterly and not too scrupulous opportunist. Where administrative decentralization was needed, she relaxed the shadow if not the substance of governmental control. She insidiously transformed the gentry into unpaid governmental civil agents, but kept their loyalty by legalizing their patrimonial privileges. This strategy involved the sacrifice of the peasantry and doubtlessly ran counter to the better side of her nature, but she resigned herself to the sacrifice. Because she had intelligence and historical vision, she favored the growth of the commercial bourgeoisie, whom she linked in interest with the great landed aristocracy, while she pitted them simultaneously against the squirearchy, of whom she was an involuntary dependent. Like Peter I, to whose policy she returned in many essential respects, she made royal absolutism a cement at home, uniting her vast territories and disparate races, but a sword abroad, cutting Russia's way to stronger frontiers and new markets.

Wily and calculating, the tsarina of the nobility was a patriot queen, like Elizabeth of England, brooding over the destinies of her country. She was almost all things to all men, except to the peasantry, who constituted a mere 94 per cent of the population. To them she was a blight and a calamity. She served the old regime, and saved it by making concessions where the exercise of plenary absolutism was impossible. She adjusted the national economy to more modern needs, broke up the rigid social classifications, and made Russia safe for aristocracy for at least another century.

v. "ENLIGHTENED LIBERTY" IN POLAND

In retrospect the years preceding the first partition of Poland seem an inevitable prelude to disaster. The crown was an anemic shadow. It lacked capital, military arms, and civil servants. It was dragged along to its ruin by the feudal nobility; and there was, to save it from decay, no body of loyal subjects steeped in the spirit of free enterprise and civic responsibility. Yet Poland was not entirely wanting in more elevated spirits. Influential voices protested against the degrading realities. Father Stanislas Konarski, the gentle Piarist priest, made himself the conscience of his country in his educational crusade for enlightened reform. Undismayed and more practical reformers rallied around the powerful "Family" of the Czartoryskis, for three generations the nursery of Polish enlightenment.[16]

In the generation before the death of the Saxon-born Augustus III in 1763, the "Family" had employed its enormous wealth, its numerous retainers, and its immense prestige to mold public opinion and leaders for a gradual and peaceful reform of the constitutional nightmare. But their spokesmen, principally the two Czartoryskis, father and son, were ardently disliked and mistrusted by the *szlachta*. Unpatriotic the Family's political outlook was not, as alleged by the National party formed by the rival Potockis and Radziwills. But it was both naïve and dangerous on their part to re-establish a native Polish dynasty, with the aid of Russian redeemers, for a struggle against reactionaries at home.

The death of Augustus III afforded an opportunity to the reformers, who at once invoked Catherine's vaguely promised assistance to place their own candidate on the throne. This opportunity to extend Russia's influence in Poland was almost too good for Catherine to miss. In the spring of that year she had already placed her candidate on the ducal throne of Courland, nominally a Polish dependency. By the treaty of April, 1764, she and Frederick II of Prussia agreed jointly to secure the election of the pliable Stanislas Poniatowski as king of Poland. Catherine's instructions to her ambassador, Count Keyserling, about the election make illuminating reading. After several

---

[16] W. J. Rose, *Stanislas Konarski. Reformer of Education in Eighteenth Century Poland* (London, 1929), chs. i-iv; vii.

pages of unvarnished advice concerning the use of bribery on a large scale, she concluded with the following declaration: "If our candidate is not elected, then without any preliminary declaration we will order our troops at once to invade Polish territory . . . , to treat our adversaries as rebels, and to destroy their goods and their property by fire and sword. In that contingency we will act in concert with the King of Prussia."[17] Under the shadow of gleaming Russian bayonets the Convocation Diet held a fine mockery of an election in September and dutifully named Catherine's ex-lover, Stanislas Poniatowski, king.

Catherine thus seemed as triumphant in her Polish affairs as she had been in ending the Seven Years' War and in composing her difficulties at home. But the interests of Frederick the Great in Poland ran counter to her own, for the Hohenzollern favored partition. Moreover, the handsome and cultivated ruler whom they had selected, presumably because he was safe, proved more obdurate than they had anticipated and ranged himself on the side of his relatives in the "Family." Catherine, who opposed partition, persevered in trying to govern Poland through the existing constitutional arrangement and instructed her new ambassador, Repnin, to utilize the ↄro-Russian faction in the country to the full. Repnin easily found pretexts for his veiled interference in the problems of the religious and political disabilities of the Dissidents. By the terms of the Russian-Prussian alliance the two countries were pledged to protect the rights of these Dissidents. There was no question that Roman Catholic Poland had been guilty of intolerant treatment of these religious minorities. But Catherine was exceedingly ill-advised from the Russian point of view at least in involving her imperial prestige in their cause, for they included Lutherans and Calvinists as well as Orthodox Catholics. In risking disorders in Poland which could only promote partition, she was playing a game whose stakes were more attractive to Frederick than to her.

For several years neither the Russians nor the Poles gained a decisive advantage. While the reformers endeavored to loosen the Russian grip by abolishing the *liberum veto*, which legalized political anarchy, Repnin countered in several ways. He used force against them and he castigated them publicly as the destroyers of Poland's glorious

17 H. Grappin, *Histoire de la Pologne* (Paris, 1922), 140.

traditions. Simultaneously, he also encouraged the Dissidents to avail themselves of the existing political practices and form armed confederations, which they did. He got wide and favorable publicity abroad for the Russian policy of toleration. At the same time he gave assurances to the ignorant and intolerant Polish populace that Russia would safeguard religious purity against the inroads of heterodoxy. Furthermore, he inflamed the same conservative political prejudices by flaunting the assumed liberal menace of the Czartoryskis' reform program. Thus he kept the country in ferment and led the conservative and reactionary Polish groups to believe that Catherine was on their side against political and religious reform. It was through his benevolent aid that a large group of some 80,000 conservative but patriotic Polish noblemen formed the armed Confederation of Radom.

Soon enough the Confederates found that they had been tricked and were expected to obey the empress. They were in accord with Repnin in his insistence upon keeping political life oppressive and stagnant; but they waxed indignant when he employed ruse and legal authority to usher in religious and political toleration. Repnin did not hesitate to employ force. He deported several of the leading Roman Catholic opponents of Catherine to Russia, and he forced the Diet of 1767 to appoint a Delegation in order to negotiate a settlement of the religious and political problems. Little time was required to convince this diet with "arguments armed with cannon and bayonets." It abrogated the few measures of reform that it had passed, maintained the *liberum veto*, and recognized in principle the justice of the Dissidents' claim for the fullest political equality and the widest freedom of religious belief, worship, and instruction. In the following year a cowed Delegation drew up the formal pact with Catherine that ratified the agreement and placed Poland under Catherine as the "protector of her laws and liberties."

At last the empress had gained the puppet state that she desired. Almost overnight Poland had won a degree of religious toleration that would have been extraordinary even in England in those days. Catherine reckoned, however, without the force of patriotic resistance. Warsaw burst out in furious opposition and was promptly placed under blockade. Undaunted, Polish patriots, led by Joseph Pulaski and Bishop Krasinski and flying the banner of *pro religione et libertate*, formed the Confederation of Bar to keep their country safe from high-handed political reform, dictated religious toleration, and Russian coercion. This confederation was the nucleus of a broad religious and patriotic revolt. However justifiable from a nationalist point of view, it was less than admirable in its religious intransigence and its violence. The nationalist revolt precipitated a civil war, for confederations similar to those of Bar sprang up elsewhere in the country. Civil war merged into foreign war, and the war of the great powers eventuated in the first partition of Poland.[18]

After the partition most trained observers shared the gloomy view of the much-traveled Archdeacon Coxe, who forecast in 1778 that Poland would be "totally swallowed up by the neighboring powers." But Poland surprised all Europe by a recovery that offered, writes a nationalist historian, "one of the most magnificent examples of national regeneration that any people has ever realized. In all domains, economic, social, political, intellectual, it was like a feverish revival, an immense effort to escape from the nightmare of yesterday, from the obsessing picture of all the ruin and all the humiliation."[19] Inspired by the liberal speculation of western Europe and stirred by the reforming activities of powerful neighbors, the Polish intellectual élite awoke from their lethargy. But only in part did inspiration come from the French and English *philosophes*. The Polish reformers drew also upon native sources, upon the writings of such men as Karwicki and Konarski, for their inspiration. In their ranks were the great figures of the abortive Polish revival: political theorists such as Stanislas Staszic and Stanislas Malachowski; the two Czartoryskis and Marshal Lubomirski; the great humanitarian, Chancellor Andrew Zamoyski, and the fervent republican, the noble-born Hugo Kollotaj. Not the least of the reformers was the monarch himself.

Poniatowski was admirably trained, as few of his compatriots were, for politics. He was also one of the most enlightened and most carefully educated Poles of his day. It is true that he was weak-willed and without firm conviction. He wavered and yielded ground when tenacity and resistance would have emblazoned his name in glory. But not a little of the great transformation stemmed from him. Before

---

18 *Vide* ch. vii for the diplomatic relations of the powers.
19 Grappin, *op. cit.*, 150.

the partition he had already placed himself on record in favor of religious toleration and the ending of the *liberum veto*. The Russian-Prussian declaration of 1766 which had formally immobilized the political anarchy in his country he countered by penning the *Considerations of a Good Citizen*, a dignified and patriotic statement of a compromise political solution on the basis of constitutional rule. But his weaknesses of character as well as his former relations with Catherine, together with the unfortunate circumstances of his election, clouded his name. In the turbulent days of the nationalist revolt, the Confederation of Bar declared him deposed from the throne; and his status with his people remained uncertain until after the partition.

After the cruel blow had fallen a new concept of liberty spread slowly through the land, seeping into many an entrenched citadel of lay and ecclesiastical obscurantism. The dissolution of the Jesuit order gave the government an opportunity for a sharp drive against the temporal claims of ecclesiastics. The spirit of Febronianism permeated the new code of church and state relations which Chancellor Zamoyski proposed.[20] A new educational commission was established in 1773. Dowered with the confiscated Jesuit property, it laid the foundations of a comprehensive educational system on the most advanced and progressive lines. Time doubtlessly was against it, but a new generation of Polish youth was being fashioned, far removed in spirit from the disruptive ideals which their ancestors had treasured under the guise of "golden liberty."

Impressive, too, was the economic revival of the country, whose main artery of trade, the Vistula, had been cut. Progressive magnates employed their rents to set up factories in a brave effort to end the country's dependence on foreign countries for manufactured goods. Towns, once half-empty, burst into new life. While the crown was not strong enough to abolish serfdom outright, it deprived the nobility of their life-and-death rights over their private serfs. The great Four-Year Diet of 1788, which shed a brilliant light upon the land soon to be blacked out, placed the serfs under the legal protection of the state. Zamoyski set an example for other noble proprietors to follow. He liberated his own serfs and generously tided them over the initial period of financial difficulty.

[20] See below, ch. x, pp. 264-268, for the anti-Jesuit and Febronian movements.

Poland's numbered hours did not permit a solution of the troubled problem of municipal self-government. Already sorely complicated by religious, racial, and financial differences, the solution of town government was not advanced by the presence of Russian troops of occupation. Nevertheless, various royal commissions labored valiantly to restore a modicum of orderly existence to towns whose government had been otherwise distinguished in the past. In national administration the terms of the Constitution of 1775 made provision for a large executive council, elected by the diet, which was to serve as advisory agent to the crown and also as administrative board for foreign affairs, police, army, justice, and finance. The single executive will of the monarchy was in this way to be supplemented in its difficult task of overcoming the entrenched authority of the hitherto semi-independent feudatories. To give additional force to this will the reformers also increased the strength of the regular army and reorganized it on the superior and efficient Prussian model. The monarchy still further strengthened its position by regaining a great deal of the alienated royal domain which had been exploited by the great feudal lords. The augmented state revenue reflected the improved economic conditions, and physiocrats were emboldened to make a plea for their cherished single tax on land. The reform movement reached its apogee in the new Constitution of 1791, which provided for a hereditary monarchy patterned after the reformed French state. But only a year later Russia, the "Protector," and Prussia, the friendly ally, swooped down like wolves upon the Most Serene Republic. The formal death of Poland as an independent state was now only a matter of time.

The causes of Poland's annihilation are indivisible, and only the crudest kind of plastic surgery on the face of history could prove that one cause alone accounted for the disaster.[21] In all likelihood Poland might have survived had it not been for the predatory ruthlessness of her neighbors. No doubt the great awakening had at first touched only the élite; the humanitarianism of Konarski and the exhortations of Zamoyski were neither readily understood nor acted upon. The discipline, the sacrifice, and the stern renunciation of older ways

21 J. Rutkowski, "Les bases économiques du partage de l'ancienne Pologne," in *Revue d'histoire moderne*, VII (1932), 363-389.

demanded by the new royal reform program overtaxed both the good will and the capacity of ignorant peasants and a gentry chained to prejudice. But with time the reforms, not all, perhaps, but the most fundamental, might have taken root. Time, however, was not on the side of the innovators. Prussia did not cherish Polish liberty. It was never part of Russia's intentions to let fresh life breathe into her vassal state. The enlightened rulers on the neighboring thrones willed Poland's destiny otherwise. In consequence the reforms that were effected have the character of museum pieces.[22]

VI. THE SCANDINAVIAN STATES: SWEDEN AND DENMARK

Enlightened despotism was only a passing phenomenon in neighboring Sweden. It was exclusively linked with the name of Gustavus III, who gained his personal ascendancy in 1772 by a mixture of ruse and coercion and lost it in 1792 by assassination. It left no permanent impress except romantic legend upon a country that was rich in its traditions of popular liberty and self-rule.[23] In the half-century that preceded Gustavus, in the "Age of Liberty" as that period is called in Swedish history, the parliamentary system had broken down in bitter factional strife among the representatives of the several estates or orders. Sweden had become the football of international politics, principally of France and Russia. France stood behind the privileged landowning aristocracy (the Hats), anxious to use the young prince Gustave to further its interests in northeastern Europe. Russia supported the burgesses and the well-to-do peasant proprietors (the Caps), eager to maintain disorder in order to fasten its grip on the country and, through Sweden, its control over the Baltic. To incorporate Sweden into his "System of the North," was the dream of Nikita Panin, even as Choiseul and Vergennes schemed to foment revolution in Sweden and make it via Gustavus a French outpost in the east. This political and diplomatic imbroglio had become complicated still

---

22 In addition to the brief, suggestive sketch in L. Konopczynski, "La liberté éclairée en Pologne," *B.I.C.H.S.*, IX (1937), 88-100; and ch. vi by Dembinski in *The Cambridge History of Poland, 1697-1935*, ed. by W. F. Reddaway and others (Cambridge, 1941); there is a more detailed treatment in the still useful work by R. N. Bain, *The Last King of Poland* (London, 1909), especially chs. vii and viii.

23 L. Stavenow, "Der aufgeklärte Despotismus des 18. Jahrhunderts in Schweden," in *B.I.C.H.S.*, V (1933), 762-772.

further in the decade of the sixties by the fierce social conflict that broke out between the Hats and the Caps.

Such was the difficult plight of the Swedish crown when Prince Gustavus received word in Paris, early in 1771, that his father, King Adolphus Frederick, had died. He was then only twenty-five years of age, a curious and dangerous blend of natural talent and charm of manner, along with romantic ambition and inconstancy of character. That he sincerely yearned to end internal strife and restore his country to the strong position it had once held is as indisputable as it was eminently praiseworthy. That he had earnestly discussed ways and means of doing so with French statesmen is also indisputable. He was a great admirer of his famous uncle in Potsdam (his mother was Frederick II's sister Louise Ulrica), and he had a wide and intimate acquaintance with the writings of the French philosophers. In common with the economic liberals he favored a physiocratic policy at home as a corrective to the exaggerated mercantilism which had overtaxed his country's resources and brought it to economic distress, financial dislocation, and social unrest. He shared with forward-looking statesmen their hope of eradicating the factional spirit of the estates and re-establishing the rule of the monarchy in the interests of the public good. He hoped to curb the dangerous independence of crown officials, discipline civil servants into efficiency and establish an *esprit de corps*, increase governmental revenues, strengthen national defenses, and simultaneously spread the blessings of religious toleration and humanitarian relief over the land.

Gustavus had the qualities to win a spectacular victory, but few qualifications to consolidate his gains permanently. Politics was to teach him circumspection and develop his talent for dissimulation and indirection. For all his gifts, he lacked real greatness. He was consumed with ambition. His impatience and his love of theatrical display prevailed over his sense of duty and distracted him from devoting his energies to a methodical superintendence of the administration. His pride and vanity were prodigious, and he was wanting in both depth and firmness.[24]

[24] A. Ritter von Arneth, *Joseph II und Leopold von Toskana. Ihr Briefwechsel von 1781 bis 1790*, 2 vols. (Vienna, 1872), I, 178, cites a letter from Joseph II in which that stern incarnation of the sober virtues calls Gustavus "a man without character . . . with a veneer of wit and information . . . a braggart and coxcomb."

Convinced by the failure of his efforts as mediator between the Caps and the Hats that his country was steadily losing its real independence to Russia, the newly enthroned ruler resolved to use force to save Sweden and restore the power of the crown. The attempt of the *Riksdag* to reduce his role to that of the "do-nothing king" was the last straw. His military plot almost miscarried, but Gustavus saved the day by his personal courage. Hailed as liberator by the populace, he delivered an invective against the factions, forced a new constitution upon the deputies, and then dissolved the parliament (*Riksdag*).[25] The Constitution of 1772 vigorously reaffirmed the royal prerogative and abolished the ruinous party system which had been responsible for much of the confusion and violence of the preceding years. It did not completely destroy the legitimate constitutional rights of the parliament. "You are deceived," said Gustavus, "if you suppose I intend anything prejudicial to your law and your liberties." The *Riksdag* replied proudly to his guarantee: "We declare anew that arbitrary power, or what is commonly called absolute sovereignty, inspires us with the greatest horror; but we believe that it is for our welfare, and at the same time a cause of glory for us in the quality of free and independent estates, making the laws and subject to them, to exist and live under the government of a king clothed with an authority limited by the laws."[26] So long as that happy accord between the executive and the legislature existed, the revolution of 1772 was successful in establishing a balanced and constitutional monarchy somewhat on the English model. The sensational revolutionary coup and the new constitution undoubtedly gave the crown extensive powers, such as the right to convoke and dismiss the *Riksdag* and limit its discussion to proposals introduced by the king. But the deputies still had the power of the purse, control over legislation, and final determination in foreign policy. The political truce lasted for a decade; and in that period came all the innovations that gave Gustavus his title of enlightened despot.

25 For the role of the great powers in this crisis, especially France, *Gustave III et la cour de France*, 2 vols. (Paris, 1867), I, ch. iii, by M. A. Geoffroy; S. W. Thompson and S. K. Padover, *Secret Diplomacy. A Record of Espionage and Double Dealing: 1500-1815* (London, 1937), 169.
26 M. Baldwin, *Gustavus III of Sweden. A Study of the Enlightened Despotism of the Eighteenth Century in Europe* (unpublished M.A. thesis, Cornell University, 1902), pp. 15-16; 33-34.

Not until 1778 did Gustavus reassemble the parliament, and then only to ratify measures already effected. Enjoying his vast popularity and seconded by able advisers, he embarked on sweeping reforms. His economic changes, inspired and directed by the two great ministers, Liliencrantz and Hermannsen, were imbued with the spirit of physiocracy. Gustavus freely acknowledged his indebtedness in economic reforms to the great Turgot, the inspiration for his own reforms. The reformers restored monetary stability by calling in the debased paper money at about 50 per cent of its market value and establishing a new system of coinage based on silver. On the basis of detailed reports prepared by government commissions they carried through a series of measures that established free internal grain trade throughout the entire country (1775-1780). They relaxed the onerous guild regulations. Without injuring the possession rights of crown tenants, tax assessments were modified in favor of the small free farmer. To increase foreign trade free ports were established on the Baltic, and free market towns were founded in the interior to stimulate domestic commerce.

Before the ruler broke with the parliament in the second decade of his reign, he also carried through other admirable reforms. In 1781 full religious toleration was granted to non-Lutheran Christians who already had the status of resident aliens. In the following year the Jews were given permission to settle in three designated large cities, engage freely in trade, and practice their religion without molestation. Between 1775 and 1778 his counselor Liliestraale sponsored long-overdue changes in law and legal procedure which in the perspective of a century a Swedish parliamentary commission still called an epoch-making juridical reform. Almost to the very close of his reign the king maintained and even extended the existing system of a free press. Despite mounting criticism of his policies Gustavus counted upon his popularity to outweigh journalistic attack.

The last decade of his rule, from 1782-1792, was far removed in spirit from the first ten years. It was a bitter era of growing unrest, social discontent, political strife, and financial stringency. There is little doubt that the mutinous attitude of the *Riksdag* of 1786, which amended or rejected most of the royal proposals, accentuated Gustavus's evolution toward absolutism. But he was not free of blame. Gustavus was a prodigal spendthrift who sank great sums of money in public building, court entertainment, theatricals and operas, and, above all, in the true style of his century, on military preparedness. It was his need of money that destroyed his popularity and reopened the long-stilled controversy with the *Riksdag*. Among the less fortunate of his expedients to meet his wants was the attempt to make brandy production a governmental monopoly. This experiment failed, the peasantry eventually regaining their right to make spirits, subject to a royal license. In the meantime the hated fiscal measure inspired methods of evasion curiously familiar to Americans with memories of bootlegging days.

Embarrassed by his soaring expenses and irritated by mounting criticism, the monarch then tried coercion to fill in the gaps of the deficit. When drastic suppression of the writings and speeches of the political opposition failed and sharp curtailment of the parliamentary power of the purse also proved no remedy for an unbalanced budget, he fell back upon the ancient expedient of an aggressive policy abroad to distract public attention from failure at home. For three years, from 1786 to 1789, he ruled without a parliament. Reforms were permanently shelved in these years and Gustavus's enlightened despotism became a thing of the past. The war against Russia into which he had so recklessly and unexpectedly plunged in 1788 gave the landowning nobility an opportunity for a classical military *Putsch* against a presuming monarch. But Gustavus played his hand more skillfully than did his aristocratic foes. Taking advantage of their personal differences and political bickering, he impressed the Act of Union and Security upon the *Riksdag*. In form it was an Appendix to the Constitution that he had already imposed seventeen years earlier. Superficially, the new document moved in the direction of bourgeois liberalism, for it restricted the privileges of the nobility while opening high political offices to commoners. Actually, it was the constitutional sacrament of his autocracy, giving him, in addition to his other powers, a free hand in foreign policy and full command of the army. Enlightened despotism as a broad policy of state had degenerated into Gustavus's personal absolutism resting upon naked force, and to his personal absolutism the outraged nobility retaliated with the weapon of assassination![27]

27 The most detailed treatment in English is still R. N. Bain's sympathetic *Gustavus III and his Contemporaries, 1746-1792*, 2 vols. (London, 1904).

The Oldenburg dynasty ruled over two million subjects in the neighboring Danish kingdom, which then comprised Norway as well as the territory of the present Danish state. The kingdom's importance was slight, and no creative stimuli flowed from Denmark to the rest of Europe. Yet its history furnished a brief but spectacular chapter in eighteenth-century enlightened despotism. From 1730 to 1766, under Christian VI and Frederick V, Denmark enjoyed both security abroad and prosperity at home. Its foreign policy, skillfully conducted by Count Johann H. E. Bernstorff, was peaceful and was grounded upon Denmark's firm resolution to remain neutral in the great international wars without sacrificing Russia's benevolent friendship. The economic counterpart of this pacific diplomacy was intense mercantilism, and the two policies between them augmented the country's wealth. Not unnaturally the major portions of the profits from state-supported industry and extensive trading relations abroad went to the new business oligarchy and the old landed aristocracy.

Ultimately, the costs of these developments appeared greater to the nation than their advantages. The merchants and the landed proprietors who had benefited most were, many of them, of German extraction. In addition to waxing wealthy from trade they were more or less unobtrusively reducing the rule of the crown to an empty formality and installing their own members into the highest administrative posts. To safeguard their interests these new bureaucrats perpetuated a viciously reactionary judicial procedure and maintained the inequalities of a rigid social classification. Dogmatists or obscurantists, most of them, in things of the spirit, they dammed up the streams of fresh speculation from abroad as much as they could and narrowly enforced the religious constraints which had been established by the Pietist rulers.[28] Preserving neutrality and subsidizing state-sponsored industrial enterprises swelled the public debt, whose carrying charges imposed a cruel burden of taxation upon a peasantry which was still largely bound to the soil and liable to heavy servile *corvées* and dues.[29]

[28] J. W. Eaton, "The French Influence in Denmark in the Seventeenth and Eighteenth Centuries," in *Germanic Review*, VI (1931), 321-362.
[29] The best printed account in English is by W. F. Reddaway, in *Cambridge Modern History*, VI, ch. xxi; but the clearest and most penetrating treatment is the unpublished doctoral dissertation of H. S. Commager, *Struensee and the Reform Movement in Denmark* (Chicago, 1928), ch. i.

The relaxation of the press censorship gave the opposition a chance to air its views. At first this opposition was centered in a small coterie of disaffected men whose personal jealousy of and hostility to Bernstorff probably had as much to do with their attitude as their more impersonal desire to improve Danish administration *à la prusse*.[30] The nominal leader of this group was the ousted war minister, the Frenchman Count de Saint-Germain, but a brilliant young German physician, Johann Friedrich Struensee, came to the fore. Struensee had first been introduced into the group to serve as a go-between at the court, where his influence was high. He was in many ways an extraordinary person. Professionally competent, elegant in manner, and licentious in behavior, he was an enthusiast of the materialistic doctrines of the French Encyclopedists and eager to put their political tenets into practice. A successful physician at Altona, he gained a great hold over the idiot king, Christian VII (1766-1808), by partially restoring his health. In time, as he ingratiated himself with the queen, he resolved to use his growing authority to bring a full measure of enlightened reform to the misruled kingdom.

Having attained power by his hypnotic influence over the monarch, he retained control through his amorous relations with the queen, who soon bore him a daughter. By the summer of 1770 Struensee was the real power behind the throne. He got rid of Count Bernstorff, and recalling to court several of his exiled boon companions, such as Enevold Brandt, he made himself an open dictator.[31] Once he emerged from the shadows, it was clear that his cardinal principle was to free the king from bureaucratic restraints and make the crown the pivotal center of the governmental system. He abolished the council of state, dismissed hostile ministers from office, and subordinated the overstaffed *collegia*, as well as their departmental heads, to the authority of a newly constituted cabinet. He made himself the unchallenged chief of this body, which became the absolute authority in the state. At least in theory he thus restored the royal prerogative. But his highhanded usurpation of power, carried to the point of issuing cabinet

30 For the enormously important Bernstorff family, cf. the authoritative studies of Aage Friis, *Bernstorfferne og Danemark*, 2 vols. (Copenhagen, 1903, 1919); and *Bernstorffske Papierer*, 3 vols. (Copenhagen, 1904, 1907, 1913).
31 W. F. Reddaway, "Struensee and the Fall of Bernstorff," in *English Historical Review*, XXVII (1912), 274 ff.

orders without the royal signature, and his illicit relations with the unfortunate and impressionable young queen only quickened resentment against him, first at court and then more generally throughout the country. The ill will provoked by his alleged brutal treatment of the mad king and his contemptuous attitude toward native customs and institutions would in any case have prejudiced public opinion against him, but he also outraged traditional feeling by his ill-considered zeal in attempting to correct within mere weeks or months the blunders and injustices that had taken years and generations to pile up.

His days were numbered. A palace intrigue, led by one of his erstwhile friends, overthrew him in January, 1772. Three months later he and Brandt expiated with decapitation and quartering both their moral delinquencies and the crime of challenging the established order.[32]

Struensee's personal rule was a mere episode in Danish history, but by outlook and intent it was linked with an insistent demand for social and economic improvement. His rule lasted only a moment, but his influence remained vital for the next half-century, first under the regency of Crown Prince Frederick from 1784 to 1808 and then under the latter's rule as Frederick VI from 1808 to 1839. His successors were also inspired by the great currents of the age to liberalize economic enterprise and replace the regime of status with free contract. The long and brilliantly successful ministry of the younger Andreas P. Bernstorff, nephew of the famous Johann, 1784 to 1797, saw the triumph of most of the Struensee program, but applied wisely and with measure. New commercial practices were introduced one by one. In 1788 the grain and cattle trades were declared free within the kingdom. The government withdrew most of its subsidies to industrialists and granted the right of free enterprise to urban merchant capitalists. The law concerning the guilds (1800) removed the shackles that had immobilized a free labor supply and established the right to set up industries without the sanction of the guilds.

It was the able and progressive Count Reventlow, long the friend of the peasants, who induced the crown prince to appoint a reform

32 Cf. Commager, *op. cit.*; and W. F. Reddaway, "Christian VII," in *English Historical Review*, XXXI (1916), 59-84; also the sympathetic and critical appraisal, *Struensee et la cour de Copenhague, 1760-1772. Memoires de Reverdil*, ed. by A. Roger (Paris, 1858).

commission in 1786, which conducted a systematic investigation into the effects of serfdom upon agricultural productivity. Bernstorff was also associated with Reventlow in bettering the legal status and economic condition of the peasantry, thus applying on a national scale the improvements that he himself had earlier effected on his private estates. The labors of the investigating commission were crowned in several memorable decrees. The fundamental juridical change was made in 1787, when the servile peasant was declared the legal equal of all other Danish subjects. In the following year serfdom was completely abolished. Within the next decade the redemption terms of the peasants' service obligations were also carefully worked out, simultaneously with the detailed provisions for dividing up the large landed estates. A chain of public credit banks was established to lend money at easy interest rates to the small peasant farmers. Through these legal enactments prosperity came to the Danish farmers, and the foundations were laid for the middle-class democracy of the nineteenth century.[33]

33 A. Linvald, "Comment le despotisme éclairé s'est présenté dans l'histoire du Danemark," in the *B.I.C.H.S.*, V (1933), 714-726, gives a stimulating account of the broader implications of the reform movement.

Chapter Six

LATIN EUROPE

I. THE ITALIAN STATES

MOST accounts in English, serenely ignoring recent Italian scholarship, depict eighteenth-century Italy as sunk in torpid slumber. From this slumber, so runs the version, the rude shock of Bonaparte's conquering ragamuffins galvanized her into life. An echo of these judgments is heard in the words of a noted living historian: "Italy, too, the Italy of Piranesi's prints was peaceful and stagnant—a land of hard-working, ragged, submissive peasants, of idle beggars, and of cultured dilettante nobles and clergy with few interests in life . . . a land strangely different from the fierce and passionate Italy of the Middle Ages, of the later Risorgimento or of modern Fascism."[1] As a generalization this statement is both vivid and well-drawn; all that is lacking is accuracy.

Italy was indeed disunited. A number of states were ruled not by the fathers of their people, but by foreign fathers-in-law. The edge of native inquiry had been dulled by two centuries of ecclesiastical obscurantism; the creative patterns of artistic expression had become stereotyped into the vacuous insipidities of Arcadia. In somnolent provincial towns sleek patricians and placid priests still cheated ennui in a dreary parade of learning. Cruelly exploited peasants were scarcely capable of looking beyond the horizon of their little world of toil and obligations. In the very age of Piranesi, however, even poetasters turned critics and began to poke fun at Arcadian vapidities and the cloying verse that sang the loves of graceful shepherdesses and their

[1] G. M. Trevelyan, in Turberville, *Johnson's England*, I, 2. In Italian for the most useful digests of recent scholarship see A. Ghisalberti, *Gli Albori del Risorgimento italiano* (Rome, 1931); A. Ferrari, *La preparazione intelletuale del Risorgimento italiano* (Milan, 1923); A. Omodeo, *L'Età del Risorgimento italiano*, 2nd ed. (Messina, 1932); and in English L. Salvatorelli, *A Concise History of Italy* (New York, 1940), ch. xvi, is a useful summary.

Sixty-One Illustrations
Drawn from Unusual Sources
and Specially Chosen by
the Author
for

FROM DESPOTISM

TO REVOLUTION

1763–1789

by

LEO GERSHOY

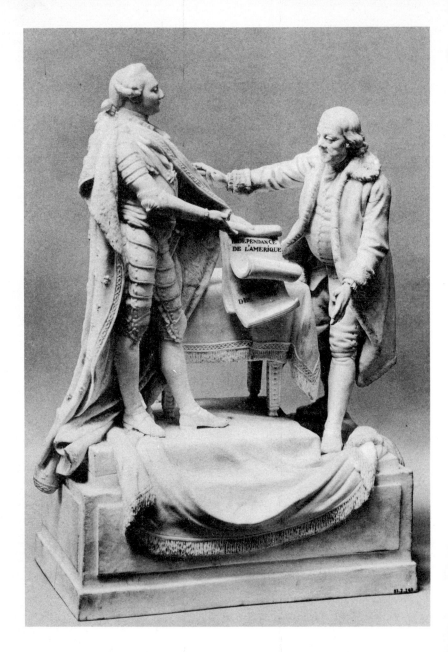

1. The Franco-American Alliance: Louis XVI and Franklin
Statuette, probably designed by Le Mire

2. Gregory Orlov
Contemporary print (Vienna)

3. Catherine the Great
Contemporary print

4. Vergennes
Engraving by Bovinet

5. Marie Antoinette in 1775
Engraving by F. G. Dagoty

RULERS AND STATESMEN

7. Stanislas Poniatowski, the Last King of Poland

6. George III

8. Maria Theresa with Her Family in 1776, Joseph at Her Left
Painting by F. H. Füger (Vienna)

9. J. F. Struensee
Contemporary painting

10. Benjamin Franklin
Engraving by E. Fisher after
M. Chamberlin

11. William Pitt the Younger
Painting by John Hoppner, R.A.

12. Charles James Fox
Painting by A. Hickel

Reproduced by the kind permission of
the National Portrait Gallery, London.

FOUR STATESMEN

13. Voltaire at Ferney
Engraving by D. Denon

14. Soirée at the Home of the Duchess Amalia of
Weimar, with Herder at the Extreme Right
Water color by G. M. Kraus (Weimar Library)

15. Operatic Performance at Esterhazy Palace, with Haydn at the Cembalo
Painting by B. E. Pollack (Vienna)

16. *Young Mozart Playing at the Temple in Paris*
Painting by M. Ollivier (Louvre)

17. Adam Smith
Wedgwood Medallion

18. Necker
Wedgwood Medallion

19. Jean Jacques Rousseau
Bust by Houdon
(The Metropolitan Museum of Art)

20. Turgot
Terracotta bust by Houdon
(Museum of Fine Arts, Boston)

FOUR PHILOSOPHERS

21. Charles III of Spain
Painting by Goya (Madrid)

22. Jovellanos
Painting by Goya (Madrid)

MONARCH AND MINISTER

23. The French Charlatan
Engraving by Helman

24. A Dancing Bear
By H. Bunbury

STREET SCENES

25. The Butcher   26. The Baker   27. The Candlestick Maker
Plates for Diderot's *Encyclopédie*

28. The Triumph of Sentiment (Butcher weeping over *Werther*)
By Thomas Rowlandson

29. Election Troops Bringing in Their Accounts
By James Gillray

TWO ENGLISH CARTOONS

30. Well-A-Day! Is This My Son Tom!

31. Be Not Amaz'd Dear Mother. It Is Indeed
Your Daughter Anne.

(Drawings by Grimm)

HOME FROM THE GRAND TOUR

32. A View of Paris, about 1750
Engraving by J. Rigaud

33. The Minuet
Painting by G. B. Tiepolo (Palazzo Papadopoli, Venice)

34. A Gaming Table at Devonshire House
Pen drawing by Thomas Rowlandson

PLEASURES OF SOCIETY

35. The Harbor at Marseilles
Painting by T. Vernet (Louvre)

36. Anchikov Palace at St. Petersburg
Contemporary print by M. Maxaeva

37. The Rialto
Painting by Guardi (The Metropolitan Museum of Art)

39. The Departure of the Monks after the Dissolution
of the Monasteries by Joseph II
Engraving after L. Defrance

40. Freemasons Initiating a New Member
Contemporary French engraving

41. Prostitutes Being Shorn and Condemned to Sweep the Streets
Contemporary Viennese engraving

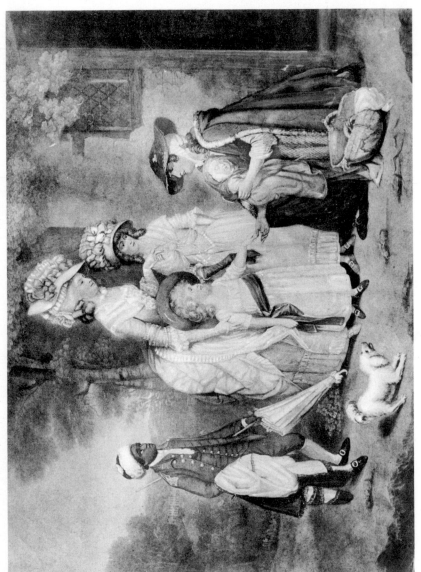

42. A Lady and Her Children Relieving a Poor Cottager

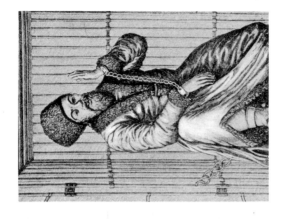

43. The Peasants' School
By Daniel Chodowiecki

44. Flogging of a Russian Peasant
Contemporary Russian print

45. Pugachev in His Iron Cage
Contemporary Russian print

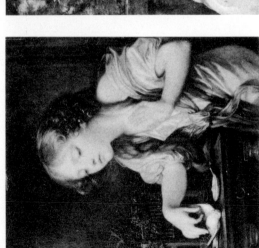

46. The Dead Bird
Painting by Greuze (Louvre)

47. Lady Cornewall
Painting by Sir Joshua Reynolds
(National Gallery of Art, Widener Coll.)
Washington, D. C.

48. The House of Cards
Painting by Chardin
(National Gallery of Art, Mellon Coll.)
Washington, D. C.

THREE CHARACTERISTIC PAINTINGS

49. Apotheosis of Homer
Wedgwood vase, with bas relief by Flaxman
(The Metropolitan Museum of Art)

50. Venus Instructing Cupid
Marble by Falconet (The Metropolitan Museum of Art)

NEOCLASSICISM IN CERAMICS AND SCULPTURE

51. Frederick the Great's Workroom at Potsdam

52. Petit Trianon Palace at Versailles
Designed by Gabriel

53. Mary Wollstonecraft
Contemporary engraving

54. Condorcet
Engraving by Levachez

TWO FEMINISTS

55. Mlle. de Lespinasse
By Carmontel (Musée de Chantilly)

56. Mme. Du Deffand
Print in Bibliothèque Nationale

TWO RIVALS OF THE SALON

57. A View of the Wilderness, with the Alhambra, the Pagoda, and the Mosque
Contemporary engraving

ECLECTICISM IN NATURE, KEW GARDENS, LONDON

58. Aqueduct in Ruins

Painting by Hubert Robert (The Metropolitan Museum of Art)

AESTHETIC ECLECTICISM AT ITS MOST LAVISH

59. Rumanzov's Victory over the Turks, August 1, 1770
Engraving after Daniel Chodowiecki

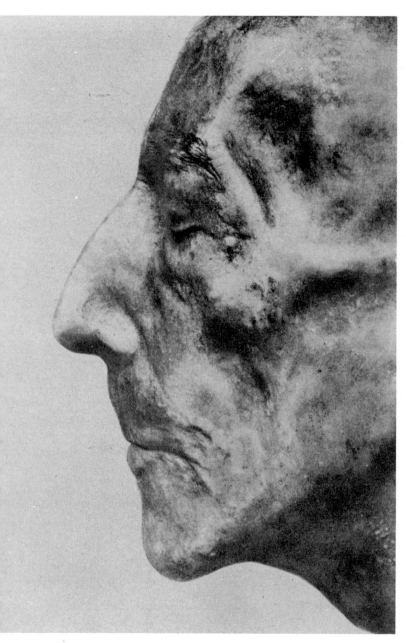

60. Death Mask of Frederick the Great
(Hohenzollern Museum, Berlin)

61. The Cake of the Kings: First Partition of Poland, 1773
Engraving by Le Mire after Moreau le jeune

swains. During the first half of the century the peninsula had been dragged into war by the power politics of its stronger neighbors. Bewildering dynastic changes in the wake of invading troops had not disturbed its tranquillity. But beginning with the Peace of Aix-la-Chapelle in 1748 Italy enjoyed for half a century the blessings of peace and territorial stabilization. Guided by Muratori, Gravina, and Vico, Italian thought was again flowing into the stream of European culture. New life was stirring in the land whose cultural traditions went back without break to the days of classical antiquity. Writers, critics, jurists, economists, scientists, and artists everywhere conducted searching inquiries into their past and propounded bold programs of improvement.

Stimulated by new economic ventures made possible by peaceful living, and excited by new ideas from France and England, latent social forces and vital civic concepts burst forth. Not universal torpor, frivolity, or cultural sterility obtained in the peninsula, but among the cultural élite a new temper and a high ferment of spirit which presaged great achievements. With good reason therefore Voltaire could write to the Prince de Ligne in 1766: "Formerly people visited Italy for its ancient glories, but today to see its thinkers who are combating superstition and fanaticism."[2] The spokesmen were not preponderantly visionaries or idealists, cut off from the tough realities of life. There were men of affairs among them, business men, lawyers, and officials, men conversant with the actualities of a civilization in flux. Nor were they mainly from the bourgeoisie, save in the north. Many of them were patricians, scions of the landed aristocracy, which had never become completely feudalized. Italian cosmopolites, traveling without undue official interference across their mountain frontier, joined with foreign visitors in blending their own native doctrines with the seminal speculation of the foreign *philosophes*. In the framework of that intellectual *risorgimento* Italy renewed her contacts with modernity.[3]

The compact kingdom of Piedmont, rich in its three million indus-

---

2 Quoted in G. Natali, *Il Settecento*, 2 vols., 3rd ed. (Rome, 1929), I, Introduction.
3 P. Silva, "Forze e iniziative nazionali & influenze straniere nell' opera dell'assolutismo illuminato in Italia," in *B.I.C.H.S.*, V (1933), 753-757; G. Gallavresi, "Aspetti del periodo storico dell' assolutismo in Italia," *ibid.*, 759-761; and H. Bédarida et P. Hazard, *L'influence française en Italie au 18e siècle* (Paris, 1936).

trious subjects and governed by the House of Savoy, offered the
spectacle of princely absolutism on the march. The prince, the diplomat, and the soldier were the creative figures and the symbols of
national unity during the century that embraced the two reigns of
Victor-Amadeus II (1675-1730) and his son, Charles Emmanuel III
(1730-1773). In Bogino and Ormea, Piedmont had the services of two
remarkable ministers whose task was of a piece with the work of
Mazarin and Richelieu and of the ministers of Louis XIV: of establishing a strong monarchical order at home and consolidating their country's position abroad. Abroad, they extended its territory into the
fertile plains of Lombardy and encroached upon the weak frontiers of
Genoa. Utilizing their strategic Alpine military location, they played the
game of power politics with a deftness that was not impeded by
stringent scruples and with a success that won envy from the Hapsburg imperialists. At home, a smoothly functioning administrative
machinery, a co-ordinated financial and taxation system, and uniform
laws and judicial procedure assured public tranquillity. Full social
justice was not realized, but the most flagrant abuses of feudalism and
ecclesiastical misrule were curbed. The administrators attacked the
church obliquely, first making clerics pay taxes to the state like any
commoner. The political and legal influence of the aristocracy was
already negligible, for the military nobility had been domesticated into
loyal state servants. The crown took the initiative, being the first
in Europe to abolish serfdom, both real and personal. Unfortunately,
what princely absolutism could do, it could also undo, and the reform
movement reached its nadir in the reign of Victor-Amadeus III (1773-
1796). Intellectuals like Baretti and Denina were imprisoned or harried out of the land; Bogino was dismissed. The Inquisition was restored and the clergy regained their influence. Barrack absolutism
reigned supreme, and Piedmont returned to its unenviable position as
the Boeotia of Italy.

Elsewhere in northern Italy only fitful reforms interrupted the steady
march of the aristocratic republics and the smaller dynastic states
toward extinction. The dead hand of the past was stretched over
great Venice and Genoa as well as over petty Modena and Piombino.
Prosperity had fled; literature and art were lifeless; and the spirit of
business enterprise was crushed. Genoa sank into its final decline,

pushed by ancient abuses at home and tugged by conflict with Corsican patriots abroad. Venice still exerted its imperishable fascination over foreign visitors. But the roots of its vitality had dried, and it moved with dignity and nostalgic charm to its close. Its industry and commerce were stagnant, the administration corrupt and inefficient, the taxation system onerous, but the clergy remained numerous, wealthy, and privileged. The capital city itself had become the great pleasure resort of Europe, and foreigners of all nationalities gathered to gamble and share in the joys of an almost perpetual carnival. Efforts at reform failed dismally, and reformers like Angelo Querini, Giorgio Pisani, and Carlo Contarini were all imprisoned by the authorities. A witty foreigner hit off the amorphous quality of the moribund republic, recording that its government was "rich and consolatory, like its treacle, being compounded nicely of all the other forms—a grain of monarchy, a scruple of democracy, a drachma of oligarchy, and an ounce of aristocracy."[4]

The Papal States elicited from enlightened contemporaries the same moral indignation that republican historians of the nineteenth century vented against the Old Regime in France. A composite picture, drawn from the travel books of the Englishmen Tobias Smollett and John Moore and the French travelers Duclos and De Brosses, gives a most piteous account of the lives of the two million inhabitants of the thirteen provinces which stretched diagonally across the peninsula. Much of the once fertile soil lay fallow. When not reduced to pestilential marshes, it had been turned to pasturage. The naturally able and industrious inhabitants were abandoned to indigence. The pope, while moved by benevolence and pity for the unfortunate, lacked financial resources and was innocent of political authority and military strength. False friends and intriguers surrounded him, all of them scheming for additional benefits for themselves but meantime keeping the Eternal City filled with idlers and beggars.

Such a picture is manifestly overdrawn and distorted by the partisan outlook of an age that saw in papal rule the fount of all injustice. If less than valuable as analysis of conditions, these travel accounts are

4 Mrs. Piozzi, *Glimpses of Italian Society in the Eighteenth Century*, (New York, 1892), 125; G. B. McClellan, *Venice and Bonaparte* (Princeton, 1931), chs. i-viii.

still immensely useful as description of the seamier aspects of life under the popes. The sober fact remains that the better part of the public energies of Clement XIII (1758-1769) and Clement XIV (1769-1774) were expended in the struggle against the Jesuits, and those of Pius VI (1775-1799), before the French Revolution, to defending the church against royal reformers like Joseph II. Nor were the travelers' accounts of economic decay unreal, for stagnation prevailed everywhere except in the bustling commercial ports on either side of the Adriatic.

Don Carlos, the Spanish Bourbon and the future Charles III of Spain, reigned in the Kingdom of the Two Sicilies from 1734 to 1759. Feudalism obtained there with a severity elsewhere untouched in Italy, for almost all the land was divided between the crown and the related lay and ecclesiastical artistocracy. Contemporary accounts depicting the un-Christian lives of the latter and the conspicuous wastefulness of the former are many.[5] The total population was almost seven million. Most of the inhabitants were peasants, fallen from the small hereditary tenancies that they or their ancestors once held to the rank of landless laborers on the great cattle ranches. Naples, a large city of 300,000 inhabitants and a center of culture and commerce, had a permanent economic minority of 30,000 beggars. Its streets swarmed with the half-naked and homeless lazzaroni who bore their dirt and disease and turbulence as the charters of birth. The ruler himself set the tone for beneficial changes, for the stanch absolutist who so devoutly respected the dogma of the church also held short shrift for ecclesiastical pretensions in taxation and justice. But he left Naples for Spain in 1759. During the regency of the minor Ferdinand IV, from 1759 to 1766, the Tuscan Bernardo Tanucci, one of the most illustrious figures of the century, became all-influential. In 1766 the young king reached his majority, but power went to his consort Maria Carolina, the daughter of Maria Theresa. Almost two decades of anti-feudal legislation and state action against monasteries eventuated with the new rulers in a reaction that undid the earlier gains. The queen was ignorant even by royal standards and retrograde even for a daughter of Maria Theresa. Dismissing Tanucci and shelving all reforms, she undertook a vigorous military policy that made her state secure for Hapsburg imperialism

---

[5] For a typical scathing denunciation, see John Moore, *op. cit.*, II, 131 ff.

and Theresian obscurantism.[6] Hapsburg influence also blighted the reform movement in the duchy of Parma, where the French minister, Du Tillot, had made Parma both a seat of culture and a center of prosperity. The coming of the Hapsburg (in consequence of the marriage of the reigning duke to another daughter of the Hapsburg mother-in-law of Europe) closed the happy chapter.[7]

Enlightened despotism reached the plains and plateaux of Tuscany in the person of the Grand Duke Peter Leopold, the younger brother of Joseph II, who ruled the duchy from 1765 to 1790. His own great achievements were not dimmed by the earlier progress effected by native Tuscan administrators such as Sallustino Bandini and Pompeo Neri, or by the energetic capitalist entrepreneurs who had taken their country's renovation in hand. With Leopold the renovation moved more rapidly; and twenty-five years of steady and cumulative changes, following the equally long preparatory period, wrought a remarkable transformation in Tuscany. Free economic enterprise became a reality with the passing of guild control and the abolition of internal dues. Francesco Gianni was the master mind in the establishment of a unified system of public finance and the institution of virtual tax equality for all classes. Radical indeed were the reforms in the administration of justice. Leopold, who was an enthusiastic admirer of Beccaria, abolished torture and the death penalty and the confiscation of the criminal's property. He strictly limited the judicial rights of the landlords and established a uniform criminal procedure for all classes. Physiocratic views also gained the upper hand in governmental circles. The right of entail was retained, but only nominally. In the minister Fossombroni the Tuscan agricultural reformers, the *Geografili*, found a champion of their efforts to introduce crop rotation and the use of artificial fertilizers. The state abolished hunting and fishing rights and began the division of common pastures (though in Tuscany as elsewhere scarcely with beneficial consequences for the poorest peasantry). While serfdom was gradually becoming a thing of the past, Gianni sponsored the memorable law of 1767 that gave Tuscany free internal

---

[6] For the earlier years, see M. Scipa, *Il Regno di Napoli al tempo di Carlo III de Borbone*, 2 vols., 2nd ed. (Rome, 1923); for the later years, B. Croce, *Storia del regno di Napoli* (Bari, 1925).

[7] H. Bédarida, *Parme et la France de 1748 à 1789* (Paris, 1928).

grain trade. Leghorn more than ever held its position as a great port of southern Europe, its harbor crowded with ships from all nations.

Under the most favorable circumstances such revolutionary changes were bound to produce a reaction; and there were reasons for the especially bitter resistance to Leopold's measures. During his earlier years Leopold had shown himself both more cautious and more flexible than his rigidly austere brother. Relying upon Tuscan advisers, he established local magistrates' benches, restored municipal self-government, and went so far as to have Gianni prepare a draft of a written constitution. Reserved and aloof, he had never been popular with his subjects. With the passage of time, however, he became more absolutist in his ways and more dogmatic in his thinking; and his secret police made his name odious. Though the propertied classes were behind him and rationalists warmly applauded his program of secularization, the uneven distribution of the gains of the emerging capitalist order did not endear his policy to the masses. Lay charity and humanitarian poor relief softened the worst abuses, but benevolence was not enough to win the ruler the support of the poor. So long as he limited himself to correcting the administrative relations of the clergy with the state, he was safe against outbursts of popular feeling. But ill-advised by his mentor, the quasi-Jansenist Bishop of Pistoia, Scipio Ricci, he altered the ceremonial ritual of church services. In attempting to invest the crown with the symbolical value of the cross, he succeeded only in throwing the masses into the arms of his most reactionary opponents. A cloud covered his work, and a clerical reaction was already under way, when he left Tuscany in 1790 to succeed Joseph on the imperial throne. His ecclesiastical renovations were seriously compromised but his other magnificent deeds were not nullified.[8]

Milan, the capital of the Austrian duchy to which it gave its name, was the center of business prosperity in northern Italy and the true focal point of the Italian enlightenment. The foundations for the revival of the Lombard middle classes were laid in the decade of the fifties. A first generation of native administrators, under the guidance of Counts Pallavicini and Cristiani, took advantage of the reforming

---

[8] The most illuminating approach is *Riforme in Toscane nella seconda meta del secolo XVIII* in A. Anzilotti, *Movimenti e contrasti per la unita italiana* (1930); A von Reumont, *Geschichte Toskanas seit dem Ende des florentinischen Freistaates* (Gotha, 1877), II, gives the details.

trends in Vienna to strengthen the central administration against town oligarchs and feudal aristocrats. The earlier work bore results in the following two decades, which were the best years of Lombard enlightened despotism. Upon Count Firmian, the Viennese representative who was governor from 1759 to 1782, fell the task of completing the administrative centralization. The broader social program that the newly trained bureaucracy carried out was largely initiated by the Lombard progressives themselves, by such great economic liberals as Pietro Verri, Cesare Beccaria, and Gian Carli. Co-operating with the Hapsburg rulers these Lombard officials and intellectuals took the lead in developing a free capitalist economy and introducing order into the fiscal administration. Under Verri's able guidance the state did away with the farming of taxes and abolished internal taxes on trade.[9] A central economic council directed the general program, while special commissions like the Giunta Economale gradually stripped the church of its fiscal privileges and prerogatives. Thanks to the thorough physiocratic program of the government, agriculture prospered; while a broad public works plan and governmental poor relief won the good will of the unpropertied. In those two decades the total population rose to a million and a half, an astounding increase of 25 per cent.

The tempered hands of Firmian at Milan and Kaunitz at Vienna lost control when Joseph II became the sole ruler. Milan and Vienna came to the parting of the ways, for Joseph's integral absolutism demanded from his Lombard associates in regeneration not co-operation but complete subordination. Thus far, they had collaborated, bound in idealism and interest, with the reforming royal absolutism against their common foes. They fell apart when the supreme absolutist emphasized his own program in the place of the reforms that they had in view for their country. The long arm of the new Council of Government reached down into the private affairs of every subject. Lombardy pullulated with officials and secret police, all impersonally ushering in the millennium by uprooting habits and ending institutional arrangements that were centuries old. In spirit and scope the Lombard decade differed in no way from Joseph's rule in the Austrian and Bohemian provinces. The well-intentioned reforms simultaneously outraged conservatives and liberals in Italy even as they did in

[9] Cf. M. R. Manfra, *Pietro Verri e i problemi economici del tempo suo* (Milan, 1932).

Austria. Abandoned by his friends and bitterly attacked by his foes, the royal leveler accomplished little more than to provoke an anti-Austrian patriotic reaction, at least for the moment. Nevertheless the Josephian era had done much by its very intransigence to mark a decisive turning point in the country's development. For all the gap between Joseph's authoritarian liberalism and the deeply imbedded democratic ways and values of the Italian progressives, the emperor bridged the road to nineteenth-century bourgeois parliamentary reform. Repudiated and a failure, his rule still linked the past with the future.[10]

II. PORTUGAL

Portugal had sunk in the eighteenth century to the rank of a fourth-rate power. Priest-ridden and racked by feudalism at home, it was fettered commercially to England. In international affairs it was the puppet of the great powers. Its small population was declining, and of its fewer than 3,000,000 inhabitants the overwhelming majority were peasants without any stake in the soil. The influence of the Jesuits was prodigious. Joined by family connections to the high aristocracy, they were immensely wealthy. Entrenched at court, they had the ear of the ruler, and by their control of key positions they were able to direct state policy at home and abroad. The crown, the clergy and the conventual establishments, and the great nobles owned all the land. Much of it was entailed and many of the proprietors were absentee owners. Divided into large latifundia, it was worked by sharecroppers who staggered under tax burdens and service obligations. The greater part of the royal revenue came from the stores of gold and diamonds in Brazil and from the tolls on the rich colonial trade. While the internal debt, royal extravagance, and the upkeep of religious institutions consumed the crown's income, private wealth was drained by specie payments abroad, especially to English merchant capitalists, more than £1,000,000 per annum on an average being exported to England.

The new ruler, Joseph I, who ascended the throne in 1750, reigned without ruling. He gave his trust, from the outset, to the most spectacu-

---

[10] F. Valsecchi, *L'assolutismo illuminato in Austria e in Lombardia*, II (1934), is the best and most recent detailed account.

lar and dynamic reformer of the century, Sebastien Carvalho e Mello. Better known by his later title of Marquis of Pombal, that great inno-vator was fifty-one years old when he was appointed minister of war and minister of foreign affairs. He was a man of ruthless will and fierce resoluteness of purpose who had formulated his views in the course of his career as diplomatic representative at London and Vienna. He had only a single aim. Actuated by hatred of the church and the great aristocracy, in which he saw the twin sources of Portugal's degradation, and driven by his fanatical belief that only the restora-tion of strong monarchical power could save the country he conse-crated himself to destroying all barriers to royal rule.

If Pombal followed the precepts of Machiavelli, the Florentine, he also emulated Richelieu and Colbert. A royalist and a patriot, he was the prisoner of a dream, perhaps a hallucination, to make the Portu-guese monarchy powerful at home and respected abroad. A thorough mercantilist, he could not conceive of economic enterprise unless it were subject to governmental regulation and direction, nor could he even contemplate economic changes unless state-sponsored or endorsed. Pombal was not, properly speaking, a statesman, who sought to evalu-ate the cost or the injury that would redound to particular interests from his grandiose scheme of concentrating all power in the prince as the custodian of public and national welfare. A man of prodigious energy, but also an intemperate servant of an absolutist purpose, he was, in his own eyes, the chosen vessel and holy grail of his royal master.

His debut foreshadowed his entire career in its ardor and its errors. Some of his first acts were salutary, such as his efforts to reorganize the royal treasury, bring about the restitution of alienated crown land, and remodel the military organization. But when he tried to arrest financial decline by fiat through prohibiting the export of specie abroad and sought to increase foreign trade by establishing a government monop-oly of the Brazil trade, he ran into a storm of protest from private traders. He weathered the storm, because he became all-powerful in 1755 through his matchless courage and resourcefulness when the great earthquake and tidal wave destroyed Lisbon.[11] Plague, famine, and

---

[11] European optimism was doubly shocked by this disaster because it also disrupted the great international market of which Lisbon was the center.

brigandage over, he directed his vigor and tenacity to reconstructing a greater capital city. From that moment on, until Joseph's death in 1777, he enjoyed the complete confidence of the king and gained complete control over all branches of the administration. He redoubled his drive against national demoralization, surpassing himself in an unceasing effort to tap the wellsprings of national enterprise. While he was engaged in these labors, whose staggering costs bore heavily upon the population, his energies were for several years deflected to the problem which he had not yet had the opportunity to solve: the radical extirpation of ecclesiastical and aristocratic influence.

After unleashing his notorious vendetta against the church and the Jesuits, he terrified the court aristocracy into submission, finding his opportunity in a plot to kill the king.[12] Though the plot was real, full proofs were lacking of the collusion of those grandees whom Pombal arrested and tortured; and no adequate evidence was ever brought forth at the hearings to involve the Jesuits as accomplices. The trial more than pointed to a political frame-up, and the punishments visited upon the condemned revived the horrors of the mediaeval past. Having made a holocaust of the aristocracy, expelled the Jesuits, whose estates he confiscated, and terrorized the remaining opposition, he returned to his earlier course of imposing a single plan of administrative salvation upon a cowed country. The nation sank under the weight of this monolithic despotism. The land was overrun by the secret police, *agents provocateurs*, and professional delators. Pombal made the courts the instruments of his vengeance and filled the prisons with 9,000 victims of his regenerating crusade. Years later, when he fell from power, some 4,000 of these prisoners were still alive to recount the horrors to which they had been subjected. It was "the resurrection of the dead," wrote the Austrian envoy.[13]

He imposed his neo-mercantilist program upon manufacturers and merchants powerless to restrain him save through tried and untried subterfuges. He founded the government Wine Company of Oporto (1756), giving it among other privileges a sales monopoly. Despite bitter opposition of private growers he put fresh restrictions upon

12 F. L. Gomes, *Le Marquis de Pombal* (Lisbon, 1869), ch. viii.
13 Comte J. Du Hamel de Breuil, "Un ministre philosophe, Carvalho, Marquis de Pombal," in *Revue historique*, LIX (1895), 17-18.

them to discourage winegrowing. Hoping to end Portugal's dependence upon foreign grain, he revived the old legislation that compelled the public sale of domestic grain under the supervision of government agents. To end its dependence on imported manufactured goods he founded and subsidized wool, silk, and cotton factories and prohibited the importation of competing French products. He invited foreign technicians into the country and instituted a Council of Commerce to co-ordinate national economic enterprises and a School of Trade to provide vocational training for learners. He also abolished internal customs dues in the country, but advanced far beyond the mercantilist program by establishing free-trading relations between Portugal and its American colonies. However beneficial the blessings of unified state control may have been still later, after a quarter of a century of unbroken effort by Pombal and his associates, Portuguese commerce still remained largely in foreign hands. Eighty per cent of the ships in the harbor of Lisbon still flew foreign flags, more than half of the total number alone being English. Lisbon was crammed with English men and women, some resident aliens, others transients, and all patronizingly superior to the native inhabitants in their extraterritorial rights. The effort to put royal finances on a solid basis, however, proved more successful. Tax collection was centralized. The governmental revenue was greatly increased and the costs were considerably reduced. A careful auditing system reduced corruption to a minimum, and Pombal's strict control prevented the royal household from wandering away from the path of rigid economy.

So long, however, as the great ultra-conservative aristocratic and clerical families were ensconced in their legal prerogatives, he could not completely loosen their hold over the country. Accordingly Pombal restricted the right of free testamentary bequest, particularly as it affected ecclesiastics and nobles, and also curtailed the right of the church to acquire new landed possessions. Henceforth, he decreed, no new ecclesiastical entails of any size or importance could be established. Deploying upon another front in his campaign, he broke up the monopoly hold of the great noble families over public offices by making the merit system the basis of the civil service. He also did away with the demeaning distinction between the so-called "old Christians" and the "new Christians," the latter being those whose ancestors were baptized Jews. Pombal realized only too well how much Portugal owed to the strong Jewish strain in its mixed population[14] and restored civil rights to the Jews. He abolished what remained of slavery in Portugal, and had in mind for future action a comprehensive recodification of the civil laws. Above all he realized fully that his work would be useless unless he reared a generation steeped in his views and prepared to support his great innovations. So without benefit of advanced pedagogical theory, but simply on the basis of experience and his own intelligence, the tireless old man drew on his pool of energy to found a modern national educational system.

The death of the protecting king in 1777 was the true end of Pombal's public career. Dismissed from his positions, exiled in disgrace to his estates, and exposed to the first wave of the avenging reaction, the embittered octogenarian lived on until 1782. In the few years that were still vouchsafed him, the new queen held the reaction in check. Meantime she made atonement for his personal acts of injustice and abrogated the most hated of his enactments. His inquisitorial factory inspectors were dismissed; and the Oporto Wine Company was abolished, together with the Brazil trading monopoly. She attenuated the full force of his edict concerning wills and testaments and restricted the arbitrary powers of the intendant of police. Within a few years after his death, however, his disciples and his ideas were driven completely underground.

Thus Pombal dramatically failed to arrest the decay of Portuguese life. His faults were many. His terrorism was its own worst enemy, for he created a ministerial despotism as crushing as the mediaeval tyranny that he had savagely extirpated. His alone was the initiative, and he permitted no one to share responsibility with him. He placed too great a strain upon the weak agricultural foundations of the country by his relentless effort to thrust Portugal forward to an economic modernity for which her population had neither the resources nor the technical equipment. Nevertheless, his work was not all in vain. His destructive fury leveled many of the old barriers blocking

---

14 Pombal's good sense and good humor were superior to the aberrations of religious fanaticism. It is told that Joseph I, yielding at an ill-advised moment to an access of anti-Semitism, gave the order that henceforth all Jews were to wear a white hat as a distinctive sign of their racial origin; whereupon his minister appeared at the palace with two white hats: one, he explained, for himself, the other for the king.

national advance. He desired nothing beyond the restoration of monarchical power; but by his sharp blows to the system of caste relations, by destroying the social pre-eminence and the legal control of the secular and ecclesiastical grandees, and by secularizing the attitude and the values of his contemporaries, he effectively cleared the way for a generation of later reformers. New forces would probably have broken through the dam of Portuguese life without him, later if not sooner, but Pombal speeded the release of new energy. Without entertaining any sympathy for individualism himself, he had caught the vision of the new secular society in which the individuals of the middle class would demand and win the right to decide their own destiny.[15]

III. SPAIN UNDER CHARLES III

Enlightened despotism was no passing episode in Spain, as it was in Sweden. On the contrary, it left a memorable impress upon the country's growth. Charles III, already a veteran reformer in 1759 by reason of his long association with Tanucci in Naples, linked the earlier improvements of the Spanish Bourbons with the later progressive movement which eventuated in the liberal uprising of his country against Napoleon and the drafting of the Constitution of 1812. While his policy united the mandate for domestic security and prestige abroad with the encyclopedist insistence upon social welfare at home, his methods similarly combined the older mercantilism with strands of the newer individualism.[16] Under any circumstances the Spanish achievements would be held considerable; but in view of the obstacles they must be deemed extraordinary.

The existing administrative system was seriously hampered by the inefficiency of a corrupt and numerous bureaucracy. At all times the unwritten and written "liberties" of provinces and the privileges of corporative groups interfered with its activity. The backward agricultural system was notorious for its wretchedness, and the poverty of the peasantry was well-nigh legendary. Manufactures remained literally

---

15 For a critical estimate, cf. J. L. d'Azvedo, *O Marquis de Pombal e a sua epoca* (Lisbon, 1909); for one more favorable, Conde de Carnota, *Marquis of Pombal,* 2nd ed. (London, 1871).
16 M. C. Alcázar, "El despotismo illustrado en España," in *B.I.C.H.S.,* V (1933), 727-752.

hand production for the near-by region or else for home use. Trade had been reduced to a mere trickle at home, and foreign commerce regularly yielded a heavy adverse balance. Cultural torpor and general intellectual stagnation matched economic decline and the utterly inadequate revenue resources of the government. The prosperous burgher or the aristocrat free to travel abroad could conceivably break through the sanitary cordon set up by the Holy Office and the Inquisition around Spain's frontiers to ward off the infection of secular learning and the contagion of scientific curiosity. It was more difficult, if not impossible, for the peasant isolated in his little vicinity to escape from the all-pervading ignorance. His sole contact with the bracing atmosphere of thought was with the man of the church. The Jesuits, with all their faults, were still the most learned of Spanish ecclesiastics; but the masses had relations not with the Jesuits but with the local priests, monks, and mendicant friars. In a country of more than 2,000 monastic establishments, the greater part of whose income went to the few titled prelates, the living standards of simple monks and parish priests averaged not much higher than those of the poor peasantry. Their intellectual outlook was not too different, for ignorance and fanaticism were also their hallmarks. In making religion real and vivid to the people they only too often tinctured what was valid in their faith with puerile and brutal superstitions.

The methodical ruler was himself a devout believer, subject strongly to the influence of his court confessor. But the shrewd English traveler who noted that Charles III did not "suffer his devotion to lay him open to the enterprizes of the court of Rome, or the encroachments of his own clergy," hit upon what was most characteristic of the king's views: his intense conviction that the state and not the church was supreme in temporal matters. For the better part of a decade he leaned heavily in state affairs upon two Italian advisers, his Genoese minister of foreign affairs, Grimaldi, and his Sicilian minister of war, Squillacci. Meantime he continued to exchange views by correspondence with his old adviser, Tanucci, in Naples. But he speedily acclimatized himself anew to his native country. After the wild outburst of popular wrath in Madrid in 1766 against foreigners and foreign innovations, he intrusted the crown to the guidance of a number of remarkable Spanish counselors whose superb remodeling of the country's institutions he supported stanchly during the rest of his rule.[17]

When the infuriated Madrid populace forced him to flee for his very life, it was the high-born Aragonese, Pedro de Bolea, Count Aranda, who saved the situation. Soldier and diplomat, patriotic royalist and cosmopolitan intellectual, this fearless and outspoken *regalista* was the true head of the government for seven years, from 1766 to 1773. Truculent by nature and uncompromising in his bitter hatred of the Jesuits, in his capacity as president of the Council of Castile he directed governmental policy at the very moment that the international crusade against the Society of Jesus was reaching its apogee. In the euphemistic phrase of Archdeacon Coxe, whose own religious impartiality was not exceptional, Aranda was thus endeavoring "to naturalize a spirit of toleration hitherto unknown in Spain." Such an unquenchable flow of energy made even his great services seem more desirable at a distance, and the king accordingly appointed him ambassador to Paris. There his vigor found free expression, and he served his country well from 1773 to 1787 by conducting a masterly campaign of playing off the French ally against the common English enemy.[18]

A far more complex personality and more important figure was Count Pedro Rodriguez Campomanes, Asturian jurist and man of letters. Of all the Spanish thinkers he most resembled Diderot in his humanity and the breadth of his intellectual and social interests. Holding in turn the important posts of director of the postal service, secretary of the treasury and, for more than a quarter of a century, from 1762 to 1789, fiscal of the Council of Castile, he exercised a prodigious though often concealed influence upon the many varied phases of Spain's evolution. He was associated with Floridablanca and the younger reformer Jovellanos in the campaign to restrict the privileges of the sheep ranchers in the Mesta. He was a powerful force in the movement to liberate industrial and commercial enterprise. The outstanding *regalista* of his day, he fought the extra-religious privileges of the church and endeavored to institute a secular and humanist

17 The most detailed and critical accounts are by A. Ballesteros y Beretta, *op. cit.*, VI, chs. i-iii; and G. Desdevises du Dézert, *op cit.*
18 R. Konetzke, *Die Politik des Grafen Aranda* (Berlin, 1929), *Vorwort* and *Rückblick*, which discuss the motives behind his activities at home and abroad.

system of public instruction. In his writing Campomanes displayed the highest admiration for English institutions. For his own country he counseled reforms from above, to be initiated by a ruler secure against the church and the landed aristocracy and consequently free to introduce those changes currently stressed by the liberal French bourgeoisie.[19]

The leading statesman in the last years of the reign was Joseph Moniño, ennobled as Count Floridablanca. Fresh from his ambassadorship to Rome, where he had guided the diplomatic battle of the Bourbon powers against the Jesuits, he devoted himself as leading minister, from 1777 on, to ushering in a happier era for humanity by royal fiat. He was strongly influenced in general by the French *philosophes* and by the physiocratic economists in particular, and he took the lead with Campomanes in the material and social renovation of the country. Trusted implicitly by the king, he gave direction to the train of reforms. In the same paradoxical fashion as illustrated by the careers of Joseph II and his brother Leopold, Floridablanca blended his overbearing, authoritarian, and suspicious personality with his solicitude for mankind and fused it with his urge to emancipate the individual.[20]

The centralizing tendencies which the new dynasty of the Bourbons had reintroduced into Spain were greatly accelerated under these officials. Of the hierarchy of councils and boards that formerly exercised such enormous influence over the central administrative system, the Council of Castile alone kept its great power and its all-embracing jurisdiction. It too was dominated by the strong personalities of its fiscals and its presidents, who made it the instrument *par excellence* of royal absolutism. The trend away from collegiate boards toward a responsible cabinet of ministers culminated in the creation of the Council of State (*Junta de Estado*) in 1783. This closely knit and compact ministry united in a co-ordinated and integrated whole the entire direction of domestic administration. The intendants and subordinate delegates, the *corregidores*, continued to batter away at old provincial and municipal privileges and prerogatives. The entrenched strength of

---

[19] G. Desdevises du Dézert, *op cit.*, LXX, 45 ff.; and his "Les lettres politico-économiques de Campomanes," in *Revue hispanique*, IV (1897), 240-265.
[20] M. C. Alcázar, *El Conde de Floridablanca* (Madrid, 1929).

the municipal oligarchy often necessitated oblique tactics, but it was apparent that the elected town officials were steadily surrendering their initiative and authority to crown officials. The centralizing and unifying spirit was applied, but with less success, to jurisprudence and legal procedure. As it was well-nigh impossible to separate administration from legal affairs, the jurists in the service of the crown wisely contented themselves with nationalizing the law and systematizing procedure slowly, by broad legal decisions and rulings, rather than by attempting more formally to codify the regional and local laws.

Spanish enlightened despotism concerned itself even more with fundamental economic reforms than it did with administrative changes. Its agricultural policy was vigorously physiocratic. For several decades the royal ministers fought to break the privileges of the great sheep ranchers of the Mesta, particularly that right which permitted their countless flocks to feed on the commons to the exclusion of needy, landless peasantry. They also attacked entails and the family trusts that effectively prevented the breakup of vast estates, which if cultivated would have appreciably improved the plight of the peasants. Ultimately, legal provisions were set up to facilitate the sale of entailed land, while it was forbidden to entail new property except with royal permission. The reformers found it equally difficult to end the continuous ravages of erosion and deforestation which were eating ruinously into the country's natural wealth. They made plans for flood control and irrigation projects, but these ventures were costly, and the peasantry could not always be counted upon to co-operate. The monarchy itself brought the wild Sierra Morena country under cultivation and established model farms at Aranjuez. As in France, numerous agricultural societies were founded and land banks set up to finance the improvements of reforming landlords. The crown also endeavored to encourage and speed up the growth of a body of small, independent peasant proprietors by parceling out confiscated ecclesiastical lands and other real property that it held. Various decrees, due largely to Aranda, allowed for the division of royal and municipal domain among the landless peasants on condition that it be cultivated. The rights of squatters who had improved their lands were protected by law. New colonists received generous tax exemptions; and the legal status of hereditary leaseholder was accorded to those cultivators whose industry and equipment made them a reasonable risk.[21]

For two decades Campomanes and Jovellanos also devoted themselves to neo-Colbertist improvement of trade and manufacture. Roads and canals were built; the system of weights and measures was nationalized; a governmental postal system was established, and with it a uniform coinage system. The internal customs dues were lowered, and in some instances abolished, while the reformers tried above everything else to break the immense power of the guilds. Under such state aid and protection, private enterprise increased by leaps and bounds. The English traveler, Henry Swinburne, commented with surprise on the intense industrial activity of Barcelona during the seventies. A decade later another Englishman, Joseph Townsend, spoke with patronizing admiration of the large-scale machine production of woolens, silks, and cottons. Free trade had its great champion in Floridablanca, who was able to introduce free internal grain trade for a brief period in 1783. Slight as the value of commerce and manufacture was compared to agriculture, the increase was still extraordinary. A number of free ports were established; and Floridablanca sought to make import duties uniform and as low as possible. All foreign trade increased fivefold during Charles's reign; the colonial trade by itself even more. The old torpor was swept aside as Spanish life reasserted its intrinsic vitality. Swinburne put it all very handsomely: "The influx of foreigners, increase of commerce, and protection granted to the liberal arts, begin to open the understanding of this people, who made great strides of late in sense and philosophy."[22]

Underwriting these projects was a heavy drain upon the royal treasury. For all the tribute that Spain received from the colonies and its income from the domain land, for all the monopolies and customs dues, tax arrangements with designated provinces, the "free gift" from the clergy, and the unquestionable but heavy indirect taxes of the *alcabala* and *milliones* on the production and sale of prime necessities, the state was always in arrears. The national wealth possibly warranted

[21] The basic study is R. Leonhard, *Agrarpolitik und Agrarreform in Spanien unter Carl III.* (Munich, 1909); cf. also D. Villar Grangel, *Jovellanos y la reforma agraria*, 2nd ed. (Madrid, 1925).

[22] For a contrary impression, gathered by Lafayette between 1782 and 1783, cf. L. Gottschalk, *Lafayette and the Close of the American Revolution* (Chicago, 1942), 405-412.

higher taxes than were levied, but on the condition of a far more equitable incidence and a drastic reduction of the costs of collection. A reorganization of the fiscal system, however, was a utopian dream so long as the existing social relations remained unchanged. Since the radical solution of a basic single tax on land had been rejected, the government was forced to fall back upon expedients, and not the most equitable.

With all these reservations in mind still the renovation of the country was amazing. Out of the income derived from confiscated ecclesiastical estates the royal reformer and his associates made heavy and for the most part wise disbursements to schools, orphanages, hospitals, and asylums, which were the chief recipients of royal generosity.[23] The conclusion drawn by an earlier student still stands: "On the whole, the result for good rivals that achieved in an equally short time in any other country; and in the history of Spain there is certainly no period which can compare with the reign of Charles III."[24]

[23] For the religious and educational policies, cf. chs. viii and x.
[24] G. Edmundson, "Spain under Ferdinand VI and Charles III," in *Cambridge Modern History,* VI (1909), 384.

Chapter Seven

WAR AND PEACE

I. THE PATTERN OF INTERNATIONAL RELATIONS

INTENSIFIED state activity was thus consistently directed toward strengthening the foundations of power at home. But the directors of state policy applied themselves with equal vigor to attaining their objectives abroad. Security and power were fast becoming the co-ordinates of national survival in the new technological order where administrative inefficiency as never before threatened the weaker state with disaster. The passage of sound laws and uniform legal procedures, the careful training of civil servants, establishment of orderly financial systems, and the enactment of countless regulations were all necessary security measures against potential aggression on the part of stronger neighbors. But this defensive mentality unavoidably coalesced with an offensive spirit. Where they could, statesmen strove for power in order to exert influence and gain control over states smaller or weaker than their own. Little was new in these relations save greater awareness and enlarged conceptions of power. And as before, the language of ideal purposes was still employed to veil the nakedness of ruthless state competition.

All the great powers described their relations with one another in terms of the ideal. "Europe forms a political system," wrote the famed Swiss jurist, Emeric de Vattel, "in which the nations inhabiting this part of the world are bound together by their relations and various interests into a single body . . . [making] of modern Europe a sort of republic, whose members, each independent, but all bound together by a common interest, unite for the maintenance of order and the preservation of liberty. This is what has given rise to the well-known principle of the balance of power, by which is meant an arrangement of affairs so that no state shall be in a position to have absolute mastery and dominate over the others."[1] Frederick of Prussia, whom no one could accuse of gilding the lily, observed more tersely: "Politics is the science of acting always by convenient ways in conformity with one's own interests." And Machiavelli himself never looked reality more openly in the face than did the veteran Count Aranda, who avowed that diplomacy resolved itself "into recognizing the strength, the resources, the interests, the rights, the fears and the hopes of the different powers, so that as the occasion warrants it, we may appease these powers, divide them, defeat them, or ally ourselves with them, depending on how they serve our advantage and increase our security."[2]

For technical reasons alone no state of the eighteenth century could yet conscript its entire manpower, draft all its resources of capital wealth and materials, and regulate production and consumption with no other aim than that of establishing a huge machine working relentlessly for military victory. Militarism, while of the essence of eighteenth-century relations, neither ate into the substance of production nor even remotely approximated the modern state's capacity for total mobilization of thought, feeling, and economic life in the interests of *Wehrwirtschaft*. The thinking of the squire who had made a career for himself in war perhaps groped toward the concept of a mobilized state. The vivifying stimuli to military tactics and strategy came, however, not from his views on the art of war, but from the actual practices, first of the colonial militia of the thirteen American colonies and then from the forces released by the French revolutionary armies. Until then the old immobility obtained, the older tactic of defensive warfare and limited operations, and the block system of strategy. For technical and not humanitarian reasons, for reasons of state, the civilian non-combatant population was spared. It was axiomatic that states waged war against political bodies but not against men; against attacking armies and fortresses but not against property.

While the intellectual backwardness of the junior officers and their unimaginative and literal adherence to regulations reinforced such barriers to a more modern military efficiency, military thought itself could not escape the impact of the pervading revolutionary changes

[1] E. de Vattel, *The Law of Nations* (1758), quoted in F. L. Schuman, *International Politics*, 2nd ed. (New York, 1937), 47.
[2] R. Konetzke, *op. cit.*, 206.

in living. Not only an iconoclast like Rousseau, but farsighted military theorists like Count Guibert, realized that modern war was becoming much too complex and too interwoven with social forces to be left entirely to the generals. They sensed that hegemony would go to that state which most effectively reorganized its military conceptions to conform to technological realities and social capacities, that the future belonged to a truly national army based upon and skillfully exploiting the enormous potentialities of bourgeois strength, wealth, and initiative.[3]

Meantime the tensions of international relations grew sharper in the period of nominal peace following 1763. The dynastic rivalries of royal houses were still real. The Junkers of all countries could still opt *ex officio* for war. Ambition and a restless urge for power still impelled individual rulers forward to aggression. Yet, to an ever-widening degree, the more modern bourgeois search for profit fortified the older vested interests in war possessed by particular individuals and special groups. The dynastic state had from the outset played the role of fairy godmother to capitalism, but now after the lapse of several centuries a maturer capitalism was on the verge of taking over the state. Everywhere in varying measure the middle classes were exchanging a passive for an active, more influential and decisive role in determining and orienting foreign policy. It was with this dynamic force of capitalist calculation in mind that Vergennes uttered his memorable ruling that "in the present state of the world commercial questions are political questions and as such within the province of foreign affairs." The vulgar prod of profit thrust blue-blooded aristocrats forward even in politically backward central and eastern Europe. Many a titled aristocrat was indeed an opulent commoner a marriage bed removed. It was the wealthy landed aristocrat who was the capitalist entrepreneur in Catherine's Russia. In France and England great noblemen were indistinguishable in thought and enterprise from mere merchant princes. Many a noble landlord had a large labor force working in his fields for the international grain market, frequently affiliating himself with manufacturers of military equipment and munitions, mining directors and shipping magnates. Where gain was meager at home, opportunities beckoned beyond the frontiers.

---

[3] Cf. the brief and stimulating article of Hans Speier, "Militarism in the Eighteenth Century," in *Social Research*, III (1936), 304 ff.

In war and peace the powers directed their diplomacy toward acquiring the great stakes of the modern economic society that was dawning: markets and monopolies; strategic harbors and vital land frontiers; furs, fish, and indispensable naval stores; grain for growing populations, and the tropical wares that were the sources of fabulous wealth. England and France renewed their imperial competition. To Austria and Prussia came no respite from struggle over the rich prize of Silesia, which merged now into the vaster struggle for military hegemony over all of central Europe. Enfeebled Poland, anarchic Sweden, and weakened Turkey appealed as incitations to plunder and partition. The Hapsburgs, with their trade outlets closed to the north and the west, and with their prestige waning among the secondary German states, tightened their contacts with the Adriatic and moved eastward into the Balkans, while neglecting no opportunity to gain possession of the Bavarian bastion in the west. Frederick of Prussia, who yearned for peace, also yearned for the East Prussian provinces of Poland. Catherine tightened the Russian grip on the Baltic for the trading opportunities with western Europe that it gave and, while biting deeply into eastern Poland, had in Potemkin and his business associates a living reminder of Peter the Great's designs upon the Black Sea and the Straits.

The best thought of the age vehemently condemned war and the competitive militarism which led to war. Alternately it ridiculed the arrogance and stupidity of the militarist outlook and recoiled in horror from the stark brutalities of mass homicide. This anti-militarist mood was strong in the Europe of the enlightenment, and visions of world peace loomed large on the horizon for the thinker and the statesman, the man of God and the man of affairs. But war and its alter ego, armed diplomacy, remained as usual the normal basis of state relations.

II. THE RENEWAL OF ANGLO-FRENCH COMPETITION

Up to the eve of the French Revolution neither Britain nor France was a force in continental diplomacy, for the interest of both then lay preponderantly with colonial matters. Choiseul, who was solidly entrenched in royal favor, was the directing intelligence behind his country's foreign and colonial policy during the decade of the sixties;

and it was his policy that Pitt the Elder had in mind when he declared that "France is chiefly if not solely to be feared by us in the light of a maritime and commercial rival." Taken individually his maneuvers to restore the imperial power of France appeared bewildering and even contradictory, an impression that perhaps had something to do with his own temperament and the secret diplomacy pursued simultaneously by his ruler. Taken together, however, his European and his colonial policies were the dual aspects of his anti-English resolution. He counted on the Hapsburg alliance of 1756 to bolster up the French sentinels in northern and eastern Europe and maintain his country's traditional position as arbiter of the continental balance, while through the Family Pact with Spain he would realize his more grandiose scheme of a joint Bourbon dynamic thrust against England, their enemy in the Mediterranean and the Caribbean. Charles III of Spain favored his plans, and in the Spanish foreign minister, Grimaldi, France had "the shadow of Choiseul's sun."[4]

Convinced of an impending revolt of the American colonies against British rule, he endeavored in advance to weaken the unity of the British empire by tightening the marriage bonds which made the Bourbon-Hapsburg network of dynastic alliances a true royal international. Joseph, the eldest son of Maria Theresa, was married to the Bourbon infanta Isabella of Parma; his sister Maria Amelia, to the Duke of Parma, and another sister, Maria Carolina, to the ruler of Naples; his brother Leopold married the Spanish Bourbon heiress of Tuscany, and his ill-starred youngest sister, Marie Antoinette, was betrothed to the future Louis XVI. At the same time Choiseul bent every energy to restoring the might of the French armed forces, which had been shattered by the reverses of the Seven Years' War. Before resigning his office in the admiralty be brought the naval strength up from 40 ships of the line to 64 and from 10 frigates to 45. New arsenals and ammunition magazines were founded in France itself, while bases for naval operations were prepared in Santo Domingo, Martinique, and Guadeloupe. As secretary of state for war he also repaired the havoc in the army. He cashiered many of the older and more incom-

4 Cf. L. Blart, *Les rapports de la France et de l'Espagne après le pacte de famille* (Paris, 1915), chs. iii, iv, and vi; and A. Bourget, *Etudes sur la politique étrangère du duc de Choiseul* (Paris, 1907).

petent officers and restored discipline in the ranks. He eradicated much of the speculation in connection with rations and payment of the men, regularized the recruiting system, and spurred the manufacture of arms. In specialists of the stamp of Bourcet, the great advocate of dispersion, and Gribeauval, the artillerist, he had extraordinarily able technicians who reorganized tactics and undertook the training of younger and more progressive officers.

His intentions to renew the struggle against England were an open secret, even to the English. The files of the ministry of foreign affairs were crammed with dossiers of his plans. The English diplomatic and espionage service followed his preparation closely, aware that his agents were stirring up discontent in the American colonies and preparing Martinique and Gaudeloupe as bases for future sweeping operations. Nor were they unaware of his extraordinarily modern project for a surprise invasion across the Channel, without a formal declaration of war but accompanied by friendly reassurances to the presumably demoralized civilian population.[5] For a brief moment William Pitt was again at the helm in the foreign office, 1766-1767, energetically alive to the need of countering the growing naval strength of the Bourbon allies, but he was followed by the more sanguine Charles Townshend.

Up to 1770 the Bourbon allies fared less than well in the west. They failed to break the trade of the American colonials and the British merchants with their own West Indies colonies and they were unsuccessful in colonizing French Guiana, which, along with the islands of the Antilles, was to have been the core of a restored colonial empire. They fared better in Europe. French penetration into Egypt threatened the eastern Mediterranean, while control of Corsica gave Choiseul an additional and highly strategic naval base in the western Mediterranean for possible operations against Gibraltar and Minorca. The climax of their aggressive moves came in 1770, when the Spaniards defiantly ousted the British garrison in West Falkland Island in the South Atlantic, whose strengthening Pitt had had the foresight to advocate. The European chancelleries smelled war, but the war failed to come. Instead, Choiseul was dramatically dismissed and his policy

5 M. C. Morison, "The Duc of Choiseul and the Invasion of England, 1768-1770," in *Transactions of the Royal Historical Society*, 3rd Series, IV (1910), 83-115.

temporarily repudiated. Justifiably or not, Louis XV used the pretext of France's diplomatic humiliation and the fiasco of the Hapsburg alliance in the impending partition of Poland to jettison his foreign minister.[6]

The last years of the reign were an anti-climax with respect to the English policy, but the accession of Louis XVI in 1774 brought to the foreign ministry the veteran of many years of diplomatic experience, Charles Gravier, Count de Vergennes. Like Choiseul, Vergennes was an unyielding Anglophobe and looked upon England as "the natural enemy of France," whose unalterable and cherished object was "if not the destruction of France, at least her degradation and ruin." Unlike his predecessor he neither cherished any easy illusions about a speedy reconstruction of the French colonial empire nor underestimated the difficulty of first breaking up the existing British empire. He differed too in the interpretation that he put upon the Hapsburg alliance. Privy to the notorious "King's Secret," he had seen at close range the grim consequences of a diplomacy that openly relied upon the Austrians and secretly opposed them. In the future he planned to employ that alliance merely as a defensive weapon on the Continent without involving France in the territorial calculations of the Hapsburg ally. On the contrary, his long-range policy of appeasement was to involve making discreet advances to Prussia and effecting a rapprochement with the estranged Russia; of giving financial aid to the Rhenish clients, such as the Palatinate and Zweibrücken; of contracting new marriage alliances, e.g., with Genoa, Piedmont, and Saxony; and of supplementing his country's diplomatic friendships with commercial alliances. The policy also entailed sacrifices, but Vergennes was prepared, if necessary, to suffer humiliations in Europe in order to attain his major goal of destroying Britain's power by drying up its source in the American trade. Once he had cut that commercial link, reasoned the mercantilist in him, Britain's general decline would begin, and with it would open a new opportunity for France to regain her preponderant position in world affairs. Patriotic fears, desire for revenge, mercantilist calculations, and commercial appetites wove themselves together into a single strong cable of action.[7]

[6] V. L. Brown, "Anglo-Spanish Relations in America in the Closing Years of the Colonial Era, 1763-1774," in *Hispanic-American Review*, V (1922), 325-483.

[7] Cf. E. S. Corwin, *French Policy and the American Alliance of 1778* (Princeton, 1916), for the motives of Vergennes.

While Vergennes was fundamentally a man of peace except for his bellicose views on England, his royal master was a man of peace without exception. He shared his minister's skepticism of the Hapsburg alliance, but he also had strong sentiments about extending open aid to the revolting American colonists. Though such assistance would unquestionably fit in with Vergennes's plans, Louis XVI reasoned not without cogency that encouraging revolutionaries, even at a distance of 3,000 miles, should not be part of the program of an absolute ruler. He even withheld his assent to mere secret aid until he was convinced that the policy of real neutrality endangered the security of France's own possessions in the West Indies.[8]

Among the various agents whom the colonists sent to get aid abroad, Silas Deane was one of the most efficacious in gaining from France the supplies of stores, munitions, and money that his countrymen needed so desperately. His great efforts were surpassed by the remarkable French adventurer, Caron de Beaumarchais, who put his tireless zeal and daring virtuosity into the cause. Backed by powerful silent partners in the French and Spanish governments themselves, his innocent firm of Rodrique Hortalez et Cie provided the Americans with a flow of indispensable funds, rifles, powder, and shoes without which the first years of conflict might indeed have overwhelmed the colonists.[9] The policy of secret French assistance also permitted American privateers to take on supplies themselves and be refitted in French harbors, a procedure that Vergennes's bland excuses never quite satisfactorily explained to the outraged British ambassador in Paris. Meantime, military and commercial circles in Paris, as well as more disinterested liberals, impatiently clamored for open support of the colonists. This was the attitude that led the English envoy to report with belabored sarcasm that "our wits, Philosophers and Coffee House Politicians . . . are to a man all warm Americans, affecting to consider them as a brave People struggling for its natural Rights and endeavoring to rescue those Rights out of the Hands of violent and wanton Oppression."[10]

The decisive change from French non-belligerency to an open alli-

8 R. Pinon, "Louis XVI, Vergennes et la grande lutte contre l'Angleterre," in *Revue d'histoire diplomatique* (1929), 37-64.
9 O. W. Stephenson, "The Supply of Gunpowder in 1776," in *American Historical Review*, XXX (1925), 277 ff.
10 Quoted in S. K. Padover, *The Life and Death of Louis XVI* (New York, 1939), 106. Cf. also B. Faÿ, *The Revolutionary Spirit in France and America* (New York, 1927), 75.

ance came in 1778. The Declaration of Independence of course made the shift possible; and it became all but inevitable after Benjamin Franklin, the bland and wily darling of Paris and the canniest amateur diplomat and propagandist that any nation ever had, set to work. The surrender of "Gentleman Johnny" Burgoyne at Saratoga in October, 1777, furnished him with an ace card in his flawless game of diplomatic poker. His delicate suggestion at that crucial juncture that the colonists might now come to terms with England—against France— achieved its intended effect, for the French negotiators quickly saw the advantages of concluding an open alliance with the Americans in order to ward off the fearful prospect of an English raid upon their Caribbean islands. Early in 1778 Vergennes cast the die. The Continent was tranquil, for thanks to his own efforts Prussian and Austrian differences over the question of the Bavarian Succession were composed. According to the old Family Pact, he was bound to act only in concert with Spain but he took a chance on his ally, trusting that Spain would be inspired by his own example to break with England. Necker warned him, even as Turgot had warned him two years earlier, that war could cost France dear, but he reasoned that the ultimate gains would be immeasurably higher than the immediate costs. So on February 6, 1778, he signed the treaties of alliance and commerce (on practically free-trade lines) with the rebellious colonists, and within a few short months his country was again openly at war with England.

Spain in the interim was very effectively pursuing the policy that Aranda delicately called "dissimulation and serenity." Spain's concern with the revolt was entirely lacking in sentimental sympathy for the cause of "liberty" against "violent and wanton Oppression." Despite the scores that Charles III had to settle with England, he never forgot that he too had colonists in the new world. Nor was he prepared, during the early years of the American revolt, to court the risk of an open break with England.[11] Confident that the prolongation of the war would exhaust both the Americans and the English, he was content to take advantage of British embarrassment without war. Consequently he hung back, resisting the inducements of Vergennes and the American commissioner, Arthur Lee, who pressed him to do more

11 Cf. R. Konetzke, *op. cit.*, for the details.

than give secret aid. The dramatically sensational developments of
1778 brought a change in his attitude, for they opened an opportunity
to play for stakes worth far more to Spain than the independence of
the colonies: the stakes of Gibraltar and Minorca in the old world and
Florida and the West Indies in the new.[12] Accordingly Floridablanca
played an astute game, both with his ally and with his future foe, and
Vergennes soared to a high pitch of moral indignation in discovering in the Spanish minister the same calculating temper that he himself possessed. But the French diplomat needed the Spanish navy to
obtain mastery of the seas, and he resigned himself to the Spanish
conditions. First, the latter offered his services as mediator to England
—in return, naturally, for Gibraltar. After England rejected the
proffered aid, as he had expected, Floridablanca put into effect
the convention of Aranjuez (1779) with France. To repay for the
urgently sought-for Spanish military alliance Vergennes reluctantly
agreed not to withdraw from the war until after Gibraltar had been
retaken for his Bourbon ally.

The two partners were then ready to act. The French navy alone
was the equal of the English in numbers, but while well officered, it
was still badly undermanned and inferior in sturdiness and speed.
The addition of the forty Spanish ships of the line gave them numerical superiority. Though their supreme naval effort, the attempted
invasion of England across the Channel, failed, Vergennes kept tightening the diplomatic net around the foe. He found his great opportunity when England declared war against the United Provinces. The
Dutch had been a thorn in England's flesh, not, to be sure, without
profit for themselves, conveying supplies to the Americans, and allowing the American privateers as well as the ships of Rodrique Hortalez
et Cie to refit in Dutch ports, especially in the Dutch island of St.
Eustatius in the West Indies. After England had declared war, Vergennes drew upon all the finesse of his long experience to complete
England's diplomatic isolation and swing the important neutral countries of Europe against "the tyrant of the seas." It was not too difficult to convince the states of the North Sea and the Baltic that

---

12 For Spain's unfriendly attitude toward the Americans, see Frank Monaghan, *John Jay*
(New York, 1935), 125 ff.; F. S. Bemis, *The Diplomacy of the American Revolution*
(New York, 1935), for the continental aspects of French and Spanish intervention.

neutrality was expedient in that fierce naval struggle which exposed their ships to the attacks of both sets of belligerents. But to have them enforce their rights as neutrals was not work for a novice diplomatist, for enforcing neutrality meant in practice doing so exclusively against England. This was especially true in the case of Russia, the bulk of whose shipping trade was menaced not by English but by American privateers.

As early as 1778 Vergennes made his bid to the neutrals with his declaration that "free bottoms make free goods," to which the English commercial and diplomatic representatives at the various capitals had countered with the more persuasive and telling argument of British naval strength to make good the English right of search and the policy of paper blockade. But as privateers, French, Spanish, and finally Dutch ships kept weakening British sea control in the course of the next two years, St. Petersburg became the seat of a great diplomatic contest. To be successful, Vergennes's project of a league of neutrals needed the adherence of Russia. His game for the moment seemed lost when Catherine proposed a league of neutrals so constituted as to protect her own commercial interests by closing the North Sea to the vessels of both sets of belligerents and impartially excluding all privateers from northern waters. But at this most critical moment his carefully nurtured policy of diplomatic conciliation bore fruit. Catherine was indebted to France for friendly aid in her imbroglio with the Turks, and a grateful empress ultimately accepted the French basis for the proposed league. In March, 1780, she signed the declaration which established the League of Armed Neutrality. By its terms contraband was narrowly restricted to munitions and arms, which freed neutral ships to carry other stores of greatly needed goods; and the neutrals regarded themselves free to navigate along the coasts and to the very ports of all belligerents. Thus constituted, the League practiced neutrality on the side of England's enemies. Along with Denmark and Sweden, Russia armed her merchant vessels to protect this interpretation of neutral rights. Almost all other neutrals engaged directly or indirectly in trade with England—Prussia, the Empire, Portugal, and the Two Sicilies—later acceded to the declaration, which completed the commercial and political isolation of England. Perhaps the League of Armed Neutrality was less effective in reality than it promised as a declaration, but the very assumption of hostility toward England was worth a great deal in bolstering up the morale of her enemies.[13]

When the general peace treaties of September, 1783, ended the fighting, England had behind her as bitter memories a long and humiliating series of reverses. At the lowest point of her fortune she had lost command of the Channel to France and Spain. Her imperial communications had been cut. John Paul Jones had set foot on her soil. Minorca and Gibraltar had both been besieged by the enemy. Ireland had threatened rebellion. While Rodney's magnificent victories restored her naval supremacy, the war had cost her terrified merchant princes 3,000 craft of all description. The suffering of the poor was more severe than in the history of living man, and an unprecedented debt seemed to threaten the very country with bankruptcy. A phrase in a letter that Horace Walpole wrote caught the mood of shame and humiliation which fell upon the country: "You must be happy now," he wrote, "not to have a son, who would live to grovel in the dregs of England."[14] And experts on the Continent, equally adept at reading handwriting on walls, also saw that the disruption of the empire was near. In that vein prognosticated Leopold of Tuscany in 1783:

Thus is the great power . . . fallen completely and forever; all its prestige and strength lost . . . and sunk to the ranks of a second class power such as Sweden and Denmark; and it will probably not be long before she too will be dominated by Russia as they are. France, delivered for all time of that formidable adversary, thereby doubles her intrinsic strength, her commerce, her authority and her prestige and, in consequence, the haughtiness of her tone in all Europe. . . .[15]

Leopold notwithstanding, France scored no overwhelming triumph at the peace table. The American colonies were irretrievably lost, a bitter and costly blow to English purse and pride. Spain recovered

[13] Belgian ports, especially Ostend, furnished more faked neutral (Austrian imperial) clearance papers to English outward-bound ships than they did to England's enemies. Cf. T. K. Gorman, *America and Belgium* (London, 1925), ch. vii; Vergennes induced the Congress to instruct the commanders of its armed vessels to conform to these principles. His importance in the formation of the League is stressed by J. J. Meng, *The Comte de Vergennes. European Phases of his American Diplomacy* (Washington, 1932).

[14] Quoted in R. Coupland, *The American Revolution and the British Empire* (London, 1930), 13.

[15] A. Von Arneth, *Joseph II und Leopold von Toskana. Ihr Briefwechsel von 1781 bis 1790*, 2 vols. (Vienna, 1872), I, 151-152.

East Florida and kept the recaptured island of Minorca, but she failed to regain the prize of Gibraltar which had lured her into the conflict. France reaped her reward in Tobago in the West Indies, trading posts in India and Senegal, and retention of St. Pierre and Miquelon in the St. Lawrence—but at the price of an intensified revolutionary spirit and a crippling debt, both of which paved the way to 1789.

III. THE FIRST PARTITION OF POLAND

While the Anglo-Bourbon duel was being fought in the west, the other great powers were perpetrating as callous a diplomatic transaction as a century not without some distinction in *Realpolitik* was to see. Neither England, harassed by her colonial problems, nor France, with her vacillating eastern European policy, could prevent or retard the first partition of Poland, or even profit from it themselves. In its immediate antecedents the Polish crisis went back to the understanding of April, 1764, which committed Prussia to common action with Russia in Poland. By its terms the two countries agreed to act in concert for the selection of Catherine's sometime paramour, Stanislas Poniatowski, as king of Poland, to defend "the peace of the Republic" against anarchic disturbances, and especially to protect the religious rights of the Dissidents (Greek Orthodox Catholics and Protestants).[16]

Neither Frederick nor Catherine signed the agreement out of choice or by inclination. Sheer expediency was the parent of that unnatural pact which pledged the late enemies to joint action in a country where their interests were mutually exclusive and hostile. Frederick's assent derived from his shrewd calculation of diplomatic probabilities. Estranged from England and enjoying only chilly relations with France, he saw his military security endangered by Joseph's steely determination to recover Silesia. He therefore courted reconciliation with formidable Russia in order to set up an immediate buffer against Hapsburg revenge. He was compelled to lay aside his own designs and play the Russian game in Poland. In return he obtained the military alliance that his country needed along with a Russian guarantee of Silesia and the promise of aid in the event that

---

16 C. V. Easum, *op. cit.*, ch. xvii, has an illuminating discussion of Frederick's difficulties immediately after 1763.

a hostile power (Austria) attacked him within his own frontiers. Catherine, who was equally isolated diplomatically, for to all intents the Russian-Austrian alliance was defunct, was conversely compelled by the Czartoryskis' challenge to her predominance to associate Frederick with her in solving the affairs of the country where Russia's predatory national interests demanded Prussia's total exclusion. Although she privately characterized the alliance as "ignominious and intolerable," Prussia as a dubious ally was preferable to no ally at all; and certainly to a Prussia friendly to the Ottoman Empire or reconciled with Austria against her. Harboring such reservations, the two mortal foes of Poland reached their reluctant understanding which either was cheerfully prepared at the first good opportunity to repudiate.

The Polish question became acute when the confederates of Bar, aided by Austrian sympathizers and a trickle of arms and ammunition smuggled to them across the Turkish frontier, attacked the rule of Russia in their country early in 1768.[17] At this point Choiseul resorted to the classical French strategy. Ably seconded by Vergennes at Constantinople, he incited the Turks to make a diversion on Russia's flank. The Porte was not loath to do so, for the Polish question had already insensibly merged with the broader "Eastern Question." When a contingent of Russian troops, pursuing the rebels, violated the Ottoman frontier and burned a Turkish town, the sultan declared war upon Catherine in his guise as the protector of Polish liberties. Thus the war broadened and during the following four years Poland was desolated by a savage and sanguinary struggle. The unhappy land was torn asunder by the throes of a strife that was at once patriotic, religious, and social. The impassioned exhortations of Orthodox priests matched the fervor of the Roman clergy's inflammatory sermons; and Ukrainian Cossacks, vying with the feared robber *Haidamacks*, massacred Jews and landlords with impartial homicidal fury.

Beginning with the spring of 1769 the Russian troops methodically pursued the offensive by land and sea. After conquering the Black Sea littoral westward of the Dnieper, and the province of Bessarabia, they hacked their way deep into the Danubian provinces of Moldavia and Wallachia clear to the Hapsburg frontier. This first campaign

[17] For the prior Russian penetration into Poland, see *supra*, ch. vi, pp. 127-130.

was anxiously followed in Vienna, for Russian penetration to the Danube threatened the Austrian flank. Though Frederick had loyally given the "accursed subsidies" to his ally, he was no more anxious than Austria to have Russia win a shattering victory and impose her own settlement. Hence he maneuvered on all diplomatic fronts. Early in 1769 he renewed until 1780 the alliance with Russia which was due to expire in 1772; and later that year he met Joseph in Silesia and sounded out the young emperor. It was a foregone conclusion that Austria would either fight to keep Russia permanently away from the Danube or else demand compensations for herself. Neither outlook was to Frederick's liking. In the event of a Russo-Austrian conflict Prussia was certain to be involved by reason of the *casus foederis*; whereas a deal between the two powers to partition the Balkan possessions of the Ottoman Empire would also do Prussia no good, since Prussia had neither interest in nor yet claims upon the Porte.

The acquisition of Danzig and West Prussia from Poland had long been axiomatic in Frederick's thinking, but at the moment he was exclusively concerned with having the war end, freeing himself from the obligation of paying the Russian subsidy, and preventing the outbreak of a general European war in which Prussia would become involved. The campaign of 1770 was outwardly most disquieting for his hopes. The Russian fleet made its way from the Baltic to the Mediterranean and in midsummer won the crushing naval victory of Chesmé over the Turks. After this blow the Russian armies advanced against several Danubian fortresses, threatening both the Turkish capital and the Crimea. In reality, the aftermath of victory found Russia as eager as Prussia to avoid a general war. Her poverty, the outbreak of the plague, and general popular discontent were strong deterrents. And the knowledge of these circumstances strengthened Frederick's diplomatic position.

At a second meeting with Joseph in Moravia he discovered that Austria was not minded to play the French game of harassing Russia. Prince Kaunitz was no more averse than Frederick to serving as honest broker, but he was handicapped by the necessity of pleasing his two royal masters, who were far apart in their views, as well as by his own complex exchange projects. Maria Theresa, who wished for neither partition nor war, had blocked his first fantastic plan of

1769. This proposal involved a joint Austrian-Prussian intervention on the side of Turkey, in return for which Prussia would obtain the territory she sought in Poland while Austria would win the retrocession of Silesia. In the face of the empress's veto Kaunitz fell back upon a simple Austrian-Prussian rapprochement by the terms of which they agreed "faithfully to keep the peace," i.e., each state guarded its freedom to act as circumstances might command.

Though the understanding greatly diminished the danger of a general European conflagration, Frederick looked ahead and also threw a "sanitary cordon" of Prussian troops around the Polish territory that he had staked out for his country. Both Germanic states then accepted a Turkish invitation to mediate in the war. Frederick may have had other designs in the back of his mind, but his correspondence makes it clear that while urging his brother Prince Henry, then on his way from Stockholm to St. Petersburg, to offer mediation, he was not actively planning partition of Poland. Indeed, the Prussian-Russian alliance seemed on the verge of dissolution in that summer of 1770 when Frederick was writing angry protests to his brother about Catherine's efforts to use the pact exclusively for Russian ends and reiterating to his envoys at the other capitals that he would steer clear of involvement in Catherine's Polish plans.

But events were relentlessly fashioning the partition as the most satisfactory solution for the two allies: for Russia, which was increasingly loath to pursue the war against both the Confederates in Poland and the Turkish troops, and for Prussia, which was equally anxious not to become embroiled in war. Though the Russians declined the offer of mediation, after the Austrians had occupied Zips in the fall of that year, Frederick renewed his diplomatic efforts and urged that the three powers should intervene jointly. In October, 1770, Prince Henry in a thoroughly informal and tentative way broached the idea of a tripartite Prussian, Austrian, and Russian action simultaneously to end the war against Turkey and make Poland pay the price of peace. This suggestion broke the deadlock and sounded the knell for Poland. Until then Catherine had been reluctant to give up the tempting prospect of retaining newly conquered Moldavia and Wallachia, as the fruit of her victories. But between the end of 1770 and January 8, 1771, she changed her mind and indicated indirectly to Frederick through Prince Henry that she was ready to act along the latter's lines.

The outbreak of epidemic at Moscow, the premonitory rumblings of peasant disturbances, the pressure of a pro-Prussian faction at court, and the thoroughly disquieting information that Austria (now secretly allied with Turkey) had called up troops with the manifest intention of falling upon the flank of the Russians if they crossed the Danube—all this had given her pause. Without knowing, as Frederick was to discover, through a studied indiscretion on the part of Maria Theresa, that the Austrian mobilization was merely a feint, Catherine reasoned that Russia would surely have to fight with Austria over the Russian conquests in the Balkans unless she joined with the Hapsburgs in partitioning Poland. But Frederick reasoned that he would get the territory his country sought in Poland, "the ointment for my burns," as the king described it to his minister in Russia, in return for his payment of the "accursed subsidies"—and all without becoming involved in a war against Austria. The domestic difficulties, together with the Austrian occupation of Zips, gave Catherine the pretext to suggest "smilingly" to Prince Henry that Prussia follow the Austrian example. Subsequently Russian statesmen made independent offers to the prince. Catherine herself, while renouncing the Danubian conquests, would get compensations along the Vistula. To return the conquered Balkan principalities, about whose retention there were the gravest of doubts, and have her moderation rewarded with a deep wedge of Polish territory was a compromise solution which Catherine could still contemplate with a measure of equanimity. Such a solution did necessitate the end of Russia's long policy of serving as the protector of Poland, and her acquiescence in the Prussian proposal may therefore have been the involuntary action of an increasingly hardpressed ally. But her own calculations under the altered circumstances were not strikingly devoid either of cold intelligence or of flexibility.[18]

Not until his brother's return to Berlin in January did Frederick abandon his coolness toward the proposed partition. When he did decide in February to follow the lead laid down by Prince Henry and

---

[18] Apart from the extraordinarily clear treatment in the Introduction of R. H. Lord's *The Second Partition of Poland* (Cambridge, 1915), which favors Catherine, there is the equally valuable chapter in Easum, *op. cit.*, which uses the political correspondence of Frederick to prove the initiative of Prince Henry and Catherine.

the empress, he began to act with great vigor. Both powers were now eager for a rapid settlement. Catherine in particular wished it, because of the growing war weariness and the increasing popular discontent at home and because of the disturbing diplomatic situation abroad, where the Austrian military threat was ominous and the rise of Struensee in Denmark and the accession of the pro-French Gustavus III in Sweden were equally menacing.

As the summer advanced, Frederick became certain that Austria would not fight, despite her military pact with the Turks. Maria Theresa had willed it otherwise. Hence he pressed Catherine to take more territory in Poland, for such aggrandizement only strengthened Prussia's own claims for compensation. His position was doubly strong, for while Catherine made no headway in her negotiations with the defeated but obdurate Polish Confederates, at the same time she realized only too well that Prussia would not stir to aid Russia in her war with Turkey. Therefore she agreed to draw up a secret Prussian-Russian plan for partition without Austria. By the time the definite terms were settled in February, 1772, the planners were convinced that Austria would accept their invitation to adhere, if only out of a sense of realism. "We have settled everything already," wrote the Russian minister of foreign affairs to his ambassador at Vienna, ". . . and it would therefore repay the court of Vienna also to make acquisitions." Kaunitz and Joseph required little persuasion, but Maria Theresa's sense of what was honorable and Christian delayed the final stroke. Kaunitz gradually overcame the scruples of "dear worthy Lady Prayerful," as Catherine unfeelingly dubbed the Hapsburg empress. During the next six months the three courts bargained vigorously about their respective shares, but not until August 5, after the final crushing of Polish resistance, were the three separate treaties signed. It was then that Frederick made his stinging observation that the more Maria Theresa wept, the more she took. Europe was slow in realizing what impended, so difficult was it to accept the fact that Russia was resigning her old role of protector in favor of the new one of partitioner. As the soldiers moved, the three courts issued public manifestoes bespeaking their firm moral resolution to preserve the peace of Europe against the infection of Polish anarchy. A whole year elapsed before Stanislas agreed to summon a diet and to give formal assent to the *fait accompli.* He yielded to military force and to the Russian threat of a still more drastic spoliation. The tragic date of the ratification was September 18, 1773.[19]

By this first partition Poland lost nearly one-third of her territory and almost one-half of her population. Frederick's share of Polish Prussia (with the exception of Danzig and Thorn) was the smallest in land and in population, but it was most valuable from the point of view of its strategic location and its political value. It closed the gap between the separated Prussian provinces, freed Prussia from the fear of a Russian attack, and gave her effective control of the basin of the lower Vistula and its enormously important grain trade. The great emporium of Danzig, however, he failed to get. To Catherine, handicapped still by her unsettled war against the Turks, went New White Russia and the territory to the Dvina and the Dnieper, i.e., the eastern part of the old Lithuanian state. Though its chief importance was the added strength that it gave to Russia's military frontier, its acquisition also had the advantage of giving Russia political as well as economic control over those eastern Polish provinces which her traders had been penetrating for a full century. To the Hapsburgs, who had betrayed both Poles and Turks, went 2,700,000 inhabitants and a huge stretch of territory that included Galicia, the northern slope of the Carpathians, and a corridor through Silesia to the new possessions. Cemented thus in interest and idealism of the higher order, the accomplices could wholeheartedly echo Frederick's measured judgment that "a new era of international justice and good feeling" had been inaugurated.

Enlightened public opinion found typical expression in Voltaire, who showered praise on one of his stars, Catherine, and bestowed congratulations upon his other luminary, Frederick. The European public was less shocked by the cynical cruelty of the proceedings than startled by the moderation of the partners, who took only a third when the whole was theirs for the asking. The states of Europe also looked on, not in "apathetic indifference," as Stanislas poignantly wrote, but in utter helplessness. While British statesmen "occasionally asked questions of their envoy [in Berlin, they] . . . paid little

---

[19] The brief account in ch. v. of the *Cambridge History of Poland* (London, 1941) is a masterly summary.

attention to his replies."[20] George III himself, with his characteristic sensitivity to spiritual forces and with not a little awareness of the troubled situation in the American colonies, saw in these developments the workings of providence and declared piously that the evil was so great that only the Almighty could set things right. French diplomats did not invoke the deity. They had court intrigues and the famous system of the "King's Secret" to account for their country's pusillanimous acceptance of the overthrow of their Polish "barrier of the East."[21]

Continuing Russian military successes soon compelled the Porte to sue for peace. By the Treaty of Küchük Kainarja (1774) the sultan recognized the independence of the Crimea, which the Russians had conquered in 1771, and ceded three of its great fortresses to Russia. He paid a heavy war indemnity, opened Turkish waters to Russian navigation, and gave Catherine a commercial treaty with the most-favored-nation clause. While Russia restored the Danubian principalities, Catherine reserved the right to intervene in their behalf against misrule. She also won the right to build an Orthodox church in the foreign quarter of Constantinople, along with a vague and therefore doubly dangerous right to make representations in behalf of its worshipers. Russia was to invoke the provisions of this treaty during the following century.

IV. DIPLOMATIC POINT COUNTERPOINT

Not only Catherine's aggressions but Joseph's restless imperialist ambitions continued to trouble the peace. Ever on the alert to round out the Hapsburg possessions and win new outlets for the trade which Prussia blocked to the north and west, he acquired Bukovina in 1775, and in the following year Fiume. A far greater opportunity knocked at his door in 1777, when the Duke of Bavaria died without legitimate issue. Austria's acquisition of the duchy was to be desired for purely

---

[20] Sir Richard Lodge, *Great Britain and Prussia in the Eighteenth Century* (London, 1923), 150.
[21] Cf. L. Jacobsohn, *Russland und Frankreich in den ersten Regierungsjahren der Kaiserin Catharinas II, 1762-1772* (Berlin, 1929), for the fiasco of the French diplomacy; and O. Brandt, in "Das Problem der Ruhe des Nordens im XVIII. Jahrhundert," in *Historische Zeitschrift*, CXL (1929), 550-564, for French diplomacy and the Russian-Danish settlement of the Holstein succession.

strategic reasons, for it would open a direct southwestern route to the Tyrol and the Hapsburg appanages in Italy. This was a prospect which the French ally did not cheerfully face. Moreover, from the point of view of Germanic relations, while compensating for the loss of Silesia, it would also augment Hapsburg influence in the struggle for domination within the Holy Roman Empire.

The variety of genealogical claims which Joseph presented as his title to the vacant duchy were not unimpressive, especially when buttressed by his troops. Nor was it difficult to persuade the elector of the Palatinate (the co-lateral heir of the deceased duke) to recognize Hapsburg claims to Lower Bavaria and the Upper Palatinate, the former of which he occupied in January, 1778. Joseph had to reckon, however, with Frederick, who wrote to Prince Henry: "I know quite well that it is only our own interests that compel us to act at this moment; but we must be very careful not to say so."[22] He filed Prussia's claim to the adjoining territories of Bayreuth and Anspach, which were already in the possession of the junior branches of the Hohenzollerns, conniving to have them revert to the direct possession of Berlin. He incited Saxony to claim part of the Bavarian territory, and above all he secretly encouraged the childless elector's heir presumptive, the cautious Duke of Zweibrücken, to assert his succession rights to the disputed inheritance. Whatever patriotic Hohenzollern historians may have made of Frederick as the protector of the rights of the small German princes, his correspondence clearly reveals that his primary concern was with checking this threat of Austrian expansion. Though reluctant to fight, he matched Joseph's military preparations, and by the spring the rival forces were stretched in hostile array over the boundary between Silesia and Bohemia. In July Frederick and Prince Henry invaded Bohemia but, unable to dislodge the Austrians from their strong position along the Upper Elbe, the Prussians waged a lusterless campaign of inactive but watchful waiting.

Although Joseph was confident that he had the situation well in hand, his faith in the French-Austrian alliance was unjustified. Vergennes had not the faintest intention either of jeopardizing his American policy by involving France in a war on the Continent to further

22 *Politische Correspondenz*, XL, 224, cited in Easum, *op. cit.*, 296.

Joseph's interests and procure a bastion for Austria to the west, or of courting a break with Prussia by acquiescing in Austrian aggression and accepting the proffered bribe of the Austrian Netherlands for doing so. He had made his attitude clear to Joseph when the emperor visited Paris in 1777, but thereafter he still had to cope with the persistent efforts of the "Austrian party" at Versailles to involve France in the European struggle. Meanwhile he consolidated France's friendly relations with the secondary states of Germany which lived under the shadow of the Hapsburg menace. It was also part of his grand strategy to have an unweakened Prussia stand as sentinel on Austria's flank, for an estranged and violated Prussia could conceivably turn for aid toward England, with whom France was already at war. Hence he rejected Austrian entreaties, circumvented intrigues at home, and threw the weight of France in the balance against Joseph, ruling that the *casus foederis* was in no way involved in the problem of the disputed Bavarian succession.[23]

The war lagged, and in the fall when the Prussian troops withdrew from Bohemia, the chancelleries began to spin their fine threads of negotiations. In the diplomatic maneuvering which ensued Frederick had the not inconsiderable advantage of knowing that Maria Theresa was vociferously pacific in her views, while the bloodless military stalemate was humiliating the bellicose Joseph. The emperor's dream of winning imperishable military glory had materialized into the tragic comedy of the derided *Kartoffelnkrieg*, where two hungry armies made a major contribution to military annals by digging up frozen potatoes to stay alive. France and Russia moved jointly for peace on the Continent, the former by interceding in Catherine's behalf in the current Russo-Turkish renewal of hostilities, and the latter by offering her mediation to the Germanic contestants. This endeavor bore its first results in a truce and their agreement to call a peace congress. The congress opened at Teschen in March, 1779, with Catherine's troops deployed for action in a pointed index of her goodwill as mediator. Since indications made it clear that Austria was the objective of Russia's military attention, Joseph was persuaded, and Austria signed the Treaty of Teschen. The Hapsburgs renounced

---

[23] For Vergennes's attitude, see G. Grosjean, *La politique rhénane de Vergennes* (Paris, 1925).

their rights to Lower Bavaria, though they saved face by retaining a small triangle of territory along the Inn River. Frederick was not without gain in this transaction, for Austria agreed to the future incorporation of Bayreuth and Anspach into Prussia. Russia's benefit from mediation took the form of gaining enormous prestige as a factor in continental relations and in establishing a precedent for her future intervention in Germanic affairs. The French mediator, Vergennes, was also rewarded—at least for the time being. He had kept his Austrian ally out of Bavaria. By courting Russia, whose fleet he needed in European waters for the successful conduct of his war against England, and by satisfying her territorial appetite at the sacrifice of the distant Ottoman Empire, he won an important move in his complex but uncomplicated design to keep Europe at peace while he was directing French energies against England overseas.[24]

While Vergennes's diplomacy swept on triumphantly to its goal of the League of Armed Neutrality and the defeat of England abroad, the snarl of continental diplomacy became utterly tangled with the threads of conflicting ambitions and claims crossing each other in bewildering fashion. Frederick's fear that the check at Teschen would only excite Joseph to fresh provocation was all too soon realized. Freed from the restraining hand of Maria Theresa, who died in 1780, and bitterly disappointed by Vergennes's unsympathetic interpretation of the Hapsburg alliance, Joseph bent all his efforts toward supplanting Prussia at St. Petersburg. He acted less out of enthusiasm for Catherine's eastern projects than out of a compelling need to have Russia as an ally against his great German rival. By May, 1781, the startling reversal of alliances had become a reality, for the lengthy exchange of letters between him and Catherine sealed the sensational shift which joined the two great empires in a defensive alliance. Their understanding called for a mutual guarantee of their existing pacts and conventions and the *casus foederis* in the event that one or the other were attacked by a third party, i.e., the Turks.

Frederick might well despair. The expiration of his alliance with Catherine removed the sheet anchor of his own security, while the cordial understanding between the two predatory powers (now that

---

24 The fullest account in English is H. W. Temperley, *Frederick the Great and Kaiser Joseph, an Episode of War and Diplomacy in the Eighteenth Century* (London, 1915).

he himself was a man of peace) not only cast a grim shadow upon the independence of their weaker neighbors, but portended Austro-Russian domination over the affairs of the Continent.[25] For Russia the diplomatic revolution signified the end of Panin's "System of the North," which was based on the Prussian alliance, and the inauguration of Potemkin's and Bezborodko's far more grandiose scheme of the "Greek Empire."[26] It implied that Russia was disassociating herself from Prussia, which was unalterably opposed to the dismemberment of the Turkish realm, in order to ally herself with the eager Joseph and presumably repay his collaboration with Russia against Turkey by co-operating with him against Prussia.

Each of the new allies sought to involve the other in a course that made withdrawal impossible or at the least extremely risky. The advantage was Catherine's from the start. Joseph was no innocent dupe of his "sister" in St. Petersburg and enjoyed the benefit of the most astute diplomatic counsel from Kaunitz as well as from his veteran ambassador to Russia, Count Ludwig Cobenzl. But he lacked the cards that Catherine held. From the very first meeting at Mohilev in 1780, when he accompanied her back to Russia, through all the succeeding years, his correspondence reveals that he had the uneasy feeling that there was always something "suspicious and deceitful in her conduct." He felt, all the time that they were exchanging proposals and counter-proposals concerning their respective shares under the "Grand Plan" for the partition of the European territory of the Ottoman Empire, that Catherine was busily "baiting the hook" to win his support for her more immediate annexation of the Crimea and the West Caucasus.[27]

[25] Cf. the *Politische Correspondenz*, XLIV-XLVI, for his frantic efforts to prevent the gradual dissolution of the Prussian-Russian alliance of 1764.

[26] For the prodigious influence of Potemkin, cf. Theresia Adamczyk, *Fürst G. A. Potemkin, Untersuchung zu seiner Lebensgeschichte* (Emsdetter, 1936).

[27] The "Grand Plan" as it was finally evolved, which Joseph accepted in principle without enthusiasm and with many misgivings, gave Russia the remaining territory east of the Dniester: the Crimea and the West Caucasus; the two Danubian principalities of Moldavia and Wallachia were to become the Dacian state (under Russian influence). Austria was to round out her possessions by acquiring part of Wallachia, part of Serbia, including Belgrade, part of Bosnia and of Herzegovina, and the Venetian territory on the Adriatic, including Istria and Dalmatia, as an outlet for her Hungarian products. The remaining territory in the Balkans, i.e., Bulgaria, Roumelia, Macedonia, and Greece, was to constitute the independent Greek Empire, with Constantinople as its capital and Catherine's grandson, Constantine, as emperor. The other countries which had interests in the Near East were to be compensated with territory or commercial agreements in the North African or the Asia Minor possessions of the Turks. For the terms, cf. A. von

She kept reassuring him that even if *"der alte Fritz"* should nerve himself to attack them while they were involved in war against the Turks, their combined forces would be more than a match for his army. Joseph replied that there were other states to consider, France, for instance. His demurrer was not irrelevant, for Vergennes had turned down the Austrian invitation that France become a partner to the grab in the east. In fact, Vergennes had hoped that with the aid of Frederick he could unite Austria and Prussia *against* Russia to prevent the annexation of the Crimea and the adjacent area. Consequently the irritated Joseph hesitated over Catherine's promptings, fearing a Prussian and French attack if he did collaborate with Catherine and the loss of the Russian alliance if he did not. With his heart still set upon gaining Bavaria he was of no inclination to alienate the good offices of his French ally. Catherine rescued him from his awkward dilemma by effecting the annexation of the Crimea singlehanded. While Europe considered her act a prelude to the final attack upon Turkey, Russia was satisfied for the moment. Joseph salved his conscience—and reserved his freedom of action—by not formally recognizing her deed. But he did nothing to oppose it, and as a just reward for his "good offices" and his "measured conduct," Catherine wrote him with tempered gratification, "I hope that the happy moment will come when I shall acquit myself of my debt to you."[28]

Vergennes too accepted reality and indeed had run ahead of it. Beset by his aim of furthering the commercial interests of France, he convinced himself that peace could best be maintained in the west by orienting aggressors to the east. He advised the sultan to cut his losses and formally concede the Crimea, the Kuban area, and Taman peninsula. The Russo-Turkish Treaty of Constantinople (1784) sealed the deed on those terms.

For a few years the "Grand Plan" was postponed. While Joseph was nursing his first disappointment over his alliance, Catherine's lukewarm behavior in the affairs of the west to which he had turned gave him a second and greater grievance. His new opportunity had come in connection with the controversy over the opening of the

---

Arneth, *Joseph II und Katharina von Russland: Ihr Briefwechsel* (Vienna, 1869), Introduction.
28 *Ibid.*, 148.

Scheldt River to Belgian navigation. Though various international agreements required that the Scheldt be kept closed, Joseph found a chance to have the issue re-examined when some armed Dutch soldiers technically violated Belgian neutrality. Simultaneously with the Scheldt issue he attempted to exchange the Belgian possessions, which he regarded as useless to Austria, for the Bavarian inheritance, which he held of pivotal importance. "I have profited by the same opportunity," he wrote to Leopold on October 31, 1784, "to inform the Comte de Merci [Mercy-Argenteau, the Austrian ambassador to France] that perhaps this will be a unique occasion for France, rent by fear of war . . . to propose the exchange with Bavaria in her own name."[29] Had the exchange taken place, it would automatically have ended the affair of the Scheldt, so far as Austria was concerned, for the Hapsburgs would no longer have been interested.

Unfortunately for his cause he was neither circumspect in his tactics nor moderate in his demands. He spoiled a good case and voided an excellent opportunity by outrageously bullying the Dutch before he had made sure of France. For a year between the autumn of 1784 and that of 1785 the peace of Europe hung by a thread, but Vergennes was not to be deflected from his single resolution to use the Hapsburg alliance for what it was worth to keep the peace in Europe while he himself pursued his other plans. He would neither add to the commercial strength of Austria by reopening the Scheldt along its course through the Netherlands nor would he abandon the United Provinces, with whom he was busily negotiating a trade treaty. He renewed the French offer of mediation, and after taking counsel with Prince Henry in Paris he further intimated that if Joseph did not voluntarily accept the offer of mediation, France would join with Prussia in compelling him to listen to reason. Joseph accepted it, persuaded into doing so by Catherine's blunt declaration that she too would not give him active military support. He dropped the idea of opening the Scheldt and agreed also to renounce Austrian claims upon the frontier city of Maestricht. Conversely, after long negotiations, the United Provinces agreed by the Treaty of Fontainebleau to demolish the barrier fortresses at the mouth of the river and indemnify Joseph for the Dutch attack on ships flying the Belgian flag. France provided half of the indemnity money, and Vergennes consolidated his victory in the cause of peace and profit by arranging a treaty of alliance with the United Provinces. Thus he gained another ally for his country and its merchants.

The complete collapse of the Bavarian exchange project was another reverse for Joseph. Again he secured the assent of the elector of the Palatinate to cede Bavaria to Austria in exchange for the Austrian Netherlands, except the provinces of Luxembourg and Namur, which would go to France as the reward for her consent. Vergennes was momentarily tempted to endorse the transaction, but soon returned to his course and refused his consent except on the condition that Frederick also agreed. Such delicate phraseology was an obvious rejection, for Frederick encouraged the Duke of Zweibrücken to withstand both Russian and Austrian pressure and refuse his consent as heir presumptive to the proposal. Here, for a second time, Catherine abandoned Joseph in his hour of need. She remained unmoved by his veiled threats that the price of his continued collaboration in the east was her loyal support in this crisis. However, by his menacing tactics Joseph played squarely into the hands of Frederick, for he gave the latter precisely the opportunity he needed to pose as the protector of "Germanic liberties."[30] By a final desperate effort the slowly dying ruler of Prussia created his League of Princes in January, 1785. With Prussia, Saxony, and Hanover as its core, reinforced later by the adherence of Brunswick, Mainz, Hesse-Cassel, Baden, and the Thuringian states, the *Fürstenbund* stood on guard so long as Frederick lived, a rampart against Joseph's aggression.

The emperor tried to break the bonds which linked him to Catherine, bitter over her failure to come to his aid. But Kaunitz gave him no encouragement from Vienna for a rapprochement with Prussia, while Hertzberg blocked all efforts at the foreign office at Berlin.[31] Accepting his fate, Joseph resigned himself to his dubious alliance. Russian-Turkish relations had steadily deteriorated since 1783. The annexed Crimean territory was a standing menace to the sultan's

[30] For a penetrating understanding of Frederick's own tactics, cf. the old work of L. von Ranke, *Die deutschen Mächte und der Fürstenbund*, 2 vols. (Leipzig, 1872).

[31] See Lord, *op. cit.*, ch. ii, for the course of negotiations; and for Prince Henry cf. in addition to the work of Easum already cited, P. Bailleu, "Graf Hertzberg," in *Historische Zeitschrift*, XLII (1879).

forces; the new town of Kherson on the Dnieper had a powerful arsenal; the naval base of Sevastopol was being built; and a Russian fleet lay at anchor in the Black Sea. To the east, Georgia had fallen under Russia's protection; while in the west, Catherine's agents were fomenting disorders in the Balkan provinces. Precarious was the peace in that autumn of 1786 when the tsarina decided to investigate conditions at first hand in the newly acquired southern provinces. Assured that she had the whip hand over Joseph, she invited him to accompany her, actually of course to inveigle him into underwriting a military campaign for the realization of the "Grand Plan." Joseph flared up over the nonchalant insolence of the "Catherinized princess of Zerbst," who had studiously added her invitation as a postscript to a letter. But wise old Kaunitz calmed him, and as the year closed the emperor sent word that he would come. His mood of rankling irritation still persisted and was to turn into deep resentment when he met Catherine in the following spring at Kherson.

It was on this occasion of their journey to the Crimea that the imaginative Potemkin surpassed himself by erecting his famous one-street villages and in staging enthusiastic welcomes to the two sovereigns.[32] Joseph was not deceived, either by the villages or by Catherine's laborious efforts to involve him. The *Memoirs* of the Prince de Ligne, and the Comte de Ségur, both Russophiles, attest his annoyance and suspicion. On reading the inscription "The Way to Byzantium" on the gates of Kherson the angry Hapsburg exploded: "What I want is Silesia, and war with Turkey will not give me that." But he was too far committed to withdraw and his freedom of choice was gone. Their flotilla reached the Crimea in June, Joseph more morose than ever; and at Sevastopol the startling news of the insurrection in Belgium reached him. Abruptly, he took leave of the tsarina and speeded back to his capital.

The difficulties of the two rulers had only begun, for the Turks were poised for action. Incited by Hertzberg and encouraged by England, they presented an ultimatum for the restitution of the Crimea and the end of Russian control in Georgia. And when Catherine rejected their demands, they declared war upon Russia (August, 1787). This brusque

---

[32] Theresia Adamczyk, "Die Reise Katharinas II. nach Südrussland im Jahre 1787," in *Jahrbuch für Kultur und Geschichte der Slaven* (Breslau, 1930), N. F. Bd., VI, 25-53.

démarche took Potemkin completely by surprise. His own preparations were far from completed. Though he wrote of evacuating the Crimea, Catherine implored him "to take courage," meaning to assume the offensive without waiting for the enemy to strike. Invoking the terms of their alliance she appealed to Joseph for military support. The emperor responded in the only way that self-consideration counseled: He deployed the finest army that Austria had turned out in the century against the Turkish line of the Danube and the Save—and he also set himself to prevent his royal ally from getting more than her share.

As for his Gallic ally, the France of Vergennes adhered to appeasement. Vergennes would let nothing, not even good faith, interfere with his long-range project of using the foreign office to advance commercial interests. Having once deserted his Turkish ally over the Crimea in 1783, Vergennes had diplomatic precedent to fall back upon for a fresh betrayal. Through Ségur he negotiated a trade treaty with St. Petersburg (January, 1787) which gave French merchants terms as favorable as those enjoyed by their British competitors. But through his ambassador at Constantinople, Choiseul-Gouffier, he excused in advance the French sacrifice of the "Turkish barbarians" to the mercy of the civilized Slavs. When the war came, France practiced neutrality for herself and counseled resignation for the Porte. This decision was worse than a crime; it was a blunder and an overwhelming diplomatic disaster.

The moment had come, with Russia and Austria engaged in war and France pursuing an ignominious diplomacy which revealed her weakness, for all those states whose security had been threatened or whose influence eclipsed by the Bourbon-Hapsburg-Russian machinations to reassert themselves. Prussian agents busily incited revolt against Joseph in Hungary and Belgium, seeking meantime to coerce Poland into ceding Danzig and Thorn. Sweden saw her opportunity to recover South Finland from the Russians; and England profited by the occasion to make her successful effort to regain the prestige in which she had been so sorely lacking for the preceding quarter of a century.

England's opportunity came with the turn of events after 1785 in the United Provinces, where the bitter factional conflict between the Republicans representing the richer merchants and the Patriots representing the more radical petty bourgeoisie was keeping the country in constant turmoil. Not only did the English envoy, James Harris, have to make his way cautiously through the intricacies of the political squabbles, but Britain itself was not ready to turn the domestic struggle in Holland to her advantage until Pitt the Younger had completed his reorganization and reconstruction at home.[33]

By the end of 1786 Britain was ready to work together informally with Prussia in utilizing the international aspects of the Dutch domestic strife to their mutual diplomatic gain. While the Patriots were the instruments of France, and French officers had helped them establish a volunteer legion to threaten the power of the Stadtholder, the Stadtholder himself, William V, was the grandson of George II, and his wife was the sister of Frederick William II, the new king of Prussia.

The crisis in the United Provinces reached its height in midsummer, 1787, when the Free Corps of the Patriots stopped the carriage of the royal princess and with stark democratic impropriety placed its royal incumbent in custody. "If her brother is not the dirtiest and shabbiest of kings," sputtered the English foreign minister with high Britannic choler, "he must resent it, *coûte que coûte*."[34] Frederick William II did resent it, to the point of threatening war. Spurred by Hertzberg's animus against the French-Austrian bloc and the personal indignation of the king, official Prussia turned markedly bellicose. Like Pitt, who was now prepared for action, Hertzberg was certain that France would not support her Dutch agent. The master improviser Vergennes had died in February, and the inept Montmorin who had taken over the foreign office lacked his predecessor's genius for negotiating profits for France. Besides, the financial crisis had deepened and his country teetered on the brink of bankruptcy. Promises or no to the Patriots, France was in no position to fight and both Prussia and England knew it.

After many years, circumstances were bringing England and Prussia together again, and the end of Britain's inglorious isolation was almost in sight. Montmorin played for time, but England hastened her naval preparations and the Prussians concentrated 20,000 troops on the Dutch

[33] For Harris, consult *Diaries and Correspondence of James Harris,* ed. by the Third Earl of Malmesbury, 4 vols. (London, 1845).
[34] Lodge, *op. cit.,* 172.

frontier. He planned to propose joint French-Prussian mediation to the contending Dutch factions, but the Prussians acted first. They presented an ultimatum to the Dutch Estates-General and speedily implemented ultimatum with invasion. For the Duke of Brunswick the campaign was a mere military procession. The anti-Stadtholder coalition collapsed, the urban merchant oligarchies repudiating the Patriots and opening the town gates to the invader. Within a few weeks' time he had routed the rebels and restored the authority of the House of Orange. The Prussian army and the English fleet then stood on guard to safeguard the victory. Pitt pressed his advantage to the full and on October 23, 1787, he compelled France to make a formal *démenti* of all intentions of giving military aid to her now sorely beaten and divided Dutch allies. This open declaration, coming together with France's diplomatic debacle in the east, completed her humiliation in Europe, where her prestige sank to its nadir. England on the other hand was again a force on the Continent. Allowing for exaggerated patriotic emphasis, Sir Richard Lodge's verdict remains substantially exact: "Europe was startled by the sudden re-emergence of a state which for a quarter of a century had stood aloof from continental affairs, and only four years before had seemed to fix the seal to its decline by the extorted grant of independence to its revolted colonists."[35]

Within a half-year Prussia and England came still closer together by concluding separate treaties of alliance with the Dutch. Only the final step of uniting them directly with one another remained to be taken. But Hertzberg had to show his monarch something more advantageous from such a move than the enhancement of British prestige. He finally evolved an infinitely convoluted plan which had the merit of remedying the difficulty from the Prussian point of view but also the defect of running strongly counter to British interests in the Near East. For at long last, British merchants, together with the imperialist-minded premier, had come to the realization that their interests were best served not by weakening but by strengthening the already "sick man of Europe."[36] Consequently Hertzberg's proposals received no encouragement at London.

35 Lodge, *op. cit.*, ch. vi.
36 For England's almost unbelievable earlier disregard of Russian moves and French intrigue in the eastern Mediterranean, see the work of Gerhard already cited, and also

Undeterred, the British envoys, Ewart at Berlin and Harris at the Hague, stuck to the main business at hand: to forge the triple alliance, not as an all-embracing agency for universal peace, but as an instrument of British security. The two youthful envoys conducted their negotiations brilliantly, overcame mutual suspicions, and on August 13, 1788, succeeded in having the definitive treaty between England and Prussia signed. Together with the two separate treaties with the United Provinces, it constituted the Triple Alliance. It was as England wished, a defensive alliance, the two countries pledging themselves to support each other in war and to uphold the settlement of 1787 in Dutch affairs. A secret clause committed them also "to act in perfect and intimate concord in relation to the war between the Imperial Courts and the Ottoman Empire," thus protecting British imperial interests in the Mediterranean.

The new alliance had its first test in the Swedish invasion of Russian Finland. It met the challenge to the peace in the north, holding Russia in leash on the Baltic, while simultaneously deterring France from interfering in behalf of Sweden. The subsequent history of the alliance, like the Russian-Austrian war against the Ottoman Empire, soon merged into the general course of European developments during the maelstrom of the French Revolution. And in this storm the older dynastic and commercial rivalries were liquidated, indeed, the very foundations of the balance-of-power diplomacy shattered, in a life-and-death struggle between the old and new ideals of human relations.

V. DEBITS AND CREDITS

All the great powers, Russia, Prussia, Austria, France, and England, profited *qua* states from their aggressive expansionism. The only victims were the lesser countries and the home populations that footed the bill of militarism, navalism, and balance-of-power diplomacy. Imperial Russia benefited greatly from the thrusts and counter-thrusts on the international stage, acquiring over 200,000 square miles of territory and nearly 7,000,000 new subjects. At the outset of her reign Catherine seized *de facto* control of Courland (nominally a dependency

---

F. Charles-Roux, *L'Angleterre, l'isthme de Suez, et l'Egypte au dix-huitième siècle* (Paris, 1923).

of Poland) with its ice-free ports of Libau and Windau. Her share in the first partition of Poland completed the century-old economic penetration of her weak neighbor's land and fortified Russia's frontier to the west. To the south she acquired a secure frontier on the Black and Azov seas (at the expense of the Porte) along with free navigation westward through the Straits and the Bosporus. Her intercession as mediator between Prussia and Austria won Russia great diplomatic prestige in central Europe. Astonishing trade increases matched the heightened military strength and diplomatic standing. The already lucrative Baltic trade profited by the addition of the two excellent harbors in Courland. The trade with the Middle and the Far East remained considerable, and the enormous potentialities of the Black Sea-Mediterranean route for linking southern Russia with southern and western Europe were still to be exploited to the full.[37]

To Prussia, Frederick brought extraordinary prestige, strategic military frontiers, and the standing of a first-rate military power. Not less valuable were Silesia and the Polish provinces for their economic assets: both rich in natural resources and fresh manpower for the army and the former boasting great textile manufactures as well. These gains notwithstanding, foreign trade lagged far to the rear of Prussia's state-sponsored industrial program and resplendent military position. The "House of Austria" fared least well of the central and eastern powers. Galicia was, of course, a valuable acquisition, as were the territories of Bukovina and Fiume. But the Hapsburgs did not regain their lost guidance of Germanic affairs. Silesia was not recovered. Twice Joseph was balked in his Bavarian exchange. The Italian appanages grew more restive, and Hungary and Belgium broke into open revolt. Neither in its trade nor in its territorial aspects did the costly *Drang nach Osten* pay the Hapsburgs dividends.

In the main France's international ledger was kept by Vergennes, who baffles easy cataloguing. Like Joseph and Catherine he faced both ways, at once nationalist and mercantilist, internationalist and free-trader. Only a reluctant physiocrat, he employed bureaucratic controls at home over non-co-operative individual traders. But an advanced critic of narrow mercantilism, he had broad views on the international economic relations of his country. Peace and trade were indivisible in

[37] D. Gerhard, *England und der Aufstieg Russlands* (Munich, 1933).

his eyes. The wider and stronger the web of commercial treaties linking France to her continental neighbors, the more effectively would
it reinforce his diplomacy of pacification. Before his victorious war of
revenge against England, peace in Europe had been necessary in order
to leave France unhampered in her military effort. After 1783 peace
was still needed in order to have France exploit the victory, and
through peace and trade regain her lost eminence in world affairs.

Consequently, alongside the patriot who had his country's greatness
as his ultimate objective there was the internationalist who knew that
his policy entailed sacrifices from individual French merchants. Despite
strong protests he persevered in the economic liberalism that increasingly alienated the provincial merchants, such as opening the colonial
trade in the West Indies to foreigners and ending the regime of
reciprocally injurious prohibitive tariffs. The famous commercial
treaty of 1786 with England was an effort on his part to consolidate the
provisions of the military settlement of 1783. Confident of France's
ultimate future, he was resigned to a temporary sacrifice of French
industry in order to divert British sentiments from military revenge
to peaceful commercial profit and concomitantly to spare the weakened
French treasury the strain of continuous military expenditure.

This policy, in its diplomatic aspects, eventuated in the tragic eclipse
of France and the resurgence of England. On the other hand, his
economic internationalism unquestionably accelerated that remarkable
increase in France's foreign trade whose value was not to be equaled
again until after the middle of the nineteenth century. Paradoxically,
it was this very flowering of private wealth that accentuated the revolutionary temper of the self-assured merchant capitalists. They turned
away from Vergennes because his economic liberalism in the service
of the absolute monarchy gave the *ancien régime* a new lease on life,
whereas what they wanted was its end.

The balance sheet was also very favorable to England, where capitalist enterprise succeeded most of all in liquidating older political
jealousies. By 1789 the country had fully recovered from war and dis-
comfitures of defeat. The gloomy prognostications of 1783 had all
been proven false. After her defeat, her oligarchy's share in the American import trade probably grew greater than it had been in colonial
days. As an ally of the United Provinces she was assured of navigation

on the Scheldt and had a necessary point of entry for trade with the Continent. As partner of Prussia and mistress of Hanover, she was in a position to build up a trading clientele in Germany. As dominant member of the Triple Alliance and as Russia's greatest customer she enjoyed preponderant influence in the North Sea and Baltic trade. With Gibraltar hers and already patron of Portugal, she held Bourbon Spain in check; and supporter of the territorial integrity of the Ottoman Empire, she had access to the eastern Mediterranean for her trade with the Far East. Through the Eden Treaty with France she gained a new market of highest value for her manufactured goods and, more even than in France, her trade increased to unparalleled heights, for the most part following the flag, but still profitable when flowing past or away from the flag.

Chapter Eight

OF HUMAN WELFARE

I. THE WELLSPRINGS OF HUMANITARIANISM

WHILE rulers and statesmen methodically guided their policies by the great mandate of the enlightenment and pursued security and power, they also gave heed to a second imperative. A dominant note of humanitarian protest swelled, as the century advanced, into the chorus of liberal democratic faith. This faith coexisted with the prevailing cultural style which made the world of man seem as orderly as the strong and clear phrases that philosophers used to describe it. It was, for the most part, a rival view to that pattern of a bandbox universe woven by Cartesian, Newtonian, classical, and baroque strands. By its insistence upon toleration of human vagaries and its kindliness of spirit toward man's foibles it stood often at the antipodes of the more sober quest for order and regularity. In itself it was not a revolt against the rational eighteenth century. It was a mood and a mode of thought that polarized many discordant tendencies and brought together many complex and incongruous strivings that were themselves as authentically eighteenth century as Diderot's *Encyclopedia*.

Eighteenth-century humanitarianism must ultimately be referred to the dynamics of social change. The shock of new economic practices, the destruction of the familiar system of communal living, the intensified inter-state rivalries, the shortening of distance and the narrowing of time, all these revolutionary changes permitting man to tap the sources of new knowledge also increased his awareness of social distress and as never before brought the evils of poverty, disease, and hunger to the level of public consciousness. This greater awareness of social injustice represented no fundamental renunciation of the accepted assumptions of business enterprise. Successful promoters of business enterprises, even as they gave serious heed to the health, security, and happiness of their fellowmen and evinced, as a contemporary phrased it, "a disposition to pry into the state of society," still by no means repudiated the tenets of free competition.

Theirs was a weighted temper of sympathy reflecting the preconception of the successful, the conviction that their own prosperity was the prior and indispensable condition for a flow of compensatory blessings to the less fortunate. Not uncharacteristic was the hardheaded and enormously successful Yankee-born Count Rumford, who, after setting up workhouses for the deserving poor, discovered that benevolence was "virtue's prize," and "exquisitely delightful," because it filled him with "inward peace and self-approbation." The social conscience of Dr. John Moore, the complete English liberal, was equally serene. After paying tribute to the resourcefulness of the prosperous merchant, he concluded not without unction that "a man of the character above described, while he is augmenting his own private fortune will enjoy the agreeable reflection that he is likewise increasing the riches and power of his country and giving bread to thousands of his industrious countrymen."[1] A thousand voices echoed Rumford and Moore, in one way or another proclaiming that the wealthy were nature's elect. With the high-minded reformer Joseph Priestley, the liberals discovered that the prosperous were virtually compelled by the laws of natural economics as well as by the dictates of their moral natures to diffuse their wealth through the "lower ranks of society" and use their riches "for the good of the whole."

The attitude toward nature was also a great determinant of the humanitarian ideal. The scientific pattern of an orderly universe, permeated with reason and directed by a benevolent and intelligent force, left little place for the mediaeval Christian cosmogony. The man of reason had no quarrel with the apostolic insistence upon the sanctity of human life or the doctrine of the universal brotherhood of man which were imbedded in Christian ethic. But he rejected all that had developed around the core: the ascetic temper, the fear of the impulses of the flesh, the dogmatic rigidity, and the deferment of man's happiness to the distant future of a celestial hereafter. The vast scientific conquests had made the seventeenth and eighteenth centuries illustrious in optics and astronomy, in botany and biology, in physics

[1] John Moore, *A View of Society and Manners in Italy*, 2 vols. (ed. of 1790), I, 327-328.

and geology. Co-ordinated, all, under the ruling idea of natural law, they revealed worlds both smaller and greater (and in any case, different) than the cosmos of Christianity. The new geography and history, with their discovery of civilizations outside (and in the eyes of many superior to) the Christian commonwealth, and the new psychology, rejecting the Pauline conviction that man was innately depraved, broke down the mediaeval assumption that man's earthly tribulations were a salutary and necessary prelude to his happiness in all eternity. This secularization of religious values gave a decisive stimulus to the trend to end man's sufferings on earth. It spurred immensely the effort to improve his lot here and now rather than prepare him for the lasting joys of heaven. It was the heartening realization of the beneficent utility of science, the invincible assurance that by its methods man could progressively discover the truth that fired his imagination. It was the hope of mastering the physical and social environment that for good or for ill determined his fate that inspired the eighteenth century with an optimism unprecedented, unparalleled, and possibly, unwarranted.

This humanitarian and humanistic temper had a long history behind it, independent of the scientific revolution. It was a reassertion of the average sensual man's cravings for the comforts and pleasures of life. The drift from the ascetic temper to the hedonistic was manifest in the seventeenth century "libertines," those rationalists who persevered in believing without benefit of dogma that the end of life was simply the enjoyment thereof. The temper was joined with the appreciation of the intuitive nature of man, as variously expressed, but perhaps most clearly in the philosophical rhapsodies of Lord Shaftesbury and Francis Hutcheson, whose researches revealed a moral sense in man, a sort of innate affection for good and distrust of evil, of which benevolence was the highest form. To be sure, the vindication of man's natural honesty and worth by an appeal to philosophy and psychology ran into hostile criticism. David Hume savagely satirized its oversimplifications, pointing out in his *Treatise on Human Nature* that human nature was infinitely complex and that man was moved by a number of primitive impulses unrelated to any desire for pleasure. It might be added for the sake of completeness that Hume's classical demolition of the psychological foundations of benevolence had as little appreciable effect upon his contemporaries as his posthumously published dialogues had in diminishing belief in deism.

Men who were anxious to put all revealed religion in the wrong refused themselves the dubious philosophical pleasure of impaling themselves on the horns of the dilemma that tormented the more profound intelligences. They refused to grapple with the problem of why the benevolent force that governed the universe sanctioned the existence of evil. The average thinker of good will was loath to concede that natural reason failed to prove the existence of natural goodness in man. He would not take his stand with Hume and aver, "A person seasoned with a just sense of the imperfections of natural reason will fly to revealed truth with the greatest avidity. . . . To be a philosophical Sceptic is, in a man of letters, the first and essential step towards being a sound believing Christian." Nor would he, convinced despite himself by the existence of evil that God was lacking in a moral sense or indeed that there was no God, move forward to materialism and proclaim despairingly with Diderot that "everything is in perpetual flux"; that "birth, life and death are just changes of shape"; that will and liberty were only "the latest impulsion of desire and aversion"; and that vice and virtue themselves had nothing whatsoever to do with reason or grace but were only the fortuitous consequences of being "born with a fortunate or unfortunate disposition."

Such nice refinements upon thought were caviare to the general. Turning away from the double-edged tool of syllogistic logic, men reexamined, as the fuller logic of living demanded they should, the infinitely various ways in which human goodness naturally expressed itself. They turned to the lessons of history and geography and applied themselves to coping with the practical exigencies of everyday life in order to find fresh examples and gain new corroboration for their conviction that virtue was indeed only "fidelity in fulfilling obligations that reason imposes." Since they were assured in advance of their quest, since they knew deep in their hearts that under all its external variations, universal human nature remained constant and good, all the routes that they followed led to the inevitable triumph of the conviction that benevolence was the distinguishing trait of that supreme creation, man.[2]

[2] Carl Becker, *The Heavenly City of the Eighteenth Century Philosophers* (New Haven, 1932), chs. ii and iii.

Most of all, however, the devotees of benevolence fell back on the promptings of the heart to corroborate their faith. The voicing of these claims of a common humanity coincided with an elusive change of atmosphere arising from sources indifferent or hostile to intellectual reasoning. The age of reason converged upon the age of sentiment. It moved toward that mood of repentance which expressed itself, as Condorcet phrased it with noble naïveté, in "compassion for all the ills that afflict the human race." This new mood, like the arguments of the rationalists, appealed for the alleviation of suffering among the poor and the oppressed. It besought men of good will to eliminate cruelty and diffuse happiness among the miserable and the wretched. It was part of the universal phenomenon that discovered the intangible and cohesive forces of national traditions and turned away from a rationalist and invertebrate cosmopolitanism. It was in large part a reproachful supplement to arid rationalism, correcting its failure to appreciate the strength of human instincts and emotions.

This revulsion against the rationalist psychology which recognized as real only things of immediate perception had many contradictory facets. Into it of course flowed the strains of the hedonists' enjoyment of living. It satisfied the urge to be generous and charitable without being spurred by dogma or prodded by calculation. The mood conveyed the protest of gentle and kindly spirits, themselves secure against adversity, who could not accept the complacency of the rich, their earthbound practicality, and the brutalities which they condoned. It contained the basic elements of a social-democratic faith, implicitly condemning existing injustices by opposing the primitive and rural folkways to the urban and classically correct. The new temper revolted alike against the admonitions of orthodoxy which bade one to suffer evil and the shallow optimism of the rationalists with their callous solution that whatever is, is right, and their evasive conclusion that all was for the best in this best of all possible worlds. To it adhered, also, the irritated grievances of respectable petty bourgeois against aristocratic skeptics who scorned their own "enthusiasm" and their yearning for a more personal and vital religious experience.[3]

This middle-class yearning for a religious faith with richer color and with an intensity deeper than the conventionalized "lively transports"

[3] Dr. Johnson's *Dictionary* (1755) defined enthusiasm tartly as "a vain belief of private revelation, a vain confidence of divine favour or communication."

corresponded to the evangelical fervor and the resurgent fundamental-
ism that swept the ranks of the poor. It coincided with the currents of
Pietism in the Germanies and of Methodism in England and the
American colonies with their fervid emotionalism and their ecstatic
glorification of piety. Consequently, the strands of a cultural counterrevolution were also woven into this pattern of sensibility. As the century waned, the dependence upon the intuitive and the personal broadened into a systematic reaction against the hopefulness of the natural-
rights philosophy. The appeal of the primitive or the original was
captured by an ideology that turned against egalitarianism and utopianism and counseled, instead, resignation to fate. But in a thousand
different ways the earlier temper probed into the wounds of society,
searching for the real man of feeling whose passions would move at
the command of virtue.

There was much bathos in this wave of *sensibilité*. Not a little of
it became an empty parade of sentiment that answered the emotional
needs of a blasé generation. There were among the well-wishers of
mankind men whose philanthropy was not unaccompanied by the
expectation of handsome financial dividends. In their midst were
utopians and egalitarians, whose despair disarmed them from positive
participation in relieving humanity's woes. Their numbers counted the
irresolute who resolved their doubts in mystic ceremonies; and they
included youthful romantics who wept for the wretched, braved the
authorities, and at thirty made their peace with the world. Yet by far
the greater number of these *coeurs sensibles* redeemed what was
mawkish in their raptures by devoting themselves with resolute
determination to making a reality of their envisioned terrestrial
paradise.

Profoundly stirred by the spectacle of human misery and convinced
that the reformation of society was the civic responsibility of every
right-minded citizen, they gave passionately of their time and energies
to the achievement of communal happiness. With myriad voices these
anonymous workers preached the moral loftiness and the social
grandeur of altruism; and in a great variety of ways their deeds
demonstrated the sincerity of their convictions.

Both the rationalists, therefore, whose sense of the dignity of human
life turned them against the stark realities of cruelty and suffering, and

the sentimentalists, whose impotent indignation turned into sorrow for the victims of civilization, contributed to a new social outlook. With an earnestness and a resolution charged with generous emotions, they renewed under a secular aegis the old messianic enterprise of human salvation. They fused into one the individualist contention of their age that the highest happiness came from altruism with the older Christian ideal that helping one's neighbor led to salvation. Frustrated, many of them, in their own lifetime, since the ideal could only be imperfectly realized, they fastened their hopes, these seekers of Utopia, on the prospect of future earthly happiness that their children and their children's children would enjoy. They synthesized the two freely flowing currents of rationalist and sentimental discontent in the appealing myth of human progress and perfectibility.

This revolutionary faith in progress and the perfectibility of man was a modern phenomenon, for until the eighteenth century only the faintest intimations of its temper existed. It was essentially the product of that century, the very core of the "new history" of the *philosophes*, and a conception utterly alien to the mediaeval image of history as the unrolling of the divine scroll. Though at its most depressing moments history may have been for Gibbon "little more than the register of the crimes, follies and misfortunes of mankind," nevertheless it remained essentially "philosophy teaching by examples." Thus construed, it became the record of man's experience, a record triumphantly corroborating the teachings of reason. The *philosophes* were least of all interested in what differentiated man from man, and most of all interested in what linked mankind together. Their concern was to extract from historical experience confirmation of the great truth proclaimed by reason: that under the distracting play of surface differences human nature everywhere remained constant in all recorded eternity. For them all Hume's "constant and invariant principles of human nature" meant constantly and invariably good—humane and generous, tolerant and just, capable in brief of assuming a rational responsibility for man's fate in an always insecure world. If such was the function of historical investigation, it was clearly not necessary to strain for pedantic fullness of factual information, or even to have the facts speak for themselves in a conventionally correct chronological order. What mattered was to have the examples of history demonstrate that wherever the fundamental attributes of human nature were repressed and denied, as for instance under the rule of tyrants and priests, then humanity itself was deprived of its birthright. What mattered even more was to have history demonstrate that where this constant and invariant human nature was allowed expression, as during those four happy ages of Pericles, the Antonines, the Renaissance, and the enlightenment, the arts and sciences flourished and man lived happily, free from strife and oppression.[4]

Thus did Voltaire re-examine the past and compose his brilliant short history of civilization, *Essay on Manners and Customs*, of which Grimm remarked that it was a truly excellent book to place in the hands of the young to teach them to love justice, humanity, and benevolence.[5] Thus, too, did Gibbon retrace, with a cadenced and majestic dignity that set off the sharpness of his ironic musings, the stages in the decline and fall of his cherished classical civilization. What a warning and reproach he conveyed to the destroyers of his own day, the new religious zealots and the *coeurs sensibles*, as in his sober pages, impregnated with learned vindictiveness, he mourned the disaster that had overwhelmed mankind when Christianity seeped into the tissues of Roman paganism. So, too, the Abbé Raynal in his rhetorical, inaccurate, and diffused compendium, *Philosophical and Political History of European Settlements and Commerce in the Two Indies*. But his was an intellectual potpourri that for all its defects, or perhaps because of its defects, scored one of the most spectacular literary successes of the century and reached the hearts of learned and untutored alike. With a relentless profusion of detail this "Bible of two worlds" depicted the cruelties and the indignities that European traders, officials, and soldiers, together with Christian missionaries, had inflicted upon the helpless Negro and Indian inhabitants of the colonies. As the reader suffered these lacerations of his sensibility, he gained from Raynal's public confession of the crimes and follies of European civilization a sense of vicarious personal forgiveness. This was the temper that Grimm unconsciously reflected in his judgment

---

[4] For formal discussions of the new history there are E. Fueter, *Histoire de l'historiographie moderne*, tr. from the German (Paris, 1914), Bk. IV; and J. W. Thompson, *History of Historical Writing*, 2 vols. (New York, 1942), II, ch. xxxviii; for more informal and more penetrating analyses, Becker, *op. cit.*, ch. iii; and J. B. Black, *The Art of History* (New York, 1926).

[5] Grimm, *op. cit.*, IV (November 15, 1766), 310.

that "since Montesquieu's *Esprit des Lois* our literature has perhaps produced no monument worthier to pass to remotest posterity and to consecrate the progress of our enlightenment."[6]
More than any other did Condorcet's history elaborate upon the idea of the progress of human enlightenment and the perfectibility of man. The idea was common intellectual coin, but its fullest formulation and elaboration came from his pen in 1794, when he himself lay in hiding from the Jacobins and the high noon of the enlightenment had already faded into the troubled twilight of the revolutionary conflict. His *Esquisse d'un tableau historique des progrès de l'esprit humain* (translated a year later into English as *Outlines of an Historical View of the Progress of the Human Mind*) was indeed the last will and testament of the age of enlightenment, mirroring all the *philosophes'* invincibly naïve faith in the intelligence and good will of man. The argument is grounded upon the premise that the evidence of historical experience proves the fact of progress and discloses the laws of human and social advance. In the body of the *Esquisse* Condorcet traces with pride the course of mankind's glorious ascent from primitive society to the age of enlightenment. But the final chapter, the "Tenth Epoch," best reveals the temper and gives the flavor of the work. There the author, projecting the progress of mankind upon the time scale of the future, concludes with a paean of rejoicing for the glories of man still to be on earth. It was a glorious vision that he conjured up for his contemporaries: a world free from military strife and the cruelties of conquest, a world liberated from ignorance and disease, a federation of man bestowing the blessings of security and prosperity upon all. It was the century's most appealing project, its most endearing myth, and the Ultima Thule of enthusiasts of human welfare.[7]

II. TOLERANCE AND EDUCATION

Deism, or natural religion, was an important way station along the highway of human progress. Rooted in the newer attitude toward

6 *Ibid.*, X (July, 1774), 453-455 for the whole passage.
7 For Condorcet's place in the development of the concept, see J. B. Bury, *History of the Idea of Progress* (New York, ed. of 1932), and for a thoughtful analysis of the *Esquisse*, J. S. Schapiro, *Condorcet and the Rise of Liberalism* (New York, 1934), ch. xiii.

nature and fortified by the new science, its tenets carried the day among the wise, the worldly, and the well-to-do. The trunk alone of religion was left after deism chopped off the gnarled branches of ceremony and ritual: only the existence of a Supreme Being; the consciousness of good and evil that permitted man to live virtuously in obedience to His will; and the reality of the future life in which the supreme architect of the universe would reward the good and punish the evil. Everything else was a pious fraud perpetrated by monks and priests.

Naturally, things were to be different with the masses. Voltaire chose his words with the care of a man who knew what he was about, when he wrote to his friend Frederick of Prussia: "Your Majesty will do the human race an eternal service in extirpating this infamous superstition [Christianity], I do not say among the rabble, who are not worthy of being enlightened and who are apt for every yoke; I say among the well-bred, among those who wish to think."[8] The "well-bred," moreover, were of no mind to go beyond the comfortable doctrines of natural religion. To flaunt, even publish, one's doubts about the validity of the deistic arguments could only frustrate the designs of rational Christianity, as John Adams once unctuously interpreted them, to make good men, good magistrates, and good subjects. To give heed to the urge for a religion charged with more stirring emotional intensity would manifestly be yielding to vulgar "enthusiasm," and transgressing the borders of what was seemly and decorous. Worse, of course, yielding to the urge would only lead to disturbance of the social peace, for what limitation to man's greed and folly, especially untutored and unpropertied man, would remain, once it was bruited about that there was no omniscient eternal ruler, sternly applying penalties against transgressors of His law?

Hume and the more tenderhearted Diderot could see clearly that deism was a way station along the road of religious disbelief as well as a milestone on the highway of progress. Helvétius and Holbach would sweep forward uncompromisingly to materialism. But such extremists were few, their adherents fewer still, and deism prevailed in fashionable and middle-class society.

The Catholic defenders hit back against natural religion, nowhere

8 Quoted in P. Smith, *op. cit.*, II, 501.

so stanchly as in France. It is only part of the folklore of liberalism to make their numerical following slight and them themselves bereft of wit and benighted in view.[9] But they fought a losing battle from the start, partly because they were forced to employ the arguments and the terminology of their adversaries and partly because the church was mined from within. The goodness of the many thousands of anonymous servants who labored in the vineyards of the Lord was outweighed, no doubt unfairly, in the eighteenth-century scales, by the evil reputation of their superiors. Bitter doctrinal disputes sapped the vitality of the church. Nepotism, pluralism, and absenteeism; luxurious and occasionally profligate living among the prelates; persecution of dissenters and ill-concealed skepticism in its own midst—such were the elements that ecclesiastics variously and gratuitously contributed to the decline of their organization and the lowering of its prestige.

The defenders were especially at a disadvantage because deism involved legal, political, and social problems for which the credo of the church had no solution. Despite the intellectual cautiousness of the deists, their alert and ambitious middle-class adherents widened the issues at stake. They rallied behind an outlook that gave intellectual certification to their worldly and secular interests. The emerging sentiment of bourgeois nationalism buttressed their commonsense positivism. This bourgeois temper was colored by a strong bias against the wealth and the fiscal prerogatives of the church as a corporation, an institution that deflected capital from public enterprise and a corporate body whose educational practices palpably disqualified the younger generation from coping with the exigencies of secular and national problems. The princes, too, profited by the opportunity to renew the struggle against their own ancient enemy at Rome, placing themselves, in the Catholic states, in charge of the struggle against the spiritual power. They did so not necessarily out of hostility to the dogma of the church, but out of the obligations inherent in their positions as secular rulers. In this modern phase of the mediaeval struggle for supremacy, in this effort to unify, centralize, and regularize the authority of the crown, the princes also had the guarded support of

---

9 The solid and discriminating study of R. R. Palmer, *Catholics and Unbelievers in Eighteenth Century France* (Princeton, 1939), far surpasses the polemical work of A. Monod, *De Pascal à Chateaubriand: Les défenseurs français du Christianisme de 1670 à 1802* (Paris, 1916), chs. viii-x.

the prelates of their own country. Under the cover of the anti-curial campaign the national episcopate revived claims that had not been successfully enunciated since the defeat of the conciliar movement at the Council of Trent, especially the right of each national church, acting through its bishops, to gain autonomy from the Roman curia.

Thus deism established itself on the Continent. Without much vitality in England, which had been its cradle, it became the lowest common denominator of belief among the French *philosophes*, who strove to reduce religious beliefs to the rules of order, as Boileau had once attempted to do for the muses. In the Iberian peninsula it joined with anti-clericalism, while in Italy it blended subtly with the attack upon the temporal claims of the papacy and pleaded for a return to the apostolic simplicity and the democratic rule of the primitive church. Militant deism sank no roots in Germany where a learned critique of revelation found no publisher during the author's life and few readers after his death, when Lessing, the famous author of *Nathan the Wise*, edited and published parts of it under the title of *Fragments of an Anonymous Work Found at Wolfenbüttel*. Lessing, the parson's son, also condemned himself to noble but sterile labor in composing the *Education of the Human Race*, in which he synthesized reason with the basic Christian doctrine and sought to convince a small public that the religious evolution of mankind was only its progressive education in the knowledge of God. For there was sustenance at other tables for his more cautious and more numerous compatriots who wished to be known as enlightened without being branded as unbelievers. They could be edified by almost any random issue of the "moral weeklies" which all century long preached a diluted Christianity to the earnest middle classes; or they could be uplifted by Gellert and Klopstock and lesser rhapsodic enthusiasts who coated their brand of substitute Christianity with sugary sentimentality.[10]

Not only did natural religion present itself in more or less diluted form, but one could arrive at deism by following other roads than reason. Rousseau, for instance, was also a deist. Unlike the philosophers whom he detested, he founded his belief in God not on reason, which

---

[10] For the two streams of deistic influence among the German vanguard, cf. C. Gebauer, *Deutsche Kulturgeschichte der Neuzeit* (Berlin, 1922), Bk. III, and G. Steinhausen, *Geschichte der deutschen Kultur*. Volksausgabe. (Berlin, 1933), ch. x.

was only "a sea of uncertainty and doubt" with "neither bottom nor limit," but on that internal sentiment which directed his belief independently of his reason. "If there is no God," he says through the mouth of his Savoyard Vicar, "the wicked is right and the good man is nothing but a fool." But not by following "dogmatic self-assertive, haughty philosophy" does he reach that conclusion. He follows conscience: "Conscience! Conscience! Divine instinct, immortal voice from heaven, sure guide for a creature ignorant and finite indeed, yet intelligent and free; infallible judge of good and evil, making man like to God. In thee consists the excellence of man's nature and the morality of his actions."

It was reserved for Kant's *Critique of Pure Reason* (1781) to go beyond Rousseau's eloquence and passion and posit the rational justification of faith. The argument by which the great German idealist philosopher establishes his distinction between the phenomenal world where the Newtonian law of causality obtained and the noumenal world which was governed by the inner law of the categorical imperative assuredly is complex. For the most part, happily, it is also irrelevant to this discussion. His conclusion, however, which linked the Rousseauist impatience with reason to the nineteenth-century repudiation of reason, is highly relevant. In concluding that we must have faith, since science can neither affirm that that which we choose to do is wrong nor conversely deny that it may be right, he wished only to prove that science had its limitations. Unfortunately, he succeeded worse than might have been wished, for by implication he seemed to give mankind intellectual validity to believe whatsoever it chose to believe, whether consonant with reason, beyond reason, or simply without reason.

With the powerful as well as the wise behind it, victorious deism demolished all justifications of religious persecution and installed the ideal of tolerance in the hearts of its adherents. The movement for religious toleration varied greatly in intensity, ranging from comparatively ineffectual campaigns in behalf of Protestants in Spain, or in behalf of both Catholic and Protestant dissenters in the Scandinavian states, to the concerted and successful effort in France to win civil status for the Huguenots. Apart from dissident Christians, the Jews were the favored-objects of the reformers' and writers' solicitude. With one accord these advocates appealed to history to show that the rights of the Jews both as men and as citizens had been denied them. Only by ending the special rules and regulations governing Jewish existence, argued the would-be emancipators, could governments convert them into good citizens contributing freely and fully to national life.[11]

The most exuberant confidence was displayed in the capacity of enlightenment to emancipate mankind from the tyranny of ignorance and persecution. The famed Italian *philosophe* Filangieri echoed this hope. Writing in his *Scienza della Legislazione*, whose very title bespeaks his temper, he said:

So long as the evils that afflict humanity are still uncured; so long as error and prejudice are allowed to perpetuate them; so long as the truth is limited to the few and the privileged, and concealed from the greater part of the human genus and from the kings, so long will it remain the duty of the philosopher to preach the truth, to sustain it, to promote it, and to illustrate it. . . . Citizen of every place and of every age, the philosopher has the whole of the universe for his country and earth itself for his school, and posterity will be his disciples.[12]

Helvétius succinctly expressed the belief of all the reformers that men could be got at from the outside by education and made into useful citizens through subordinating their private interests to the public good. There was a pedagogic science, he claimed, of achieving this felicitous end, a science whose principles were as certain as those of geometry. The physiological differences among men were unimportant. All men had the same interests and the same senses, and all that they were depended on how those interests were served and those senses appealed to. "If I could demonstrate that man is but the product of his education, I should have undoubtedly revealed a great truth to the nations. They would then know that they hold within their own hands the instrument of greatness and happiness, and that to be happy and powerful is only a matter of perfecting the science of education."[13]

Rousseau's *Emile*, which was a counterblast to Helvétius and the

[11] Cf. C. W. Dohm, *Uber die bürgerliche Verbesserung der Juden* (Berlin, 1781), tr. into French in 1782 under the title of *De la réforme politique des Juifs.*

[12] Quoted in F. de Sanctis, *History of Italian Literature*, 2 vols. (New York, 1931), II, 831-832.

[13] Quoted in E. Halévy, *The Growth of Philosophical Radicalism* (New York, 1928), 18 ff.

sensationalist psychologists, cannot be evaluated correctly unless one understands from the start that Rousseau was writing of man under the aspect of eternity: of what education should be in that same ideal state of nature which would be administered politically under the terms of the social contract. The work was an instrument for venting his scorn at the environmentalists, whose educational assumptions, he argued, failed utterly to recognize the true nature of man. Essentially, the educational system advanced in *Emile* is a series of negative commandments, the intent of which was to safeguard the healthy primitive impulses of the child against the mischievous tamperings of the intellectualists. Characteristically exaggerating his position, Rousseau almost hysterically refutes Locke's thesis that virtue is put into the mind by instruction. He assumes that the natural instincts of the child are both correct and good. Hence the function of education "consists, not in teaching virtue or truth, but in preserving the heart from vice and the spirit from error." The assumption animating the somewhat fantastic training to which the young Emile was exposed was therefore his right to conduct his own self-education. For all its shortcomings—and no professional educationalist has had difficulty in pointing them out—the insistence that the primary concern of education should be the development of the unique potentialities and the flowering of the full personality of the child was a long and important step forward in emancipating children from the tyranny of adults. And in Rousseau's clear recognition of the profound significance of adolescent change in the growing child and his great stress on the practical and the useful, on physical education, and on learning through doing, he inspired a major movement of educational reform.

It is unfortunate that the battle over *Emile* has thrown out of focus Rousseau's more sober and practical views on what was possible and immediately desirable in educational practice. The heretic who roundly rejected the environmentalists' thesis that the obstacles to man's advance were largely external did not also reject their trust in the state as a great agency of education. On the contrary, his other writings abound with the most fruitful suggestions for stimulating national consciousness and carry perhaps the most fervent plea of the entire age to make education a handmaiden of patriotism. In *The Social Contract* he places stress on the theory of public education, and in his writings on Corsica and Poland he gives practical illustrations of how that national education could serve patriotism. Both the environmentalists and Rousseau, when he talked about the education of the citizen rather than of abstract man, were in perfect agreement that society could not control its own destiny unless the state itself assumed the cardinal responsibility of educating its subjects in citizenship. Rousseau insisted repeatedly that the true foundation of active political life could not be a flaccid cosmopolitanism or a tenuous love of humanity. Citizenship had to be grounded in the particular cultural heritage of each separate nation. Love of the *patrie*, moreover, could be sustained only by national institutions that treasured and kept alive the genius or the spirit of the nation. Of these institutions none was so vital as a state system of instruction, for it was only by this means that the young citizens could be taught from their earliest years to focus all their emotional loyalty upon the fatherland. Both by implication and by positive enunciation Rousseau ridiculed the view that the individual could effectively be linked to the larger community of the state by obligations inherent in his position as a member of a corporative group or through the coercive power of a prince. In all these writings he vehemently affirmed that the spiritual cement that held men together was nationalist sentiment, love of the fatherland. Thus, with a singleness of purpose that was unmatched outside France, educational theorists and reformers steeped in his views directed their protest against all systems of instruction and all links and ties that prevented the realization of their hopes to bind the citizen to the larger community of the state.[14]

The key words, consequently, to the specific educational projects were nationalization and centralization. What was prolix and diffuse in Rousseau's *Social Contract* became concrete and compact in the *Essai d'éducation nationale* (1763) of La Chalotais, influential administrator and foe of the Jesuits, who specifically advocated a state educational system, "because every nation has an inalienable and imprescriptible right to instruct its members." Many other treatises sounded identical notes. Turgot, for example, envisioned a central board for a

---

14 Apart from the treatises on education, cf. the relevant pages of A. Cobban, *Rousseau and the Modern State* (London, 1934); and C. Budde, "Die Pädagogik Rousseaus in Ihrem Verhältniss zu seinen kulturphilosophischen, politischen und religiösen Anschauungen," in *Neue Jahrbücher für Wissenschaft und Jugendbildung*, V (1929), 198 ff.

system of governmental education which would supervise all grades of instruction, co-ordinate the curriculum, and even furnish free of charge government-inspired textbooks designed to inculcate in the minds of the pupils their obligations and their duties as citizens of the state.[15]

While in pre-revolutionary France the reformers tested the existing bases of social relations, indeed repudiated them in favor of a new and challenging concept of national ties, England remained singularly barren of original or creative educational theorists, as it was of suggestions that would deprive private and local bodies of their control over instruction. The Continent took over what was possible or expedient from the French and adapted its borrowing to national needs. Except in the most advanced intellectual circles social and educational criticism still rested on the proposition that the growth of national sentiment and acceptance of princely authority were but the two sides of the same shield.

III. HEALTH, WEALTH, AND HAPPINESS

Abolition of the scourge of war was another of the millennial hopes which fired the imagination of eighteenth-century man. The humanitarian and utopian Abbé de Saint-Pierre early in the century composed a *Project for Perpetual Peace in Europe* (condensed in 1729 into an *Abrégé*) which aroused the enthusiasm of many admirers and the sneers of Frederick the Great at the very moment that the great wars were giving the deathblow to its expectations. But the majority of the *philosophes*, who hated the horrors of what Bentham called "mischief on the highest scale," had little faith either in projects, such as Saint-Pierre's or those of Penn, Crucé, and Sully before him, or in federations of princes to do away with warfare. They took their stand on the laws of nature and reason to end organized violence. They pinned their faith on the diffusion of enlightenment and on the improvement of social institutions to convince all men, including rulers, of the stupidity and the futility of war.

---

[15] For the text of La Chalotais' *Essai* and for the examples of similar proposals, see F. de la Fontainerie, *French Liberalism and Education in the Eighteenth Century, La Chalotais, Diderot and Condorcet* (New York, 1932).

In a more sober and realistic vein economists and financiers calculated the costs of war and concluded that the stimulus supplied to
economic enterprise by incessant preparation for war was an extraordinarily heavy price to pay for progress. Therefore, to end the threat
of war raised by competition for markets and empire, they would
abolish all tariff restrictions and institute free international trade. Self-
interest would lead them to buttress this enlightened economic internationalism with a kind of union of proprietors, a league of nations
bound by considerations of property and profit to keep the peace. Le
Mercier de la Rivière put the thought very succinctly, if not crassly:

A common and evident interest for all nations holds them naturally
and necessarily federated one with the other to consolidate the rights of
property and liberty by a common guarantee. This natural and general
confederation . . . imposes upon each nation the duty to aid in the maintenance of the rights of other nations; but also, by this same duty, each
purchases the right to call in its turn upon the strength of other nations
for the defense of its [own] rights.[16]

As usual, Rousseau approached the problem from his own angle of
vision. While the men of affairs stumbled forward to a double-entry
economic internationalism, he injected democratic values into his condemnation of militarism. He held that peace in his time was thwarted
by the aggressive and provocative war machines of the great powers,
which made for the war of all against all. Europe was in other respects already united—in culture and mores and economic interdependence—but war and the grim specter of conflict kept it disunited.
So he reasoned in his revision and condensation of the famous *Project*
of the Abbé de Saint-Pierre.[17] This militarism which so warped the
thinking of man derived from a manifest aberration of the spirit. It
stemmed from the perverted view that might made right. Destroy that
concept, pleaded Rousseau, destroy it at its source in the twisted assumption that state unity rested upon the cowed obedience of subjects
and consequently in the subordination of the civil to the military
branch of the government. Humanize and democratize society, and
establish a citizen army fired by love of the *patrie* and possessing the
democratic authority to co-operate with other citizens in the determina-

16 Le Mercier de la Rivière, *op. cit.*, 329-330.
17 *A Lasting Peace and the State of War*, ed. by C. E. Vaughan (London, 1917).

tion of national policy. In that way the present Hobbesian international anarchy would disappear and war would become a thing of the past.[18] The same critical temper was directed against the evils of serfdom at home and slavery and colonial subjection abroad. In the economically more mature cultures of the west serfdom had either disappeared or was being eliminated under the joint attack of administrative action and literary condemnation, but even in central and eastern Europe where it was solidly entrenched serfdom could rally few spokesmen to its defense. Anti-slavery propaganda was rife in England where the public mind was prepared for it by the cult of the "noble savage," philosophical deism, the zeal of missionaries, Quakerism, and the evangelical piety of the Methodists. Of the many literary attacks in France the *Réflexions sur l'esclavage des nègres* of the tireless Condorcet (sometime president of the Anti-Slavery Association) and Raynal's *History of the Two Indies* easily exercised the most influence in fashioning public opinion.[19] Other writers condemned the political and economic mischief of colonial rule. What Bentham expressed in his brochure, *Emancipate Your Colonies*, was variously intoned by Turgot and a hundred others as part of the general physiocratic repudiation of the mercantilist system. It was in many respects an inverted form of enthusiasm for colonial America.

America appeared on the horizon of European liberals early in the century, an alluring prospect dazzling the imagination of the discontented, the aggrieved, and the dreamers. As travel and postal facilities across the Atlantic improved, as protracted wars dimmed the prospects of radical reform in Europe, and as disillusionment grew about the much vaunted British model of secular salvation, a swelling flood of writings swamped the old world with the glories of colonial America. In all countries America was depicted as a primitive land, a country in the "state of nature," whose inhabitants were consumed by a passion

18 E. V. Souleyman, *The Vision of World Peace in Seventeenth and Eighteenth Century France* (New York, 1940), chs. vi-ix; and C. L. Lange, *Histoire de la doctrine pacifique et de son influence sur le développement du droit international*, forming XIII of *Recueil des Cours* of the Académie de Droit International (Brussels, 1926), ch. ix.
19 For general accounts, F. J. Klingberg, *The Anti-Slavery Movement in England* (New Haven, 1926); and E. D. Seeber, *Anti-Slavery Opinion in France During the Second Half of the Eighteenth Century* (Baltimore, 1937); for Raynal, A. Fougère, *Un précurseur de la Révolution: l'abbé Raynal, 1713-1796* (Angoulême, 1922); and also D. H. Irvine, "Abbé Raynal and British Humanitarianism," in *Journal of Modern History* (1931), 564-576.

for liberty and endowed by nature with all the attributes required to make real the visions of the reforming philosophers. In Britain the periodical press expounded the ineluctable advantages of migrating to a land whose various regions were the most healthful, the most pleasant, the most fertile in the world; where the new European colonist could easily supply himself with the necessities of life, secure his own possessions, enjoy unmolested the fruits of his labor—in brief, escape from the yoke of the malefactors of society.

The white settler gradually took on the lineaments of the natives of the blessed land. Through an easy process of wish transference European commentators discovered that the American descendants of European settlers possessed the simplicity, the dignity and the physical perfection, as well as the virtues of tolerance, justice, and liberty, that the noble Indian savage himself possessed.[20] Of all the American colonials who at different times approximated the perfection of the American Indian, the Quakers of Pennsylvania most consistently embodied all his virtues. Indeed, they shone with heightened resplendence in Pennsylvania, which somehow became synonymous with all America, a veritable Utopia where concord and justice reigned.[21] This identification of the American colonial with the noble savage was a relatively simple transference compared to the identification of the Indians with the citizens of classical antiquity. It was not enough for the disgruntled and idealistic to melt in admiration for the patriotic republican Greeks and Romans of antiquity. In the alchemy of their faith, they made the astounding discovery that the American Indians of the present resembled the pagan heroes of old. The hero of yesterday and the idol of today were alike fervid patriots, public-spirited and high-minded citizens, imbued with a consuming love of liberty, fighting with coolness and bravery, and ever prepared, for the cause of freedom, to sacrifice themselves and their children rather than to bow down before tyranny.[22] Much of this excessive adulation of classical antiquity, "noble savages," and virtuous Americans seemed, in France at least, to be a species of vicarious patriotism. Actually, it was not so much in America itself that the *philosophes* and their fol-

---

20 H. N. Fairchild, *The Noble Savage* (New York, 1928); G. Chinard, *L'Amérique et le rêve exotique dans la littérature française au XVIIe et au XVIIIe siècles* (Paris, 1913).
21 Edith Philips, *The Good Quaker in French Legend* (Philadelphia, 1932).
22 H. T. Parker, *The Cult of Antiquity and the French Revolutionaries* (Chicago, 1937), chs. ii-iv; also the stimulating essay of M. Kraus, "America and the Utopian Ideal in the Eighteenth Century," in *Mississippi Valley Historical Review*, XXII (1936), 487-504.

lowers found the realization of their dreams as in the more tenuous
world of their imagination, which they peopled with figures from
Plutarch, inhabitants of America, and every other conceivable and
laudable type of *âme républicaine*.

When the very existence of the glorious new world in America was
threatened, this patriotic-utopian impulse was transferred from the
realm of the imagination to the real world. The liberals of Europe
who militantly rallied to support the American colonists were fully
conscious that they were fighting for their own liberties as much as
for the liberties of peoples far across the seas. Only through the preservation of the liberty, the equality, the religious tolerance, the economic
security, and the humanity that prevailed in America—or seemed to
prevail—could they keep alive the hope of advancing the cause of
freedom in their own land. Even in Germany, as Goethe recalled in
his *Autobiography*, the generous and the idealistic, the liberal and the
patriotic wrote vigorous defenses of America: "We wished the Americans all success, and the names of Franklin and Washington began
to shine and sparkle in the firmament of politics and war." English
liberals agitated, and Irish malcontents eloquently bespoke their
solidarity: "We should never for a moment forget this important
truth," exclaimed Horne Tooke, "that when the people of America
are enslaved, we cannot be free. . . . We are stones of one arch, and
must stand or fall together." It was only natural, too, that a turbulent
France, which was giving an enthusiastic welcome to Raynal, should
fall rapturously upon Crèvecoeur's *Letters of an American Farmer*,
devour Chastellux's *Voyages . . . in North America*, and turn eagerly
to Brissot, Lafayette, Ségur, and all the other philo-Americans. No
enthusiast of colonial independence was so enraptured by the turn of
events as Condorcet. He took the American victory almost as a personal triumph, as if the emancipation was a magnificent corroboration
of those laws of social progress which he was to elaborate fully in the
Esquisse but which he was currently revealing in his *Letters of a
Citizen of New Haven* and *Letters of a Citizen of the United States*,
as well as in his pamphlet, *The Influence of the American Revolution
on Europe*.[23]

23 In addition to Schapiro, *op. cit.*, ch. xii, see B. Faÿ, *The Revolutionary Spirit in
France and America* (New York, 1927), ch. i; and F. Monaghan, *French Travellers in
the United States, 1765-1832* (New York, 1933).

It was only in the last quarter of the century that the repression of the American colonists enkindled the wrath of the liberals, but the sanguinary cruelties of criminal law and procedure were a constant source of indignant protest. Capitalist merchants and producers stood squarely behind the reform movement, anxious to safeguard their investments by eliminating both criminal and legal violence. Philanthropists joined with evangelical reformers, and rationalist philosophers with jurists and statesmen, in denouncing the harsh practices of criminal law and in suggesting ways of ameliorating the procedures and systematizing and humanizing the many varieties of penal legislation. Discussion groups and public-minded private citizens vied with one another, and with rulers and ministers as well, in offering prizes and propounding solutions for those stupidities and deeds of inhumanity that have made eighteenth-century justice so malodorous.[24] Even in England, where no demand for codification existed and liberals proudly cherished the illusion that their judicial institutions were *sui generis*, hence models to be followed abroad, a powerful current swept the country for reform of prison conditions and legal procedure.

That reforming wave accomplished the formidable feat of shaking the lethargic Jeremy Bentham out of his languor, stimulating him into publishing a truncated section of his philosophy of penal law in his *Introduction to Politics and Morals*. His views may have been richer than Beccaria's, but his outlook had already been anticipated in the latter's epochal *Trattato dei delitti e delle pene* (1764). Translated two years later by Abbé Morellet into French, and in 1767 into English, the *Essay on Crimes and Punishments* remains as memorable a landmark of eighteenth-century liberalism as Adam Smith's *The Wealth of Nations*. It was in a sense even more influential. Apart from the rapturous plaudits that it brought to its learned Milanese author, it served as the inspiration for all subsequent writings and most of the practical reforms of his and the following century. Nor is it a lessening of Beccaria's contribution to state that he incorporated in his little treatise many ideas that had been variously presented by individuals as diversely separated as Voltaire and Hume, Rousseau and Montes-

24 The standard work is C. L. von Bar, *A History of Continental Criminal Law*, in *The Continental Legal History Series* (Boston, 1916).

quieu, Hutcheson and Helvétius.[25] Its fundamental assumptions were characteristically utilitarian. Crime was an injury to society whose prevention was more important than its punishment. Indeed, Beccaria's insistence that the punishment must fit the crime rested upon the supposition that punishment deterred people from committing criminal deeds. A rational person, knowing in advance from the provisions of the criminal code that the prescribed punishment for wrongdoing outweighed the maximum possible benefits of crime, would refrain from doing evil. "The criminal," muses a witty commentator, "presumably is to consult the book before committing a crime."[26] This philosophy was typical of the age in its emphasis upon the utilitarian conception of moral arithmetic. Fortunately, too, it was of its age in its humane and merciful provisions for the treatment of the imprisoned, its strong appeal for public judicial procedure, and its condemnation of torture. Mankind owes much to Beccaria for the prosaic common sense that made it possible for him to present his principles systematically and prepare the way for the remarkable improvements that followed.[27]

The vast literature of social protest reveals that these currents of discontent also washed against all other institutionalized evils. However reluctant the protestants may have been to come to grips with their problem, however much they shrank back from the implications of their own analyses, never before had there been so determined, so concerted, and so comprehensive an endeavor to cast the light of reason and spread the balm of mercy over the wretched of the earth. The indignation that seared religious intolerance and the mass homicide of war, and the generosity of spirit that inspired men to reform the criminal procedure and succor the unfortunate inmates of pestilential prisons, were also directed in an attack upon poverty and disease. From one end of the Continent to the other, private individuals and co-operative associations multiplied their efforts to establish hospitals and maternity homes, dispensaries and orphanages. Municipal authorities and state administrators bestirred themselves in behalf of the unem-

[25] For a discussion of Beccaria and his predecessors, see M. T. Maestro, *Voltaire and Beccaria as Reformers of Criminal Law* (Columbia University Press, 1942).
[26] W. Seagle, *The Quest for Law* (New York, 1941), 240-243.
[27] E. Halévy, *op. cit.*, is very useful for Beccaria and the young Bentham; also C. Phillipson, *Three Criminal Law Reformers: Beccaria, Bentham, Romilly* (London, 1923).

ployed, devising plans for public works and creating various agencies
to supplement or, if need be, supplant the mere altruism of the
benevolent but often all too helpless individual employer.

As knowledge of the appalling extent of poverty grew greater, as
understanding deepened concerning the wide ramifications of the social
problem, it became increasingly evident that poverty and crime, unemployment and inhuman criminal legislation, ignorance and vagrancy,
disease and mendicity, were all interrelated aspects of the great economic dislocation. More was required to keep the social peace than
extending alms to the "deserving poor." More was necessary than
administering poor relief in local bastilles for such of the disinherited
as evinced the requisite high moral temper or showed themselves
properly grateful for the cold cup of charity. The newer attitude of
practical reformers on the Continent represented a shift in emphasis
from mercantilist-cameralist preoccupation with the good of the state
itself to a humanitarian concern for the recipients of state aid. Enlightened self-interest still prompted rulers and statesmen to dispense
charity, but philanthropy or lay charity, doing good for the sake of
humanity, came to the fore. Destitution was now also regarded as
human, and nothing human was alien to the comfortable.

IV. THE STATE AND THE INDIVIDUAL

While humanitarianism blended with cultural nationalism, cultural
nationalism was first appropriated by disgruntled bourgeois liberals
who made it a carrier of their political hopes. Protests against royal
absolutism before the mid-century had either been confined in France
to criticism of the methods employed or else, like Fénelon's famous
Télémaque, evaded reality. The basic reason for the continuous popularity of that idyllic picture of the philosopher-king may very well have
been the manifest unreality of Fénelon's conception, which afforded
the engrossed reader the twofold advantage of maintaining his present
dynastic loyalties while yielding to the illusion of hypothetical future
gains.

Montesquieu's timorous groping toward constitutionalism was, on
the other hand, a step toward the distant ideal of political democracy.
He stood in the line of the political speculators who sought in natural

law limitations on the power of any government over the life, property, and possessions of its subjects. The central theme of *The Spirit of the Laws*, on which his immense influence rested, is its hatred of monarchical despotism. Legislation should be no exclusive prerogative of the monarch, but in a well-ordered state would arise from "the necessary relation of things," reflecting and corresponding with the manners and customs of citizens and being of their making. To guarantee liberty thus attained, the authority of the crown was to be held in restraint by the separation of its powers, by an elaborate system of checks and balances, and by the institution of intermediary bodies which would serve as the conservative custodians of the fundamental laws of the realm.

Montesquieu's was assuredly an affirmation of the rights of citizens against the Leviathan state. Yet it is with infinite caution that he advanced his view that the foundation of the state is the liberty of the individual and the goal of good government the preservation of the priceless rights of religious and civil freedom. Repeatedly he insists upon the rule of the law, but he means the law of the propertied, for the noble magistrate shrank from the prospect of the rule of *demos* as much as he feared the tyranny of royal absolutism. His reasoning is colored by the emotional prepossessions of a social conservative, and there is little doubt that in arraigning the absolute monarchy he was pleading *pro domo*. Perhaps the road runs straight from Montesquieu to Edmund Burke and the triumph of prescriptive rights. Nevertheless, this thinly veiled apologia for the restoration of a loose corporative society based on the rule of the humane and enlightened landed aristocracy contributed to weakening the claims of the absolute state. He led to Burke, but he derived from Locke; and of the lineage of Locke there was also the revolutionary figure of Jean Jacques Rousseau.[28]

All the important writings of that disordered genius, except the *Confessions*, had appeared by 1763: the two *Discourses*, the *Nouvelle Héloïse*, *Emile*, and *The Social Contract*. However widely interpreters

[28] For the great popularity of Montesquieu in the middle decades cf. E. Bonno, *La constitution britannique devant l'opinion française de Montesquieu à Bonaparte* (Paris, 1932); and for favorable and hostile appreciations cf. respectively, E. Carcassonne, *Montesquieu et le problème de la constitution française au xviiie siècle* (Paris, 1927) and A. Mathiez, "La place de Montesquieu dans l'histoire des doctrines politiques du dix-huitième siècle," in *Annales historiques de la Révolution française* (mars-avril, 1930).

of his thought may differ, they are agreed that he stands at the gateway of the present, and that his influence has been prodigious over the cast of modern life. It is no simple task to devise a formula that will embrace the totality of his speculation. His detractors have branded him as psychopathic and indecent, when not merely false and stupid; and his admirers hail him for his enthusiasm and vision, his sympathy with the lowly, and his intuitive grasp of forces deeper than reason. For some he leads straight to prescriptive traditionalism in politics and, via Kant and Hegel, to the Catholic revival in religion; or, what was perhaps worst of all, to an invertebrate literary romanticism. Others see him with pride as the inspired prophet of democracy or, with anger, as the fatal theorist of state despotism. He was indeed a paradoxical and contradictory figure, but nonetheless a protean figure in whose writings any reader can readily discover all that he dislikes most, leaving for a reader otherwise persuaded to discover in the same passages conclusions agreeably different.[29]

Certainly, profound differences set him off from the other *philosophes*. Without disdaining the appeal to reason and historical experience, he also argued as he himself wrote, from some "interior sentiment that directs my belief independently of my reason." A neurotic frustrate, ravaged by a sense of inferiority toward the self-composed and assured men and women whom he encountered in society, a hypochondriac in many respects utterly despicable, he rationalized his groping for spiritual peace in an involuntary revulsion from solutions that were intellectualist in origin. When he condemned civilization *en bloc*, as he did in the first *Discourse*, contrasting natural society to existing civil society and opposing the natural impulses of the heart —benevolence, good will, reverence, and the like—to the distorted and depraved sentiments of men living in society, he was laying a rhetorical gloss over the doubts and fears that gripped him. In each new work, however, he clarified his thinking and presented different aspects of that same problem of the spiritual dislocation which tormented the more sensitive of the learned as well as the unlearned. The latter were the men who were torn up by their roots by the revolution in living habits and stripped of the security that the old mediaeval mutualism had given them and their fathers. The schemes of cosmic betterment

29 For a useful résumé of the different interpretations, see Cobban, *op. cit.*, ch. ii.

propounded by the major *philosophes* largely neglected their interests. Their old spiritual guides only too often failed them, unable to make old answers fit new problems. They were set adrift, the petty urban bourgeoisie and proletariat, in a new world indifferent to their wants. It was for such men that Rousseau spoke, passionately enjoining them to have faith in the emotions which moved them and to trust in their instincts rather than in the poisonous teachings of the rationalists.[30]

It is the sheerest misreading of his attitude to suppose that he regarded the state of nature as an actual primitivist shelter to which he could flee for refuge from the miseries of a corrupt civilization. However much his earliest writing approached such a conception, in the maturity of his thinking he used the state of nature as synonymous with the full rounded development of man's capacity. In *Emile* and in *The Social Contract* it was equivalent to the uninhibited expression of those virtuous instincts that he himself in his calmer moments enjoyed, but whose full realization society as then organized automatically thwarted. In these works he was no longer looking back to a non-existent lost paradise. More pathetically still, he was looking ahead to an unattainable Utopia. Moreover, while he reasserted the primacy of the emotions and related their harmonious satisfaction to good living, he did not in the slightest degree deny the claims of reason. Very explicitly, he insisted that the truly virtuous man was he who held his impulses in leash. There is in *The Social Contract* a conception of the categorical imperative which Kant himself could not have better phrased:

> What man loses by the social contract is his natural liberty and an unlimited right to everything he tries to get and succeeds in getting; what he gains is civil liberty . . . which is limited by the general will. . . . We might, over and above all this, add, to what man acquires in the civil state, moral liberty, which alone makes him truly master of himself; for the mere impulse of appetite is slavery, while obedience to a law which we prescribe to ourselves is liberty.[31]

The profound significance of Jean Jacques rests then on the fact that his writing echoed and made articulate the mood of the petty

[30] In all his writings there is nothing to equal the lengthy passage on the Creed of the Savoyard Vicar in his *Emile* (Everyman ed.), 228-278, for a sustained passionate exposition of these doubts and fears.
[31] *The Social Contract* (Everyman ed., 1927), Bk. I, ch. viii, 19.

bourgeoisie of small traders and shopkeepers, landless rurals, and land-hungry, tax-ridden peasant proprietors, all the world of the lowly. His style, that "mixture of rodomontade and vulgarity," as the classicist in Voltaire so graciously described it, was thoroughly in keeping with his person and his purpose. It was precisely by his sentimentalism and his false heroics, his platitudes and his attitudes, and by less frequent but beautifully sustained passion-laden phrases, that he conveyed the yearnings of the simple, the poor, and the weary, the bitterness of the disinherited, the urge toward tenderness, the starved longing for richer emotional experience, the revolted feeling against the regulated artifices of social life, and the hope of the oppressed and forgotten for liberty.

In an age when physiocrats and Encyclopedists advocated legal absolutism, when the dominant note of political speculation still ex-tolled the rule of the enlightened prince, Rousseau vigorously rejected the doctrine that the state was a big family and the king the father of his people. He insisted that in every well-ordered state the individual should be subject only to the laws that were rightfully established and that he could freely accept. "Do not talk to me any longer of your 'legal despotism,' " he once wrote impatiently to the elder Mirabeau. "I could not stand it, let alone understand it, and for me these are only two contradictory words."[32] He had at first concerned himself most with castigating the faults of existing civil society. As his thinking became clearer, he sought to discover whether there could be any sure and just rules of administration in civil society, "taking men as they are and laws as they might be." Thus *The Social Contract* goes far beyond Locke. Locke had made government depend on the con-sent of the governed, but had failed to provide any effective machin-ery for the testing of public opinion short of revolution, the revolution already consummated in 1688. Rousseau sought to establish constitu-tional means for the expression of popular consent; and he found them in his concepts of the social compact and the general will.

The question whether he actually believed in the historical reality of the social contract is highly irrelevant to an understanding of his position. It might be stated in passing that he himself regarded the question as such. His great contribution was to contend that acceptance of the principle of consent gave validity to the social structure while

32 C. E. Vaughan, ed., *The Political Writings of Rousseau* (New York), II, 161.

the failure of acceptance made society despotic. His language occasionally confuses his meaning and he is guilty of begging questions, but in the main his thought is clear. Condorcet, who stood in the very stream of Rousseauist thought, comprehended that his purpose "was not to propose practicable measures but to present great principles with force and energy." Sovereignty, the right to power, belongs to all the people, even though in practice its application always requires an executive instrument called government. Sovereignty is inalienable, indestructible, and indivisible. The general will, the prime mover of all just governments, is the sole repository of the interests of society as a whole. It is born of the social contract: "In place of the individual personality of each contracting party, the act of association creates a moral and collective body . . . receiving from the act its unity, its common identity, its life and its will."[33] Its standards are imperiously binding over all the rights of the individual, yet whatever sacrifices man made, when in the transition from natural to civil society he sank his personal will into this general pool, the citizen into which he was metamorphosed still remained free. True freedom consists in obeying the restraints of law, but in obligating himself to obey the general will he actually obeys only his higher moral self.

Here then was the fierce rumble of individualism against the absolute state. The state is no longer conceived as a providential creation set apart from and above the lives of its citizens. Nor is it an entity guided by and subject only to the will of the enlightened prince. The state becomes a form of public association designed to serve the general welfare. The individual is transformed from a subject obeying a will alien to his desires into a citizen governed by the law that he and his fellows established. It is true that Rousseau's Genevan cast of thought made him establish the general will as a new absolute, its authority coercive over all society. Moreover, Rousseau has been criticized for failing to explain how and when the general will, whose expression theoretically should always have been unanimously supported since it derived from the entire social body, was legitimate if it had only the support of a majority. Actually, the criticism lacks relevancy, for it touches upon the mechanism of determining popular sovereignty, whereas Rousseau was concerned with establishing the principle. By

[33] *The Social Contract* (Everyman ed.), Bk. I, ch. vi.

insisting upon this principle he reduces government from a mysterious dispensation removed from the lives of the ruled into a device for
effecting social adjustments. Government becomes geared to the social
mechanism, its most essential part, but still a part controlled by the
many for their mutual good.[34]

Iconoclastic as Jean Jacques Rousseau's views were, this first great
spokesman of democracy was no uncompromising egalitarian. He
abhorred the fashionable cult of luxury and he bitterly condemned
the gross inequalities of fortune, but he never went so far as to propose the leveling of possessions. Holding property sacred, he proposed
no more than the regulation of the extremes of wealth and indigence.
It was his aim to make existing agrarian capitalism as safe in the
future for the small proprietor as it was for the great landowner; to
safeguard the petty craftsman against the opulent merchant, the captain of industry, and the princely financier. His demands were social-
ized versions of the petty-bourgeois domesticity that Richardson was
currently preaching in his interminable and mawkish novels. Rousseau
cherished all those desiderata—the comforts of the hearth, the simple
pleasures of family life, the innocence of dress and speech, and, perhaps too often, the naïveté of thought as well.

The full political impact of Rousseau came belatedly during the
Revolution. Meanwhile other theorists carried his democratic tenets
far beyond the stand that he himself took. With the Marquis de Condorcet, "the individual rises to face the state armed with his rights," in
the words of an admirer. Only in the realm of thought, it should be
added. The intellectual leveler who summarily rejected Montesquieu's
checks and balances, who exposed the deficiencies of the vaunted
British constitution, who extolled the American Revolution as the
model for France to follow, drew back when the test came during the
French Revolution.

Among the other lesser prophets, the egalitarians and idealists whose
pity for the meek, the weak, and the unhappy drove them far beyond
Rousseau's petty-bourgeois and nationalist democracy, there was the

34 Of the several sympathetic appreciations of Rousseau, Cobban, op. cit., is the most
detailed, and G. D. H. Cole's introductory essay to the Everyman edition of The Social
Contract is the most readable and understanding; for his influence, see David Williams,
"The Influence of Rousseau on Political Opinion, 1760-95," in English Historical Review
(1933), 414 ff.

little-known figure of Morelly. His *Code de la Nature* (1755) was a testament of communism which anticipated Fourier and the ideal collectivist society arranged around uniform phalansteries of the elect. "Destroy property," he proclaimed, "the blind and pitiless self-interest which accompanies it, wipe out all the prejudices and the errors which maintain them, and . . . there are no more furious passions, ferocious actions, notions or ideas of moral badness." There was also the Abbé Mably, who belonged to the liberals by reason of his detestation of the existing order, but who went beyond them in his lack of faith in their panaceas. His *Doutes . . . proposés aux philosophes économistes* (1768) bitterly assailed the physiocratic theses, but he also lacked faith in the re-creation of his ideal society of primitive collectivism that civilization had destroyed. He was deficient in confidence for the masses whom he would have succored. Degraded by their poverty they were incapable of regaining their rights, and only disorder and disorder alone would be the net consequence of any effort to tear up the root of evil in private property.[35]

Still more violent were the diatribes against private property from the pen of the famous lawyer and publicist, Simon Linguet. Disbarred from legal practice, Linguet shot a stream of analysis and invective against both the iniquities of the present and the timid reform proposals of the bourgeois liberals. He was contemptuous of the middle-class reformers who would win merely legal equality for their exploited fellow men. His own fundamental proposition was that since property had originated in violence and was perpetuated through legal coercion, the state had no other function than to employ its power to preserve the claims of the few upon the labor of the many. Men were hardly free, he caustically observed, irrespective of whatever political rights they might have gained, so long as they had to go upon their knees to a rich man to get permission to increase his wealth. In his manual of disenchantment, *Théorie des Lois*, he poked sardonic fun at the hopes held out by the *philosophes* for the emancipation of humanity:

[35] For Mably and Morelly, consult the thoughtful essays by C. K. Driver in F. J. C. Hearnshaw, ed., *The Social and Political Ideas of Some Great French Thinkers of the Age of Reason* (New York, 1930), ch. ix; also, A. Lichtenberger, *Le socialisme au dix-huitième siècle* (Paris, 1895); and H. Girsberger, *Der utopische Sozialismus des 18. Jahrhunderts in Frankreich* (Zurich, 1924), for all the utopians.

Ah, cruel philosophy, how sad are your consolations. . . . What then is the purpose of your speech? I suffer and yet according to you, I could, I even ought, to be freed of suffering. I am perishing in my chains and you cry out to me that no one has the right to keep me in irons. What then is your design? Is it to force my heart to feel my injustice and my slavery all the more keenly? How much wiser would it be to have a terrible but salutary voice say to me: "suffer and die in chains; there is your destiny."[36]

He had no illusions and he sought no followers, and his contemporaries misunderstood him as completely as he scorned most of them. Not until he was rediscovered, in the following century, as a forerunner of Marxian socialism, was it seen that the man who so savagely satirized the "sentimental parades" of the liberals, that the "apologist of tyrants" who grimly recommended resignation, did so only in the despairing spirit of Diderot, who held it less inconvenient to be mad among madmen than to be wise all alone.

There was nothing elsewhere on the Continent to approach the spirit of advanced French political speculation. In Italy the political thought of the northern and central parts of the peninsula was more congenial to liberalism than that in the south, which cherished neither the memory of communal liberties nor the tradition of Roman imperial legislation. Of all the many Italian thinkers who shed luster upon the cultural *risorgimento*, it was only the Milanese group around Pietro and Alessandro Verri, men like Beccaria, Gian Carli, Longo, and Frisi, who even remotely prepared the minds of their contemporaries to welcome the literary gospel of middle-class revolution. Blending foreign doctrines with native views and tempering their ideas to the patriotic purpose of unifying the country and emancipating it from the Austrians, the Italian liberals achieved much to earn the gratitude of their compatriots. But original and decisive contributions to the body of European liberalism did not come from them.[37]

The Germans, on the whole, successfully avoided taking political thought. The literati couched their writing under the aegis of eternal

---

[36] Quoted in J. Cruppi, *Un avocat journaliste au XVIIIe siècle, Linguet* (Paris, 1895), 165; also H. R. G. Greaves, "The Political Ideas of Linguet," in *Economica*, X (1930), 40-55.

[37] In addition to the works of Ruggiero and de Sanctis, there is the admirable little study of H. Bédarida and P. Hazard, *L'influence française en Italie au 18e siècle* (Paris, 1935), and the classic study of G. Natali, *Il Settecento*, 2 vols., 3rd ed. (Milan, 1929).

values, and lesser mortals took refuge in mysticism, physiognomic readings, and other forms of the esoterical. The high-minded Kant soared into the empyrean, above mundane distractions. Several critical batteries there were that did not fire blank shells, but they limited themselves to correcting concrete abuses rather than suggesting basic solutions. Apart from journalists like Schlözer, whose *Staatsanzeigen* was consulted regularly even by Maria Theresa, and Christian Schubart, editor of the influential *Deutsche Chronik*, there were only Justus Möser (1720-1794) and Johann Gottfried Herder (1744-1803) to challenge the regnant cameralist precepts. Both occupy positions of importance in German political speculation because they were the harbingers of the romantic reversion to the teachings of historical experience as a corrective for the presumed anti-historical and abstract preconceptions of natural law. They belong to liberalism, therefore, somewhat in the manner of the French egalitarians, linked by the most tenuous of ties. They were negativists, fiercely at odds with existing society but also hating enlightened despotism and convinced that to heighten state activities was to give a wrong answer to present ills.

The political thought of Möser, publicist and embittered petty official in the ecclesiastical principality of Osnabrück in northwestern Germany, was rooted in the historical experience that he thought he discovered when he studied and wrote about the development of his native state in his *Osnabrückische Geschichte*. Proud discoverer and militant defender of the institutions that had served Germany so well, he inveighed against the absolute state that had dissolved the ancient social and cultural community. His conception of the state as a sort of democracy of small peasant possessors was sterile and unrealistic, for it idealized and rationalized a feudal social order that was dying. If in his traditionalism he had the defect of not being able to anticipate a Germany unified by Prussia, he also had the merit rare among his contemporaries of daring to criticize the existing Prussian order.

His young contemporary, Herder, while attuned to him in spirit, was far more influential. All the movements of the last quarter of a century bear the impress of Herder's fecund intelligence. Without wishing to be a romantic he was a precursor of literary romanticism. He was the intellectual parent of German nationalism, for inspired by his mystic teacher Hamann and by his reading of Möser and Rousseau, he evolved a brilliant concept of the organic growth of cultures. His significance in political theory rests on the fact that while elaborating his pre-romantic notions of nationality, he also injected into them a profound aversion to the pre-eminence of the state over the individual. A Prussian by birth, he hated Junkerdom and despised and feared Frederick's feudalized militarism. Though he was the foremost of Germany's anti-state political theorists, rejecting the Hobbesian and Machiavellian theories, the man who so cordially hated the absolute state for its tyranny had himself no explicit ideas on the actual structure of political relations. "If you have to, serve the state; and if you can, serve humanity," he counseled. In the last analysis he advised obedience to the ruler, resigning himself to absolutism as a necessary evil, still indispensable to safeguard the health, wealth, and good fortune of its subjects.[38]

English liberalism, reflecting the entire English historical past, was full of a number of trends and tendencies, not all of which were compatible. It included the penetrating speculation of an Adam Smith and also smug adherents of *laissez faire*, lacking in the master's humanist temper and true benevolence. Liberalism permeated the criticism of Dissenters like Priestley and Price; and its followers also included aristocrats like Shelburne and Rockingham, radicals like Jebb and Cartwright, and humanitarians like Sharp, Howard, and Wilberforce. It embraced a cultural nationalist like Burke, whose amplification of Locke's principles all but illustrated how thesis could be transformed into antithesis. John Wilkes was in the camp, the friends of India and the Irish malcontents must be included, and even Dr. Johnson had his moments of liberal weakness. Jeremy Bentham was still engrossed by his admiration for enlightened rulers and particularly for his "dear Kitty" of Russia, but the Zeus from whose head philosophical radicalism sprang full grown certainly cannot be excluded from the roster. In fact, eighteenth-century English liberalism was most contemporary in its combination of opposites; and it already faced both ways, back to Locke and 1688 and forward to Fabianism and the Webbs.

[38] More elaborate than Aris, *op. cit.*, chs. vi and vii, are Peter Klassen, *Justus Möser* (Frankfort, 1936); and R. E. Ergang, *Herder and the Foundations of German Nationalism* (New York, 1931).

The freedom of enterprise for which Adam Smith argued so eloquently had largely been won in England when *The Wealth of Nations* made its appearance in 1776. Industrial regulation had long since broken down, discredited in practice by the visible injury that it inflicted upon the aggregate national welfare and by the corruption that it engendered. Commercial policy changed more slowly than industrial, but what the great international merchants could not obtain legally by licenses and exemptions they were taking without permission of the government through smuggling and extra-legal devices. Theory had also turned against the assumptions of mercantilism, and its trend could be followed, even as Smith doubtlessly followed it, in the writings of the French physiocrats and not a few economists at home. He might well have read in the pages of Dean Tucker a generation before his day that "the self-love and self-interest of each individual will prompt him to seek such ways of gain, trades, and occupations of life as, by serving himself, will promote the public welfare at the same time."

Whatever its indebtedness to others, *The Wealth of Nations* is incontestably one of the great masterpieces of eighteenth-century individualism. It was the full flowering of the economic arguments that paralleled both the emancipation of the individual from political absolutism and his fierce struggle to win religious toleration. It was the first full-length and systematic treatise against state intervention. When, by his appeal to the evidence of history, Adam Smith completed his case against "the folly of the human laws" that impeded the play of the individual's enlightened self-interest, no intellectual obstacle blocked his conclusion that private and public interests harmonized and that social progress resulted from the free play of man's natural instincts. In his most famous passage he argued how economic man co-operated with providence: He "neither intends to promote the public interest nor knows how much he is promoting it . . . he intends only his own security; and by directing that industry in such a manner as its produce may be of the greatest value, he intends only his own gain, and he is in this, as in many other cases, led by an invisible hand to promote an end which was no part of his intention."

To go beyond Smith's contribution and underscore some of the ends which were reached in practice is manifestly unfair to a man who could scarcely be expected to anticipate the problems of the age of machinery. Nor would it be just to the economist who was in no way unaware of "the pernicious effects" to which merchants put their economic power, who lamented their control over the lives of the workers, and regretted their influence over Parliament. With fewer defects than most, Smith was the supreme representative of an age which identified the liberation of the individual with the cosmic forces making for the good life. His Magna Carta of commercial capitalism, which restricted the role of the state to that of a policeman keeping order in the economic arena, had behind it the sanction of victory already won.[39]

The English Nonconformists, it has been said, rediscovered Locke in the pages of Montesquieu and Rousseau. The observation is doubtless correct, but they never gave up or went much beyond their discovery. Priestley's once well-known *Essay on the First Principles of Government* (1768) may in truth have been "an edition of Rousseau for English Nonconformists," but its fidelity to Locke was not less characteristic. It was an elaboration on utilitarian grounds of Locke's defense of revolution, but a revolution that had already occurred almost a century earlier; and it clung to a premise that was demonstrably inaccurate even when Locke enunciated it: the premise that England was a society of proprietors vested with sacred rights which they were resolved to safeguard against attacks from an irresponsible ruler and the turbulent masses. What Priestley only broached and half-enunciated became articulate with Burke, who contended that without the rule of the wealthy, leisured, and cultured aristocracy England would either relapse into the government of a corrupt court faction serving an arbitrary ruler or else sink under the mob rule of the "swinish multitude." Such fears possibly lurked in Priestley too, but they never came to the fore and luckily do not mar his humanist defense of complete civil and intellectual liberties against the encroachments of the government.[40]

The radical reformers, Jebb, Cartwright, and Wyvill, also enlarged upon the revolutionary traditions of 1688, but they did so notably

---

[39] A fuller discussion of Adam Smith will be found in the following volume of this series.

[40] A. Lincoln, *Some Political and Social Ideas of English Dissent, 1763-1800* (Cambridge, Eng., 1938).

in the realm of action rather than of speculation. Of all the liberals, the most influential, the most complex in intelligence, and perhaps the most flagrantly illiberal in temperament, was Edmund Burke. His acceptance of the tradition of revolution, the bloodless English revolution, was real and sincere. By stressing in all his writings the broad principles of political relations, he helped modernize Locke and bring him up to date. It was his great achievement to make a sound and active party system the touchstone of working constitutionalism. But by his attitude toward contemporary revolutions, especially the revolution in France, he bridged the illiberal seventeenth century with the conservative nineteenth. By his *Reflections on the Revolution in France* he, who had been anathema to the crown, won the praise of monarchs and conservatives. In what was to have been a tempered and judicious defense of English parliamentarism he largely idealized the British constitution and gave an almost religious consecration to the belief that government was a sacred trust, that one ought to preserve and improve rather than to change.

At the great crisis that 1789 symbolized in modern history the law of nature almost ceased to be for him part of the design of the supreme architect of the universe, and it no longer served as a rational standard for the testing of existing institutions. Nature lost its classical identification with the rational. The natural pointed in one direction, and the rational led elsewhere. Nature became a changing, complex, and evolving force, and Burke found sense in life only by bending himself to it, by a reverent acceptance of the world as it is, and by co-operating with forces unknown and unseen, including those of his own more than rational human nature. His temperament had always predisposed him toward religious piety, but now, caught in the coils of his fear of disorder, he moved forward to the high-water mark of emotionalism, averring that "we ought to venerate where we are unable presently to comprehend."

Since Burke persuaded himself that the awful contriver of the world wished man to accept his destiny, he could also readily feel that it was part of providential dispensation to keep humanity divided into the rich and the poor. He maintained that we ought "manfully to resist" the thought that government *qua* government could do anything about inequality or that the rich could "supply to the poor those necessaries which it has pleased the Divine Providence for a while to withhold from them." We may not tamper with the decrees of providence, and all that remains is to appeal to "the jurisdiction of mercy," by which he meant private charity.[41]

Reviewing the humanitarian mandate as a whole, in its complexity and its incongruities, it stands forth unmistakably as a many-sided anticipation of liberal democracy. It was clear to many observers that the dissolution of the old order and the disintegration of old values were well under way in the era made dramatic by the final blazing up of the glories of royal absolutism. Yet the formulators of the new values did not cut themselves off from the old. Determined to deserve well of humanity, yet not unreasonably solicitous of their security in the present, they adapted themselves to two worlds. Their statement of the liberal credo was marked by caution and timidity. They suffered from a compelling fear of the unpropertied. Individualists to the core, they at no time dared or wished to reject all state intercession. Adam Smith left education, military training, and the application of a public works system in the hands of the state. Rousseau, secular Calvinist apostle of individual rights, kept the state, albeit the all-powerful people's state, as his ideal political structure. Saving only the unrealistic French egalitarians, none of the liberals systematically formulated solutions for the dilemma of the unpropertied, rural and urban alike, whose numbers were constantly being swelled by the new capitalism. More disturbing still, the basic elements of a rival outlook were deeply imbedded in the liberal faith; for humanitarianism and philanthropy carried the germs of that nineteenth-century cultural counterrevolution which worked itself out in the irrationalism, primitivism, and emotionalism of the romantic revival.[42]

[41] From his *Thoughts on Scarcity*, quoted in H. J. Laski, *The Rise of Liberalism. The Philosophy of a Business Civilization* (New York, 1936), 229-230. For other treatments of his illiberalism, consult A. Cobban, *Edmund Burke and the Revolt against the Eighteenth Century* (London, 1929), ch. i; and Willey, *op. cit.*, 240-253; whereas A. M. Osborn, *Rousseau and Burke* (New York, 1940), takes an opposing view.

[42] Fr. Meinecke, *Die Entstehung des Historismus*, 2 vols. (Munich, 1936), deals sympathetically with that transition.

Chapter Nine

LITERATURE AND THE ARTS

I. THE FIRST STIRRINGS OF SENSIBILITY

CULTURAL cosmopolitanism made Europe one, and the tides of sentiment and sensibility washed over the Continent. Intellectuals and men of letters had long dismissed national patriotism as a constraining force, tending to impair the true solidarity of all citizens of the world; and many of them felt with Lessing that to be a zealous patriot was an honor that they could cheerfully forgo. Everybody who could, traveled in this age of improved communications: "kings and desperate men," scholars and artists, students and merchants, refugees from religious persecution and young gentlemen on the *grand tour*. Everybody cherished Italy in an age of classical revival and archeological excavation. Everybody also admired London, if only from a distance; but it was France, particularly Paris, that was most enshrined in the good European's heart.

Paris was the arbiter *sans pareil* of elegance and taste. It retained its place as the café and the resort of Europe, but it was also the world center of intellectual speculation, where all ranks were leveled in the freemasonry of the spirit. Scholar and aristocratic patron met in salon and club to sharpen their speculation and their wit in an easy exchange of ideas. They sat together at the sessions of the Academy and relaxed after dining at the theater or opera. From this hub of Europe, itself cross-fertilized by English thought and manners, dress and even food, the values of individualism radiated to central and eastern Europe. Only in the last decades, when English culture supplanted French, was the grip of the latter relaxed over German life. Even so, it was still the Berlin Academy which, in 1784, gave the highest prize to Rivarol for his discourse on the *Universality of the French Language*.[1] French and English influences also co-operated and con-

[1] Cf. L. Reynaud, *L'histoire générale de l'influence française en Allemagne au dix-huitième siècle* (Paris, 1922), chs. v. and vi; and A. Kelly, *England and Englishmen in German Literature of the Eighteenth Century* (New York, 1921).

tended in the Iberian and Italian peninsulas, while Gallomania at first swept all before it in Russia. Mid-century Russia teemed with Frenchmen: artists and scholars, adventurers and publicists, cooks and lackeys. France reigned supreme in the court and in the kitchen, the boudoir and the parlor, the salon and the school; and as the century waned, here also Anglomania superseded the cult of France.[2]

Creative literature and the arts mirrored both this cosmopolitanism and its momentous confusion of patterns. Poetry and political oratory, the new comedy and the domestic tragedy, the novel and the historical treatise carried the challenging protest of social evangelism. The poets discovered the tremulous joys of melancholy and thoughts by night. They found that death had its voluptuous charms, but they were equally entranced by the innocent beauties of rosy-fingered dawn. In scornful protest against the artificial canons of taste that denied the beauties of nature and its seasons, they stepped out of the salon into the fresher air of the carefully non-cultivated English garden. Tarrying only a moment, they fled out into the open landscape, where they drank in the scent of flowers and listened to birds that sang. After discovering the mountains and the oceans, they embarked on the long journey to the dreamland overseas: to the America of the noble savage and the glorious revolutionist, to the serenely wise Orient, to the home of the ever living heroes of classical antiquity; and best of all to the refuge of the unspoiled children of primitive simplicity who lived and loved in the idyllic islands of the Indian and Pacific oceans. Others still explored their own historic past, that vital tissue of memories and traditions which fused the present with what had been and what was still to be. The warp of this literature was the new humanitarianism, but the skilled and cunning artifices of literary craftsmanship made up its woof. It was indeed everything that literature always is and always must be: an anodyne to pain and a spur to action; an evocation of restful days in the sun and a blaring trumpet calling men to battle. And all of it carried the message of sensibility.[3]

2 For the Gallomania, see the classic study of E. Haumant, *La culture française en Russie* (Paris, 1910), especially pp. 42-158; and for the contrary phenomenon of Russian influences in France, D. von Mohrenschildt, *Russia in the Intellectual Life of Eighteenth Century France* (New York, 1936); for the reaction in favor of England, E. J. Simmons, *English Literature and Culture in Russia, 1553-1840* (Cambridge, 1935), chs. iv-viii.

3 For America see R. B. Heilman, *America in English Fiction, 1760-1800* (Louisiana State University Press, 1938); and J. T. Hatfield and E. Hochbaum, "The Influence of

Addison and Steele were its first great spokesmen. Creators of a periodical press that counted many imitators, they echoed the views of the new middle-class readers who had triumphed, at least after a fashion, in the glorious revolution of 1688; and they took up problems that neither a lingering Restoration theater nor a formalized Town literature could adequately solve. Their salutary essays expressed that troubled sense of disquiet which fashionable vice imparted to men of sober mien, and they conveyed a deeply rooted urge to improve humanity by fortifying their readers in advance against the time-consuming and unprofitable affectations and frivolities of society. The underlying assumptions of the *Tatler* and *Spectator* essays were of a piece with the new sentimental comedy, such as Colley Cibber's *Love's Last Shift*, and the contemporary domestic drama like *The Rival Brothers*. The essence of the proposed solution of human affairs was to make real the "natural rule of honesty and worth" within the human heart by appealing forcefully to man's feelings and tapping the sources of his natural goodness.

For some time the appealing note remained muffled, and perhaps fortunately so, considering its later resonance. Kindliness remained as rare in literature as it was still in real life, and public morality long continued coarse and calculating, despite or perhaps because of the high artifice of sophisticated society. But as innumerable voices took up Hogarth's sorrowing refrain over his compatriots' callousness, even the most complacent found it difficult to lull themselves into a comatose inactivity by intoning that all partial evil was universal good and that whatever was, was right. The satirical *Gulliver's Travels* of Swift and the urbanely cynical letters of Lord Chesterfield insinuated the thought that something after all was wrong in this best of all possible worlds; George Lillo's realistic *The London Merchant* and David Hume's blunt philosophical reflections were fresh thrusts against smugness, while meantime the sensibility that was streaming into real living overflowed into the poetry of Thomson and Young and Blair that discovered nature, and into the novel that taught the passions to move at the command of virtue.[4]

the American Revolution upon German Literature," in *Americana-Germania*, III (1899-1900), 338-385.
    [4] Leslie Stephen's *English Literature and Society in the Eighteenth Century* (London, 1903), remains a readable and delightful account, despite its Brahman-like overtones.

The tides of change were also lapping against old bulwarks in France. Here too the waves of sentiment were at first gentle, but they soon beat more heavily, eroding conventional forms and improvising literary genres more appropriate to the new mood. Classical tragedy was of course much too stilted, too artificial in its content, and too divorced from actuality to serve its needs. The high comedy, fashioned by the genius of Molière, was too cutting in its vivisections of human frailties for the tastes of the prosperous burghers who now thronged into the theater. What these stout citizens most assuredly did not want on the stage was the great master's full-bodied raillery or his savage probing into the maniacal recesses of humanity. They relished easily recognizable pasteboard types, a manikin appealingly labeled Virtue whom they could rapturously applaud while he decimated his opposite number, the evil puppet, Vice. Criticism of society thus prettified drew them to the theater.

The "whining comedy" of Destouches and La Chaussée gratified such superior artistic tastes. It was in fact comic, at least up to a point; but it also gave a generous measure of those full-blown aphorisms, high-sounding platitudes, and facile dicta of morality that compensated the predominantly bourgeois audience both for the insecurity of their position as *nouveaux riches* and the subservience that the protocol of aristocratic social relations still imposed upon them. However mawkish and stereotyped in its depiction of character, the *comédie larmoyante* enjoyed great popular appeal because of the diversity and complications of its plots and its shrewd hits at human foibles. To a degree unparalleled in England, it effectively speeded the democratization of social relations. Even Voltaire could not escape its appeal; and the prince of satirists unbent sufficiently not only to dramatize Richardson's virtue-laden *Pamela* but to serve "Virtue" so movingly in his own sentimental comedy, *Nanine*, that none other than Jean Jacques Rousseau himself was constrained to praise his rival's work "because in it honor, virtue, and pure natural sentiments are preferred to the impertinent prejudices of rank."[5]

It was the novel, however, that gradually emerged as the ideal literary form for the new temper. At first structurally thin and

---

[5] The standard treatment of the sentimental comedy is E. Bernbaum, *Drama of Sensibility* (Cambridge, 1915).

vacuous in content, it soon borrowed the attributes of older and more mature genres and so transcended its earliest limitations. Because of its almost limitless flexibility of form, it became the perfect medium of expression in an epoch that was uniquely, incessantly, and often most aggressively preoccupied with formulating the ideal of peaceful human relations. One of the most popular forms in the early century was the novel of manners. Most of these works were technically bad, even for their own time; but they possess great value in reflecting the living habits of different social groups as seen by the carping eye of the middle-class moralist. For example, these profusions of literary mediocrity have the merit of enabling a student to reconstruct a picture of the vanished social past wherein priests were inveterately shown as deceitful when not also lecherous, the holy church recreant to its trust, the military proud and haughty, and the multi-millionaire financiers rapaciously cruel. The snob novel, the novel of "*la bonne compagnie,*" which Crébillon *fils* made peculiarly his own, was a variant form of the novel of manners, popular among sophisticates for its suave intimations of eroticism.

In this same early period, Marivaux and Prévost traced the beginnings of the sentimental novel. Marivaux's lacy and gossamer-like *Vie de Marianne* and Prévost's poignant *Manon Lescaut* are both fascinating and thoughtful studies of the *jeune fille amoureuse*. Self-conscious and gifted technicians, they carefully calculated their effects when they plucked at the strings of emotion. But also sincere men of feeling, they reveled in the primacy of sentiment. For both of them reason was a snare and a delusion, "*un grand visionnaire,*" as Prévost said. What Marivaux accomplished through the charm and delicacy of his portraiture and his subtle analysis of the young girl's nascent emotions, Prévost obtained by flaunting and exaggerating self-pity and depicting the turbulence of a love that led ineluctably to the grave. Social significance was not their chosen theme; but quite consciously they prepared the public for the release of inhibitions and a facile display of tender feelings.[6]

The novel of propaganda developed concurrently, linked to the sentimental novel by the deadly earnestness of its social reformism. Perhaps

---

[6] P. Trahard, *Les maîtres de la sensibilité française au xviiie siècle*, 3 vols. (Paris, 1931), I, *passim*, is valuable even at its most didactically repetitious.

not unnaturally the masters of the early propaganda novel were the titans of *la philosophie*. Montesquieu's *Persian Letters* was literally only on the fringe of the novel form, but its propagandist effectiveness compensates for its technical deficiencies. That witty and malicious satire can still be read with pleasure and amusement, for he wrote in the great tradition of the analysts of human personality. Montesquieu's successes inspired a host of imitators to flood the literary market with satiric epistles supposedly written by Indians, wise Chinese, even by Peruvians and Turks, all of them different but sharing a common nullity. "*Le roi* Voltaire" meantime had devised the *conte*, or philosophical tale, to flay religious fanaticism and cruelty. Whatever the particular form, whether the oriental tale with its improbable picaresque adventures, like the fantastic and high-spirited *Zadig*, and the *Princesse de Babylone*, or the inspired morality tale, the imperishable *Candide* of coruscating wit and humor, his moral purpose remained ever the same. The generous Diderot, too, carried on biting propaganda against *l'infâme* in his lengthy (and posthumously published) novel, *La Religieuse*. A realistic psychological study of the unnatural restraints of monastic life and a tirade against involuntary vows, it was the novelistic counterpart of his more profound philosophical dialogues such as *D'Alembert's Dream*, the *Supplement to the Voyage of Bougainville*, and the masterly *Rameau's Nephew*.

Most of these novels of propaganda were both poor novels and poor propaganda, and the form reached its apogee of concentrated dullness in the *Contes Moraux* of Marmontel. A more mature French novel of sensibility was developing, fed by the new native comedy and drama but also greatly influenced by the evolution of the English novel. Across the Channel the genius of the humdrum bookseller, Samuel Richardson, was carrying the sentimental novel to its highest pinnacle.[7] The modern reader doubtlessly is revolted by Richardson's smug self-righteousness and his self-revealing conception of virtue as a sort of cloak that one donned and doffed at will, but such aesthetic or psychological fastidiousness is almost ungracious and certainly irrelevant in the face of Richardson's unparalleled success and the unprecedented sway of his influence. With *Pamela, Charles Grandison*, and above all *Clarissa Harlow*, he consummated the English triumph of

[7] B. W. Downs, *Richardson* (London, 1928), is a readable brief study.

the moral and the sentimental. He had a spectacular cult in France too, where his directive genius brought together into a single stream various feebler currents and lesser eddies. The full-blown French novel of sensibility came to life out of the union of these forms: the psychological novel of Marivaux, Prévost's tender and tragic tales, the popular pre-romantic novels of feminine novelists, like Madame de Tencin's *Comte de Comminge*, the sophisticated novel of voluptuous high life in the school of Crébillon *fils* and Duclos, and not least the influence of Richardson.[8]

II. THE FLOWERING OF SENSIBILITY

Sensibility was in full flower by the mid-century. The ironic Henry Fielding could mockingly write that the only thing on earth superior to the sun in all its majesty was "a human being replete with benevolence," and oppose his own mellow raillery and humanistic tolerance to the more strenuous biblical morality of Pamela's creator. But Richardson's hold over his immense audience remained unloosened.[9] Sensibility of course is not to be confused with social revolt. Without question the sentimental deluge conveyed the troubled mood of all who realized that justice did not reign. But there was nothing in its works to indicate a departure from that continuous and slowly fashioned social pattern which seemed the very essence of England's stability and pre-eminence. The stern Dr. Johnson breathed some of his dour reflections on the futility of endeavor and the hollowness of achievement into his *Rasselas* (1759). The misconception that new manners were bad morals gave a kind of querulous vitality to Brown's jaundiced *Estimate of the Manners and Principles of the Time* (1757). But neither was exactly a voice of revolt. Thomas Cowper, too, fulminated against spurious civilization, the rank abundance that destroyed rural simplicity and bred sloth and lust, wantonness, and gluttonous excess. But he was an evangelical reformer, a curious composite of old-fashioned Christian fervor and the tender humanitar-

---

8 Apart from the formal accounts in the standard manuals, the most valuable treatments are in F. C. Green, *French Novelists: Manners and Ideas from the Renaissance to the Revolution* (New York, 1929), and the same author's brilliant study of French and English literature, *Minuet* (London, 1935).

9 A. Dobson, *Henry Fielding: A Memoir* (London, 1900), and the monumental study, W. L. Cross, *The History of Henry Fielding*, 3 vols. (New Haven, 1918).

ianism of a Robert Burns, who sorrowed for all suffering. George Crabbe, who recoiled in irritation from the current pretty idealizations of rural life and in *The Village* gave a grim and uncompromising picture of the villager's path as it led to the pauper's grave, did indeed strike a more rebellious note. Still he protested almost as ardently against the spiritual degradation of man as against the injustice of man-made institutions. The only authentically revolutionary novel of the entire century was William Godwin's *Caleb Williams*, and even Godwin's revolutionary appeal for social justice was distorted by his rhetorical exaggeration and was drained of vitality by its utopian sentimentalism.

This ambivalence of open sentimental sorrowing and inner acceptance of social evils also came to light in Lawrence Sterne's masterpiece, his prodigiously successful *The Life and Opinions of Tristram Shandy* (1759-1766). This interminable work subsequently provoked violent disagreement among critics. Some virtually swooned in appreciation of the author's delicate sensibility, his subtlety, and his impish humor; while others were revolted by his mawkish lachrymosity and his studied mountebank antics. Whichever appreciation is more nearly correct, it is less apposite than the simple fact that for the rest of his life Sterne was enthroned as high priest of sentimentalizing morality.[10]

He had a host of imitators, most of whom diligently copied his faults. Among the better ones was the versatile Scot, Henry Mackenzie, who in 1771 published *The Man of Feeling*. Its astounding success still compels reluctant admiration. Mackenzie's own statement of his purpose throws some light on its nature: "It consists," he wrote to a friend, "of some episodical adventures of a Man of Feeling where his sentiments are occasionally expressed and the features of his mind developed as the incidents draw them forth. It has, however deficient in other respects, I hope, something of Nature in it, and is uniformly subservient to the cause of Virtue." All the stock characters of a long century appear and reappear in its pages: the faithful servant and the not less loyal house-dog; the philosophical mendicant and the impostor, benevolent of mien; and naturally the wicked seducer and the repentant prostitute who, though ruined by reading bad novels borrowed

10 See the excellent study of W. L. Cross, *The Life and Times of Lawrence Sterne*, 2 vols., new ed. (New Haven, 1925).

from a circulating library, still pulsated harmoniously with the behests of Virtue. Perhaps this statement of the purposes and the cataloguing of the dramatis personae sufficiently explains the great acclaim of the novel.[11]

The sentimental novel reached its apogee in Oliver Goldsmith's *The Vicar of Wakefield*. Loosely constructed throughout and absurdly incredible in its climax, it still holds its place as the finest English novel of sensibility. It is full of stereotypes and groans with copy-book maxims. Yet its feeling is tinctured with wit; and the pity and the charity of the ineffably benevolent Dr. Primrose are nicely sheathed in satire and relieved from inanity by Goldsmith's irrepressible gaiety. While this perennially charming book also had its numerous inferior imitators, a new school of the novel was arising. Meantime the anti-quarianism of Percy's *Reliques* and Macpherson's *Ossian*, along with Chatterton's literary frauds and Burke's speculation on the beautiful and the sublime, came together with Walpole's early Gothic tale, *The Castle of Otranto*, to mark the reawakening of wonder, terror, and romanticism.

While the English novel was thus advancing to the romantic via the new novel of terror, the French sentimental novel reached maturity with Rousseau.[12] *La Nouvelle Héloïse* clearly owed a great deal to Richardson. But it was also indebted to French antecedents. Above all its unique distinction came from the genius of Rousseau himself. Intensely personal and subjective, it was a lyrical work of the creative imagination. It welled forth from his deep frustration, from the thwarted passion of an accredited man of feeling who had only recently experienced the bitter joys of being caught in the coils of burning but alas unrequited love. The Saint-Preux of the novel, who is first the tutor and then the secret lover of Julie d'Etanges, is the fictionalized figure of the real Rousseau, the unsuccessful and slightly ridiculous claimant to the heart of the beautiful Elizabeth Sophie d'Houdetot of real life. He is at first knightly in his feelings

---

11 H. W. Thompson's *A Scottish Man of Feeling, Henry Mackenzie* (New York, 1931) is an attempt both learned and gay to rescue Mackenzie from his limbo of bathos.
12 The controversy concerning Richardson's influence over the French novel in general and Rousseau in particular is given an anti-Richardson turn in Green's *Minuet*, ch. xiv. It is a convincing refutation of Joseph Texte's famous thesis that Richardson changed the destiny of the French novel; cf. the latter's *Jean Jacques Rousseau and the Cosmopolitan Spirit in Literature*, tr. by J. W. Matthews (London, 1899).

and his language is decorous and restrained. As passion grips him, his tone alternately becomes pleading and imperious; and he is at length swept off his balance into violating the precepts of the moral law. But the Julie who yields to his embraces, who, in her delicate phraseology, is responsible for her own sorrow, lives on triumphantly to vindicate virtue's law. Renouncing her guilty passion, she expiates her sin in a heavy self-imposed penance; and she gradually ripens into a model wife, a perfect mother, and an insufferable bore. In the narrative of their guilty passion, Rousseau is the supreme lyricist of his day. In the story of Julie's redemption, the other side of Rousseau is revealed—the untrained but searching psychologist and the unbending moralist.

There were many haunting echoes of this ethical religiosity and this gospel of true if extra-ecclesiastical repentance. *Paul et Virginie*, Bernardin de Saint-Pierre's little masterpiece of escapism, discovered the lost paradise of the innocent and the romantic. A preposterous pastiche, it is still a moving and idyllic tale of the unhappy love of two children who live in the unspoiled simplicity of the island of Mauritius, weeks distant by sail from corrupt Europe. For Bernardin, as for Rousseau, the primitive is the natural and the beautiful. *Paul et Virginie* is the fictional counterpart of Raynal's strained philosophical thesis that the terrestrial Eden had been corrupted by the serpent of European and Christian civilization. The tale is replete with the maudlin pathos of Greuze, and the accents of utopianism and the exotic dream haunt its pages.

Escapism degenerated in Florian's *Fables* into bathos that proved almost too much for its own generation. By some providential system of compensation, the new realistic novel soon arose, not unlike the novel of terror in England. It too paraded its moral purpose, even when, to insensitive readers, a work like Choderlos de Laclos' *Dangerous Relations* (1782) seemed little more than a disguised manual of seduction. Choderlos' contemporary, the gifted Rétif de la Bretonne, who penned many narratives of carnality which fanciers are reputed to esteem, also disclaimed pornographic intent. Indeed, the conclusion to his *Paysan Perverti* (1775) is irreproachably edifying: "Beware, my children. Let us stay in our hamlets and not seek to destroy our blessed ignorance of the pleasures of the large cities. Vice gives us a taste for them, irreligion spurs us to give ourselves to them, crime gives us the opportunity; and misery and disgrace . . . are often their consequence."

In the meantime, the English theater was recovering painfully from the low state to which it had sunk. Interest in the stage ran high and the London theaters all prospered. Scarcely a large provincial town failed either to have its own local theater or to attract a troupe of strolling players. To be sure, not even the genius of a David Garrick or a Mrs. Siddons could entirely rescue Shakespeare from those who purified his language and improved his thoughts. Nor did true comedy exist. Although cross-fertilized by the superior French comedy and infused with the new talent of its own writers, the English comedy failed to regain the sparkle of Congreve and Wycherley. It remained, in some respects, an auxiliary of the pulpit. As Garrick avowed in the prologue to Hugh Kelly's widely acclaimed comedy, *False Delicacy*:

> For our fine piece, to let you into facts,
> Is quite a sermon, only preached in acts.

A promising young playwright could lampoon a dramatization of *Pamela* and put on the boards a broad burlesque with an inner puppet show, styled *The Handsome Housemaid; or Piety in Pattens—wherein a Maiden of low Degree, by the mere Effects of Morality and Virtue, raised herself to Riches and Honours*. Yet the same audience that laughed at this skit or chuckled at *False Delicacy* preferred inspirational and elevating plays like Cumberland's *The West Indian* and *The Jew*.

Oliver Goldsmith and Richard Sheridan never successfully destroyed this empire of the sentimental. True, *The Good Natured Man* ridiculed contemporary posturing and attitudinizing. Miss Hardcastle, the robust, lusty, and unshockable heroine of *She Stoops to Conquer*, was a vast relief after simpering and virtuous maidens. Tony Lumpkin's hearty and irreverent guffaws released a long-imprisoned spirit of merriment. But Goldsmith was no satirist lashing his victims in a purifying wrath. He laughed gently and poked tender fun at his victims without destroying or wishing to destroy the kindly attitude toward human nature which was at the core of the sentimental comedy. Sheridan's brilliance shone brighter and his wit was more biting. He had an extraordinary comedy sense and he was a master of situation. Yet in both *The Rivals* and the *School for Scandal* he showed that he too was "no stranger to the finer feelings," as one of his contemporaries put it. His impelling motives, and those of his characters, also stem from humanitarianism. His satire could corrode the pharisaical Joseph Surface, but he admired the charitable prodigal, Charles Surface, and extolled Sir Peter's kindly forbearance. Perhaps Goldsmith and Sheridan succeeded in strengthening the comic element but they manifestly did not eliminate the sentimental element of the combination.[13]

French sentimental comedy failed to realize its early promise, for it increasingly sacrificed its comic spirit to the didactic. It degenerated into the domestic tragedy, or *drame*, for which the protean Diderot supplied an edifying aesthetic. According to his famous *Entretien sur le fils naturel, Dorval et moi* (1757), the social situation was to take precedence over characterization, and individuals were to step backstage, allowing their personal problems to be overshadowed by the impersonal dilemmas of social reformation. The name of the new theater, *le genre sérieux*, was not inappropriate to its purpose of safeguarding the purity of the family hearth. Except the improvements that he suggested in more realistic acting and stagecraft, Diderot's disservice to the theater was not inconsiderable. His own plays in the improved style, *Le fils naturel* and *Le père de famille*, had all the merits of intelligence and most of the defects of prodigious dullness.

This bourgeois drama never developed a playwright of talent in the several decades that it flooded the stage with pathos. In the fullness of time a true theatrical genius, Beaumarchais, arose. His task to rescue the comic muse was similar to Sheridan's, and he accomplished it more successfully. *The Barber of Seville* (1775) and the more satiric *The Marriage of Figaro* (1784) revealed a rare talent. His plays kept and fused the best elements of several varying traditions, but the final product was Beaumarchais, gay and witty, stamped by high resourcefulness and originality of plot, and marked by a brilliant and versatile command of stagecraft.

13 Cf. Green *Minuet*, ch. vi; Bernbaum, *op. cit.*, chs. viii-xiv; and G. H. Nettleton, *The Major Dramas of Richard Brinsley Sheridan* (New York, 1906), Introduction.

The memorable *première* of *The Marriage of Figaro* was one of the greatest triumphs in the entire history of the French stage. Much of its success was due to the transparently disguised satire. Still, to attribute the play's astounding run entirely to Beaumarchais' political criticism and to see in him the harbinger of revolution is to turn as sentimental as the very victims of his wit. *The Marriage of Figaro* was far more comedy than sociology. Figaro, in many ways Beaumarchais' alter ego, vigorously strikes back at his social superiors who seek to abuse and exploit him. While railing at the abuses of the social order, he seems as much distressed over the fact that he himself does not stand at its summit. One almost has the feeling that were he in the position of his master, he would treat his own Figaro thus; and that his own servant moreover would imperturbably continue to cheat and deceive him without entertaining any revolutionary desire to plant trees of liberty while doing so.[14]

III. ESCAPE FROM FREEDOM—GERMAN STYLE

Sensibility first penetrated German literature as censure of princely and aristocratic mores. The many weeklies imitative of *The Spectator* and *The Tatler* also followed their English originals in compromising with ugly realities. Anacreontic poets and the enthusiasts of nature soon sounded their tender dissent against life's hardships, but throughout all the earlier decades, dominated by the influence of men like Gottsched and Gellert, the body of creative and critical writing was marred by weak sentimentalism and shallow rationalism.[15]

The decade of the sixties displayed a more manly temper and a greater national self-consciousness. Frederick's military victories over the French were put to cultural service by the emerging middle classes, who cast off the French cultural yoke almost as though they were retorting to Voltaire's cruel taunt that Germans used their native language only to address servants and animals. While the younger generation was experiencing that exhilarating sense of emancipation

---

[14] Cf. Green's interesting argument to this effect in *Minuet*, 182-191.

[15] In English see K. Francke, *History of German Literature as Determined by Social Forces*, 4th rev. ed. (New York, 1907), chs. vii and viii; in German H. Hettner, *Geschichte der deutschen Literatur im achtzehnten Jahrhundert*, ed. by Witkowski (Leipzig, 1929), and the more convenient work of A. Koester, *Die deutsche Literatur der Aufklärungszeit* (Heidelberg, 1925), chs. iv and v.

coupled, however, with the sinking awareness that life was depriving them of opportunities for assuming their rightful responsibilities, the many-sided Lessing was leading the Berlin circle of rationalists in cultural reforms. In fighting against vacuous and insipid art and musical forms, Lessing fought for his country's spiritual emancipation and for a national literature as free from dependence upon foreign models as it would be innocent of religious intolerance and class snobbery. But his own plays are unreal, soaring above actual living. For all the sincerity of *Emilia Galotti* and *Nathan the Wise* and all the delightful humor of *Minna von Barnhelm*, they never came to grips with the problems they presented.[16]

By a curiously ironic twist of fortune this sober intelligence, whose services to German cultural development were so great, speeded the coming of the *Geniezeit* and the *Sturm und Drang*. Inspired but also profoundly disturbed by Winckelmann's pamphlet, *Thoughts on the Imitation of Greek Works in Painting and Sculpture* (1755), Lessing countered vigorously with his *Laocoön, or the Boundaries Between Painting and Poetry* (1766). He carefully analyzed Winckelmann's brilliant argument that nobility of soul manifested itself in stoical restraint, as shown by the example of Laocoön, but he thoroughly rejected the conclusion that "the noble simplicity and serene greatness" of Greek statues were also the true characteristic of Greek literature in its best period. He advanced in its stead the contrary argument, derived also from Greek examples but applicable universally, that while art, which dealt with bodies, attained its supreme expression in statuesque repose, poetry was in no wise subject to the restraints and the boundaries of the art form. Poetry, which deals with action and movement, he argued, if it were to be true to its inner essence must pulsate with energy and be vibrant with life. And his scholarly and dramatic work reached its climax when he symbolically separated the two forms and restored freedom of motion to poetry.

Thus the *Laocoön* emancipated poetry—not poetry in general but German poetry in particular. It was Lessing's destiny to disassociate the idea of sublimity from its identification with the noble, the beautiful, and the serene, and to prepare for the Storm and Stress by

16 E. Schmidt, *Lessing, Geschichte seines Lebens und seiner Schriften,* 2 vols., 4th ed. (Berlin, 1923).

expounding an aesthetic that placed the seal of artistic approval upon the painful, the tearful, and, above all, upon the passionate.[17] Goethe recounts in his *Autobiography* how his group at Strasbourg threw themselves during those very years "into living knowledge, experience, action, and poetizing." Wieland was too cynical for these nature-drunk youths, too much the detached and satirical novelist. Only Klopstock, the "divine Klopstock," remained a hero. Their *Weltschmerz* was of course highly personal, an aspect of adolescent adjustment. It also articulated with the prevailing temper. It fed on their discovery of Shakespeare's tragic turbulence; Rousseau harrowed their minds; and they all shuddered with guilty pleasure over the dark and forbidding effusions of *Ossian*, its fantastic and weird figures and its forebodings of disaster and death.

The Sorrows of the Young Werther was thus a perfect expression of the thwarted longings and collective frustrations. Werther's tirades against "people of sound understanding"; his interminable posturing, his adoration of Homer, and his cult of the silver-tongued Ossian; his kindly and well-publicized benevolence toward the gentle villagers; his morbid joy in torturing himself after Lotte's marriage to another; and finally his suicide—all these effusions made pleasurable inroads upon the serenity of Goethe's contemporaries. Despite all governmental discouragement, the Werther fever raged through young Germany, eventuating occasionally in a dramatic and needless suicide, but for the most part working itself out more peacefully in Werther costumes, Werther engravings and embroidery, low reliefs and medallions, and even wafting its essence into a perfume called *"Eau de Werther."* The English and French also devoured the book in translation; and an impressionable young Corsican named Napoleone Buonaparte read it seven times, he avers, weeping copiously at each reading.

This collective adolescent romanticism imbued, at least in part, the sybilline utterances of Hamann, the self-styled Magus of the North It pervaded Herder's literary reconstructions of the Germanic past; and it inspired Lavater's science of physiognomy, whose students were to make the valuable discovery that a pure benevolent physiog-

17 For the entire argument, see Miss E. M. Butler, *The Tyranny of Greece over Germany* (Cambridge, Eng., 1935), chs. i-iv.

nomic type did exist. It played havoc with the less robust, who lashed themselves into frenzies of letter writing, alternating this epistolary exercise with cults of friendship and sham suicide pacts, all of which it became fashionable to regard as superior manifestations of tenderness and pity.[18]

For two decades dramatists, novelists, and poets poured out works contrasting the aesthetic ideal of emancipated humanity and free individuals to the decadent moral corruption, aristocratic tyranny, and social injustices of the sad present. The theme was ever the same, whether expressed in Friedrich Stolberg's *Ode to Liberty*, the ballads of Bürger, Heinse's half-utopian and half-despairing novel, *Ardinghello*, or any of the fiery *Sturm und Drang* plays. All these youthful works warred on authority. They repudiated the sober conventions of society and extolled only the primitive, the original, and the incorruptibly simple. Goethe's own rebellious champion of humanity— robber baron Goetz von Berlichingen, who defied empire, church, and death—fired deeply the imagination with his super-teutonic masculinity. This humanitarian melodrama reached its climax with the young Schiller's conception of the sublime criminal. The hero of *The Robbers* (1781), Karl Moor, set himself not to reform society but to destroy it. "The law has never yet formed a great man, but freedom breeds colossuses and giants," boasts Robber Moor. The bombast and the fury were only foils, for Schiller had a thoroughly moral purpose in mind. The play was a dramatic narrative, whose scheme required that several characters should offend the finer feeling of virtue. But, the preface continued, "Whoever proposes to discourage vice and vindicate religion, morality, and social order against their adversaries, must unveil crime in all its deformity; and place it before the eyes of men in its colossal magnitude." Consequently, after a career of stupendous crime, Robber Moor gives himself up to the representatives of law and order.

Karl Moor's surrender to the police was symbolical, not of Schiller alone, but of the entire Storm and Stress movement. Schiller himself was already wafting his bark down the quieter waters of philosophical resignation, settling down to the study and writing of history. The

---

18 Cf. the old work of E. Sierke, *Schwärmer und Schwindler zu Ende des XVIII. Jahrhunderts* (Leipzig, 1874).

movement culminated in a final empty blare. The words of the young rebels ever had the ring of revolutionary calls. Their poses were always warm with the glow of resentment at the exploitation of the poor; yet never did their bombast, their heroic defiances, their blood and thunder, incite to revolt. The writers were careful to key their protest, if not above human reality, at least recognizably removed from the geographic reality in which they themselves lived. They had no direct and immediate contact with the perplexing needs of life. They had no tug from reality. They simply did not know the poor whose annals they recorded; and their benevolence was in the main offensively patronizing. The unconscious class snobbery that Goethe alone reveals in *Werther* is truly monumental.

The waves of the Storm and Stress spent themselves in such heroics. Gradually, the aging young men made their peace with society. They discovered in the all-prevailing and all-pervading Graecomania eternal and universal standards in aesthetics, literature, and the arts which could lift man above life's tribulations and give him consolation of a loftier order for its dangers and discordance. The *Humanitätsideal* found a comfortable terrestrial home in the benevolent duchy of Weimar, where Goethe, now full of his Italian journey, was preparing for his long rule as cultural director of Parnassus.

The devotees of the transcendental truths of Greek culture warmed themselves at the hearth of that temple. They were nourished by a steady flow of supplies from the excavations at Pompeii and Herculaneum, the teachings at the University of Göttingen, and the writings of the revered and prematurely departed Winckelmann. For them beauty was truth and truth, beauty. For the benighted incapable of soaring there remained the salutary household stuff of literature: almanacs, useful recipes and remedies, and compendia of moral aphorisms.

Rediscovering classical antiquity was only one of the ways in which the century renewed the ties with its own historic past. To be historical-minded was, in some instances, a superficial craze, like the fashion for English gardens, Chinese pagodas, or Gothic furniture. It was also a trend that connected with the dawn of enthusiasm and the liberation of poetry from philosophy. Pervaded by a new aesthetic and romantic protest, by that tentative willingness to suspend disbelief which Burke's *Philosophical Enquiry Into the Origin of Our Ideas of the Sublime and Beautiful* significantly revealed, it was above all a dominant chord in the symphony of the romantic rebellion, a curiously aberrant and anti-rationalist individualism. The mood was waning that saw history as philosophy teaching by examples, a record of experiences corroborating reason's dictum that under surface differences the principles of human nature ever remained "constant and invariant." A new tone was sounded at the very moment that Raynal and Gibbon were bringing the rationalist interpretation of history to its apogee. Rousseau had been led by his personal insecurity into eloquently ringing the changes of human personality; and Burke's fears impelled in him a respect bordering on religious reverence for those historical processes that he was "presently unable to comprehend."

But the great heralds of the new historical temper were Möser and Herder. Möser's *Osnabrückische Geschichte*, in particular its reverberating introduction, together with Herder's *Ideen zur Philosophie der Geschichte der Menschheit*, graphically illustrated that "rebarbarization" of literature in which Pascal had discovered the distinguishing mark of true cultural vitality. Möser's idealized and loving picture of the German middle ages as resting upon a foundation of a free peasant democracy was a flagrant distortion. Still, by directing attention to the Germanic past as the expression of an evolving folk culture of sturdy independent peasants, he did much to efface the rationalist historians' equally abstract conception of the middle ages as one long and unredeemed Gothic night of a thousand years. His *Osnabrückische Geschichte* and his *Patriotische Phantasien* were strong appeals for the writing of living history conceived on a broad social basis and founded on the idea of growth and change.[19]

While he was laying down the premises of the genetic method, his younger and more gifted contemporary, Herder, was elaborating the implications of the basic idea. With a breadth of learning and an intellectual vigor that made him one of the greatest seminal forces of modern German culture, Herder traced the evolution of man's diversified cultural activities in literature and the arts, language and religion,

---

[19] Cf. W. J. Bossenbrook, "Justus Möser's Approach to History," in *Mediaeval and Historiographical Essays in Honor of J. W. Thompson*, ed. by J. L. Cate and E. N. Anderson (Chicago, 1938).

not as independent expressions but as closely correlated manifestations of national culture. A passionate nationalist, he yearned to rescue his beloved German mediaeval lyric and epic from the scorn that the admirers of classical forms vented upon them. In national poetry, the untutored and uninhibited folk song of primitive peoples, he heard the voice of his race and saw the reflection of its soul. He saw in Shakespeare's dramatic intensity the full expression of Teutonic genius, and he heard in Ossian's dadaist melodramatics the authentic echo of the spirit of the north. In his *Fragmente über die neuere deutsche Literatur* he had already supplied the Storm and Stress with its literary creed. His *Über den Ursprung der Sprache* anticipated the scientific study of comparative philology. His canons of artistic taste, laid down in *Kritische Wälder*, were aesthetic counter-blasts to classicist enthusiasts in the lineage of Winckelmann who denied the beauties of the Gothic. He was one of the first students to trace the origins of religion back to the mythological beliefs of primitive people.

The four volumes of the *Ideen* and the many tomes of his *Briefe zur Beförderung der Humanität* were encyclopedic efforts to elaborate the idea of organic growth in the whole of recorded human development. Those diffuse studies were the Veda of the new historical faith. Herder had moved far away from the rationalist interpretation of history as a panoramic epic where under different names and shifting locales, unimportant in themselves, a timeless struggle raged between reason and superstition. He turned away from the *philosophes'* arid conception of the individual as a sort of manikin moved by intellectual springs and progressing logically toward the nirvana of human perfectibility. The individual re-emerged in his atavistic nakedness, a prisoner of emotional promptings and the pawn of a destiny that was moved by a logic greater than the reasoning of any one man. He did not re-enter the pages of Herder's history alone, separated from his fellows. At all times and on all levels of historical experience he belongs to his community. The national genius fashions him and gives direction to his individual strivings, even as his very person incorporates the spirit of the group. Moreover, this genius or spirit of each racial group was unique, the product of the interplay of time and place with protoplasm, material resources, and social relations. Each stage of evolution, by this line of thought, was rationally perfect and perfectly rational because it corresponded with an inner rationale of growth. Finally, just as the individual belonged to the nation, so each nation belonged to humanity, by its distinct culture contributing richly to the harmonious evolution of all mankind.

Herder's creative speculation was the dying century's span to the new age. It was the spiritual foundation of the strangely etherealized and distorted Germanic version of idealism. Precisely as Condorcet's picture of human progress was the last will and testament of eighteenth-century European rationalism, so Herder's learned apologia for the intuitive, the emotional, and the irrational was the *summa* of German escapism. To a world tortured in the travail of democracy German political thought preached the gospel of subordinating individual longings for the greater glory of the national state. As German burghers let life go by, consoling themselves, by a nice respect for the proprieties of status, for their exclusion from a share in real civic responsibilities, so Herder's magnificently sustained and learned misconception of the past administered the balm of solace for present humiliations. Since the individual found immortality in the undying group spirit, he was always, theologically speaking, in a state of grace. The bitterness of existence where circumstances still compelled men to choke in public the doubts that assailed them in private was somehow assuaged by the learned doctrine that private misfortune also contributed to the national good.[20]

IV. MUSIC AND THE AGE OF ENLIGHTENMENT

Music also moved toward the romantic. The graceful epilogue of rococo that attended the culmination of the earlier mathematical idiom in the magnificent compositions of Bach and Händel was little more at first than the counterpart of the *style galant* of Boucher and Lancret. It was, with its delicate tone colors and modulated volume, a gay reproach to the grandiose extravagance of baroque, a reflection of the prevailing aesthetic that corrected the unrealities of

20 In addition to the study of Ergang already cited, cf. E. Fueter, *L'histoire de l'historiographie moderne*, tr. and rev. ed. (Paris, 1914), 507-512; Fr. Meinecke, *Die Enstehung des Historismus*, 2 vols. (Munich, 1936); and the searching article of C. A. Beard and A. Vagts, "Currents of Thought in Historiography," in *American Historical Review*, XLII (1937), 460-483.

the salon with the greater artificialities of a nature peopled by nymphs and shepherds. But as the disciples of rococo's great theorist, Rameau, elaborated its fuller implications, rococo emerged in its own creative right as a significant interlude pointing to modern musical aesthetic.

The Mannheim school of composers clustered around Stamitz, together with the Viennese instrumentalists, rendered great service in furthering the emancipation of music from its bondage to other art forms. Substituting the tenet that harmony rather than melody should be the determinant of structural form, they did much to modify the existing conception of instrumental compositions, whether solo or concerted, as auxiliaries of poetry, theater, and the dance. While technological genius was devising the modern pianoforte of steel frame and high-tension strings as a substitute for the wooden frame and brass strings of the older harpsichord, the innovators were preparing for the symphonic form by adding new instruments and mixing strings, woodwinds, and brasses in concerted compositions. Subtly changing the quality of tone and heightening dramatic effect by adding the contrast of color, they broadened the range and swelled the volume of instrumental performances. Under the combined impact of technological, social, and aesthetic change music was slowly evolving from a purely domestic art into a platform art, soon to edify large public audiences drawn mainly from the ranks of the well-to-do middle classes.

Structural changes and evolving tastes also effected a revolution in the opera. Despite a contemporary critic's rule that:

> La musique doit, ainsi que la peinture,
> Retracer à nos yeux le vrai de la nature

there was no unanimity in interpreting the nature of "la nature." In lyrical tragedy and ballet opera it was taken to mean the sentimentalized and insipid nature à la Rousseau. But in Christoph Wilibald von Gluck's restoration of naturalness to the serious opera nature was conceived in the aesthetic of Winckelmann. The natural became synonymous with the classical Greek ideal of symmetry and dignified simplicity. Gluck's famous preface to *Alceste* was a resounding blast against the current operatic vacuity. Music and drama were to complement each other. Music was to support and strengthen the poetic sentiment and accentuate the dramatic intensity of the plot without interrupting the action or weakening it by superfluous ornament. His own great operas—*Alceste, Orpheus and Eurydice, Iphigenia in Aulis*—where both pantomime and an augmented orchestra fully exploit the emotional possibilities, were exciting realizations of his credo. The best of his melodies have a sculptural plasticity; his plot is skillfully drawn; the dramatis personae are real characters; and the choruses swell and advance the dramatic incidents.

The various currents of change flowed together in the restlessly creative musical intelligence of Joseph Haydn. In music his glory rests on his contribution to the sonata form, on his greatness as the creator of the string quartet, on his position as father of the symphony, and not least on his decisive influence in the development of the modern orchestra. In the broader stream of eighteenth-century culture, however, Haydn symbolizes a truer return to nature, a nature more real than that of the gallants and less intensely studied than that of Gluck. The son of a Croatian peasant, he brought a breath of fresh air into "the patchouli-scented atmosphere of the salon." The melodic strain of native folk songs ran through his own highly structured compositions; and he addressed himself consciously to the humble of the earth, hoping as he phrased it that "the weary and the worn, or the man burdened with affairs, may enjoy a few moments of solace and refreshment."

His pupil and younger contemporary, Wolfgang Amadeus Mozart, baffles stereotyped labeling. His brief personal career belongs to musical history. It was an unhappy existence, beginning with the precocity of a *Wunderkind*, whom an exacting father condemned to exhausting tours, and ending with years of humiliating labor in order to discharge crushing debts. The career of the great genius also belongs to the cultural development of his age. Only naïve misunderstanding can hear his compositions as the expression of a graceful placidity. He does not, it is true, strike poses and brave the lightning. Nor does he, like so many of the melancholy young men who were his contemporaries, flamboyantly advertise a head bloody and unbowed under the bludgeonings of chance. Happily one would seek and not find in his works mawkish or moralizing sentimentalism. He is neither a dupe of nor a propagandist for the verities sociological.

The truth of the matter is that Mozart was thoroughly eighteenth century in his style, the balanced, measured, and beautifully proportioned style that typified the ideal and rarely the reality of true sophisticates and aristocrats. His great dramatic operas are overwhelming proof that his talent and forte lay in the delineation of personality. He represents the deep and persistent humanist concern with the eternal verities of human nature. The serenity and the clarity of his great string quartets and the peerless last symphonies are hardly synonymous with shallowness or simplicity of spirit. Perhaps the physical limitations of the eighteenth-century orchestra accentuated the sense of measured strength and tranquillity that his genius imparted of itself to those undying compositions. But his limitless melodic outpourings evidence an undeniable inward urge to surmount the deficiencies of his medium and escape the vestiges of baroque formalism. The romantic is not distant from the classicist in Mozart; the diversity and the conflict of his age are only concealed; and the fires of the *Sturm und Drang* smolder in his restraint.[21]

V. THE ARTS AND CRAFTS

Rococo's day was ending in the sixth decade, its role fulfilled, especially on the Continent. Chinese civilization had contributed much to it and the decorative arts, too; and at a given moment no one who pretended to be in the mode could do without his precious Chinese pottery, his lacquer-covered furniture, his walls hung with Chinese paper, or his priceless Chinese silks. For the very rich or the regal there were Chinese gardens and pagodas, pavilions and grottos; for the learned, the writings of the sage Confucius to study; and for all, the opportunity to watch the performances of Chinese shadow plays.[22]

The vogue of classical antiquity swept all before it in the declining years of rococo. The excavations at Pompeii and Herculaneum stim-

21 Of the more conventional histories of music, Cecil Gray's astringently intelligent *The History of Music* (New York, 1928) is easily the most valuable; H. Leichtentritt, *Music, History, and Ideas* (Cambridge, 1938), chs. vii and viii, is very suggestive in its rarefied, conceptual way; and P. H. Láng, *Music in Western Civilization* (New York, 1941), chs. xii-xiv, is a magnificent pioneering work, with all the virtues and some of the defects of such difficult endeavors.

22 A. Reichwein, *China and Europe. Intellectual and Artistic Contacts in the Eighteenth Century* (New York, 1925).

ulated the new interest. The *grand tour* fed it. The publication of Winckelmann's *History of Art*, along with the seven stout volumes of the Count Caylus' *Recueil d'Antiquités* and the lavishly illustrated *The Antiquities of Athens* of Stuart and Revett, virtually made it irresistible. Even the uncompromising British patriot Tobias Smollett succumbed to the craze and confessed a "most eager curiosity to see the antiquities of Florence and Rome . . . to view those wonderful edifices, statues and pictures, which I had so often admired in prints and description. I felt an enthusiastic ardour to tread that very classical ground which had been the scene of so many achievements."[23]

Curiously, neo-classicism, while repudiating rococo and reflecting the Renaissance admiration for antiquity, also pointed toward the romantic future. This merger with pre-romanticism is difficult to explain. Somehow the first rapturous poetic discovery of nature's simple delights swelled under these contradictory influences into the cult of a nature at once more sublime and more pathetic. People's minds gradually accepted not only ruined classical temples, theaters, and palaces as constituting nature, but also bleak heaths, cataracts leaping in glory, the splendor of castle walls, and snowy summits old in story. The evolution of the garden from the geometrically classical design of Le Nôtre to the newer natural style conveys a sense of the astounding aesthetic confusion in which the Chinese and the Gothic, the neo-classical and the romantic, combined in an extraordinary artistic eclecticism. For at its most "natural" the eighteenth-century garden could effect an awe-inspiring combination pillaged from a luxuriant choice of arbors and secluded grottos, hermitages and ruined temples, miniature hills, neatly piled rocks cut negligently by rippling cascades, and peaceful canals winding through open lawns.[24]

The graphic and plastic arts reflected this joint invasion of the neo-classical and the sentimental. Richard Wilson, the "father of English landscape painting," skillfully adapted the hybrid form to his native soil and profitably ransacked nature for moving effects. The canvases of George Morland dripped with sentiment, colored engravings of his scenes of village life for years remaining treasured adornments in many

23 Tobias Smollett, *op. cit.*, II, 2.
24 E. Manwaring, *Italian Landscape in Eighteenth Century England* (London, 1925); and B. Sprague Allen, *Tides in English Taste*, 2 vols. (Cambridge, 1937).

a humble home. While lesser artists cultivated the penchant for the picturesque topographical scene, the popular and capable George Stubbs painted sporting scenes which successfully met a public demand for high-bred horses and lovable dogs.[25]

Italian painting of the later eighteenth century remained undistinguished. The canvases of the two Canaletti faithfully reproduced continental urban activities. While the Venetian Tiepolo did decorative scenes with talent, and his compatriot Longhi observed keenly and commented ironically, the neo-classical Pompeo Batoni remained fashionably uninspired. Landscape painting in France had the conscientious Joseph Vernet to strip nature for its melancholy effects; while Hubert Robert, the *"Robert des Ruines,"* who studiously set his edifying moments of everyday life against a background of classical ruins, adorned it with archeology. Even Fragonard, the painter of *scènes galantes* in the sophisticated manner of Boucher, was sufficiently infected by the mood to paint idyllic scenes of bucolic joy.

Sensibility came most to its own, however, in the painting of manners. Chardin's canvases of middle-class domesticity, like his *"La Mère Laborieuse"* and *"La Vieille Femme Cousant"* radiated tenderness and gleamed with the high moral rectitude that the *drame bourgeois* was currently defending on the stage. Of his many admiring followers Lépicié was the most notable, and surely the most sociologically valuable if not invariably the most aesthetically enjoyable. But the stupendous straining of Greuze eclipsed all previous efforts for sentimental effect. As an artist he possessed unusual technical competence, which he exploited in a sedulous cultivation of a true emotionalism and a barely concealed eroticism. His talent served him well, for he enjoyed the plaudits of extraordinary popularity. He was in truth a pictorial evangelist of petty-bourgeois felicity; and his famous paintings—"The Father of the Family Reading the Bible," "The Paralytic," "The Happy Mother," and "The Village Bride"—were all powerful sermons in oil.

English portrait painting was dominated by the two great figures of Sir Joshua Reynolds and Thomas Gainsborough. If only by reason

[25] *Georgian Art (1760-1820)*, ed. by Roger Fry and others (New York, 1929); and S. Sitwell, *Conversation Pieces. A Study of English Domestic Portraits and their Painters* (New York, 1937), ch. v.

of its subject matter, aristocratic portraiture was less likely to reflect the vogue, though on occasion the martial Roman toga consorted anachronistically with the lordly Georgian periwig. Reynolds was in his personal life a thorough opportunist, tough-minded and calculating, resourceful and tenacious, and as urbane as any occasion demanded. He was the portrait painter par excellence of the nobility, in part because of his artistic talent, but even more because his own values gave him rare psychological insight into the personality of his sitters. Their world was one: the universe of strength, power, and wealth. By the prestige of his success and his authoritative position as president of the newly established Royal Academy, Sir Joshua was to maintain his influence over English painting for half a century after his death. His late contemporaries and successors, Romney, Hoppner, Opie, and Sir Thomas Lawrence, all gravitated more or less faithfully in his orbit. On the other hand, Thomas Gainsborough expressed a more sensitive mood. Technically as competent, he was deficient in that keen calculation which made Sir Joshua the eminently successful pictorial promoter that he was. By training as well as by temperament Gainsborough was a lover of nature, its different moods and the chiaroscuro of its twilights. His greatest portraits are suffused with the values of landscape, because his sitters are treated integrally with the background. A careful observer, he meticulously recorded details that eluded less patient artists, capturing fleeting expressions with quick, suggestive strokes, often the mood of perplexity or doubt that lay under the surface of aristocratic assurance.[26]

French portraiture, which had been dominated by the impressionistic and psychological analysis of Quentin de la Tour, also became impregnated with sensibility. Aristocrats of ancient lineage and parvenu farmers-general, popular actresses, and merchant princes continued to sit more or less condescendingly for their portraits. The poses, though not improved, were new. Duplessis introduced the first wave of dreamers and pensive readers, most of them melancholy. With Mme. Vigée Lebrun in her first vein came upper-class milkmaids and romantic gardeners posing self-consciously for posterity, and loving mothers, too, with adoring children clinging to their satin skirts. In her

26 Sitwell, op. cit., ch. vi; and R. H. Wilenski, English Painting (London, 1933), chs. viii and ix.

last phase this excellent artist, who knew her public well, revealed her sitters in the fashionably diaphanous costumes, negligent scarves, and gracefully flowing veils of dear departed Greeks and Romans.[27]

Sculpture followed the general evolution of taste. The frivolous and artificial gaiety of Boucher lingered insipidly in Clodion, even in Falconet, who could range also from delightful miniatures to heroic statues in the style of his contemporary Pigalle. But insidious government pressure—for the influence of the state was still great over the corporative structure of the licensed artists—combined with the trend of taste to discredit the allegorical and the frivolously sensual, and antiquity won the day in sculpture with a hybrid neo-classical and sentimental genre. Pigalle crowded Paris with the statues of the famous of both sexes and Houdon flooded it with his representations of the political and intellectual leaders of the time. The decadence of sculpture remained on the whole unbroken outside France. Canova's productive period as a truly great restorer of classical art was only beginning in 1780, as was the fertile creative painting genius of Goya. The absence of originality and real talent did not diminish the popularity of Joseph Nollekens, though John Flaxman was a more significant innovator of classicism. In his early career he had worked for Wedgwood, modeling both classic and domestic friezes and plaques, ornamental vases, and medallion portraits for the great potter. That that experience proved invaluable for his later career was revealed in his memorial sculpture, which at its best admirably combined the contemporary sentimentalism with classical simplicity.

Architecture in the classical style developed via the mannered rococo from the massive Palladian and the baroque to Winckelmann's ideal of "the noble simplicity and the serene greatness of the ancients." Everywhere, and most of all in England, the century experienced a protracted building boom. Successful professional men in the towns and prosperous men of affairs in the larger cities lavished their wealth upon comfortable homes and decorations. Along with country mansions and small town houses for the well-to-do, architects and builders like the two Woods, Gibbs, Holland, and Dance also began town

---

27 Cf. R. Schneider's useful manual, *L'art Français. Dix-huitième siècle* (Paris, 1926); also the more detailed A. Leroy, *Histoire de la peinture française, 1700-1800* (Paris, 1934), and R. H. Wilenski, *French Painting* (London, 1931), Pt. IV.

planning and public housing for the poor. More than any other architect, however, since the days of Wren, Robert Adam changed the face
of London. In Lansdowne House and Stratford House, in the charming unit of Kenwood, and most of all in the now vanished Adelphi,
he remodeled the building style of the capital on the models that he
had so carefully studied in his apprentice days in Italy. Gabriel and
Soufflot and their school met a similar demand in France. Countless
private mansions and public buildings arose—theaters, administrative
centers, hospitals, ample municipal squares, and public promenades—
which pleased yet dazzled the eye with a stylistic catholicity born of
an unnatural union of predominantly Graeco-Roman and classical
Renaissance forms with imperial Egyptian and contemporary Italian.

Prosperity also expanded the demand for furniture and decorative
adornments for the home. The ideal of craftsmanship was never
higher, for the unconscious connoisseurs who appreciated good, clean
design and honest quality would not tolerate either meretricious workmanship or inferior quality. In all countries the century was a great
period for furniture designers and cabinet workers. The great French
craftsmen and designers of the "style Louis XVI" had their leaders in
Riesener and Roentgen, whose graceful furniture was soberly elegant
in design and superbly executed in its workmanship. In England the
sturdy yet graceful "Chinese-Gothick" of Thomas Chippendale was
slowly giving way to the classical elegance of Hepplewhite and the
willowy delicacy of Sheraton. In furniture, silverware, and most articles
of household adornment, it was neither a furniture maker nor a silver-
smith who set the designs for England. It was the extraordinarily
gifted Robert Adam. Together with his brother James, this great
architectural genius designed practically all kinds of decorative ob-
jects; and often even the humble artisan working for a client with
modest purse unwittingly executed forms that Adam had created for
his aristocratic patrons.[28]

The large-scale manufacture of serviceable earthenware illustrated
even more graphically than the vogue of household adornment the
shift in patronage from the aristocratic few to the prosperous many.
The earliest English experiments at Chelsea and Bow to produce por-

[28] M. Jourdain, *Decoration and Furniture in England during the Later Eighteenth
Century, 1760-1820* (London, 1922).

celain resembling the Chinese or the Saxon and competing with them in quality or price proved unsuccessful. Meantime, however, the English potters mastered the secret of producing excellent native porcelain, and subsequent experimentation at Derby and Worcester paved the way for the reign of Wedgwood at Staffordshire.

Josiah Wedgwood was not only a man of high aesthetic taste, but a production genius of the first order. By using new material, utilizing the newly invented steam engine for the grinding of clays, employing precision tools, and introducing modern specialization of labor, he revolutionized pottery production practically singlehanded. He popularized English ceramics so thoroughly that the inexpensive and tastefully designed wares bearing his name spread from English homes to those of the middle classes in all of western Europe. Economic progress thus spread prosperity among many thousands of honest burghers, giving them the means to indulge their taste and stimulating that taste for the artistic and the comfortable.

Chapter Ten

FAITH, HOPE, AND CHARITY IN SECULAR DRESS

I. SECULAR SALVATION

HUMANITARIANISM gradually pervaded life, even as it flooded literature and the arts, and lay reformers worked assiduously to realize their ideal of happiness on earth. But their efforts to attain secular salvation, to spread the greatest possible benefits among the greatest possible number, were held in check, they averred, by the institutionalized strength of the revealed religions and most of all by the prestige and the power of the "advanced sentinels of the court of Rome," as they called the Jesuits. The anti-clerical rationalists in France were by no means the only foes of the Jesuits, nor was the attack upon them directed solely on grounds of dogma. Rationalists moved by humanitarian liberalism against the cultural authoritarianism of Catholicism joined with nationalist patriots who strongly resented papal influence over state policy; and the Gallican episcopate aspiring toward ecclesiastical autonomy within their own country came together with the Jansenists, whose opposition to the Jesuits derived largely from ethical considerations.[1] Hence in all Catholic countries the Society of Jesus was the focal point of attack.

The first overt blow fell in Portugal, where the violently anti-Jesuit minister Pombal was already engaged in methodically leveling the obstacles to royal absolutism; and from Portugal the wave of hostility spread to the other Catholic states. Finding a pretext in the alleged complicity of the Jesuits in a plot against his monarch, Pombal unleashed a fierce vendetta against them. Ignoring papal pleas and remonstrances, he sequestrated their possessions, dissolved their organization, and expelled their members from all Portuguese territory. By

[1] E. Préclin, *Les Jansenistes du XVIIIe siècle* . . . (Paris, 1929), and V. Martin, *Le Gallicanisme politique et le clergé de France* (Paris, 1929).

way of crowning that crowded year of 1759, he broke off diplomatic relations completely with Rome.[2]

A bitter factional dispute, born of the reopening of the perennial Jesuit-Jansenist controversy, set the stage for action in France. The leading minister, the Duc de Choiseul, fervently disliked the Jesuits, while the rationalist anti-clericals reasoned that the "mutual rancor of priests" offered a golden opportunity for them to discredit all defenders of revelation with objective impartiality. So far as the fate of the Jesuits was concerned, matters came to a head with the institution of legal proceedings against a bankrupt but sometime flourishing Jesuit sugar enterprise in Martinique. These proceedings had begun as simple law suits on the part of creditors against the director Père Lavalette in order to recover their immense financial losses, and the original legal point at issue had been whether the director individually or the Society collectively was responsible for the debts involved.

When the Society was found guilty, it appealed in due form from the verdict of the lower court to the appellate jurisdiction of the Parlement of Paris. The move was a serious, indeed, a fatal, tactical blunder, for that high court was the very citadel of the Gallicans and the Jansenists. The Parlement first upheld the financial verdict. Then, examining the statutes of the Society, it obtained requisite legal evidence to rule that the Jesuits were automatically bound by their oath to obey regulations which were subversive of the "fundamental laws" of the realm. This fateful verdict sealed the doom of the Society in France. By an implementing resolution of the Parlement the state took over the Jesuit property in 1762, dissolved their foundations, and closed their schools. Their power was thus struck at its source. Two years later a royal edict condemned the members to exile from the country, though in actual fact Louis XV permitted many of them to remain in their capacity of private individuals acting "in conformity with the laws of the realm."[3]

The fall of the Jesuits in France was the prelude to a similar fate in the other Bourbon states. Charles III of Spain dramatically shut down all their establishments in the mother country and the American

---

[2] Carnota, *op. cit.*, 103 ff.; and L. Gomes, *Le marquis de Pombal* (Lisbon, 1869), ch. x.

[3] For two varying interpretations cf. P. Gaxotte, *Le siècle de Louis XV* (Paris, 1933), ch. ix, and F. Olivier-Martin, "Les pratiques traditionelles de la royauté française et le despotisme éclairé," in *B.I.C.H.S.*, V (1933), 705-708.

colonies and harried their inmates out of the land to find such refuge as they could elsewhere. When his long reign ended in 1788, the Spanish church was for all practical purposes a department of state and the priest a governmental agent for affairs of the spirit.[4] Ferdinand of Naples and the Duke of Parma also drove them out, supported by their Bourbon relatives in France and Spain against the protests of Clement XIII (1758-1769).

For several years the princes and the still more obdurate ministerial foes of the Jesuits put heavy pressure upon the newly elected pontiff, the Franciscan cardinal Ganganelli, who had taken the name of Clement XIV (1769-1774), to dissolve the Society. He yielded to the overwhelming insistence in 1773 and signed the brief *Dominus ac Redemptor*. This writ was a death warrant, for after more than two centuries of power the Society of Jesus with its 22,000 members was extinguished. "Thank God," exclaimed the Spanish rationalist, Azara, "we have finished with the Jesuits"; while Joseph of Austria declared in similar vein that "Clement XIV has acquired eternal glory by suppressing the Jesuits." These apostrophes were the words of intransigent monarchists, but the sentiment was echoed by many secular priests and members of other religious congregations for whom the dissolved order was equally objectionable not on grounds of faith but by reason of its wealth and privileges and its worldly practices. The expelled Jesuits found shelter in the Papal States, in the Russia of the Orthodox Catherine, and in the Lutheran sanctuary of Prussia. Frederick ostentatiously invited them to his land, meanwhile maliciously commenting that "since my brothers, the very Christian, faithful and apostolic Catholic kings, have driven them out, I, very heretical, gather up as many of them as I can."[5]

It was in the Hapsburg realm during the feverish decade of Joseph's sole rule that militant anti-papalism reached its apogee. Joseph could reinforce his own scorn of papal rule by dipping into a treasury of anti-curial arguments that lay conveniently at hand: the theses of his lay advisers, such as Sonnenfels, Martini, and Riegger; the doctrines of theologians, such as Abbot Rautenstrauch, and of his early instructor,

4 For a succinct but penetrating account, M. C. Alcázar, "El despotismo illustrado en España," in *B.I.C.H.S.*, V (1933), 739 ff.

5 The most recent account is by the great Catholic historian, L. von Pastor, *Geschichte der Päpste seit dem Ausgang des Mittelalters* (Freiburg, 1931-1932), XVI, Pts. I and II.

the jurist Beck; and above all the classical treatise of Febronius, entitled *On the State of the Church and the Rightful Power of the Roman Pope*[6] (1763). *"Los von Rom"* became the rallying cry of all the emperor's adherents. He forbade the Austrian episcopate, except with previous royal approval, to receive papal bulls and decrees or to honor rescripts. He annulled the dispensing power of the bishops and denied them the right to appeal to Rome in matters of conscience. They were required to take an oath of fidelity and submission to the emperor. Prospective ecclesiastics were obliged to receive their training at newly founded seminaries supervised by the state. While completing the reorganization of diocesan boundaries and nominating native Austrians selected for their loyalty to the vacant sees, Joseph also established many new parishes, hoping in that way to have the parish priests make real his dream of restoring Catholicism to its pristine purity. In the interim *"Los von Rom"* emancipated the Austrian clergy from papal control in order to bind them more securely to the secular state.

His reforming zeal embraced the regular clergy as well. Everywhere in Catholic Europe precedents existed for state regulation of conventual establishments. The French edict of 1749, curtailing the establishment of new ecclesiastical foundations and their right to acquire property, was indeed the most notable in a long series of restrictions. The creation of a supervisory commission for the regular clergy in 1766 and the harsher edicts of the next decade were clearly punitive in intention and execution.[7] Maria Theresa, whose piety was beyond cavil, and even the papacy itself, in the persons of Clement XIV and Pius VI, endeavored also to correct the financial abuses of notoriously lax and corrupt monastic establishments. Joseph's more violent corrective measures were blended of benevolent and utilitarian considerations. He planned to sequestrate these rich possessions so as to swell the revenues of the treasury with the income of the wealth held in inalienable mortmain. It was also his hope to convert the monk into "a useful citizen," absolved of his unnatural vows.

The sweeping royal decrees of 1781 abolished all monastic establishments devoted to the contemplative life: those belonging to the Carthu-

---

[6] Febronius was the pseudonym of Hontheim, the coadjutor bishop of Trèves. Cf. J. Kuntziger, *Fébronius et le fébronianisme* (Bruxelles, 1889), for a careful analysis of this enormously influential work.

[7] Suzanne Lemaire, *La commission des réguliers. 1766-1780* (Paris. 1926).

sians, Carmelites, Capuchins, Cistercians, Franciscans, and Augustinians. The government commissions that executed the decrees registered the designated foundations and took inventories with scrupulous exactness. More than 700 establishments out of a total of 2,163 were closed, and some 38,000 monks and nuns out of a total of 65,000 were absolved of their vows and given a choice either to enter the secular clergy or to leave the imperial dominions. The income on the capital of the confiscated property—the huge sum of 60,000,000 florins—was turned over for administration to a religious fund and earmarked for education and poor relief, salary increases to parish priests, and pensions to the former inmates of the abolished orders.

Pius VI showered the Hofburg in Vienna with protests, but he did not dare to push his remonstrances too far, lest the Austrian episcopate sever the remaining links that held it to Rome. But he quit the sacred soil of the Eternal City and journeyed to the imperial capital to make a direct personal appeal to Joseph. While his visit won him the enthusiastic acclaim of the Viennese, the month-long negotiations yielded only studied affronts from Chancellor Kaunitz, and the emperor remained unyielding in his granite obduracy. After the pope's departure Joseph wrote jubilantly to Leopold in Tuscany: "At last I have packed off the pope. . . . I am really delighted at his departure . . . in view of his wiles and wheedlings. . . ."[8] Twice again a rupture of papal-imperial relations impended, particularly after several of the leading archbishops subscribed to the virtual declaration of episcopal independence called the Punctation of Ems (1786). But the papacy held firm, and the thin strand of mutual distrust and dislike which linked emperor and pope was not cut.

The effort to win toleration for dissenters was perhaps the single most important function of the anti-Jesuit and anti-papal crusade. In the years immediately following the Seven Years' War the eyes of the Continent were turned to France, where Voltaire was bringing to a victorious close his most dramatic conflict with religious fanaticism. Late in the autumn of 1761, Marc-Antoine Calas, the son of a Huguenot merchant, had committed suicide at Toulouse. The father, Jean

---

[8] A. von Arneth, *Joseph II und Leopold von Toskana. Ihr Briefwechsel von 1781 bis 1790*, 2 vols. (Vienna, 1872), I, 103; and H. Schlitter, *Die Reise des Papstes Pius VI. nach Wien* (Vienna, 1892).

Calas, was shortly after charged with his murder, committed allegedly to prevent the son from espousing the Catholic faith. It subsequently transpired that the young man, who was moody and desperate because of personal affairs, had taken his own life with no intention of changing his religious beliefs. While the deceased was posthumously taken into the church, the wretched father, together with his family, was tried for murder in an atmosphere charged with religious hatred. Despite the absence of evidence and his own protestations of innocence, he was found guilty and sentenced to death under cruel torture. Voltaire, like most liberals, had at first taken the guilt of Calas for granted. But an examination of the proceedings speedily convinced him that a gross miscarriage of justice had taken place, and for the next three years the great prince of tolerance dedicated all his resources and energy to an inspired publicity campaign for the reopening of the case and the reversal of the verdict. Three years after the execution he had won the hard battle of *l'affaire Calas* (1765). A superior court reversed the verdict of the Parlement of Toulouse and acquitted all the accused. For the father it was a belated vindication; for the living it was relief from suffering and ignominy. It was, above all, the most illustrious triumph of the century over bigotry and fanaticism, a milestone in the history of religious freedom.[9] The movement in behalf of the Protestants was not to be stemmed in France.

The *de facto* status of Huguenots was already appreciably better than their position under the law, and neither Louis XV in his last years nor Louis XVI in his early reign pretended literally to observe the coronation oath to extirpate heresy. At length, in November, 1787, the ruler gave his signature to the edict of toleration which had been prepared by the noble humanitarian, Malesherbes. Though it still excluded the Protestants from political life, it restored their civil rights, opened professional careers to them, legalized their marriages while legitimizing those already contracted, and, above all, re-established their right to private worship.[10]

The lot of dissenters varied from country to country. A royal ukase lightened the disabilities of the oppressed Old Believers (*Raskolniki*)

9 For a somewhat different interpretation see R. R. Palmer, *op. cit.*
10 J. M. Allison, *Malesherbes, Defender and Reformer of the French Monarchy, 1721-94* (New Haven, 1938), chs. vi and vii.

in Russia (1785),[11] while religious toleration had long been practiced in Protestant Sweden and Denmark, the Swiss cantons, and the United Provinces. In England only Roman Catholics and Unitarians among the Christian sects were still denied the liberty of worship which the Act of Toleration (1689) extended to Presbyterians, Baptists, Congregationalists, and Quakers. To be sure, the discriminatory legislation was not strictly enforced, and after Holland, England was the most tolerant country in Europe. Methodism, too, had established itself, and the day had long passed when the fashionable despised it or the mob turned furiously upon its remarkable apostles. When Wesley died (1791), he had 70,000 converts in England alone, mainly among those whom the state church in its comfortable complacency had ignored. Popular fanaticism was, however, only covered by a thin surface of forbearance, as the wild Gordon riots of 1780 against the small minority of Catholics emphatically disclosed.[12]

Religious tolerance in the Germanies had its official champion in the light of the age, Frederick himself. In a variety of religious opinions Frederick saw not danger but benefit to the state, provided the expression was carefully controlled. But the enlightened ruler's attitude was innocent of warmhearted sympathy for people whose conscience put them into the ranks of the heterodox. Reasoning that all religious belief was more or less absurd, he felt that the public order was best assured by not ridiculing the expression of faith. Herder, who spoke from experience, hit off the king's cool attitude even toward the Lutheran clergy in his ironic quip that "a pastor is only entitled to exist now under state control and by the authority of the prince as a moral teacher, a farmer, and a secret agent of the police."[13]

The Jews of the ghetto were the great beneficiaries of the liberation movement. In all states of the Continent the central authorities dealt with organized and quasi-autonomous Jewish communities. Supplementing the regular municipal officials, these special Jewish councils, centered about the rabbinate, administered the local affairs of the ghetto and through their own elected intermediaries took care of all matters relating to taxation and the enforcement of their co-religionists'

11 F. C. Conybeare, *Russian Dissenters* (Cambridge, 1921), 225-231.
12 N. Sykes, *The English Church in the Eighteenth Century* (London, 1926).
13 Quoted in Bruford, *op. cit.*, 225.

general public obligations. This arrangement, however, ran counter to the forces that were completing the internal unification of the modern state. To many people the ghetto was an absurd anachronism. Many administrative reformers, even those sympathetically inclined, were as loath to perpetuate the existence of this particular corporate group, set aside by its religion, as they were reluctant to tolerate other corporate groups, based on class, functional, or geographical loyalties. Indeed, they were especially averse to maintaining the ghetto, which denied its denizens the natural and inalienable rights and duties of citizens which should have been common to all men, and forced them to lead isolated lives and pursue professions unworthy of their humanity.

Such reasoning obtained among Christian friends and well-wishers. But the Jews themselves were not of one mind. Most of them, who congregated apart and were intellectually inoculated against the ideas of change, were historically conditioned neither to stimulate nor yet to respond to the emancipation movement. Nor is it surprising that the orthodox leaders showed themselves adamant to innovations tending to weaken sacred dogma and modify the hallowed ritual. On the other hand, a small minority of well-to-do Jews who were playing an increasingly significant role in economic affairs in the western European states chafed at the governmental restrictions. Not that they wished to abjure their faith. They were secular in spirit, like their non-Jewish associates, and they held that only by giving up their special status and assuming the obligations of all citizens could their co-religionists attain equal civil rights. Under the banner, therefore, of this humanitarian nationalism, liberal Jews of the stamp of the famous Moses Mendelssohn challenged the discriminatory regulations and demeaning edicts and sought by personal example and persuasion to adapt the language, the customs, the traditions, and the aspirations of their people to the country of their birth.[14]

This philo-Semitic movement made uneven headway. Catherine's sure sense of political reality prompted her to give wealthy Jews the right of holding municipal office. It also prompted her to go no further on the road of emancipation. The issues were lengthily debated also in

[14] The fullest treatment is in S. M. Dubnow, *Histoire moderne du peuple juif*, 2 vols., tr. from the German (Paris, 1933); the best treatment in English is S. Baron, *A Social and Religious History of the Jews*, 3 vols. (New York, 1937), II; cf. also his "Ghetto and Emancipation," in *Menorah Journal*, XIV (1928), 515-526.

post-partition Poland, but the reformers never went beyond words. Gustavus of Sweden was well-disposed, giving the Jews permission to settle in several designated towns, engage in trade, and practice their religion without molestation. Denmark was an even brighter haven, for there the Jews enjoyed full freedom of public worship. Ghettoes were unknown, and neither poll taxes nor restrictions upon mixed marriages disturbed their tranquillity. Step by step they were admitted into the guilds, the schools, and the military service, and were accepted freely in society. Though the English colonies in America established *de facto* religious toleration for all citizens, in England itself the failure of Pelham's effort in 1754 to open the political city was decisive until the reforms of 1829. France, too, did not grant the Jews full civic emancipation during the Old Regime, though the efforts of such sympathizers as Malesherbes and the Marquis de Mirabeau forced the abolition of the special poll tax in 1784.[15] As for Prussia, despite a curious tradition to the contrary, Frederick was no philo-Semite. The admirer of Voltaire did not persecute Jews, naturally, any more than he did the Catholics. But he despised them as "useless to the state" and feared them as enemies of the Christian small business man, even as his father had done before him without benefit of enlightenment. He merely discriminated against them by imposing special extortionate taxes on them and excluding them as much as he could from the professions and public services.[16]

Joseph too entertained no overwhelming personal regard for the dissenters, but his compulsion to serve humanity made him the foremost royal champion of religious emancipation. This inclination was not unaided by his realistic awareness that the good will and the economic skill of Protestants and Jews were considerable assets in Austria's struggle against Prussia. In 1781, against the demurrers of most of his advisers, he issued a series of revolutionary edicts that established the widest freedom of worship in the hereditary dominions and the Netherlands. Only deists and the insignificant handful of actual atheists were excluded. Almost all the non-Roman Catholics—

15 P. Sagnac, "Les juifs et la révolution française," in *Revue d'histoire moderne et contemporaine*, I (1899-1900), 5-23; 209-229.
16 See H. Braunschwig, "L'Aufklärung et le mouvement philosémite en Prusse à la fin du dix-huitième siècle," in *Annales historiques de la Révolution française* (sept.-oct., 1935); also Frederick's *Political Testaments* of 1752 and 1768 for expressions of his dislike.

Protestants of Bohemia, Greek Orthodox believers, and the scorned Jews—were granted the right to worship freely at their own centers and prayer houses and to meet openly without molestation from the authorities. They were permitted to own property in full legal right, build schools and engage their own schoolmasters, enter the professions, and be eligible for all political and military offices. For the Jews in particular the edicts meant the welcome end of the humiliating obligation of wearing the distinctive yellow patch and the not less onerous burden of paying a special poll tax. By every standard of measurement those generous edicts were the greatest and the most beneficial of Joseph's reforms.

In the interim, the gratuitous modifications that he imposed on Catholic ritual and practices seriously jeopardized the success of his more judicious measures. Behaving somewhat after the manner of a secular bull in an ecclesiastical china shop, he attacked "superstitious practices," such as pious pilgrimages to sacred shrines, celebration of saints' days, and some of the traditional ceremonies of ordinary religious services. Even during his lifetime a violent reaction undid most of the religious reforms in the rebellious Hungarian provinces, the good along with the extreme. In the Netherlands his subjects unleashed a fierce independence movement against both political and religious changes. Nowhere else, however, did he suffer such sweeping reverses. Under the tactful but firm rule of his brother Leopold, Joseph's legislation was preserved in its main features in the Austro-Bohemian crown lands. The toleration edicts were not repealed. Though Leopold restored the tithe and did away with the new general seminaries, he enforced the police and judicial power of the state over ecclesiastics and retained the obligation of the episcopal oath of loyalty to the crown. Monasteries already dissolved were not restored, nor was their property restored. Even church services were simplified much as Joseph had wished, except for some of his extreme innovations.[17]

On the whole, the advocates of the new secular faith did little more

---

[17] Of the general histories and biographies Mitrofanov and Kerner are most critical, and Padover most favorable; Beidtel, *op. cit.*, is frankly hostile, while the monograph of Sister Mary Clare Goodwin, *The Papal Conflict with Josephism* (New York, 1938), especially ch. iii, is scrupulously accurate and vehemently Catholic in its point of view; the Protestant point of view is expressed in G. Frank, *Das Toleranz-Patent Kaisers Josef II* (Vienna, 1881).

than scratch the surface of intolerance, except among the minority of the cultivated elite. The bulk of the reform edicts were singularly ineffectual in their effect upon popular mores. The masses neither cherished Voltaire nor knew his *Traité sur la tolérance*. For the many millions of peasants the mysterious universe peopled by the devil and his phantom associates had lost very little of its terrifying reality. The great evangelical revivals that swept the Protestant countries were retrograde in their theology. Neither Methodism nor Pietism can be construed as tokens of the advance of science. Charlatans and high priests of mumbo-jumbery still found a lucrative profession in the larger towns and the cities by playing upon the credulity of the idle rich, the blasé, and the fearful. Yet that is only part of the story. The light of reason did brighten many areas of the human mind darkened by superstition. The warmth of lay charity dissolved much of the frigidity of fear and hatred. Voltaire had not lived in vain. For all that the union of absolutism and enlightenment left undone, it deserved well of mankind. Demonology and magic were scorned by the cultured vanguard. Persecution passed out of fashion as a normal instrument of civil intercourse. The brotherhood of man became a living credo. With the rulers, statesmen, and the intellectual and social elite already won over, it remained the glorious task of educational reform slowly but of course triumphantly to complete the spiritual emancipation of humanity.

II. EDUCATION AND THE GOOD LIFE

Never had hopes run so high that knowledge would set man free, nor had there ever been so many sweeping projects to eradicate illiteracy among the masses, disseminate the liberating learning of scientific truth, and make secular education the instrument for training good men and good citizens. The fall of the Jesuits and the overthrow of their control over the schools greatly swelled these expectations, particularly in France and Austria. But neither the Rousseauist emphasis upon the role of personality nor the various plans for nationalizing the educational system were realized in France. Primary instruction remained in the hands of religious congregations, and the inculcation of piety retained precedence over more mundane objectives of instruction. Instruction was miserable and the teachers themselves were at best nondescript. The *cahiers* of 1789 vividly disclose the over-whelming illiteracy of the rural population, the wretched limitations of instruction, and the lamentable shortage of schools.[18] The old established universities, meantime, had degenerated into bastions of learned ignorance. The curriculum at its best retained its mediaeval character, lagging many decades behind the remarkable scientific and philosophical speculation of the century. The spirit of the enlightenment only washed around these citadels of obscurantism. Unable to breach them, it engulfed them with extra-academic teaching and research institutes of the most progressive nature. Paris boasted of its famous Musée, Musée scientifique, and Lycée, where distinguished scholars and *philosophes* gave public lectures and offered regular courses to large and enthusiastic audiences. The provinces had their many *académies*, which developed during the course of the century into cultural centers of wide influence. For adults beyond the age of formal schooling and for the youth who found the universities sterile, there were also available the many discussion clubs (*sociétées de pensée*) and the seven hundred Masonic lodges, all of them making the humanitarian and utilitarian mandates of "*la philosophie*" the uncriticized premise of their social and political speculation.

The new spirit found a more welcome home in the secondary schools. Ecclesiastical censorship compelled the retention of outmoded subjects of study and equally outmoded manuals in the various secondary schools conducted by the religious brotherhoods, the private boarding schools, and the hundreds of *collèges* associated with the provincial universities. But history and geography, French and modern languages, biology, chemistry and physics, and the elements of social studies crowded their way into the curriculum. From these schools the graduate could go on to the great technical institutions that were making France the European center of professional instruction: to the state-controlled School of Mines, the School of Bridges and Highways, the schools of artillery and engineering, the Jardin du Roi, and the reorganized Collège de France.[19]

18 E. Allain, *L'Instruction primaire en France avant la Révolution* (Paris, 1881); and F. Brunot, *Histoire de la langue française des origines à 1900.* (Paris, 1926), VII.
19 F. B. Artz, "L'éducation technique en France au dix-huitième siècle," in *Revue d'histoire moderne* (sept.-dec., 1938); L. Liard, *L'enseignement supérieur en France* (Paris, 1882); D. Mornet, *Les origines intellectuelles de la Révolution française* (Paris, 1938), Pt. III; and Brunot, *op. cit.*, 90 ff.

Nevertheless, the state failed to turn the intellectual capacities of the younger generation to its own account. Not stanch partisans of the old order emerged from the schools, but searching critics imbued with attitudes that were not to be reconciled with the *status quo*. Conscious of the glaring defects of the existing regime and convinced of their ability to establish a better order, the young sons of the middle classes were living illustrations of Chateaubriand's famous paradox that the revolution was accomplished before it occurred. Reform was blended in their thinking with progress, and national patriotism with humanity. Every association that retarded the establishment of a sovereign national state grounded upon the civil liberty of the individual and the sanctity of private property became an obstacle in the path of liberty.[20]

The Austrian reformers were the familiar figures of the *Aufklärung*, and the two rulers themselves, Maria Theresa and Joseph, though miles apart in their religious views, stood together in their conviction that education was the concern of the state and the foremost agency for rearing useful and obedient subjects. The reorganization of instruction had begun before the dissolution of the Jesuit schools, but their destruction and the release of vast funds for teaching purposes paved the way for the promulgation of the epochal *Allgemeine Schulordnung* of 1774.[21] This famous educational edict, written by the Silesian theorist, Abbot Felbiger, co-ordinated the existing facilities into a national and centralized system. On the elementary level it provided for grade schools (*Trivialschulen* or *Volkschulen*) to be supported by local funds, and by state subsidies where those resources were inadequate. There was nothing in all Europe to compare with them. For children, schooling for the first time became a pleasure instead of a drudgery. Their treatment was kind and considerate, the school day short, and vacations long. The teachers were competent, every effort being made to recruit their personnel from the normal schools. The regulations—which could not be enforced—made stringent provisions for compulsory attendance, and Protestants and Jews were admitted,

20 See B. C. Shafer's interesting essay, "Bourgeois Nationalism in the Pamphlets on the Eve of the French Revolution," in *Journal of Modern History*, X (1938), 31-50; and A. Sicard, *L'éducation morale et civique avant et pendant la Révolution*, new ed. (Paris, 1913).

21 The fullest account of Jesuit instruction is in B. Duhr, S.J., *Geschichte der Jesuiten in den Ländern deutscher Zunge im 18. Jahrhundert*, 2 vols. (Munich, 1928).

both as pupils and as teachers on terms of equality. Religious instruction, consonant with the faith of the pupils, was by no means neglected, but the regnant spirit was secular and the supervision of instruction was put in the hands of local state officials who saw to it that the inculcation of patriotic loyalty was not slighted.

The emperor's obsession with creating "respectable moral citizens" was more evident still in his attitude toward secondary education. Apart from the normal schools for the training of future teachers and *Hauptschulen* for training in the most necessary technical skills, the reform edict also provided for Latin schools (*Gymnasien*) in every district. They prospered more during the co-regency than in the period of Joseph's sole rule, when the number of students fell off very sharply. He shifted the emphasis from the original broad curriculum and stressed instruction in technical subjects. Determined to discourage educational overproduction of graduates, for whom careers would be lacking, he intensified state supervision over both students and teachers. Their conduct and activities were meticulously recorded by local officials and transmitted to the central files of the *Hofcommission* at Vienna.

State control reached its apogee in higher instruction. Not only was Joseph unable by temperament to encourage the play of free speculation, but the utilitarian and bureaucrat in him compelled him to advocate that "nothing must be taught the youth which in later life they would use very rarely or perhaps not at all for the benefit of the state." He envisaged the university almost entirely as a school of public administration. At the University of Vienna the theological faculty became practically superfluous after the establishment of state-controlled seminaries. Instruction in political science was transferred to the law faculty, which became the cornerstone of the educational arch. Since the training of future civil servants was the primary objective, the German language was made compulsory for all lectures, and all other modern languages except Bohemian were dropped. Only official textbooks were allowed and standard methods of instruction were prescribed for the faculty. Still further to centralize the procedure, and to spare the students the burden of carrying conflicting ideas in their heads, Joseph ordered that several provincial universities be reduced to the level of *Gymnasien*.

The defects of this rigid and over-regimented system were only too glaring. Professors were left without a voice in the determination of courses and in the interpretation of the material they were obliged to present. Subject completely to the supervision of government-appointed directors, they were overburdened with work and paid beggarly salaries. The students fared equally badly. "Good God," exclaimed Mirabeau, "even their souls are to be put in uniform!" Again it was the historic role of Leopold to correct the harshest features of his brother's reforms. Yet the unimaginative and harsh regime served Austria well. There was more than mere uncritical enthusiasm in the gesture of one of Joseph's councilors, who stretched his hands to the light and exclaimed that Vienna now drew the attention of all Europe as the new center of learning and culture. The initial shock shattered the somnolence of Hapsburg cultural existence, while in time the younger generation shook off the emperor's own dogmatic and exclusive preoccupation with the severely practical and successfully preserved what was best in his ideals against the religious-romantic reaction of the early nineteenth century.[22]

The Iberian peninsula also made a vigorous attempt to institute far-reaching changes. After the expulsion of the Jesuits the sometime provincial academy at Azcoitia (in the Basque region), transformed in 1766 into the Sociedad de Amigos del Pais, obtained possession of one of their colleges near by at Vergara and established there a seminary which soon became a center of anti-clerical instruction. Court protection, together with the success of this first secular school, led liberals to establish some forty other similar societies all over Spain. Intellectuals read Raynal's *Philosophical History* and Diderot's *Encyclopedia* in acceptable translations, and not a few members of the army and the upper classes became Freemasons.[23] While the generous intentions of Jovellanos, Campomanes, and Floridablanca, like those of Pombal in Portugal, broke on the entrenched superstitions of the masses, the retrograde universities also contrived without difficulty to circumvent curricular provisions for their improvement. More or less as in France, it was the sons of the urban middle classes who benefited

22 G. Wolf, *Das Unterrichtswesen in Oesterreich unter Joseph II* (Vienna, 1880); also the severely critical and valuable account in Mitrofanov, *op. cit.*, II, 802-840.
23 *Latin America and the Enlightenment*, ed. by A. P. Whitaker (New York, 1942), 13-14 and 25-27.

most, attending schools founded by the Economical Societies, enrolling in provincial academies, utilizing the royal institutes for medicine, veterinary science, mineralogy, and natural history, and patronizing the new museums, libraries, and observatories.[24]

Russia's educational experimentation had only the native defects of superficiality to balance the advantages of a good press in western Europe, where Catherine's salaried friend, Baron Grimm, hailed her lyrically as a new Prometheus or at times more prosaically as "*Universal-Normalschulmeisterin.*" The Academy of Science, founded in 1724, maintained a loose connection with the learned world of the west. The vogue of travel during the later years of the century introduced Russians to more serious aspects of the French enlightenment than their country had known in the early days of Elizabeth's reign when the rococo ideals of elegance and worldliness prevailed. St. Petersburg and Moscow opened public theaters; the University of Moscow was established; and Freemasonry spread rapidly among the urban intellectuals.

The technical schools that Peter had founded at the beginning of the century did not long survive his death, and the education of the masses was only a dream of enthusiasts. The first flowering of Russian culture had its roots in the deep soil of popular ignorance. "Pagan sprites and spirits," writes G. T. Robinson, "still haunted the black forest and the grey waters that lay between the log-built village and the pseudo-classical manor house of the landlord, and in the peasant huts young men were nurtured and old men consoled by the repetition of folk songs and folk tales which often bore the mark of a dual pagan-Christian faith."[25] At the outset of her reign Catherine had given verbal approval to several educational projects and discussed reforms with her usual high vivacity. But apart from founding a small number of technical schools, she did very little of a serious nature until the last years of her rule. In 1786 she signed the recommendation of a school commission for the establishment of a national system of elementary instruction. The provisions were wholly laudable, being drafted by a Serbian pedagogue who was associated with Abbot Felbiger in the reform of Austrian schooling. Their enforcement

---

[24] Cf. G. Desdevises du Dézert, *op. cit.*, in *Revue hispanique*, LXXIII (1928), 210 ff.
[25] G. T. Robinson, *op. cit.*, 45.

lagged. When the new Prometheus died, Russia's entire educational apparatus comprised the University of Moscow and the provincial academies; the Smolny Institute for the daughters of poor but deserving noblemen; some technical schools and gymnasia for the well-to-do; a large number of miserable village schools kept by the clergy; and private schools established by benevolent landlords for their own serfs. Of free public elementary schools there were in the entire vastness of Russia only slightly more than 300, staffed by only 600 or so teachers. The ingenuous conclusion drawn by one of Catherine's biographers still holds: "Since the masses did not count and the middle class hardly existed, there was no serious question of doing more than raise the level of studies at the top of the social scale."[26]

Until the founding of the University of Halle in 1694, the educational system of Protestant Germany remained substantially what Luther and Melanchthon had made it, save that the gap between formal instruction and living reality steadily widened. The dynamic personality of the great rationalist, Christian Thomasius, gave distinction to the new institution. An admirer of French secular culture, he sought to break down the barriers that separated the learned professions and the ordinary citizen and to make knowledge truly useful to the greatest number. Together with the foremost German *Aufklärer*, Christian Wolff, who joined him, he made Halle the very citadel of the rational, the useful, and the practical. The changed curriculum provided a suitable response to the demand for more realistic knowledge and greater practical contact with life. Latin yielded its primacy to German and modern languages, while scholasticism was superseded by geography and history, mathematics and the sciences. The realization of the new program made Halle the leading training school of the century for the great Prussian civil servants.

The Pietist, A. H. Francke, was also associated with Halle in its formative years. He too was on the side of the moderns in this Germanic version of the contemporary French and English "quarrel of the ancients and the moderns." A foe of the dead formalism and the dogmatic subtleties of conventional religion, he sponsored a broad

26 C. Waliszewski, *Le roman d'une impératrice*, 2nd ed. (Paris, 1893), 484. Apart from the general histories and biographies there is very little material in English on this subject. V. Simkhovich's "History of the School in Russia," in *Educational Review*, XXXIII (1907), 496-504, belies its title.

program of popular education. The pedagogic centers that he set up at Halle kept his ideals alive and trained disciples who spread his influence for progressive social change over Germany.

A second new institution of higher learning, the University of Göttingen (founded 1737), was meantime correcting Halle's undue neglect of the humanities. Two teachers of genius, J. M. Gesner and C. Heyne, who dominated it in succession, rescued the ancient classics from the fate of disappearing altogether from the curriculum. As modern in their way as their Halle colleagues, they adapted the teaching of the humanities to the needs of the age. They abandoned the study of the Greek and Roman masterpieces for their presumed value as definitive statements of immutable philosophical and aesthetic truths and taught them critically, employing them as source material for training the judgment and the taste of eighteenth-century German students. They also attacked the mediaeval curriculum from other angles, and thanks to their labors Göttingen built up a rich library, established admirably equipped laboratories and diversified museum collections, and placed the advanced study of jurisprudence and history, the mathematical sciences and medicine on a level nowhere approached either in Germany or elsewhere in Europe.

Yet for all the stimulus Halle and Göttingen supplied to creative scholarship and academic freedom, the temper of higher learning remained singularly lacking in the critical ferment that marked French speculation. The students dutifully attended the universities for the concrete advantages that specialized training gave: the richer students to prepare themselves for future careers in the civil service, and the poorer ones in the church. Students and professors alike discharged their obligations without imagination and without raising the question of the validity of those institutional relations that made professional careers possible for them.

The force of inertia also retarded the rapid development of a challenging system of secondary education. The old Latin schools—town grammar schools and state schools—drew their clientele from the families of humble merchants, successful craftsmen, and lesser officials. Under the Pietist influences emanating from Halle, and later from the example of Göttingen, they shifted the emphasis away from Latin, religion, and the husks of the trivium and quadrivium. French and even German crept into the curriculum, though largely as extras to attract progressive pupils; and then mathematics and physics, history and geography. But the changes did not affect the private boarding schools and the fashionable academies to which the wealthy urban merchants and the aristocracy continued to send their sons.[27]

The proposed reforms of J. B. Basedow (1724-1790) and J. H. Campe (1707-1768) were far more realistic. Like the lesser-known F. G. Resewitz (1725-1805), author of several works on civic training, they were middle-class theorists who introduced the ideals of the progressive bourgeoisie into the structure of the absolute monarchy. Basedow, who came to pedagogy from theology, lived to become the foremost advocate of non-sectarian schooling directed to practical ends. The amazing farrago entitled *Elementarwerk* (1774) was a diffuse elaboration of his doctrines of "reason" and "nature," while the Philanthropinum, which he established that same year at Dessau as a model school, gave him an opportunity to try out his neo-Rousseauist theories. The school could not overcome the handicap of Basedow's temperament and shut its doors two decades later. But the new methods of combining work with play, stressing physical exercises and manual training, using the school as a true social community, and inculcating patriotism through such devices as group games and festivals did survive, and the philanthropinist movement spread widely over Germany.[28]

Its emphasis upon civic training and practical learning and its advocacy of state supervision over education had already been anticipated in the work of his younger contemporary Hecker. Like Basedow, he too approached educational reform from theological experience, in this instance from the Pietist group of Christian sociologists. Apart from his renown as the author of the plan that was enacted as the famous Prussian *Landschulreglement* for elementary education, he stood forth as the leader of the *Realschule* movement in secondary education. On the basis of his earlier experience with the use of pri-

---

27 In addition to the excellent brief accounts in Steinhausen, *op. cit.*, ch. x, and Bruford, *op. cit.*, Pt. III, chs. iv and v, see the standard longer treatment in F. Paulsen, *Geschichte des gelehrten Unterrichts*, 2 vols., 3rd ed. revised by R. Lehmann (Leipzig, 1919-1921), II.

28 A. Basedow, *Johann Bernard Basedow: Neue Beiträge, Ergänzungen und Berichtigungen zu seiner Lebensgeschichte* (Berlin, 1924); and G. Franke, *Geschichte des Staatsgedankens in Schule und Erziehung* (Leipzig, 1912).

mary schools as centers for social reform, he founded the influential *Ökonomisch-mathematische Realschule* in Berlin in 1747. It was primarily intended to supply systematic practical training to students who did not plan to go on to universities but wished to pursue careers in industry, commerce, and trade. The *Realschulen* enjoyed the financial support of the government and spread widely. The explanation is apparent: Hecker's reform was deeply colored by his patriotic nationalism; and his schools were admirably calculated to draw upon and discipline the intellectual energies of the petty bourgeoisie—even as the universities drew upon the upper classes—in the interests of utilizing Prussian economic resources and furthering the mercantilist ideal of national self-sufficiency.[29]

No advance was possible during the first turbulent half of Frederick the Great's reign over the elementary-school instruction that Frederick William I had established in 1723. The enactment of the *Landschulreglement* in 1763 and the vigorous activities of K. A. von Zedlitz as Minister of Public Instruction (1771-1788) have been interpreted as evidences of real improvement in the latter part of his rule. Actually, with all the best will in the world—which was lacking—it would still have been impossible to make the provisions of the *Reglement* effective. The poverty and apathy of the villagers, the penury of the government, and the lack of a trained teaching personnel made it inevitable that the ideals should be more honored in the breach than in the observance. For all its acclaim the Prussian elementary system remained far inferior to the Austrian.

Perhaps what most defeated the expectations of its champions was the unalterable social purpose to which the Frederician state attached to it. Frederick himself was a perfect reflection of the undemocratic conservatism which held that a little learning was not a dangerous thing, provided, however, that it was very little.

It is a good thing [he declared] that the schoolmasters in the country teach the youngsters religion and morals. . . . It is enough for the people in the country to learn only a little reading and writing. . . . Instruction in the country must be planned so that they only receive that which is

---

29 K. Friedrich, *Die Entwickelung des Realienunterrichts bis zu den ersten Realschulgründungen* (Berlin, 1913).

most essential for them but which is designed to keep them in the villages and not influence them to leave.[30]

In brief, the goal of all public instruction, from the universities down to the *Volksschule*, was the methodical training of students for the efficient fulfillment of the various obligations inherent in the social group to which they belonged. The universities could not do other than fortify loyalty to the state as it was. The state endowed them, paid the professors their salaries, and gave financial aid to qualified students. It supervised the activities of both for the public good. Unquestioning loyalty was the price higher learning paid for its survival. To instruct the peasantry in religion and morals was to take out a form of insurance against possible social discontent and simultaneously to invest their status with a sanction even more binding than the will of the earthly ruler.

In England there was no pedagogic reformer of the eminence of Rousseau or Pestalozzi, Basedow or Felbiger. The most scientifically minded and the most technologically advanced country in Europe, England gained peculiar distinction by perpetuating a school system that with one notable exception magnificently ignored useful knowledge and disregarded modern studies. For the scion of the aristocracy there was still a private tutor or an exclusive public school to prepare him for a pleasant sojourn at either Oxford or Cambridge. These famous old institutions had long since lost their intellectual vitality, the Jacobite citadel at Oxford even more acutely than Cambridge. Life was difficult there for the poor scholarship students, but the young men of birth and wealth fared well, their consciences absolved "from the toil of reading, or thinking, or writing." If the idleness, frivolity, and dissipated ways of the students had become by-words, the reputation of the professors was hardly better. There were professors known never to have lectured at all, and tutors who had never experienced the bracing challenge of meeting their students. Both places still retained the obsolete exercises for degrees that dated back to the statutes of the sixteenth century. Still, in view of the bigotry and pedantry of some of the instructors, the lethargy and mental crassness

[30] Quoted in K. S. Pinson, *op. cit.*, 138-139; cf. the detailed treatment in F. Vollmer, *Die Preussische Volksschulenpolitik unter Friedrich dem Grossen* (Berlin, 1918), and F. Weinstein, *Die Preussische Volksschule in ihrer geschichtlichen Entwickelung* (Berlin, 1915).

of others, and the snobbery of all, it is doubtful if much was lost by not exposing superior students to their trust. Gibbon, who wrote from personal experience as a student at Oxford, was not far off the mark in his taunt that Oxford and Cambridge were founded in "a dark age of false and barbarous science" and still bore the taints of their origin.

Some slight progress relieved the gloom of this black picture. The dictatorial Master of Trinity College, Cambridge, the bellicose Richard Bentley, breathed fresh life into the study of the humanities. The Master of Peterhouse, in his turn, endeavored, with some success, to introduce general university examinations for all the undergraduates. Beginning with 1755, Cambridge offered a prize for the best essay on economics. It established a chair of chemistry in 1766, another of "natural and experimental philosophy" in 1783, and a professorship of English law in 1788. At Oxford there was keen agitation for the abolition of useless professorships and for more lectures from professors who remained, as well as for an increase in the number of college tutors.

In secondary instruction the old public schools remained substantially unchanged, that is to say, divorced from living reality. The town grammar schools still offered Latin and Greek as their main courses, though in time they made slight concessions to the demand for the newer subjects. Many of the newer private schools, commonly designated as "academies," prepared shopkeepers' sons for "business" and the "office" without concerning themselves unduly with broader instruction. The best of the academies were those conducted by the Dissenters and were thoroughly alive to the needs of the industrialized society whose growth the Nonconformists themselves substantially furthered. Open to all students—unlike the universities—without oath or subscription to the Thirty-nine Articles of the Church of England, they were the most vital centers of English learning; and it would be difficult to overestimate their services in the study of history and modern languages, mathematics and the new sciences.

At best little could have been accomplished in class-ridden England for the children of the industrial poor. In the early century the charity schools, sponsored by the Society for Propagating Christian Knowledge, had held forth some promise of developing into a national system of elementary education. But they declined for lack of public support, and in any case their missionary zeal attenuated their pedagogic usefulness. As a contemporary tract righteously put it, the paramount consideration was to rescue the pupils "from the vile company of those that curse and swear, rob and steal [and] from fatal temptations to drunkenness, lewdness and vile intemperance." It did not indicate how this lofty ideal was to be achieved without first removing the causes that gave birth to the undeniable moral degradation of the poor.[31]

While the Sunday school movement of the eighties renewed the effort to combine elementary instruction with moral uplift and religious philanthropy, the vast network of Methodist chapels performed a still more useful service in the slum areas of the new industrial towns and mining communities. The solid merits of this effort to save the working population from temptation and bring present cheer and hope of salvation to their wretched lives assuredly should not be minimized. The isolated worshiper, often cut off from his family, made new friends at the meetings. The reading of the freely distributed tracts strengthened his religious understanding, and his soul was doubtless greatly fortified by fervent prayer and the group singing of robust hymns. But the Methodist gospel condoned social injustice. Preaching resignation to existing hardships, its evangelical revivalism deflected working-class thought from analysis of the causes of those hardships, while it turned existing resentment into hope of future moral redemption. It helped to safeguard the immemorial privileges of the free-born Englishman: of the prosperous to enjoy life as he found it, and of the poor to be uplifted and saved.[32]

III. THE POOR AND THE SICK

Not only the godly but also the prosperous took in hand the salvation of the poor. A growing economy of plenty was emancipating England from the specter of want; and the giant presses of science and wealth were hammering out a new social stereotype among the well-to-do. A thousand voices, diaries and letters, novels and magazines, changes in

[31] M. G. Jones, *The Charity School Movement: A Study of Eighteenth-Century Puritanism in Action* (Cambridge, 1938).
[32] W. J. Warner, *The Wesleyan Movement in the Industrial Revolution* (New York, 1930).

attire and decoration, tell the story of a gradual assimilation of manners and customs. The new stagecoaches and the provincial inns were breaking down the country's isolation from the town; and in the town itself, the theater and the concert hall, the circulating library and the discussion society, even gardening and the craze for commercialized sports, were helping to level old distinctions.

This trend was more pronounced in England than in France; and in France it was more noticeable than in the Germanies or the eastern and southern European states. And in all cases it applied to those who were living well above the subsistence level. This quasi-democratization of habits was slowly effacing older class ways among the prosperous, but concurrently the changes in agriculture and industry were also revolutionizing the conditions of peasants and city workers. But neither uniformly nor even predominantly for the better. In the dawning era of free enterprise the living habits of rich and poor moved along diverging roads, even as they had done before the capitalist revolution.

As the age became alive to ugly social realities, its more sensitive members applied themselves to eradicating the unseemly spectacle of human misery in the midst of a growing plenty. The "state of the poor" question aroused passionate debate, and the controversies that raged everywhere raised a voluminous crop of criticism, inquiry, and suggestion. Even the Tory temper of Dr. Johnson was ruffled; and Boswell has him querulously insisting that "a decent provision for the poor is the true test of civilization."

The international counterpart of this search for social justice at home was the quest for peace abroad, but the decades of strife inaugurated by the French Revolution made Bentham's and Kant's and Rousseau's projects for everlasting peace on earth seem tragically ridiculous. Nor was the related campaign to emancipate colonial possessions and free Negro slaves crowned with any success in the days before 1789, even though the anti-colonial arguments of the physiocrats and Adam Smith's followers survived to furnish learned ammunition for the nineteenth-century freetraders. The government of Louis XVI took steps to exclude Negro slaves from the soil of metropolitan France (for purely selfish reasons); but Frenchmen in general were in no haste to end the exploitation of Negro slaves or the trade monopolies on which colonial prosperity depended.[33] Spain emancipated her South American colonies only when successful revolt in the nineteenth century compelled her to do so. In England, William Wilberforce and his parliamentary followers, "The Saints," were more successful. The British abolished the slave trade in 1807, and the emancipation of the slaves themselves in British possessions became a reality in the year of Wilberforce's death in 1833.[34]

The foes of serfdom meantime pressed for its abolition. In eastern and southern Europe they made little headway. But even before the revolutionary emperor in Austria and the revolutionary nation in France swept away the abomination, a few private landowners and the kingdom of Piedmont had already pointed the way. Widespread unemployment and mendicity were more baffling problems. As early as 1601 England had made a first comprehensive effort through the famous Poor Law to cope with the vagrants and beggars and unemployed who swamped the country after the breakdown of feudalism and the dissolution of the monasteries.[35] The legislation provided that each parish should levy a rate, or a tax, to be collected by church-wardens and overseers of the parish, appointed by and responsible to local magistrates. For poor children it provided free technical instruction on a very elementary level. For "impotent beggars"—the old, infirm, and disabled—it authorized relief in "convenient houses of dwelling." "Sturdy beggars"—the able-bodied but unemployed vagrants—were to be "set on work" in workhouses whose establishment the law authorized. As Elizabethan England, like all the continental states, was beset by fears of scarcity, the law provided severe penalties for all who could but would not work, or at least were judged as falling into that category.

The provisions were not mandatory, and the state supervision of the parishes was characterized, say the Webbs, by "remarkable neglect."

[33] C. L. Lokke, *France and the Colonial Question* . . . (New York, 1932), Preface; and M. Besson, "La police des noirs sous Louis XVI en France," in *Revue de l'histoire des colonies françaises*, XVI (July-Aug., 1928), 433-446.
[34] In addition to Klingberg, *op. cit.*, chs. iii-iv, see also R. Coupland, *The British Anti-Slavery Movement* (London, 1933), 70 ff.
[35] There is much valuable material covering all European countries in two older works: Sir Henry C. Burdett, *Hospitals and Asylums of the World*, 4 vols. (London, 1891-1893), I and III; and L. Lallemand, *Histoire de la charité*, 4 vols. (Paris, 1902-1912), vol. IV in 2 parts.

Only a few workhouses were founded, and beggary and vagrancy grew apace. The evils were not arrested by the seventeenth-century changes made under the theory that larger workhouses should be established through a union of smaller parishes and administered by new officials, the Incorporated Guardians. In these establishments the aged and the infirm would be humanely treated, while the able-bodied would be "profitably employed," thus ending the problem of vagrancy and simultaneously enriching the national wealth by their productive efforts. Apart from the economic delusion of believing that the costs of thus employing the poor would be less than that of outdoor relief, and apart from the wholly impracticable idea that a pauper community could be made self-supporting, very few parishes in any case formed the desired union. Where they did, the superintendence of the Incorporated Guardians was a bleak story of corruption, embezzlement, and coercion. And at all events, what the larger workhouse did was inadvertently to establish the means test, whereby maintenance could be offered to the able-bodied applicant on such conditions as to dissuade him from accepting it. This rejection in turn brought down the demand for relief and consequently the cost to the parish.

The General Act of 1723 empowered the separate parishes to establish workhouses, but it tended, like the larger mixed workhouses, to lump together into a single group all classes, ages, and sexes of the unfortunates, the healthy and the sick, the law-abiding and the criminal. The basic defect of the eighteenth-century system, however, was its intense parochialism, for between 12,000 and 15,000 parishes administered the poor laws more or less independently of one another. But the parish had become utterly inadequate as the unit of administration in consequence of the increase in trade and the founding of new towns. The overseers and the churchwardens were neither competent nor interested and rarely honest; and at all times the urgency of giving doles or pensions to the paupers was sacrificed to the taxpayers' clamor to keep down the steadily rising rates they had to pay. Overseers had the right to remove not only the actual poor from their parish by invoking the vagrancy laws and the Law of Settlement of 1682, but also those who might become chargeable at some future date. They indentured pauper children and youth as apprentices and saddled them upon other parishes. The various forms of relief, both in and out of the poorhouses, gave cruelly insufficient aid to the needy and the helpless. The legal provisions to furnish employment to the able-bodied paupers could not be enforced, despite the ingenious efforts of project-makers to "set the poor on work." The workhouses themselves were too small and too lacking in equipment, while the odious practice that grew up of farming out the inmates for outdoor relief placed the paupers under the mercy of various contractors too often endowed with a maximum of resourcefulness in finding work for and a minimum of conscience in the treatment of their charges.

The increased vagrancy caused by the system itself, together with the sharp suffering that agricultural and industrial change brought about, finally galvanized men into action to end the gap between the statutory provisions and the grim reality of "unfettered local autonomy." The act that Thomas Gilbert steered through Parliament in 1782 was the first fundamental change since the Elizabethan legislation. It was no true solution, but it had the great merit of reflecting the demand for more effective aid to the needy. It clearly recognized the out-moded character of the small parish unit and authorized parishes to form larger unions and pool their financial resources for the founding of more adequate poorhouses. But the new establishments would harbor only the aged, sick, and infirm, together with their dependent children, who were in this way rescued from the dens of horror in which they had been mixed with all other paupers. The act also lowered the status of the overseers to that of mere rate collectors and intrusted responsibility to elected guardians of the poor, upon whom it also devolved to find employment for the able-bodied, failing which the justices of the peace were empowered to give them poor relief in their own homes until work was available. Wholly beneficial as the new act was for the aged and the sick, the experience of the following two decades showed that it was impossible to find employ-ment for the able-bodied. In practice, consequently, the justices of the peace were compelled to make free use of their power of ordering outdoor relief. This dole, in addition to that customarily given to the sick and the aged, developed, under the "double panic of famine and revolution" that swept England in 1795, into a regular system of relief allowance or "rate in aid of wages," which was steadily to depress English living standards during the next generation.[36]

The English experience and the English trends have been treated in some detail, because they were substantially similar to those on the continent of Europe. In Protestant Germany the administrative unit, apart from isolated church, guild, or landlord relief agencies, was either the parish or the commune; and in a Germany composed of many independent states the parochial rivalry necessarily grew even keener than in England. The Prussian royal edict of 1748, though markedly repressive and punitive in form, was also an attempt to co-ordinate poor relief on a national basis. This first effort was a failure, and not for half a century, until the promulgation of the National Code (*Allgemeines Landrecht*), did Prussia make further progress. The code distinguished between those eligible for communal relief on the basis of settlement and civic responsibilities and those whom the state should take care of. For the former it authorized the establishment of large workhouses, where local funds were to provide work facilities for the able-bodied. The latter, mainly the vagrant infirm, aged, and disabled, were to be succored by the state out of its *Vagabundenfonds*. These new provisions undoubtedly reflected a more charitable temper, but unfortunately the actual practices more closely followed the coercive regulations of earlier days.[37]

The same general pattern both in administration and in attitude also obtained in the Catholic states, where again Austria and France took the lead in improving facilities for the poor. The imperial rescript of 1781, which Joseph issued largely under the influence of Sonnenfels, established communal poor institutes (*Armeninstitute* or *Pfarrerinstitute*) whose animating and generous spirit was the principle that every person, whether disbarred by reason of age, illness, or disability from earning his own living, or without family support, could legitimately claim relief from the authorities without sacrificing his

---

[36] Both S. and B. Webb, *English Poor Law History: Part I. The Old Poor Law* (London, 1927), especially chs. iii and iv, in their exhaustive *English Local Government* series, and D. Marshall, *The English Poor in the Eighteenth Century* (London, 1926), are classic treatments.

[37] For the poor laws of Prussia and the secondary states of Germany, cf. A. Emminghaus, *Poor Relief in Different Parts of Europe*, tr. from the German (New York, 1873); also "Armenwesen," in *Handwörterbuch der Staatswissenschaften*, ed. by L. Elster *et al.*, 4th ed. (Jena, 1923), I, 949 ff.

self-respect. The funds were to come from more or less voluntary local contributions, supplemented by the budget of the State Poor Fund, and were to be administered jointly by ecclesiastical and secular officials. The institutes soon spread widely throughout the central imperial provinces, though financial stringency later militated against their full success. As much as any other country imperial Austria refrained from practicing the cruel periodic man hunt of paupers and beggars, who were elsewhere either incarcerated for stipulated periods or else brutally punished for their idleness.

The scourge of beggars and vagrants was never so great in France as in the last generation of the Old Regime. In 1767 a great national roundup yielded a catch of 50,000 human wretches, most of whom were imprisoned in those refuges of despair called *dépôts de mendicité*. Outraged contemporaries protested vehemently against the indiscriminate grouping of beggars, criminals, prostitutes, and even the insane in these poorhouses. But they were not abolished, and indeed were put to full use in the long years of economic crisis immediately before the outbreak of revolution. Life was increasingly hard for the workers and the small craftsmen in these years that saw prosperity for larger merchants and industrialists. Contemporary evidence, public and private, political and literary, and the record of violence, strikes, and boycotts in the towns, reveal that for most of the urban workers, as for the majority of the rural population, standards were declining rather than rising.

The poor parishes were powerless to relieve the burden of mass indigence, and the remarkable efforts of a handful of high prelates and wealthy laymen also provided no lasting solution. The realization gradually dawned that only the state itself could adequately tackle the problems of unemployment and poor relief. Reforming ministers, most notably Turgot and Necker, openly took the stand that society owed protection and aid to its members. During their ministries and at the hands of an admirable group of progressive provincial intendants greater public assistance did materialize, largely in the form of increased opportunities for work relief in road building as well as in large-scale municipal improvements.[38]

[38] P. Ardascheff, *Les intendants de province sous Louis XVI*, 2 vols. (Paris, 1909); S. T. McCloy, "Some Eighteenth Century Housing Projects in France," in *Social Forces*

The benefactors of man also bestirred themselves to improve the conditions of public health. Behind these pioneer figures in the administration of public health were the great scientists whose researches made the progress possible: Black, Cavendish, Priestley, and Lavoisier in chemistry; Franklin, Galvani, and Volta in physics; Buffon, Linnaeus, Bonnet, and Spallanzani in biology; and Boerhaave, Haller, Morgagni, and the two Hunters in medicine. Medical schools like Leyden, the home of the great Boerhaave, or Edinburgh, where for the first time in British history a university had a direct hospital connection, gave luster to the century. The much-maligned eighteenth-century doctor had the quality of his defects, despite the pomposity and pedantry of the typical practitioner. The young doctor usually learned little enough at the university and obtained his most useful information during his apprenticeship to an older man, but medical instruction constantly improved as hospitals and clinics were established in London and the provincial towns. These new institutions, together with public dispensaries, poor and dependent on voluntary contributions as most of them were, became the crowning glory of the English medical service in behalf of the infirm poor.

Similar observations unfortunately could not be made for the leading states of the Continent, where conditions ranged from the merely bad to the horrible. With one accord everyone condemned the French hospitals. An English traveler, visiting the vast municipal hospital in Paris, the Hôtel Dieu, which housed nearly 3,000 patients, found four patients in a bed and heard of cases of six or seven "and among these the dying with the dead."[39] The horrified testimony of the great scientist Cuvier made it clear that provincial hospitals were no improvement over those in the capital: "The sufferings of hell can hardly surpass those of the poor wretches crowded on each other, crushed, burning with fever, incapable of stirring or breathing, sometimes having one or two dead people between them for hours."[40] Joseph II's edicts made almost adequate provision for municipal hospitals in the larger towns, public health officers, and public instruction in prevention

(May, 1938); and "Flood Relief and Control in Eighteenth Century France," in *Journal of Modern History* (March, 1941), 1-18.

[39] Townshend, *op. cit.*, I, 35.

[40] Quoted in M. Bloch, *L'assistance et l'état en France à la veille de la Révolution* (Paris, 1909), 83-84.

of disease; but, as in most of the associated welfare efforts, funds were not available to give force to the provisions.

Nor could the Continent match England's revolutionary advance in the science of midwifery and the care of newborn children. The large cities founded well-equipped lying-in and maternity hospitals. The insistence upon higher qualifications for the attending physicians and the hygienic care given to the patients considerably reduced the death rate both for mothers and for children. The tireless John Howard focused public attention upon smallpox and typhus, which raged in the prisons that he so patiently inspected for more than twenty years. And even as scurvy yielded to a treatment of citrus juices and fresh vegetables, so those two old scourges of mankind gradually yielded ground before the new medical tactics of disinfection and quarantine, inoculation and segregation. Pinel's researches in Paris were also ultimately to introduce more humane treatment of the insane, but decades elapsed before any real relief came for the poor asylum patients, whom the age consigned to the care of criminals, exhibited publicly to sightseers for a fee, and subjected to almost every conceivable inhumanity.[41]

The attack upon dirt and disease immensely altered the appearance and improved the sanitary provisions for the care of the large cities. Dr. Johnson, whose own standards were not elevated, once described London as fit only for a colony of Hottentots. But with the passage of time it became one of the healthiest cities in Europe. The English merchant aristocracy inhabiting the new provincial towns were not slow in taking over the improvements made in the capital. They too widened their streets, installed public lighting, and equipped themselves with modern water and sewage disposal systems. While the early years of the following century saw a partial undoing of these improvements, the later eighteenth century has to its credit the distinguished achievement of introducing preventive medicine, banishing the plague, wiping out scurvy, and greatly minimizing the ravages of malaria, typhus, and smallpox.[42]

The public health program coincided with the reform of civil litigation and the amelioration of the cruelties of criminal law and pro-

41 Burdett, *op. cit.*, I, chs. ii and iii.
42 This account of England derives in the main from Margaret C. Buer, *Health, Wealth and Population in the Early Days of the Industrial Revolution* (London, 1926), ch. ix. to the end.

cedure. More and more the reformers appreciated the interdependence of poverty, disease, and crime. Goethe recalled in his *Autobiography* how in his youth punishments were lightened and prisons improved, and attorneys and magistrates vied with one another in philanthropic and humanitarian endeavor. His memory did not entirely play tricks upon him, but many fine pronouncements also died on the lips of their makers. The quality of mercy remained strained indeed when European liberals could sincerely admire the draconic practices of English law and leave unchallenged Blackstone's smug boast that English law was "with justice supposed to be more nearly advanced in perfection than in any other land." Though the "eccentric but truly worthy" John Howard, as a contemporary quaintly called him, aroused his readers to keen indignation by his vivid pictures of prison horrors, most of the evils he described remained uncorrected in his lifetime.

Without question the European poor of the eighteenth century fared badly, and their health, wealth, and happiness were sacrificed in the progress that brought prosperity and comfort to the few. Yet not only the warmest hearts but the coolest brains clearly recognized society's obligation to minister to the wants of the needy. Measured in terms of absolute social justice the humanitarian effort was calamitously inadequate; judged as an index of a new spirit, as a token of a humanity greater than that which Europe had ever experienced, it represented a memorable advance. Calculation and fear, even mere prudence, made the spokesmen of social reform shrink from the logical implications of the stand that they took; but with all that they left undone, with all their patronizing acts of mercy, they contributed to the furtherance of an ideal which our own advanced civilization has still to realize. They endeavored to make society conscious of its responsibility to its members, even the humblest, not for the sake of God but for the sake of man. Never before in Europe's history had so many people at one time felt so generously and sought to act in accordance with their feelings.

Chapter Eleven

CONSTITUTIONAL LIBERALISM AFFIRMED

I. ENGLISH CONSTITUTIONALISM

WHILE enlightened despotism prevailed on the Continent, bitter political disputes at home merged with imperial problems abroad to rock English public life to its foundations. They fell upon an England undergoing a unique and unprecedented social transformation, that disruptive "Industrial Revolution" whose cumulative effect was bringing the world of old agricultural England to a close and establishing a new industrial and capitalist civilization. Agricultural improvements had begun earlier in the century, but a cruelly accelerated movement of enclosures during the reign of George III provided a new framework both for the old attack upon mediaeval tillage and animal breeding and for the trend toward consolidating small farms into large. The worst hardships were to come later, during the wars against revolutionary and Napoleonic France, but the new England was already dawning before the exceptional circumstances of war and blockade, huge governmental expenditures, mounting taxes, and inflationary prices gave the landlord fresh opportunities.

Six million acres of commons were enclosed in the course of the century: meadow, pasture, and wasteland as well as arable soil. The processes of enclosure were various. The most common method was through an act of Parliament. But the landlord could break tenant rights to the commons by refusing renewals of copyholds, or by raising rents to impossible figures when leases fell in, or by intimidating or bribing the freeholder to sell out his holding. Often he gained his ends without the confirming act of Parliament. Merely by obtaining what passed for the consent of the majority of owners the landlord could take over the village wasteland on which the landless had established definite squatters' rights. The logic of historical development made Parliament his ally, for Parliament was largely a "landlord's club."

Public opinion also had no answer to the patriotic plea that fields be joined and enclosed and scientifically cultivated in order to yield larger crops for the needs of a rapidly growing population. Sound economic principles, too, impersonally commended enclosures, and assuredly personal expectations of higher rentals and tithes were no deterrents to action.

In theory, all villagers with legitimate claims could demand a share in the redistribution when the common land, whether wasteland or arable field, was being enclosed. The reality was otherwise. Apart from the difficulty of evaluating the individual equivalent of common rights, to share in the allotment meant also sharing in the costs of lawyers' fees and the expenses of road making and fencing. Comparatively few of the villagers could stand such expenses. In practice, therefore, the enclosure movement resulted in the destruction of the mediaeval village community, the annihilation of its old co-operative customs and traditions, and the wrecking of the lives of many thousands of cultivators.

Much can of course be said in defense of enclosures. They contributed in an important manner to the great increase of the country's grain and meat supply which saw England through the war crisis. The enclosure of the common wasteland amounted in many respects to a great reclamation program which afforded farm laborers opportunities for employment that did not exist before. Yet, by the end of the century even the stanchest advocates were forced into the realization that along with its good the enclosing zeal had done irreparable harm. By itself the enclosure movement did not make the small landowners extinct, for the cottager and the yeoman landowner survived well into the nineteenth century, and their elimination had begun before the enclosures. But the enclosures speeded up their extinction. The enclosure of waste rather than common tillable fields swelled the number of landless farm hands condemned to work for wages on land they did not own. In an age of the most rapid economic change the triple alliance of enclosures, consolidation of holdings, and large-scale production for the market broke up the village solidarity that earlier centuries had cemented. By destroying the customary, even if non-legal, usage of the commons the combination removed the anchorage of the poor. The old England with its "green hills far away" still lived on in an unfamiliar countryside of hedges and hedgerows. But the newer agricultural society of landless laborers and non-cultivating landlords had come; and the non-propertied poor were paying the cost of progress.[1]

Parliamentary support helped provide for safer and more rapid means of transportation, and the improved facilities made their contribution to revolutionary change. Road construction established a new record, but even that achievement was eclipsed by the construction of three thousand miles of canals for the shipment of bulky goods. While internal trade increased only greatly, foreign trade improved in almost unbelievable proportions. In the forty years preceding 1760 exports had already doubled, and they were to double again from 1762 to 1792, rising from £14,500,000 to 31,000,000. Imports, which had risen slowly in the first period, shot up almost fourfold from £9,750,000 in 1760 to 37,750,000 in 1789. The volume of shipping kept pace with the rise in the value of goods carried. Exclusive of the smuggling trade, which was not inconsiderable, some 1,269,000 tons cleared from British ports in 1800 as against the 471,241 tons in 1760. The proportion going to lands outside Europe rose from less than one-quarter in 1700 to almost one-half by the end of the century. It was the increased imports of raw cotton and the export of finished cotton goods that accounted in great measure for the astonishing gains.[2] The country which had also once feared underpopulation was now greatly perturbed lest the utterly startling rate of increase (from 6,000,000 in 1750 to 7,500,000 in 1780 and to just under 9,000,000 in 1801) run dangerously ahead of the available food supplies. Hence the export of grain was repeatedly suspended after 1765, and the new Corn Law of 1773 allowed imports at a comparatively low rate.

The vast capital wealth required to finance extensive industrial enterprise came from these profits of trade. Wealth created wealth. Prosperity, not necessity, was the cradle of revolutionary change. The modern England of machines and steam, factories and large-scale

---

1 H. L. Beales, *The Industrial Revolution, 1750-1850* (London, 1938), ch. iii; R. E. Prothero (Lord Ernle), *English Farms, Past and Present,* 4th ed. (London, 1927), chs. vii-ix; and J. L. and B. Hammond, *The Village Labourer, 1760-1832,* 4th ed. (London, 1927), chs. i-iv.

2 While the export of manufactured cloth increased fivefold in volume between 1764 and 1788, the poundage of imported cotton rose in the same period from 2,976,000 to 42,576,000, and the value from £45,786 to £1,875,046. Cf. Slater, *op. cit.,* 132.

industries, did not come into being overnight; and both the pace and the geographical area of change were widely diversified. But the series of inventions which ushered in the age of modern technology was soon to sweep aside as unimportant relics the older ways in textile production, metallurgy and engineering, and the dark, underground world of mining. The new inventions and improved techniques came to a country abundantly blessed with resources of raw materials, money, and manpower. Inventors and promoters, along with the economic philosophers, all worked together in an atmosphere of highest expectancy. With the leveling of village independence the last barrier to rapid industrialization was eliminated, and as the bewildered contemporaries watched the deserted village and the abandoned countryside pour their inhabitants in a steady stream to the new towns of the industrialized Midlands and the north, they could well believe that an industrial revolution was overpowering them.

Until the wars with France large-scale factory and power-driven industry was in its infancy. The astonishing transformation of the cotton industry from a dispersed cottage craft to an intense factory production was no true epitome of the entire industrial development, because the other textile industries lagged far behind. Nor was the development of the highly specialized pottery industry under the magic wand of Josiah Wedgwood representative of the first stages of change. Iron production and coal mining were indeed becoming major industries, but the two were not yet fully joined in their modern technological nexus. Even Watt's improved rotary steam engine, which was just beginning its penetration of industrial life, was still far more appreciated as a source of economy for fuel than as a source of motive power.

Nevertheless, the delicately interrelated body of folk customs was breaking down. The new urban community of the proletariat of machine culture had come, and with it the new problems of food and sanitation, education and recreation, and, most unhappily of all, relief. Just as the enclosures did not by themselves end the village community, so steam power, machinery, and the concentration of labor in the factory did not invent the exploitation of women and children or create the long hours of exhausting toil. Reinforced by the legal endorsement that Parliament gave to the widening disparity between the helplessness of the workers and the power of the employers, they helped fatally to generalize and systematize hardships that once were localized and particular. The demon of gain had already swept the possessing classes off their balance before the conflict against Napoleonic France accelerated the march of industrial change and aggravated its evils.[3]

Such was the background for the political convulsions. The fierce squabble precipitated by Bute's peace had deepened by 1764 into the fiercer storm of the controversy over John Wilkes. "That devil Wilkes" was doubtlessly a good deal of a wastrel in his private life, but he was also a man of courage and tenacity who embodied the old English temper that while the kingship was itself inviolable, the king was only the first magistrate of the country, bound by his responsibilities to the people.[4] Arrested by the king's order on a general warrant because George III accused him of libeling the royal speech in No. 45 of his *The North Briton*, Wilkes pleaded privilege as a member of Parliament and obtained his release on a writ of *habeas corpus*. The courts won a strong point against the crown, when the chief justice ruled against general warrants permitting search and arrest of persons and the seizure of property not specifically named. An accommodating House of Commons, however, maintained that the famous issue of *The North Briton* was in fact libelous. Arguing that privilege did not extend to libel, it ordered Wilkes's expulsion. And for his obstinacy in reprinting an annotated copy of the condemned issue he was outlawed, though he was already in personal safety in France where he had fled after engaging in a duel.

The popular demonstrations in his favor revealed the average Englishman's troubled sense that right was on the side of the accused. It is also true that the severe deflationary hardships following the end of the war did not dampen the turbulent spirits of the London mob. For several years the growing sharpness of the dispute with the American colonies crowded Wilkes off the center of the political stage.

---

[3] J. L. and B. Hammond, *The Rise of Modern Industry*, 3rd ed. (London, 1937), chs. i-v; and E. Lipson, *Economic History of England*, 3 vols. (London, 1931), III, chs. iv and v.

[4] For the system of the "King's Friends," which attempted through organized corruption to strengthen the royal prerogative at the cost of undermining well-established constitutional practices and precedents, cf. ch. 1, pp. 17-20.

The controversy was reopened in 1768 when Middlesex returned him to the House of Commons, his outlawry in the meantime having been reversed. On the wholly astonishing grounds that his former conduct rendered him unfit to serve, the House refused to seat him. Twice again the voters returned him, and each time his election was quashed. A third time, though he had snowed under a governmental candidate, the House still would not allow him to take his seat, alleging that the other candidate, a Colonel Luttrell, "ought to have been returned." This extraordinary procedure created a grave constitutional situation. Most certainly the House of Commons could in law and by custom pass on the qualifications of its members; but it could do so only in accordance with legal requirements and not against them. By its vindictive exclusion of Wilkes for acts for which he had already been punished the House indulged in an intolerable subversion of representative government. David Hume could complain during the crisis that "licentiousness, or rather the frenzy of Liberty, has taken possession of us, and is throwing everything into confusion," but the cry of "Wilkes and Liberty" that surged forth from the aroused populace was an eloquent indication that the public mind had grasped the significance of the issue far more clearly than had the philosophical historian.

Though Wilkes still remained unseated, all was not lost. On the contrary. The storm caused by his shabby treatment did not die down with the demonstrations of the populace. The anonymous *Letters of Junius* excoriated the monarchy and the "King's Friends," revealing to a wide reading public the enormous range and the wretched depths of political corruption. Edmund Burke penned one of his most masterly essays, *Thoughts on the Causes of the Present Discontent*, which elevated the quarrel to the heights of political philosophy. Simultaneously, practical reformers, such as Horne Tooke, created the Society of Supporters of the Bill of Rights and laid the precedent for organizing popular opinion outside Parliament. The court ruling against general warrants had already put the monarch in the position where he had to get specific legal authority for his acts. In 1771 a more independent House of Commons permitted full press publicity to parliamentary debates, thereby indicating that political criticism was henceforth immune from prosecution. Three years later, in 1774, when

Wilkes triumphantly took his seat, the principle was vindicated that a duly elected representative could not be disbarred, irrespective of previous convictions or present opinions. England had shown its determination to preserve the rights of political democracy.

Not for some years to come did the crown suffer any diminution of the royal prerogative. Under the direction of the able and affable Lord North, who became the leading minister of George III in 1770, the king's system—now quite indistinguishable from a thorough Tory system—remained for thirteen years the closest formal approximation to enlightened despotism that England was to experience. In form it virtually destroyed the independence of the ministry, which was organized to serve as the executive agency of the crown and enforce the royal policy. Lord North, it is worthy of note, never took the title of prime minister, always regarding himself as the chief responsible agent for "the king's business." His mentality was continental, and his phraseology, mediaeval. It was the king himself who laid down the work of the executive departments and supervised it, even down to the minutiae. The king it was, too, who watched over parliamentary proceedings, arranging when needed the humblest details of patronage and personally controlling perquisites. Whatever else may be said of him, George III himself never doubted the full legality of his system. What was more revealing was that for many long years the influential aristocratic circles seemed to share in his aberration.

The system broke down, partly because of the heavy handicap imposed upon it by the king's intellectual shortcomings and emotional instability. It broke down, too, because the best political brains of the country refused to debase themselves before a blurred royal carbon copy of continental absolutists and surrender without struggle the nation's hard-earned constitutional rights. Most likely George III was innocent of any formal attempt to extend the royal prerogative. But his strategy of transferring authority from the Whig magnates to his own person strongly conveyed the impression that he was encroaching upon the rights of Parliament. Historians may agree to differ in interpreting the "causes" of the American War of Independence, but there can be no disagreement over the pivotal importance of the war in giving the royal system its decisive blow. Only a handful of Dissenters and merchants outside Parliament and a few parliamentary critics like Burke, Fox, and Dunning in the House of Commons and Whigs like Rockingham, Shelburne, Chatham, and Grafton in the House of Lords were originally in the opposition to the government's American policy. They held that the king's attitude was subversive of every constitutional principle that they cherished and they were agreed that his victory over the colonists would be fatal to any reform movement at home. The great Whig peers also desired, by ending the king's system, to remove the threat that it and its Tory beneficiaries held to their entrenched control over local political life.

Demands for change came more vigorously from the so-called radical reformers outside Parliament than they did from the nominal political representatives. Inspired by the democratic practices of the Americans and stimulated also by the generous abstractions of French political speculation, the militant band of political democrats waged their campaign for reform through their clubs, pamphlets, and the press. Granville Sharp wrote his pamphlet, *A Declaration of the People's Natural Right to a Share in the Legislature*. Four years later, in 1778, Major John Cartwright penned his still sharper *Take Your Choice*; and John Jebb, the most advanced of the reformers, vented his scorn on the niggardly and inadequate proposals of the fiscal reformers in Parliament by proclaiming that "moving the People of England to carry so small a Reform would be tempting the Ocean to drown a fly." Lord Rockingham could retort in kind by stating that the radical proposals "would furnish matter for disputation in the school of Utopia till time was no more,"[5] but the radical proposals were actually not very radical. The redistribution of seats and the broadening of suffrage rights were all that the radical reformers asked for.

It took the shock of military defeats, the revelation of incompetence and corruption, the distress of the masses, the heavy burden of taxation upon the well-to-do, and what seemed like threatening bankruptcy to bring the two wings of the opposition together. Sensing that their moment had come, the Whig peers and commoners co-operated in the attack upon the government with Wyvill's County Association, Tooke's Society of Supporters of the Bill of Rights, and Cartwright's Society for Promoting Constitutional Information. They were reconciled to

[5] G. S. Veitch, *The Genesis of Parliamentary Reform* (London, 1913), 75-76.

using the organization of the non-parliamentary reformers, for they were sanguine of re-establishing their own control over parliamentary and administrative life once the destruction of the king's capacity for corruption had been consummated.

The tenuous agreement of the rival groups was reached between the time of the American-French alliance in 1778 and the fall of Yorktown in 1781; and by March, 1782, they overturned Lord North's ministry. Popular expectation reached its height with the establishment of the Whig ministry of Rockingham in the place of Lord North's. Petitions rained in upon Parliament, and the coalition strove, as Fox put it, "to give a good stout blow to the influence of the Crown." The stout blow fell, but the high expectations were not realized. It could not have been otherwise. The Whigs were the inheritors and indeed the defenders of a great constitutional tradition, but they were no innovators of political change. They could not broaden the bases of political democracy or extend its frontiers, because they were blinded by the limitations of their social vision into believing that once they were in control again a few practical reform measures would suffice to correct the situation. Burke, who held the post of paymaster of the forces in the ministry, effected some slight economic reforms. The official record was expunged of the resolution rejecting Wilkes on the entirely correct grounds that it was "subversive of the rights of electors." The youthful paragon, William Pitt, introduced a motion for a parliamentary inquiry, but relaxed when it was lost. Otherwise nothing was altered. On Rockingham's death a few months later, Shelburne formed a new ministry including Pitt as chancellor of the exchequer, but excluding Fox, Burke, and Sheridan. It was speedily overthrown by the most unnatural political combination of Lord North and Fox. The future of reform already lay in the past.

At this point George III showed his political shrewdness and snatched the initiative from his opponents. He was burning to get rid of both the recreant North, who had basely "deserted" him, and Fox, whom he detested and feared in equal proportions. Through a reliable intermediary he approached the already politically experienced younger Pitt, in whom he saw a pliable tool, and promised him a majority at the next general election if Pitt would agree to form a ministry on the overthrow of North and Fox. The existing government fell, when the powerful commercial interests scuttled Fox's bill to reform the government of India, and Pitt formed a new ministry. Parliament was dissolved when his own India bill was rejected, but he remained confident that the forthcoming election would give him a majority. Nor was he mistaken. The general election of 1784 veritably decimated Fox's following in the House. But to interpret the verdict at the polls as a spontaneous expression of an indignant public opinion repudiating royal corruption and punishing the political trickery of Fox and North by putting an unblemished Pitt at the helm to restore purity to political life is as much mythology as the Whig version of the Lord Bute-George III plot. The election was a polished piece of political trickery. It represented little more at the moment than the victory of royal intrigue and patronage and the skilled financial manipulation of the powerful business interests.[6]

After nearly a quarter of a century the struggle between the crown and a curiously unreal and loosely joined combination of aristocratic Whigs and ideological radicals thus ended in a seemingly dramatic popular rebuke to the king. This first impression was false at the time, and only Pitt's remarkable public achievements during the first decade of his administration were to give it a kind of belated and spurious validity. He remains the hero of the great epic of national revival and recovery from the humiliations of military defeat and diplomatic isolation.[7] He carved a niche for himself in the hearts of all his countrymen who had faith in progressive Toryism. To a country torn by social distress and discontent he gave a sound business administration on progressive lines and furnished it with the economic strength and the financial sinews to carry on the life-and-death struggle against France. As a follower of Adam Smith he applied the economic ideas of the master both in his reform of the tariff and in his trade treaty with France. He borrowed from the Nonconformist clergyman and economist, Dr. Price, for his procedure of funding the national debt. The funding operation, along with his other fiscal reforms, brought an appreciative country a balanced budget and annual surpluses. A benevolent imperialist, he took over from Fox and Burke

6 Cf. W. J. Laprade, "Public Opinion and the General Election of 1784," in *English Historical Review*, XXXI (1916), 224-237; and the same author's "William Pitt and the Westminster Election," in *American Historical Review*, XVIII (1913), 253-274.

7 Cf. the eulogistic J. H. Rose, *William Pitt and the National Revival* (London, 1911).

their most practicable suggestions for imperial reorganization. He was sincerely sympathetic to the "Saints" in their crusade against the slave trade; and he was tolerant to fully as much as the minimum program of the parliamentary reformers.

From the constitutional point of view, too, his advent to power proved itself in time enormously significant. While the election engineered by the king himself could hardly be construed as a victory over the king's system, the high hopes George III may have harbored of finding in Pitt a supple instrument, a second Lord North, were definitely and decisively thwarted. Only in that sense was the famous general election of 1784 a famous popular victory. It is assuredly to Pitt's credit that he re-established and strengthened the obligations of the ministry to the premier rather than to the king, and the responsibility of both to Parliament. But he still kept the administration supporters in Parliament in line by as deft a disbursement of preferments and perquisites as the king would have done and had already done for his own followers. It was his good fortune to be able to end the constitutional arrangement practiced by George III and Lord North without injuring the nation's needs, the interest of the commercial and financial groups, or his own personal standing.

Manifestly, the Whig aristocracy was bitterly disappointed by its failure to reap the political rewards of the campaign against the king. The peers could not rejoice over his measures favoring the merchants or his progressive fiscal reforms. But if Pitt represented the new financial and commercial interests, he was no enemy of the great landed aristocracy. He did not alienate the landlords with his political conservatism. When his modest proposal for parliamentary changes was rejected in 1785, he shelved the dangerous question of political reforms for good. The years that followed were lean ones for the sponsors of change. Social reforms were honored with neglect. On such terms the Whigs could rest tolerably satisfied with the creator of the new Tory party. The stranglehold of the aristocracy and the squirearchy over the whole of local political life remained unloosened. Land remained king, and the specter of social unrest seemed laid for many years to come. Constitutionalism under the aegis and for the benefit of landlords and the business aristocracy had prevailed over social and political radicalism and royal authoritarianism. England was happily rescued from its unmourned experiment in unenlightened despotism.[8]

II. FRANCE AND THE FAILURE OF ENLIGHTENED DESPOTISM

France too underwent a sweeping industrial development accompanied by a fierce political struggle. But the outcome of strife in France differed enormously from the settlement in England. The fruits of victory in France were not shared by the two wings of the anti-monarchical opposition. The rewards went to the more powerful new business interests, to the upper bourgeoisie of industry and finance, who exploited their triumph against their momentary allies among the old landed aristocracy as well as against the Old Regime monarchy.

The phenomenal growth of free industrial capitalism in France paralleled the far better known successes of the early Industrial Revolution in England. French industrialization also depended upon an antecedent expansion of commercial capitalism and an ample supply of money and credit. As in England, the internal trade rose sharply during the second half of the century, here too aided by improved road, river, and canal facilities. Though France was far from being the unified trading area that England and Scotland represented, the free exchange of agricultural goods made headway, and on three separate occasions the government decreed free internal trade in grain.

This domestic increase was dwarfed by the growth of foreign trade. What India and the American colonies were to the British, the semi-tropical Antilles were to French merchant capitalists. The West Indies trade in sugar, coffee and cocoa, indigo, spices and drugs, cotton and wood in 1788 reached one-quarter of the total value of foreign commerce. Merchants and shippers, brokers and bankers, particularly along the Atlantic seaboard, made colossal fortunes out of colonial trade, slavery, and other associated activities. They built huge warehouses to store the colonial wares, distilleries, refineries, and factories to process them, and enlarged existing shipyards to handle the increased

---

[8] C. G. Robertson, *England under the Hanoverians*, 10th ed. (London, 1930), chs. ii and iii and the Appendix; and P. A. Brown, *The French Revolution in English History* (London, 1924), ch. i.

volume of trade. From 1713 to 1756 foreign trade had increased three-fold from 215,000,000 francs to 600,000,000. The grim reverses of the Seven Years' War decimated France's merchant marine and nullified most of the gain. But within a quarter of a century the value of foreign trade had soared to over 1,000,000,000 francs, a striking index of the remarkable economic vitality of pre-revolutionary France.

To a far greater extent than in England French capitalists used their wealth either to purchase government offices and securities or to buy titles of nobility. More than enough remained from the profits of world-wide trade to finance a feverish outburst of industrial activity during the last decades of the Old Regime. The presence of capitalist promoters and economists in the government administration, men of the stamp of Gournay, the two Trudaines, and Turgot, spurred industrial progress. On their initiative the government removed or greatly relaxed the older Colbertist regulations concerning methods of production. In many instances this governmental action was little more than a legal recognition of an existing reality. Through its central council of commerce and the regional intendants and inspectors of manufactures the government also strove to improve and modernize the technique of production. French industry, unlike the English, owed much to active government intervention and subsidy. It was linked in spirit with English enterprise, but the existence of many privileged state factories and government-authorized or regulated monopolies also attests that in the pattern of its economic life France still resembled the other police-states of the Continent.

Thus stimulated by governmental aid and supported by public opinion, French industrial capitalism experienced a first bloom. For the joint benefit of the state and private enterprise public administrators established spinning schools for the training of the rapidly increasing rural population, founded local economic societies, set prizes for technological inventions, and despatched technicians abroad to England for training, while simultaneously luring English specialists to France. The promoters lacked neither capital nor experience in handling large labor forces. Trade profits supplied the former, and the well-developed putting-out or "domestic" system of textile production, the latter. Rural industry organized on this entrepreneurial basis continued its rapid advance in the provinces of northern France, but at the same time factory concentration became the rule in more than one-half of the enterprises producing woven cotton. Technical reasons also necessitated the congregation of workers in the cotton print industry, and by the end of the Old Regime there existed more than 100 factories organized mostly as joint-stock companies and producing more than 12,000,000 francs' worth of prints per annum. Machinery was installed in the great manufactories at Amiens, Orléans, and Louviers almost immediately after England had adopted Arkwright's and Cartwright's inventions for her own use. Most of all, the metallurgical industries and coal mining illustrated the scope of industrial capitalism. Large-scale enterprise could indeed be called a reality when iron mining enterprises like the Creusot stock company existed, with a capital fund of 10,000,000 francs, not to speak of the heavily capitalized Alais and Anzin coal mine companies, which set thousands of workers to carefully specialized tasks.[9]

Large-scale industry was still exceptional, even in the new "factories," for most of the latter were modest enterprises. Craft-guild production for the local market and manufacture in the literal sense for home use still obtained in the feeding, clothing, and housing for most of France. In fact, French economy remained predominantly agricultural, and the old perplexing problem of the peasantry grew more difficult in the years of industrial expansion. Contrary to long-held belief, the evidence of living costs, wages, and land rents proves that the great majority of the peasants, like the urban workers, suffered rather than gained from the long upward cycle of prosperity that lasted from 1771 to 1789. If one uses the living costs for the relatively stable period from 1726 to 1741 as the norm, the evidence shows that the over-all price increase for some 24 basic commodities was 45 per cent during the last two decades. The increase was abnormally high in the case of peasant necessities like food and raw material, which reveals indirectly that the indisputable absolute increase in agricultural production was still relatively insufficient for the consumption needs of an even more rapidly growing population. As the average peasant was a marginal cultivator, rarely having even in good years a cash crop

9 Cf. H. Sée, *Economic and Social Conditions in France during the Eighteenth Century* (New York, 1927), ch. viii, for an admirable digest, and E. Lavisse, ed., *Histoire de France*, IX, Bk. IV, ch. v, for a more detailed account; and Charles Ballot, *L'introduction du machinisme dans l'industrie française* (Paris, 1923), ch. i, for governmental initiative.

over and above his fixed needs and charges, this appreciation of prices was at all times injurious to his interests. It was catastrophic when bad harvests forced him to buy seed and fodder at market prices that touched scarcity level until the new harvest was ready. The evidence also shows that wages for farm labor lagged behind prices during the entire period of expansion, and that the spread was most sharply pronounced during the short-cycle depression beginning in 1786 and lasting until the outbreak of the Revolution. By using the same norm, real wages stayed at 122 during that unemployment crisis, but the shortage of commodities due to crop failures and the curtailment of transportation inflated the general price level to 165 and bread prices higher still.[10]

The campaign to deprive the villagers of their common rights coincided with this devastating rise in prices and the all too rapid population growth that made France with its 25,000,000 or 26,000,000 inhabitants one of the most densely populated countries in Europe. From the sixties on, key governmental administrators like the Bertins, the elder Trudaine, Turgot, and Ormesson put the full authority of the central administration behind the efforts of the local agricultural reformers and innovators. The motives inspiring the private land-owners and their physiocratic sponsors were substantially those which justified the English enclosures. While the details of their endeavor belong to the specialized history of France, the general trend and the social attitudes were a European phenomenon—"an exact pendant," writes a French student, to the Hammonds' sad account of the English movement.[11] The inspiration to save the nation from the menace of a food shortage by instituting scientific farming, which deprived pos-sessors and squatters alike of their usages in the wasteland and the woods, their gleanage rights, and their common fields, was never too distant from the calculation of profit from the sale of increased pro-duction. The expectation of higher rentals was also present, and the hope that the dues in kind paid by the tenants would have a higher market value.

10 G. Lefebvre, "Le mouvement des prix et les origines de la Révolution française," in Annales historiques de la Révolution française (1937), 289-329, analyzes and condenses the exhaustive researches of Labrousse.

11 M. Bloch, "La lutte pour l'individualisme agraire dans la France du dix-huitième siècle," in Annales d'histoire économique et sociale (1930), 329-384; 511-557.

The movement was least successful in the grain-growing eastern provinces where much violent peasant resistance attended the reform efforts. The reformers accomplished most in the north, having good results in Picardy and Brittany, particularly in reclaiming swamp land and heath for cultivation. These good results from the point of view of national production were in the main only evils from the villagers' point of view. The social consequences of agricultural improvement cannot be understood unless one constantly bears in mind that most of the peasantry, by reason of their tenure relations, were predominantly involved not as producers eyeing profits but as consumers watching prices. To them the common rights were just as sacred as private rights were to the large proprietors. The introduction of high capitalist farming did not, as in England, destroy the immemorial solidarity of village civilization without adequate compensation to the peasantry. But it widened the gap between the well-to-do farmers and the numerically far greater marginal cultivators and increased the insecurity while lowering the living standards of small proprietors, small tenants, sharecroppers, and the landless farm hands. On the eve of the Revolution the number of the rural proletariat was truly shocking. According to the region involved the proportion of marginal cultivators varied from one-third to three-quarters of the total peasant population.[12] This acute distress of the rural and urban masses assuredly cannot be ignored as a paramount factor in causing the Revolution to come when it did.

But they were unorganized as well as wretched, and the contention that the powerful middle classes brought on the Revolution has more to commend it. The bourgeoisie destroyed the absolute monarchy, runs one line of argument, when, by its orientation to an "undesired economic liberalism," the crown turned against their interests.[13] If one is puzzled to understand why business interests already represented by influential governmental spokesmen who were pressing their efforts for capitalist agriculture and large-scale industry should have com-

12 G. Lefebvre, "La Révolution française et les paysans," in *Annales historiques de la Révolution française* (1933); and A. Mathiez, "Notes sur l'importance du prolétariat en France à la veille de la Révolution," *ibid.* (1930), 497-524.

13 Cf. F. L. Nussbaum's articles for that argument: "American Tobacco and French Politics, 1783-1789," in *Political Science Quarterly*, XL (1925), 497-516; and "The Revolutionary Vergennes and Lafayette versus the Farmers General," in *Journal of Modern History*, III (1931), 592-613.

plained of such a trend, the answer is that economic liberalism was only one of the several things to which the bourgeoisie objected in the absolute state.

A small group nearly all the time opposed the government for its failure to carry out a comprehensive reform of the entire social structure. Another minority bitterly criticized the government not for its liberalism but for its support of monopolists, as when it failed to capture the tobacco trade in particular and the colonial American trade in general. Above all, the great international merchants who opposed the government's economic liberalism did so because such a policy kept the Old Regime viable. What they wished was to shatter its foundations. They opposed governmental initiative and state intervention not mainly for the implied liberalism but because the conception was governmentally inspired. It was the old *étatisme* writ new to which they took exception, the revival of the policy of keeping them in leading strings to public administrators who were not themselves and who put the new policy to the old end of perpetuating the existing system of political and social relations which were based on production relations then rapidly disappearing. The renewed governmental intercession seriously compromised the desired "hands off" policy by which the great capitalists could also prevail over small-scale enterprises and at the same time crush whatever labor resistance developed to low wages that were becoming increasingly standardized.

Hence their anger over the government's efforts to incorporate their own paid lobbyists, the salaried agents of the federated provincial merchants, into a national network controlled by the central administration at Versailles.[14] For these reasons they opposed the establishment of national regulations to govern mail and passenger service abroad, a national postal system, and governmental marine insurance. Because of such views they contested the opening of the colonial trade in the West Indies to foreigners and the draft of the liberal commercial accord with England, both of which measures the government sponsored to further its own political and diplomatic ends. On these grounds, too, they resisted the reconstruction of the East India Company as a government monopoly, because Vergennes was subordinat-

14 F. L. Nussbaum, "The Deputies Extraordinary of Commerce and the French Monarchy," in *Political Science Quarterly*, XLVIII (1933), 534-555.

ing considerations of profit to France's diplomatic maneuvers against England in the Middle East.[15]

It would therefore obscure the true position of the merchant princes to dwell on their opposition to governmental economic liberalism. It was never at odds with the ideological position expounded by the great bourgeois publicists. The Abbé Siéyès' inspirational response that the Third Estate was "nothing" may have been stirringly effective as an appeal to the emotions; but it was manifest nonsense as an answer to his own rhetorical question. The upper bourgeoisie was not yet the desired "everything," but it was certainly a great deal by 1789. Indeed, the social and cultural history of pre-revolutionary France turns precisely on the evolution of the bourgeois attitude from the acceptance of the conception of a corporative and absolutist state with its roots in status and privilege to the adoption of a new social order, the conception of a nation of citizens. This *nation* or *patrie*, as they came to call it, had for a long time been evolving in their minds as an alternative pattern of social relations superior to the restrictive polity of the *ancien régime*. By 1789 the revolution in their thinking had been completed, and to be a "Patriot" or a "National" was thus to be a reformer striving to establish a new regime happily freed of old abuses.[16] As shown by the many pamphlets of 1788-1789 which summarized these aspirations, their goal was not to keep the historic chain of provinces constituting the French state but to create a true nation of Frenchmen. Their aim was not to perpetuate a state uniting its subjects by force but to establish a *patrie* founded on the voluntary adherence of citizens cheerfully accepting their civic responsibilities under the law of their own making. These responsibilities they would cheerfully accept, because their government would rest upon the inviolable liberties of men like themselves and would have its foundation in the sanctity of private property.

For all these desires they needed the good will and the manpower resources of the entire Third Estate; hence by annexing peasant

15 The same author's "The French Colonial Arrêt of August 31, 1784," in *South Atlantic Quarterly*, XXXVII (1927), 62-78; and "The Formation of the New East India Company," in *American Historical Review*, XXXVIII (1933), 475-497.

16 Cf. two fertile articles on this evolution: R. R. Palmer, "The National Idea in France Before the Revolution," in *Journal of the History of Ideas*, I (1940), 95-111; and B. C. Shafer, "Bourgeois Nationalism in the Pamphlets on the Eve of the French Revolution," in *Journal of Modern History*, X (1938), 31-50.

grievances to their own demands they gained the end that they sought. To trace the routes that they traversed while moving toward their goal is to recapitulate the familiar vicissitudes of the monarchy in its last days, to itemize anew the disparate elements already discussed that constituted the ingredients of their faith. It would entail, too, reviewing the many agencies among the discussion and reading societies, the provincial academies and the circulating libraries, and the many hundreds of masonic lodges with their 30,000 members, all of which passed on the articles of the faith in diluted form to the lower social levels.[17] By 1789 the hour of crisis had struck for the "republican souls" to move back from distant or non-existent realms to the pulsating realities of France. When that moment came, when they would have either to fight or renounce forever their vision of a nation resting upon the rule of law, enlightened despotism had already abdicated its claims. With the failure of Turgot to make enlightened despotism the instrument of a peaceful bourgeois revolution, a revolution by consent, the middle classes had no choice but to go forward and make one for themselves.

Everything that followed from the downfall of that great reformer to the outbreak of the Revolution had a familiar ring, as though seen or heard before. The note of remembrance was authentic, for his reforms were the pattern to which all his successors necessarily returned for guidance when it was too late for compromise. He became controller-general and leading figure in the administration almost simultaneously with the accession of Louis XVI to the throne in 1774. These two men, the darling of the *philosophes* and the economists, and the new monarch, with his youth and good intentions, augured for the best. Events belied the augury. The young ruler weakened the prestige of the crown by his ill-considered restoration of the refractory *parlements* that Chancellor Maupeou had abolished three years earlier.[18] Worse still, by re-establishing the magistrates under reservations which they speedily nullified, he compromised Turgot's reform efforts at the outset. By surrendering the first governmental redoubt to the monarch's stanchest opponents without getting any guarantees for the crown in

---

[17] For the dissemination of the liberal credo, cf. D. Mornet, *Les origines intellectuelles de la Révolution française* (Paris, 1933), Pt. III, ch. vii.

[18] J. Flammermont, *Le chancelier Maupeou et les parlements* (Paris, 1884).

return, he re-established an equilibrium of hostility between the defenders of the *status quo* and the reforming critics which made Turgot's own position precarious before he assumed direction.

Turgot's policy represented the most ambitious endeavor of the century in France to transform the inefficient absolutism into an enlightened despotism permeated with the new ideals of social progress. He planned a rational system of taxation and an administration of the public debt that would shift the burdens off the weakest backs and spread at least some of them to the backs of the hitherto exempted groups. He did not go so far as to introduce the cherished single tax, dear to the agricultural economists, but he had in mind the establishment of a comprehensive cadastral register that would be the necessary preliminary to such a tax. He abolished the forced road labor (*corvée*), which was borne exclusively by the peasantry, introduced free grain trade, and sought to open careers to talent by doing away with the craft guilds. But by reducing pensions and court expenditures he roused the ill will of the court "drones," while his curtailment of leased taxes awakened the fury of the farmers-general. The "devout faction" already detested him for his heterodox views (he had once been a distinguished student of theology), and the magistracy feared him for his advanced social outlook. While he was drawing plans for a network of freely elected assemblies, ranging from small local bodies to a national assembly, and speculating over the details of a national system of public instruction, the king dismissed him from office.

Turgot fell because his tactics made his actual program and his assumed intentions the football of court intrigues that a well-intentioned but irresolute ruler could neither curb nor control. It is true that he alienated all the powerful vested interests simultaneously. The story of his political tactlessness and ineptitude is nevertheless highly exaggerated, the work of his enemies. All successful revolutionary reformers faced and surmounted similar opposition from their opponents. Not his tactics, but his grand strategy, was at fault. While he miscalculated badly on Louis XVI, he fell principally because he lacked the daring to act upon the implications of his program. A patrician by birth and an intellectual aristocrat by training and inclination, he shrank, for all his social vision, from appealing directly to the petty bourgeoisie and the peasant proprietors. Lacking when he needed it most the organized strength of a following united by a great sense of identity, he was prevented by his very belief in the efficacy of gradual enlightenment from creating and placing himself squarely at the head of a mass movement that alone could have given him the required support.

Perhaps the strategy suggested would also have failed, because it might have been premature for the circumstances of the struggle. In any case, he did not attempt it, and the failure of what he did attempt discredited enlightened despotism even more fully than it ruined his personal position. The monarchy never recovered. When it jettisoned its would-be savior, it effectively sealed its own death warrant.[19] After Turgot's fall the French monarchy slid irresolutely down the road of annihilation, alternating between velleities of reform and bursts of obstinate steadfastness. The practical business man, Necker, who took over control of the finances, lived on borrowed time and capital for several years before events finally caught up with him. So long as his huge flotations were covered by French, Dutch, English, and Swiss financiers, his routine administrative economies did not matter much to investors. God still seemed in His heaven, even though in inscrutable fashion He had called upon a foreigner and a Protestant heretic to perform the providential services. But when Necker took advantage of his immense personal popularity and turned reformer in the style of Turgot, he too was dropped.

The agony of the monarchy began in 1781, when the king abandoned him to his critics. While the government settled ever deeper into a morass of debts, pushed down also by the expenditures it incurred in aiding the American colonists against England, the general expansionist and inflationary movement entered into a brief but sharp cycle of depression. Hard on the heels of the free-spending administration of the enterprising Calonne (1783-1787) came the triple crisis of commercial and industrial unemployment, the threat of governmental bankruptcy, and the failure of the crops. The efforts of Loménie de Brienne from 1787 to the summer of 1788 to undo Calonne's financial prestidigitation and stave off bankruptcy were nullified by the conjunction of the threefold crisis. Exceptional circumstances prompted

---

[19] D. Dakin, *Turgot and the Ancien Regime in France* (London, 1939), is an indispensable guide.

extraordinary developments, not the least ominous of which for the monarchy was the formation of a working union between the conservative nobility and the militant bourgeois "Patriots."

Again a royal edict struck at the *parlements* even as the Maupeou act had two decades earlier. But the Lamoignon edict came much too late, and even then it was not to be upheld. The judicial and fiscal officials called upon their subordinate associates in the lower courts and their followers in the legal profession to resist the edict and suspend the administration of justice. All was confusion throughout the land, as court nobles protested a reduction of their pensions, the clergy voted to reduce their "free gift" to the crown, and the military nobility joined with the magistrates, the financiers, and the organized "Patriots" in a true rebellion. On all sides, if for different calculations, the clamor was renewed for the summoning of the Estates General. The king yielded in midsummer of 1788 and agreed to call the Estates General, fixing the opening date of its deliberations for May 1, 1789. He recalled Necker to gain funds from the financiers, and he agreed to Necker's conditions that the law reforms be rescinded and the *parlements* reinstated. The country settled down, after a fashion, into composing the revealing pamphlets and the invaluable *cahiers* which were the testamentary legacies of the Old Regime.

The revolution was at hand, but the fortuitously united revolutionaries had fallen apart. The conservative opposition could not reap the victory, because in an emergency which was nothing less momentous than the painful birth of a new social order it had only to offer an outmoded corporative solution, grotesquely inadequate and grimly offensive for the circumstances. All power went to the bourgeoisie, because by then the middle classes had completed the organization required to convert their social blueprints into reality. In the deepening hardships, when the commercial treaty with England augmented the miseries of unemployment, when the failure of the crops destroyed the purchasing power of the small peasant producers while food prices rose to famine heights, and when the cruel rigor of the 1788-1789 winter, the coldest of the century, gripped the populace—at that terrible moment, it was only to the leaders of the middle classes that the masses could turn. The interests of the two social groups were not similar. But the peasantry and the urban workers gave their support to the bourgeois reformers because the governing classes by their misrule and the revolutionists by their strength and organization gave them no other way out. And the bourgeois leaders went on to establish under their own guarantees the political system and the economic relations of the capitalist democracy that lay embedded in Turgot's version of enlightened despotism.[20]

III. ENLIGHTENED DESPOTISM IN REVIEW

Definitions of enlightened despotism break against the profusion of its contradictory strivings and its incompatible realizations. Most clearly it was not a mere phase in the internal development of any particular country. It was a broad and complex European phenomenon, a distinctive stage in European historical evolution during the course of which enlightened despotism not only modified its ideals but redirected its objectives.[21] While the century during its entire course moved away from the pattern woven out of the elements of absolutism, fiscalism, mercantilism, and cameralism, the enlightened despotism of post-1763 differs markedly from the earlier period when Prussia was its principal seat and Frederick II its shining examplar.[22] In its latter phase, less under the influence of Rousseau, whose political impact was slight until the Revolution, than under the prodigious influence of the Encyclopedists and the economists, it swept over all Europe.[23] The physiocratic credo, for all its contemporary emphasis

20 Even more valuable than the vigorous brief analysis of the crisis in A. Mathiez, *The French Revolution* (New York, 1928), chs. i and ii, is the longer and more balanced account in the little-known G. Lefebvre, *Quatre-Vingt-Neuf* (Paris, 1939).

21 For the fullest elaboration of this point of view, cf. M. Lhéritier, "Le despotisme éclairé, de Frédéric II à la Révolution française," in *B.I.C.H.S.*, IX (1937), 181-225; while F. Hartung, "Die Epochen in der absoluten Monarchie in der neueren Geschichte," in *Historische Zeitschrift*, CXLV (1931), points out that the older German economists like Roscher and Schmoller and the older historians like Treitschke, Meinecke, and Koser regarded it largely as a German phenomenon in which the Frederician state represented the summit of German absolutism.

22 G. M. Dutcher, "The Enlightened Despotism," in American Historical Association, *Annual Report for 1920*, 187-198, and "Further Considerations on the Origins and Nature of the Enlightened Despotism," in *Liberty and Persecution. Essays in Honor of George Lincoln Burr* (New York, 1931), 375-405, contrasts the practices of despotism with the theories of enlightenment and concludes that the period between 1774 and 1789 represents a repudiation rather than a fulfillment.

23 For the influence of the physiocratic economists, especially of Le Mercier de la Rivière, cf. P. Dubreuil, *Le despotisme légal* (Paris, 1908); and G. Weulersse, *Le mouvement physiocratique en France depuis 1756 à 1770*, 2 vols. (Paris, 1910). F. François-Olivier, "Les pratiques traditionnelles de la royauté française et le despotisme éclairé," in *B.I.C.H.S.*, V (1937), 701-713, identifies the physiocratic ideas with the practices of

upon "legal despotism," was itself a fertile seed-plot of middle-class liberalism. Consequently, the enlightened despots were different embodiments of the changing spirit of the age, as various as that spirit and their own historical heritage and as individual as their personalities.

In its most significant aspect the eighteenth century was the great testamentary executor of the English legacy of the preceding century. In political relations it took over the bases of obedience established by the "bloodless revolution" of 1688 and built upon them the democratic speculation of Rousseau and the utopians. While many of its spokesmen renounced their cosmopolitanism in favor of cultural nationalism, the century itself reached one climax in the storm of revolution. The religious beliefs of the age advanced from the prudential deism of the English rationalists to a more vital secular faith, even, among a minority of freethinkers, to atheistic materialism. The *philosophes* cut the cord binding ethics to revelation and made social utility the criterion of morality. They appropriated the great scientific conquests of the earlier age, and in an atmosphere where fear of the mysterious universe yielded increasingly to confidence in nature as a great benefactor, they revolutionized agricultural and industrial production, bestowing wealth and power on the middle classes. Most important of all, they elaborated upon the dawning hopefulness that the facts of progress and the new psychology of human behavior and man's capacity had engendered, and they created the appealing myth of human perfectibility. "*Sapere aude!* Dare to use your own understanding! is thus the motto of the Enlightenment," proudly proclaimed Kant.

But this evolution was retarded by the inertia of inherited relations and deflected toward other goals by the play of hostile outlooks. The strength of the *Herrenstaat* was a powerful deterrent. The rule of caste and the entrenched legal "estates" held back the realization of the ideal of a nation of citizens. Economic progress, and the social reclassification that that progress entailed, was slow in areas lacking in the fluid wealth that came from world-wide trade. Vast sectors of the

---

enlightened despotism in order to place both in sharp contrast with the traditional practices of the French crown.

Continent lay blacked out under religious superstition and cultural darkness.

Even where the old internal relations were least touched, the power relations of states grew more competitive as the new technology intensified and transformed the dynastic rivalries into fiercer capitalist competition. States were compelled to strengthen their internal position, the weaker merely to survive and the stronger to be able to participate in the struggle abroad. Whether to prepare for vigorous participation abroad or to ward off the menace of social disturbances at home, the rulers more than ever before needed order, tranquillity, and security. Translated into terms of instruments, that meant greater revenue; efficient administration; reliable police; stable judicial procedures; sound laws; larger armies and newer tactics and strategy; skilled diplomacy; and not least, a policy of social welfare. The whole content of enlightened despotism turned therefore on the solutions given by the different states to their needs and aspirations. It hinged on whether the ruler adjusted his policy to satisfy the demands that were demonstrably new or subordinated them to the interests of older social groups and kept the bases of public relations intact. Though in some ultimate sense the decision may have been made by institutional forces, the immediate role of individual rulers or their leading ministers was of paramount importance.

Much that our age holds dear was manifestly served by the triumph of an enlightened despotism whose ultimate ends were realized through revolutionary means in 1789. Its deeply embedded humanist and humanitarian liberalism was subsequently fused with and "corrected" by the less ingenuous economic liberalism of nineteenth-century free enterprise; but together they eventuated in parliamentary democracy, utilitarian ethics, classical economics, and the Concert of Europe.[24]

The English triumph over absolutism was consolidated when the objectives of the commercial oligarchy were served by the governmental authority of the landed interests. Enlightened despotism in France culminated in the violent overthrow of the old order and the painful establishment of precedents for parliamentary, middle-class

---

[24] Cf. P. Sagnac, "Les grands courants d'idées et de sentiments envers 1789," in *Revue d'histoire politique et constitutionnelle* (July, 1938); and the same author's "La rénovation politique de l'Europe au dix-huitième siècle," in *Mélanges d'histoire offerts à Henri Pirenne* (Brussels, 1926), II.

constitutionalism. The French and the English examples together remained during the following century the inspiration and the criteria to which the secondary states of western Europe—Spain, Portugal, Belgium, and Holland—constantly referred. Catherine of Russia, on the other hand, made the best of two worlds. She strengthened the old bases and bequeathed to nineteenth-century Russia its heritage of autocracy, aristocracy, and orthodoxy. She also linked Russia more firmly with the west and widened the doors already ajar for the entry of European liberalism. Joseph of Austria died brokenhearted, convinced of his failure. But his Caesarian absolutism inflicted a galvanic shock on old traditions. The repudiation of his methods did not destroy his ideals, for these remained the source of Austrian liberal and democratic strivings.

The combination of enlightenment and despotism also served other functions than preparing for the ultimate triumph of liberalism. Least enlightened was the Prussian embodiment of the mandates of the age. Measured in terms of progressive social aspirations it was a dismal failure. Frederick as ruler, distinguished from Frederick the emancipated intellectual aristocrat and cynic, faced the past. He was utterly sincere in regarding himself as the first servant of the state wherein his power was legitimized by the duties that he assumed. But his improvements were consecrated to buttressing an antiquated edifice. There is no evidence to warrant the conclusion that his militarized state, whatever its power and prestige abroad, bestowed benefits upon the aggregate whole. He continued the process of unification begun by his ancestors but only by perpetuating their conception of legal relations. His program of social welfare was grounded on a primary calculation to stimulate productive effort in order to augment the power of the state rather than increase the store of public welfare.[25] Tested in terms of his own postulates of action Frederick did not succeed too well. Authoritarianism during his lifetime did little to alleviate inner rivalries and stresses. Its efficiency was won at the price of much corruption and still more coercion. And twenty years after his death the

---

[25] Even a well-disposed German historian of the Third Reich, writing in the "coordinated" *Historische Zeitschrift*, concedes that his social solicitude was designed to serve the state *an sich* and that his policy progressively estranged the *"Volk"* from him: cf. W. Mommsen, "Zur Beurteilung des Absolutismus," in *Historische Zeitschrift*, CLVIII (1938), 52-76.

Frederician state collapsed ignominiously under the shock of the military disaster at Jena.

Authoritarian rule pursued its course, both under its beneficent guise as efficient Napoleonic Caesarism and in its more naked form as administrative, bureaucratic absolutism resting upon the loyalty of new financial and industrial interests joined with old landed and military groups. These two modern versions of the *Polizeistaat* also devoted themselves to serving the greatest happiness of the greatest number, but too often security was purchased at the sacrifice of liberty. The administration of justice and finances retained, especially in central and eastern Europe, more of the eighteenth-century ideal of orderly efficiency than it did of equality of incidence. The opening of careers to talents went together with an unparalleled concentration of economic power and the aggravation of social distress. The Concert of Europe was never entirely free from the threat of renewed strife. Public instruction became the appanage of secular national states that guarded their authority as jealously as had the ecclesiastical directors of instruction whom they superseded. The eighteenth-century fear of educating the masses above their station in life died a lingering death, while the decay of religious intolerance was accompanied by the slow rise of racial and nationalist hatreds. The triumph of deism was equaled by the sweep of fervid evangelical revivalism. Though the enlightenment bequeathed to the future its confidence in reason, it also left a legacy of despair arising out of the philosophical conviction that whirl was king. Feeling increasingly displaced logic, and environmentalists were challenged by intuitionalists. The philosophy of the natural rights of man was already on the defensive against the doctrines of the historic rights of nations before the terror created by the Revolution put the seal of victory on the romantic reversion to traditionalism and irrationality.

BIBLIOGRAPHY

Bibliographical Aids
(Revised as of November, 1957)

THIS section does not cover manuscript material. Much valuable bibliographical information can be found in works which do not profess *per se* to deal with problems of bibliography. Such are the various national histories, biographies, and monographs which in the main are listed under their appropriate headings. By way of exception certain works are included in this section because of their great bibliographical richness: *Le XVIIIe siècle*, 2 vols. in the *Clio* series. Vol. I by E. Préclin and V. L. Tapié and vol. II by E. Préclin (Paris, 1952); J. Godechot, *La Grande Nation. L'expansion révolutionnaire de la France dans le monde*. 2 vols. (Paris, 1956); P. Smith, *A History of Modern Culture: The Enlightenment, 1687-1776* (New York, 1934); E. Lavisse, ed., *Histoire de France*, VIII, 2e partie, by H. Carré, and IX, by H. Carré, P. Sagnac et E. Lavisse (Paris, 1926); W. Goetz, ed., *Das Zeitalter des Absolutismus, 1660-1789*, forming vol. VI of the *Propyläen Weltgeschichte* series (Berlin, 1931); and the preceding volume in this series, W. L. Dorn, *Competition for Empire, 1740-1763* (New York, 1940).

Among the formal bibliographies, *A Guide to Historical Literature* (New York, 1931), ed. by W. H. Allison, S. B. Fay, G. M. Dutcher, and others, is basic for older works; P. Caron and others, eds., *International Bibliography of the Historical Sciences* (Zürich and New York, 1926) 22 vols. to date, is invaluable for recent literature. H. Higgs, *Economic Bibliography* (London, 1935), is standard. The *Bulletin of the International Committee of Historical Sciences,* hereafter cited as *B.I.C.H.S.,* has printed the articles submitted by the leading European scholars constituting its "Commission pour l'histoire du despotisme éclairé." Most of these reports are accompanied by exceptionally useful bibliographical references: Consult *Bulletins* no. 5 in vol. I (Paris, 1929); no. 9 in vol. II (1930); no. 20 in vol. V (1933); nos. 34 and 35 in vol. IX (1937); and no. 37 in vol. X (1938).

Of the special guides for the particular countries, for Germany consult F. C. Dahlmann and G. Waitz, *Quellenkunde der deutschen Geschichte,* 2 vols., 9th rev. ed. (Leipzig, 1931-1932), and G. Franz, ed., *Bücherkunde zur Weltgeschichte* (Munich, 1956); for Prussian bibliography, M. Lhéritier and G. Pagès in *Bulletin de la Société des professeurs d'histoire et de géographie,* nos. 65 (1930), 85 (1935), 89 (1936), and 90 (1937); for

Austria, R. Charmetz, *Wegweiser durch die Literatur der österreichischen Geschichte* (Stuttgart u. Berlin, 1912); for Belgium, H. Pirenne, *Bibliographie de Belgique,* 3rd ed. (Brussels, 1931); for Hungary, R. Gragger, *Bibliographia Hungariae,* I and II (Berlin, 1923-1926), which list many titles of publications from 1861-1912 on Hungarian history in other languages than Magyar. For England, there are S. H. Pargellis and D. J. Medley, *Bibliography of British History: The Eighteenth Century* (Oxford, 1951); J. B. Williams, *A Guide to the Printed Materials for English Social and Economic History,* 2 vols. (New York, 1926); E. Power, *The Industrial Revolution, 1750-1850* (London, 1927). On France there is Vicomte Charles du Peloux, *Répertoire général des ouvrages modernes relatifs au XVIIIe siècle français, 1715-1789* (Paris, 1926); and his *Supplément* to the above (1927). R. J. Kerner, *Slavic Europe* (Cambridge, 1918), is basic for works in western European languages; and for works in Russian there is V. I. Picheta, *Vvedenie v Russkuiu Istoriiu, Stochniki i Istoriografia* (Moscow, 1922). For Italy, F. Lemmi, *Il Risorgimento, guide bibliografiche* (Rome, 1926), which covers the period 1748-1871; and the bibliography in E. Rota, *Questioni di storia del Risorgimento e dell' unità d'Italia* (Milan, 1951); and for Spain, B. Sanchez Alonzo, *Fuentes de la historia española* (Madrid, 1919). In addition to these guides, which are valuable for older works, there are the occasional lengthy review articles on current studies in the specialized historical reviews, such as *Revue historique, Journal of Modern History,* etc.

Europe During the Second Half of the Eighteenth Century

General Works. Among the briefer accounts there are M. Beloff, *The Age of Absolutism, 1660-1815* (London, 1954); the useful F. E. Manuel, *The Age of Reason* (Ithaca, 1951); the facile little volume of R. B. Mowat, *The Age of Reason* (New York, 1934); the crisp survey of G. Bruun, *The Enlightened Despots* (New York, 1929); the two older, detailed works on the eighteenth century: A. Sorel, *L'Europe et la Révolution française,* 8 vols. (Paris, 1885-1904), I; and J. Jaurès, *Histoire socialiste de la Révolution française,* 8 vols., new ed. by A. Mathiez (Paris, 1922-1924), V, must be supplemented and corrected by *Le XVIIIe siècle* of Préclin and Tapié, cited above; P. Sagnac, *La fin de l'Ancien Régime et la Révolution américaine,* vol. XII of the *Peuples et Civilisations* series (Paris, 1941); R. Mousnier and E. Labrousse, *Le XVIIIe siècle,* forming vol. V in the *Histoire Générale des Civilisations* series, ed. by M. Crouzet (Paris, 1953); and the remarkable survey in G. Lefebvre, *La Révolution française,* vol. XIII in the *Peuples et Civilisations* series (Paris, 1951), Bk I; and L. Just, *Der Aufgeklärte Despotismus* (Darmstadt, n.d.), a useful text. Of manuals on diplomacy there are the familiar

E. Bourgeois, *Manuel historique de la politique étrangère*, 2 vols., new ed. (Paris, 1926), I; M. Immich, *Geschichte des Europäischen Staatensystems, 1660-1789* (Munich, 1909); R. B. Mowat, *A History of European Diplomacy, 1451-1789* (New York, 1929); and G. Zeller, *Les temps modernes, de Louis XIV à 1789*, forming vol. III in *Histoire des relations internationales* series, ed. by P. Renouvin (Paris, 1955).

The comprehensive and more modern *Encyclopedia of the Social Sciences*, to which leading European scholars contributed, obviates the usual references to French and German works of that nature. Note, however, W. Andreas and W. F. Scholz, eds., *Die Grossen Deutschen, Neue Deutsche Biographie*, 5 vols. (Berlin, 1935-1937), which is a handy, if nationalistic, compendium based on recent monographs.

Economic evolution is treated exhaustively in W. Sombart, *Der moderne Kapitalismus*, 3 vols., 3rd ed. (Munich, 1928), II; and J. Kulischer, *Allgemeine Wirtschaftsgeschichte des Mittelalters und der Neuzeit*, 2 vols. (Munich, 1928-1929), II. Less encyclopedic for English readers are F. L. Nussbaum, *History of the Economic Institutions of Modern Europe* (New York, 1933), which is based on Sombart; the very useful H. Heaton, *Economic History of Europe* (New York, 1936); G. Renard and G. Weulersse, *Life and Work in Modern Europe* (New York, 1926); P. Mantoux, *The Industrial Revolution in the Eighteenth Century* (New York, 1928); H. Sée, *Esquisse d'une histoire du régime agraire en Europe aux 18e et 19e siècles* (Paris, 1921).

European Society. As the cosmopolitan eighteenth century was the great age of travel, it is exceptionally rich in travel accounts, diaries, letters, which in one way or another record the traveler's observations, impressions, and philosophical notions about what he saw. The creative literature of the age is similarly a mine of information on the living habits, housing, food, attire, and recreation of the period. Among the general accounts, there are R. S. Lambert, ed., *Grand Tour, a Journey in the Tracks of Aristocracy* (New York, 1937); and M. von Boehn, *Modes and Manners. The Eighteenth Century*, tr. from the German (London, 1935). A. Goodwin, ed., *The European Nobility in the Eighteenth Century* (London, 1953), is a useful study.

For England, J. B. Botsford, *English Society in the Eighteenth Century, As Influenced from Oversea* (New York, 1924), is a remarkably stimulating study; A. G. Turberville, ed., *Johnson's England*, 2 vols. (New York, 1933), however uneven in its contributors, is a valuable work of reference; A. E. Richardson, *Georgian England* (New York, 1931), R. Bayne-Powell,

Eighteenth Century London Life (London, 1937), and J. J. Hecht, *The Domestic Servant Class in Eighteenth Century England* (London, 1956), are interesting social accounts. J. Telford, ed., *The Letters of the Rev. John Wesley,* 8 vols. (London, 1931), and J. Beresford, ed., *The Diary of a Country Parson, The Rev. James Woodforde . . . ,* 5 vols. (London, 1924-1930), are inexhaustible repertories by native Englishmen; while C. P. Moritz, *Travels through Various Parts of England in 1782* (London, ed. of 1886), is a shrewd appraisal by an intelligent foreigner.

For France, L. Ducros, *French Society in the Eighteenth Century* (New York, 1927), is less critical than one might expect of its learned author; and H. Simpson, *The Waiting City: Paris, 1782-1788* (London, 1932), being only an abridgment of L. S. Mercier's *Le tableau de Paris,* is necessarily also a literary exaggeration. C. Maxwell, ed., *The English Traveller in France, 1698-1815* (London, 1932), serves to introduce the interesting J. Moore, *A View of Society and Manners in France, Switzerland, and Germany,* 2 vols. (London, 1780), and J. Andrews, *A Comparative View of the English and French Nations in Their Manners, Politics, and Literature* (London, 1785), both of which are filled with awe over the advantages of being born an Englishman. The best of the recent studies on Germany is W. H. Bruford, *Germany in the Eighteenth Century* (New York, 1935), a thoughtful work which corrects but does not entirely supersede the magnificent old classic of F. C. Biedermann, *Deutschland im achtzehnten Jahrhundert,* 4 vols., 2nd rev. ed. (Leipzig, 1880-1884). Of the many travel accounts in Italy, J. Moore, *A View of Society and Manners in Italy,* 2 vols. (London, 1781), and C. Duclos, *Voyage en Italie* (Paris, 1769), are informative and interesting as reflections of liberal disapproval of Italian backwardness. H. Swinburne, *Travels . . . through Spain in the Years 1775 and 1776* (London, 1778), and J. Townshend, *A Journey through Spain in the Years 1786 and 1787,* 3 vols., 2nd ed. (London, 1792), are both careful observers; while C. E. Kany, *Life and Manners in Madrid, 1750-1800* (Berkeley, 1932), is a lively social history of both charm and value. W. Coxe, *Travels into Poland, Russia, Sweden and Denmark,* 3 vols. (London, 1784), is one of the most popular works of an indefatigable voyager. The too keen observations of V. Radishchev, *Reise von Petersburg nach Moskau* (1790), tr. from the Russian (Leipzig, 1922), earned the author a free continuation of his journey to Siberia. For a full annotated list of travel accounts to Russia, consult the informative D. S. von Mohrenschildt, *Russia in the Intellectual Life of Eighteenth Century France* (New York, 1936).

The Mandates of Thought and Feeling

The Climate of Opinion. For the general temper, in addition to ch. V of Dorn, cited, and his bibliography, P. Smith's work, cited; the excellent survey in J. H. Randall, *The Making of the Modern Mind* (New York, ed. of 1940); B. Willey, *The Eighteenth Century Background* (New York, 1940); A. Wolf, *A History of Science, Technology and Philosophy in the Eighteenth Century* (New York, 1939); and A. R. Hall, *The Scientific Revolution, 1500-1800 . . .* , 2nd. ed. (Boston, 1956); E. Cassirer, *The Philosophy of the Enlightenment,* tr. from the German (Princeton, 1951); P. Hazard, *European Thought in the Eighteenth Century: From Montesquieu to Lessing* (New Haven, 1954); L. Réau, *L'Europe française au siècle des lumières* (Paris, 1938); A. Reichwein, *China and Europe. Intellectual and Artistic Contacts in the Eighteenth Century* (New York, 1925). In addition to J. B. Bury, *The Idea of Progress,* new ed. (New York, 1932), chs. vii-xiii; and the subtle C. Becker, *The Heavenly City of the Eighteenth Century Philosophers* (New Haven, 1932), there are C. Frankel, *The Faith of Reason: The Idea of Progress in the French Enlightenment* (New York, 1948); M. Ginsberg, *The Idea of Progress: A Revaluation* (Boston, 1953); and R. V. Sampson, *Progress in the Age of Reason* (Cambridge, Mass., 1957). The reflection of this temper in historical thinking and writing is treated soberly by E. Fueter, *L'histoire de l'historiographie moderne,* tr. and rev. from the German (Paris, 1915), Bk. IV; and J. W. Thompson, *History of Historical Writing,* 2 vols. (New York, 1942), II, chs. xxxviii-xl. J. B. Black, *The Art of History* (New York, 1926), is a sympathetic appreciation of four characteristic rationalist historians; while F. Meinecke, *Die Entstehung des Historismus,* 2 vols. (Munich, 1936), is a highly important pioneering study on the transition from eighteenth-century to nineteenth-century modes of historical thinking.

For France in English: K. Martin, *French Liberal Thought in the Eighteenth Century* (New York, 1929); R. G. Havens, *The Age of Ideas* (New York, 1956); D. Echeverria, *Mirage in the West* (Princeton, 1957); N. N. Schargo, *History in the* Encyclopédie (New York, 1947); and, in French, D. Mornet, *Les origines intellectuelles de la Révolution française, 1715-1787* (Paris, 1933). L. Stephen, *English Thought in the Eighteenth Century,* 2 vols. (New York, printing of 1927), still remains the most comprehensive treatment for England though it is outmoded in several instances; see also B. N. Schilling, *Conservative England and the Case against Voltaire* (New York, 1950); and E. C. Mossner, *The Life of David Hume* (Austin, 1955). G. Natali, *Il Settecento,* 2 vols., 3rd ed. (Milan, 1930), is a treasury of Italian culture and thought; also the brief H. Bédarida and P. Hazard, *L'influence française en Italie au 18e siècle* (Paris, 1935); A. Ferrari, *La preparazione intelletuale del Risorgimento italiano (1748-1789)* (Milan, 1923). The Russian background is suggestively presented in P. Miliukov, *Outlines of Russian Culture,* ed. by M. Karpovich, 3 parts (Philadelphia, 1942); E. Haumant, *La culture française en Russie, 1700-1900,* 2nd rev. and corr. ed. (Paris, 1913); and E. J. Simmons, *English Literature and Culture in Russia, 1553-1840* (Cambridge, 1935). On Germany, in addition to the works of Biedermann and Bruford already cited, W. Dilthey, *Studien zur Geschichte des deutschen Geistes,* vol. III of *Gesammelte Schriften* (Berlin, 1927); G. Steinhausen, *Geschichte der deutschen Kultur,* in the convenient one-volume *Volksausgabe* of 1933, chs. x and xi; in the brief H. Ermatinger, *Deutsche Kultur im Zeitalter der Aufklärung* (Potsdam, 1935); and the challenging H. Brunschwig, *La crise de l'état prussien à la fin du xviiie siècle* (Paris, 1947). L. Reynaud, *Histoire générale de l'influence française en Allemagne,* 2nd ed. (Paris, 1922), chs. v and vi, is interesting but biased. For Spain, the broadly conceived R. Altamira, *Historia de España y de la civilizaciòn española,* 5th ed. (Barcelona, 1935), IV; and the brief P. Mérimée, *L'influence française en Espagne au 18e siècle* (Paris, 1936), must be supplemented by J. Sarrailh, *L'Espagne éclairée de la seconde moitié du xviiie siècle* (Paris, 1954).

Cameralists and Physiocrats. The various shades of political authoritarianism may be traced in the old classic, H. Michel, *L'idée de l'état* (Paris, 1896), pp. 1-104; the scholarly F. Meinecke, *Die Idee der Staatsräson in der neueren Geschichte* (Munich, 1924); and K. Wolzendorff, *Der Polizeigedanke des modernen Staats* (Breslau, 1918), chs. i and ii. The political views of the mercantilists and cameralists are analyzed in P. W. Buck, *The Politics of Mercantilism* (New York, 1942), chs. iii and v; A. Small, *The Cameralists, the Pioneers of German Social Polity* (Chicago, 1909); L. Sommer, *Die Österrechischen Kameralisten in Dogmen geschichtlicher Darstellung,* 2 vols. (Vienna, 1921-1925); R. Aris, *History of Political Thought in Germany from 1789-1815* (New York, 1936); and G. de Ruggiero, *Il pensiero politico meridionale dei secoli 18 e 19* (Bari, 1922). For the French Encyclopedists and physiocrats, there are W. H. Wickwar, *Baron d'Holbach, A Prelude to the French Revolution* (London, 1935); I. L. Horowitz, *Claude Helvétius, Philosopher of Democracy and Enlightenment* (New York, 1954); the brief H. Higgs, *Six Lectures on the Physiocrats* (London, 1897); and the summary G. Weulersse, *Les Physiocrates* (Paris, 1931). The latter's two-volume *Le mouvement physiocratique en*

France de 1765 à 1770 (Paris, 1910), and *La physiocratie sous les ministères de Turgot et de Necker* (Paris, 1950), are the definitive studies. See also Lotte Silberstein, *Lemercier de la Rivière und seine politischen Ideen* (Berlin, 1928). The most important writings of the physiocrats are in E. Daire, ed., *Collection des principaux économistes du XVIIIe siècle* (Paris, 1846).

Political Liberalism. Of the general works, C. E. Vaughan, *Studies in the History of Political Theory before and after Rousseau*, 2 vols. (London, 1925); and F. J. C. Hearnshaw, ed., *Social and Political Ideas of Some Great French Thinkers of the Age of Reason* (London, 1930); H. J. Laski, *The Rise of Liberalism. The Philosophy of a Business Civilization* (New York, 1936), ch. iii; see also G. de Ruggiero, *History of European Liberalism* (London, 1927), Pt. I. A. Cobban, *Edmund Burke and the Revolt against the Eighteenth Century* (New York, 1929), and A. M. Osborne, *Rousseau and Burke: A Study of the Idea of Liberty in Eighteenth-Century Political Thought* (New York, 1940), are variant interpretations, both interesting. G. Bonno, *La constitution britannique devant l'opinion française de Montesquieu à Bonaparte* (Paris, 1932), traces the evolution of French Anglophilism, while F. Acomb, *Anglophobia in France, 1763-1789* (Durham, N. C., 1950), treats the contrary phenomenon. H. N. Brailsford, *Voltaire* (New York, 1935), stresses the social conservatism of Voltaire, while C. Rowe, *Voltaire and the State* (New York, 1955), stresses his political liberalism. For Montesquieu, see also P. Barrière, *Un grand provincial . . . Montesquieu* (Paris, 1946). On Diderot, there are L. G. Crocker, *The Embattled Philosopher. Biography of Denis Diderot* (Lansing, 1955); and A. M. Wilson, *Diderot: The Testing Years* (New York, 1957). For Rousseau, A. Cobban's *Rousseau and the Modern State* (London, 1934), is a sympathetic analysis; *The Citizen of Geneva: Selections from the Letters of Jean-Jacques Rousseau,* ed. by C. W. Hendel (New York, 1937), utilizes the twenty-volume *Correspondance générale de J. J. Rousseau,* ed. by T. Dufour (Paris, 1924-1934); E. Cassirer, *The Question of Jean-Jacques Rousseau,* translated with notes and an introduction by P. Gay (New York, 1954); A. Derathé, *Jean-Jacques Rousseau et la science politique de son temps* (Paris, 1950); and F. C. Green's vivid biography, *Jean-Jacques Rousseau . . .* (London, 1955). J. S. Schapiro, *Condorcet and the Rise of Liberalism* (New York, 1934), is the standard work. A Lantone, *Histoire de la franc-maçonnerie française; la franc-maçonnerie dans l'état* (Paris, 1935), supersedes the earlier studies of Freemasonry by G. Martin and G. Huart. The negative German liberalism is brought out in R. E. Ergang, *Herder and the Foundations of German Nationalism* (New York, 1931), and P. Klassen, *Justus Möser* (Frankfurt, 1936). For Italian liberalism, the works of G. Natali and A. Ferrari already cited. For Poland, C. Dany, *Les idées politiques et l'esprit public en Pologne à la fin du XVIIIe siècle* (Paris, 1901); and for Germany, F. Valjavec, *Die Entstehung der politischen Strömungen in Deutschland, 1770-1815* (Munich, 1951); and M. Boucher, *Le sentiment national en Allemagne* (Paris, 1947).

Humanitarianism and Philanthropy. H. Girsberger, *Der utopische Sozialismus des 18. Jahrhunderts in Frankreich* (Zürich, 1924), supplements and corrects but does not entirely replace A. Lichtenberger, *Le socialisme français au 18e siècle* (Paris, 1895); G. Chinard, *L'Amérique et le rêve exotique dans la littérature au XVIIe et au XVIIIe siècles* (Paris, 1913); B. Faÿ, *The Revolutionary Spirit in France and America* (New York, 1927), ch. i; M. Kraus, "America and the Utopian Ideal in the Eighteenth Century," in *Mississippi Valley Historical Review,* XXII (1936), 487-504. The carefully documented E. V. Souleyman, *The Vision of World Peace in Seventeenth and Eighteenth Century France* (New York, 1941), chs. vi-ix, should be complemented by C. L. Lange, *Histoire de la doctrine pacifique et de son influence sur le développement du droit international,* forming pp. 176-422 of Académie de Droit International, *Recueil des Cours,* XIII (Brussels, 1926); also A. Vagts' interesting *History of Militarism* (New York, 1937), and the challenging J. U. Nef, *War and Human Progress* (Cambridge, Mass., 1950). For anti-slavery agitation E. D. Seeber, *Anti-Slavery Opinion in France during the Second Half of the Eighteenth Century* (Baltimore, 1937); F. J. Klingberg, *The Anti-Slavery Movement in England* (New Haven, 1926); and R. Coupland, *The British Anti-Slavery Movement* (London, 1933). B. Rodgers' interesting *Cloak of Charity; Studies in 18th Century Philanthropy* (London, 1949), is confined to England.

R. R. Palmer, *Catholics and Unbelievers in Eighteenth Century France* (Princeton, 1939), is an admirable monograph. J. Küntziger, *Fébronius et le fébronianisme* (Brussels, 1889), and L. von Pastor, *Geschichte der Päpste* (Freiburg, 1931-1932), vol. XVI, Pts. I and II, are solid and exhaustive studies which together give both sides of the attack on the papal curia and the Jesuits. The two most suggestive studies of British and German evangelism are K. S. Pinson, *Pietism as a Factor in the Rise of German Nationalism* (New York, 1934), and W. J. Warner, *The Wesleyan Movement in the Industrial Revolution* (New York, 1930), the former of which shows the relationship to emotional cosmopolitanism and the latter, to social and political conservatism. S. W. Baron, *A Social and Religious*

History of the Jews, 3 vols. (New York, 1937), II, is a comprehensive and scholarly account of the movement to emancipate the Jews. On educational theory, W. Boyd, *The History of Western Education,* 3rd ed. (London, 1932), ch. x, is a valuable compendium. For reforms of criminal law and procedure, W. Seagle, *The Quest for Law* (New York, 1941), chs. xiv-xviii, is a work of ripe scholarship and literary discrimination; and M. T. Maestro, *Voltaire and Beccaria as Reformers of Criminal Law* (New York, 1942). Robert Anchel, *Crimes et châtiments au 18e siècle* (Paris, 1933), is a work of "vulgarization" in the best French tradition. The diffuse L. Lallemand, *Histoire de la charité,* 4. vols. (Paris, 1902-1912), IV, Pts. I and II, and Sir Henry C. Burdett, *Hospitals and Asylums of the World,* 4 vols. (London, 1891-1893), I and III, both contain basic information not readily available elsewhere.

Literature and the Arts. F. C. Green, *Minuet. A Critical Survey of French and English Literary Ideas in the Eighteenth Century* (London, 1935), replaces older studies. On English literature the old-fashioned chapters of the *Cambridge History of English Literature,* X and XI (New York, 1917), give substantial information, as do the more recent volumes of Oliver Elton, *A Survey of English Literature, 1780-1880,* 4 vols. (London, 1920), I. Time has only slightly withered the effortless urbanity of Leslie Stephen, *English Literature and Society in the Eighteenth Century* (London, 1903); while Austin Dobson's *Eighteenth Century Vignettes,* 3 vols. (London, 1894), remains as charming and unessential as ever. For the novelists, there are B. W. Downs, *Richardson* (London, 1928); the two monumental studies by W. L. Cross, *The History of Henry Fielding,* 3 vols. (New Haven, 1918), and his *The Life and Times of Lawrence Sterne,* 2 vols., new ed. (New Haven, 1925); and the learned and lively H. W. Thompson, *A Scottish Man of Feeling, Henry Mackenzie* (New York, 1931), which seeks to extricate Mackenzie from his limbo of bathos. G. Lanson, *Histoire de la littérature française,* 12th ed. (Paris, 1912), Pt. V, while full of gentility, is the most valuable comparatively brief survey; C. A. Sainte-Beuve, *Portraits of the Eighteenth Century, Historic and Literary,* 2 vols., tr. from the *Causeries* (New York, 1905), is often penetrating and always charming; *Correspondance littéraire . . . ,* ed. by M. Tourneux, 16 vols. (Paris, 1877-1882), is a virtually inexhaustible mine of literary chit-chat, much of which is very revealing. For the novelist, P. Trahard, *Les maîtres de la sensibilité française au XVIIIe siècle,* 4 vols. (Paris, 1931-1936), I; and the sprightly and scholarly F. C. Green, *French Novelists: Manners and Ideas from the Renaissance to the Revolution* (New York, 1929).

A. Koester, *Die deutsche Literatur der Aufklärungzeit* (Heidelberg, 1925), especially from ch. iii, is a concise account, more serviceable than K. Francke, *History of German Literature as Determined by Social Forces,* 4th rev. ed. (New York, 1907), chs. vii and viii. Lessing's biographer is E. Schmidt, *Lessing, Geschichte seines Lebens und seiner Schriften,* 2 vols., 4th ed. (Berlin, 1923). For the romantic qualities of Goethe, consult G. Santayana, *Three Philosophical Poets* (London, 1912); and for the Greek influence on him and his contemporaries, E. M. Butler, *The Tyranny of Greece over Germany* (Cambridge, 1935), chs. i-v. C. S. Mirsky, *A History of Russian Literature* (New York, 1927), ch. iii, is less detailed than M. Hofmann, *Histoire de la littérature russe depuis les origines jusqu'à nos jours* (Paris, 1934), Bk. II, which also gives copious excerpts from the authors. For Italy, F. de Sanctis, *History of Italian Literature,* 2 vols. tr. (New York, 1931), II, chs. xix and xx.

P. H. Láng, *Music in Western Civilization* (New York, 1941), chs. xii-xiv; H. Leichtentritt, *Music, History and Ideas* (Cambridge, Mass., 1938), chs. vii and viii, are the most serviceable works on music, Lang's being the most ambitious attempt made to relate musical development to the broader streams of culture. M. Osborn, *Die Kunst des Rococo,* and G. Pauli, *Die Kunst des Klassizismus,* forming vols. XIII and XIV in the *Propyläen-Kunstgeschichte* series, 18 vols. (Berlin, 1925-1933), and A. Michael, ed., *Histoire de l'art,* 8 vols. (Paris, 1905-1928), VII, Pts. I and II, are standard co-operative studies, erudite and sober. T. Hamlin, *Architecture through the Ages* (New York, 1940), chs. xxiii-xxv, is a brief, unostentatiously sound treatment. A Leroy, *Histoire de la peinture française au XVIIIe siècle* (Paris, 1934), chs. vii to end, is more specialized than the more comprehensive R. Schneider, *L'art français, dix-huitième siècle* (Paris, 1926), but less nationalistic in tone and also more cognizant of environmental influences. L. Réau, *Histoire de l'expansion de l'art français . . . ,* 4 vols. (Paris, 1924-1934), is a panoramic view of artistic Europe with emphasis upon French influence. S. Sitwell, *Southern Baroque Art; a Study of Painting, Architecture and Music in Italy and Spain of the Seventeenth and Eighteenth Centuries* (London, 1924), is a delightful literary effort, as is *German Baroque Art* (London, 1927), by the same writer. G. G. Dehio, *Geschichte der deutschen Kunst,* 4 vols., rev. ed., and 4 vols. of plates (Berlin, 1919-1934), III, is academic scholarship at its most presentable; also A. Feulner, *Skulptur und Malerei des 18. Jahrhunderts in Deutschland* (Potsdam, 1929). For England, *Georgian Art (1760-1820),* by R. Fry and others (New York, 1929), is an excellent survey of the arts and crafts. R. H. Wilenski, *English Painting* (London, 1933), chs. v-xi, is more systematic than S. Sitwell's exceedingly interesting and opinionated studies: *Conversation Pieces. A Study of English Domestic Portraits and Their Painters* (New York, 1937), chs. iii-vi, and *Narrative Pictures. A Survey of English Genre and Its Painters* (New York, 1938), ch. iii. There are also W. T. Whitley, *Artists and Their Friends in England, 1700-1799,* 2 vols. (London, 1928), useful on the history and surroundings; the extraordinarily learned and undigested B. S. Allen, *Tides in English Taste, 1619-1800,* 2 vols. (Cambridge, Mass., 1937); and M. Jourdain, *Decoration and Furniture in England during the Later Eighteenth Century, 1760-1820* (London, 1922).

The Enlightened Despots at Work

As this volume and the one preceding it in this series complement each other both chronologically and topically, the author has eliminated titles already listed in the former work which normally should also appear here.

Prussia. The sources are listed and utilized in R. Koser, *Geschichte Friedrichs des Grossen,* 4 vols., 7th ed. (Berlin, 1921-1925), vols. II-IV for this period. A work of great scholarship, it is more sympathetic to Frederick than the following four biographical studies: G. Ritter, *Friedrich der Grosse: Ein Historisches Profil,* rev. ed. (Heidelberg, 1954); G. P. Gooch *Frederick the Great. The Ruler, the Writer, the Man* (New York, 1947); P. Gaxotte, *Frederick the Great,* tr. from the French (New Haven, 1942); and A. Berney, *Friedrich der Grosse. Entwicklungs-Geschichte eines Staatsmannes* (Tübingen, 1934). For a vigorous presentation of the defects of Prussian enlightened absolutism, see the work of Brunschwig, cited p. 330. C. V. Easum, *Prince Henry of Prussia. Brother of Frederick the Great* (Madison, 1942), is written from the sources and also throws much light on Frederick. W. L. Dorn, "The Prussian Bureaucracy in the 18th Century," in *Political Science Quarterly,* XLVI (1931), 402-423; XLVII (1932), 75-94; 259-273, is admirable on the administration. Both R. E. Ergang, *The Potsdam Fuehrer* (New York, 1942), and R. A. Dorwart, *The Administrative Reforms of Frederick William I of Prussia* (Cambridge, Mass., 1953), show how much Frederick II owed to his father. A. Zottman, *Die Wirtschaftspolitik Friedrichs des Grossen* (Leipiz, 1937), is valuable in spite of its nationalist bias; also the older R. Stadelmann, *Preussens Könige in ihrer Tätigkeit für Landeskultur* (Berlin, 1882), II; M. Springer, *Die Coccejische Justizreform* (Berlin, 1914); F. Vollmer, *Die Preussische Volksschulpolitik unter Friedrich dem Grossen* (Berlin, 1918); F. Paulsen, *Geschichte des gelehrten Unterrichts,* 2 vols., 3rd ed., ed. by R. Lehmann (Leipzig, 1919-1921), II.

Austria and the Empire. More extensive bibliographies, including sources, are given in the works listed below of Mitrofanov, I, 3-77; Kerner; Uhlirz; and Valsecchi. Of the manuals, K. and M. Uhlirz, *Handbuch der Geschichte Oesterreichs und seiner nachbarländer Böhmen und Ungarn,* 2 vols. (Graz, 1927-1939), II, remains the most useful. F. Valsecchi, *L'assolutismo illuminato in Austria e in Lombardia,* 2 vols. (Bologna, 1931-1934), I: *I Domini Ereditari,* is admirable. The essays in *B.I.C.H.S.,* IX (1937), 22-38; 68-77; 135-147, are stimulating, as are the general observations in J. Droz, *L'Allemagne et la Révolution française* (Paris, 1939). Among the biographies, there are the older E. Guglia, *Maria Theresia,* 2 vols. (Munich, 1917); H. Kretschmayr, *Maria Theresia* (Gotha, 1925). Of more recent biographies there are C. L. Morris, *Maria Theresa. The Last Conservative* (New York, 1937); the essays of G. P. Gooch, *Maria Theresa and Other Studies* (New York, 1951), which make use of correspondence; S. K. Padover, *The Revolutionary Emperor: Joseph II* (New York, 1934), a scholarly work of great interest; the hostile P. Mitrofanov, *Joseph II, seine politische und kulturelle Tätigkeit,* 2 vols., tr. from the Russian (Vienna, 1932); the searching E. Benedikt, *Joseph II (1741-1790)* (Vienna, 1936), and the popular F. Fejtö, *Un Habsburg révolutionnaire: Joseph II. Portrait d'un despote éclairé* (Paris, 1953). Of the specialized studies, I. Beidtel, *Geschichte der österreichischen Staatsverwaltung, 1749-1816* (Vienna, 1894); K. Pribram, *Geschichte des österreichischen Gewerbe-Politik, 1740-1798* (Leipzig, 1907); A. Beer, "Die österreichische Industriepolitik," in *Archiv für österreichische Geschichte,* LXXXI (1895), 1-135, and his *Die österreichische Handelspolitik unter Maria Theresia und Joseph II.* (Vienna, 1899); K. Grunberg, *Studien zur oesterreichischen Agrargeschichte und Agrarpolitik* (Vienna, 1896); and the careful monograph of E. M. Link, *The Emancipation of the Austrian Peasant (1740-1788)* (New York, 1949). G. Frank, *Das Toleranz-Patent Kaisers Joseph II.* (Vienna, 1881), from the Protestant point of view, and Sister Mary Clare Goodwin, *The Papal Conflict with Josephism* (New York, 1938), from the Catholic; G. Wolf, *Das Unterrichtswesen in Oesterreich unter Joseph II.* (Vienna, 1880). Two different aspects of enlightened despotism in the smaller states of the Empire are elaborated in M. Braubach, *Die vier letzten Kurfürsten von Köln* (Cologne, 1931), which gives a picture of Rhenish culture; and W. Windelband, *Die Verwaltung der Markgrafschaft Baden zur Zeit Karl Friedrichs* (Leipzig, 1916), which analyzes administrative reforms. For more general accounts of the Empire, G. P. Gooch, *Germany and the French Revolution* (London, 1920), ch. i; also Jaurès, Braunschwig, and Droz, already listed.

Russia. The most useful introduction to the sources and the bibliography of works in Russian is in Préclin and Tapié, I, 301-309. Of the most recent large-scale histories, there are V. O. Kluchevsky, *A History of Russia,* 5 vols. (New York, 1911-1931), V, chs. i-xiv; K. Stählin, *Geschichte Russlands von den Anfängen bis zum Gegenwart,* 4 vols. (Berlin, 1923-1935), II; P. Milioukov, Ch. Seignobos, and others, *Histoire de Russie,* 3 vols. (Paris, 1932-1933), II, chs. xi and xii by Kizevetter; and M. T. Florinsky, *Russia, A History and an Interpretation,* 2 vols. (New York, 1953), vol. I. K. Waliszewski, *Le roman d'une impératrice* (Paris, 1903), and *Autour d'un trône* (Paris, 1894), by the same author (also in English translation), are based on wide research and are far stronger on personalities than on institutional changes. E. A. B. Hodgetts, *The Life of Catherine the Great of Russia* (London, 1914), and G. P. Gooch, *Catherine the Great and Other Studies* (New York, 1954), are useful among the modern works, while of the older biographies the German translation of B. Bilbassov, *Geschichte Katharinas II.,* 3 vols. (Berlin, 1891-1893), is the most valuable.

The English text of Catherine's famous "Instruction" is made available in W. F. Reddaway, ed., *Documents of Catherine the Great: The Correspondence with Voltaire and the Instruction of 1767 in the English text of 1768* (New York, 1931). G. Sacke, "Zur Charakteristik der Gesetzgebenden Kommission Katharinas II. von Russland," in *Archiv für Kulturgeschichte,* XXI (1931), 166-191; "Katharinas II. im Kampf um Thron und Selbstherrschaft," *ibid.,* XXIII (1932), 191-216; "Adel und Bürgertum in der Gestezgebenden Kommission Katharinas II. von Russland," in *Jahrbücher für Geschichte Osteuropas,* III (1938), 408-417; "Adel und Bürgertum in der Regierungszeit Katharinas II. von Russland," in *Revue belge de philologie et d'histoire,* XVII (1938), 815-852, are brilliant efforts to link Catherine to the broad European movement of middle-class enterprise. J. Mavor, *Economic History of Russia,* 2 vols., 2nd ed. (New York, 1925), I, is a veritable encyclopedia in which details occasionally obscure the main features; D. Gerhard, *England und der Aufstieg Russlands* (Munich, 1933), is a careful correlation of foreign relations and economic history; G. T. Robinson, *Rural Russia under the Old Regime* (New York, 1932), chs. ii-iv, based entirely on Russian materials, is a masterly presentation. The documents (in Russian) on the Pugachev rebellion are in V. Martinov, ed., *Vostanie Emeliana Pugacheva, Sbornik Dokumentov* (Leningrad, 1925); and R. Portal, "Pugačev: une révolution manquée," in *Etudes d'histoire moderne et contemporaine,* I (1947), is an illuminating study. Religious protest is treated in F. C. Conybeare, *Russian Dissenters* (Cambrige, Mass., 1921), 261-370.

Poland, Sweden, and Denmark. The co-operative *The Cambridge History of Poland, from August II to Pilsudski (1697-1935),* ed. by W. F. Reddaway and others (Cambridge, 1941), chs. iii-vi and ix, mainly by Polish scholars, gives a rounded treatment of Poland in the eighteenth century and replaces every other general history. R. N. Bain, *The Last King of Poland and His Contemporaries* (New York, 1909), outmoded in interpretation but still valuable for details, should be supplemented by J. Fabre, *Stanislas-Auguste Poniatowski et l'Europe des lumières* (Paris, 1952). On constitutional development, see Ladislas Konopczynski, *Le Liberum Veto. Etude sur le développement du principe majoritaire* (Paris, 1930). Jan Rutkowski, *Histoire économique de la Pologne avant les partages* (Paris, 1927), and *Le régime agraire en Pologne au 18e siècle* (Paris, 1928), by the same author, are the only two detailed studies on this subject in a western European language. W. J. Rose, *Stanislas Konarski. Reformer of Education in Eighteenth Century Poland* (London, 1929), is far more a social-cultural history than its title suggests.

The two most serviceable general histories of enlightened despotism in Sweden are C. Hallendorf and A. Schuck, *History of Sweden,* tr. from the Swedish (London, 1929), 318-366, which emphasizes political and foreign affairs more than does R. Svanstrom and C. F. Palmstierna, *A Short History of Sweden* (Oxford, 1934), 189-284. In Swedish, E. Hildebrand and L. Stavenow, eds., *Sveriges Historia till Våra Dagar,* 13 vols. (Stockholm, 1919-1926), IX and X, written by Stavenow, cover the eighteenth century and represent the most recent scholarship. R. N. Bain, *Gustavus III and His Contemporaries, 1746-1792,* 2 vols. (London, 1904), remains indispensable. For Denmark virtually nothing else in English is comparable to the excellent sketch in *Cambridge Modern History* (New York, 1919), VI, ch. xxi, written by W. F. Reddaway. A. Linvald, "Comment le despotisme éclairé s'est présenté dans l'histoire du Danemark," in *B.I.C.H.S.* (1933), V, 714-726, is a brilliant exposé in French by a leading Danish scholar, while in the study of A. Friis, A. Linvald, and others, *Det Danske Folks Historie* (Copenhagen, 1928), VI, Pt. I, he gives his views in some detail. A. Friis ed., *Bernstorffske Papirer,* 3 vols. (Copenhagen, 1904-1913), which is mostly in French, gives an interesting picture of society; A. Friis, *Bernstorfferne og Danmark,* 2 vols. (Copenhagen, 1903 and 1919), of which the first volume has been translated into German, is an informal cultural history. The administrative acts are in H. Hansen, ed., *Kabinetsstyrelsen i Danmark, 1768-1772, Aktstykker og oplysninger,* 3 vols. (Copenhagen, 1916-1923), in Danish. H. Hansen, ed., *Inkvisitions-kommissionen af*

20 Januar, 1772, 4 vols. (Copenhagen, 1927-1936), contains invaluable papers relating to Struensee's ideas on government. In addition to the brief and sympathetic W. F. Reddaway, "Struensee and the Fall of Bernstorff," in *English Historical Review,* XXVII (1912), 274 ff., there are the memoirs of the royal preceptor, *Struensee et la cour de Copenhague, 1760-1772. Mémoires de Reverdil,* ed. by A. Roger (Paris, 1858), distinguished by lucidity and understanding. An informative study in English, H. S. Commager, *Struensee and the Reform Movement in Denmark,* unfortunately is an unpublished doctoral dissertation, University of Chicago, 1928.

Italy, Spain, and Portugal. The conclusions of modern Italian scholarship are conveniently summarized in English in L. Salvatorelli, *A Concise History of Italy,* tr. from the Italian (New York, 1940), ch. xvi; and in Italian, A. M. Ghisalberti, *Gli albori del risorgimento italiano* (Rome, 1931), a brief, popular account. More recent and detailed are the following: the essay by F. Valsecchi, "Despotismo illuminato," in *Questioni di storia del Risorgimento e dell' unità d'Italia,* ed. by E. Rota (Milan, 1951), with bibliography; the two works of Rota, *Le origini del Risorgimento (1700-1800),* 2 vols. (Milan, 1938), and *Questioni di storia moderna* (Milan, 1948), of which he is editor. L. Bulferetti, *L'assolutismo illuminato in Italia (1700-1789)* (Milan, 1944), is a good anthology with critical introductions to the excerpts. For the decline of Venice, in English, G. B. McClellan, *Venice and Bonaparte* (Princeton, 1931), chs. i-viii; and in Italian, M. Petrocchi, *Il tramonto della repubblica di Venezia e l'assolutismo illuminato* (Venice, 1950), and M. Berengo, *La società veneta alla fine del Settecento. Ricerche storiche* (Florence, 1956). For Tuscany, A. Anzilotti, *Movimenti e contrasti per l'unità italiana* (Bari, 1930); while for Lombardy, F. Valsecchi, *L'assolutismo illuminato in Austria e in Lombardia,* 2 vols. (Bologna, 1931-1934), II, *La Lombardia,* is a definitive work. For Naples, B. Croce, *Storia del regno di Napoli* (Bari, 1925); and H. Acton, *The Bourbons of Naples. 1734-1825* (London, 1956).

In addition to Sarrailh and Altamira, already cited under *The Climate of Opinion,* A. Ballesteros y Beretta, *Historia de España,* 6 vols. (Barcelona, 1918-1932), V and VI, with exhaustive bibliographies; G. Desdevises du Dézert, "L'Espagne de l'ancien régime," in *Revue hispanique,* LXIV (1925), 226-656; LXX (1927), 1-556; LXXIII (1928), 1-488; and F. Rousseau, *Règne de Charles III d'Espagne (1759-1788),* 2 vols. (Paris, 1907). Special aspects are treated in Desdevises "Les lettres politico-économiques de Campomanes," in *Revue hispanique,* IV (1897), 240-265; Molina G. Alcázar,

El Conde de Floridablanca (Madrid, 1920); R. Leonard, *Agrarpolitik und Agrarreform in Spanien unter Carl III.* (Munich, 1909). Both Sir George Young, *Portugal, an Historical Study* (Oxford, 1917), ch. v, and T. Legrand, *Histoire du Portugal* (Paris, 1928), 78-117, are good introductions. F. L. Gomes, *Le Marquis de Pombal* (Lisbon, 1869), is less voluminous but more critical than either Conde de Carnota, *Marquis of Pombal,* 2nd ed. (London, 1871), or J. Du Hamel de Breuil, "Un ministre philosophe, Carvalho, Marquis de Pombal," in *Revue historique,* LIX (1895), 1-35, and LX (1896), 272 ff. In English there is the sketchy M. Cheke, *Dictator of Portugal. Life of Marquis of Pombal (1699-1782)* (London, 1938). The most critical study is in Portuguese, J. Lucio d'Azevedo, *O Marquez de Pombal e a sua epoca* (Lisbon, 1909), which utilizes the Pombal collection at Lisbon.

France and Belgium. For France during the Old Regime the volumes of the Lavisse series cited under *Bibliographical Aids* and the relevant chapters in the general works given. Also P. Sagnac, *La formation de la société française moderne* (Paris, 1946), vol. II; G. P. Gooch, *Louis XV, the Monarchy in Decline* (London, 1956); D. Dakin, *Turgot and the Ancien Régime in France* (London, 1939); B. F. Hyslop, *A Guide to the General Cahiers of 1789* (New York, 1936); and M. B. Garrett, *The Estates General of 1789* (New York, 1935). For the reformers, see P. Allengry, *Turgot* (Paris, 1942); E. Chapuisat, *Necker* (Paris, 1938); and P. Jolly, *Calonne, 1734-1802* (Paris, 1950). F. Olivier-Martin, *L'organisation corporative de l'ancien régime* (Paris, 1938); P. Ardascheff, *Les intendants de province sous le règne de Louis XVI,* 2 vols. (Paris, 1909); H. Hintze, *Staatseinheit und Föderalismus im alten Frankreich und in der Revolution* (Stuttgart, 1928); and F. L. Ford, *Robe and Sword: The Regrouping of the French Aristocracy after Louis XIV* (Cambridge, Mass., 1953), all deal with the central administration and the provincial opposition.

H. Sée, *Economic and Social Conditions in France during the Eighteenth Century,* tr. from the French (New York, 1927), and *L'évolution commerciale et industrielle de la France sous l'ancien régime* (Paris, 1925), by the same author, are very useful manuals by a leading French scholar. E. Levasseur, *Histoire des classes ouvrières et de l'industrie en France avant 1789,* 2 vols., 2nd ed. (Paris, 1901), II, must be supplemented by C. Ballot, *L'introduction du machinisme dans l'industrie française* (Paris, 1923), ch. 1. For the urban workers, there is E. Martin Saint-Léon, *Histoire des corporations de métiers,* 3rd rev. ed. (Paris, 1922). For agricultural improvement, M. Bloch, *Les caractères originaux de l'histoire rurale française,* rev. ed. (Paris, 1953); and A. J. Bourde, *The Influence of England on the French Agronomes (1750-1789)* (New York, 1933). The remarkable E. Labrousse, *La crise de l'économie française à la fin de l'Ancien Régime et au début de la Révolution* (Paris, 1943); and G. Lefebvre, "Le mouvement des prix et les origines de la Révolution française," in *Annales historiques de la Révolution française* (1937), 289-329. A stimulating sociological study is E. G. Barber, *The Bourgeoisie in Eighteenth-Century France* (New York, 1955).

M. Marion, *Dictionnaire des institutions de la France au XVIIe et XVIIIe siècles* (Paris, 1923), is a mine of information on all institutional aspects of the Old Regime. The most systematic introduction to the vast literature on religious development is in Préclin and Tapié, *op. cit.,* I, 403-414, for France; and II, 685-705, for Europe in general; the work of R. R. Palmer, already listed. For anti-slavery and anti-colonial opinion, see C. L. Lokke, *France and the Colonial Question, 1763-1801* (New York, 1932). The reforms of education are presented in F. de la Fontainerie, *French Liberalism and Education in the Eighteenth Century* (New York, 1932), and F. Brunot, *Histoire de la langue française des origines à 1900* (Paris, 1926), VII. For social welfare and poor relief see C. Bloch, *L'assistance et l'état en France à la veille de la Révolution* (Paris, 1909); and S. McCloy, *Government Assistance in Eighteenth-Century France* (Durham, N.C., 1946). Penal law and practice is discussed authoritatively by A. Esmein, *A History of Continental Criminal Procedure with Special Reference to France,* tr. from the French (Boston, 1913).

For Belgium, H. Pirenne, *Histoire de Belgique* (Brussels, 1920), V, Bks. III and IV, unrivaled for breadth of scholarship and balanced judgment. S. Tassier, *Les démocrates belges de 1789* (Brussels, 1930), Pt. I, emphasizes the revolutionary background. The researches of H. Schlitter, *Die Regierung Josephs II. in den österreichischen Niederländer* (Vienna, 1900), must be modified by the searching study of Austrian rule by G. de Boom, *Les ministres plénipotentiaires dans les Pays-Bas, principalement Cobenzl* (Brussels, 1932). Also P. Bonenfant, "Le régime autrichien (1716-1792)," 479-512 of *Grande Encyclopédie de la Belgique et du Congo* (Brussels, 1939); *B.I.C.H.S.* IX (1937), 38-48; L. Dechen, *Histoire économique et sociale de la Belgique* (Paris, 1932), 258-339; A. Puttemans, *La censure dans les Pays-Bas* (Brussels, 1935); and P. Bonenfant, *Le problème du pauperisme en Belgique à la fin de l'Ancien Régime* (Brussels, 1934).

England and Holland. The old classics, W. E. H. Lecky, *History of England in the Eighteenth Century,* 7 vols. new imp. (New York, 1921), and *A History of Ireland in the Eighteenth Century,* 5 vols. (London, ed. of 1913), are still valuable. The more recent scholarship is admirably summarized for popular reading in M. Dorothy George, *England in Transition* (London, 1931); and J. H. Plumb, *England in the Eighteenth Century* (London, 1951); and in more scholarly fashion in C. G. Robertson, *England under the Hanoverians,* 14th ed. (London, 1944), ch. iv. G. D. H. Cole and R. Postgate, *The Common People, 1746-1938* (New York, 1938), sections 1 and 2, stress the social aspects and costs of progress. The uneven and brilliant E. Wingfield-Stratford, *The History of British Civilization,* 2 vols. (New York, 1928), I, deals with culture and the arts. L. Kronenberger, *Kings and Desperate Men* (New York, 1942), is a delightfully written, unpretentious study that gives the flavor of the age.

The Structure of Politics at the Accession of George III, 2 vols. (London, 1929), and *England in the Age of the American Revolution* (London, 1930), both by L. B. Namier, are the standard works. K. G. Feiling, *The Second Tory Party, 1714-1832* (New York, 1938), demolishes some Whig historical legends. On the constitutional struggle, see also D. G. Barnes, *George III and William Pitt, 1783-1806* (Stanford, 1939); and E. Eyck, *Pitt versus Fox: Father and Son,* tr. from the German (London, 1950), For local government, there is S. and B. Webb, *English Local Government,* 9 vols. (London, 1906-1929), I-III. T. S. Ashton, *Economic History of England in the 18th Century* (London, 1955), is useful; see also the detailed and balanced account of E. Lipson, *Economic History of England,* 3 vols. (London, 1931), III, ch. iv-v; the compassionate monographs of J. L. and B. Hammond: *The Rise of Modern Industry,* 3rd ed. (London, 1927), chs. i-v; *The Village Labourer, 1763-1832,* 4th ed. (London, 1927), chs. i-iv; *The Skilled Labourer, 1763-1832* (London, 1919); also Lord Erle (R. E. Prothero), *English Farming, Past and Present,* 4th ed. (London, 1927), chs. vii-xiv, the classic work. For humanitarianism in action, the excellent account of religious revivalism in Lecky's *England,* III, ch. viii; reforms of elementary education in M. G. Jones, *The Charity School Movement: A Study of Eighteenth Century Puritanism in Action* (Cambridge, 1938); the serviceable introduction in Sir F. B. Mackinnon, "The Law and the Lawyers," in *Johnson's England,* II, ch. xxv; M. C. Buer, *Health, Wealth, and Population in the Early Days of the Industrial Revolution* (London, 1926); D. Marshall, *The English Poor in the Eighteenth Century* (London, 1936). Also S. and B. Webb, *English Poor Law History: Pt. I. The Old*

Poor Law (London, 1927), and their *English Prisons under Local Government* (London, 1922), in their series, *English Local Government.*

For Holland, P. J. Blok, *History of the People of the Netherlands,* 5 vols. (New York, 1898-1912), V, chs. x-xiv; E. Baasch, *Holländische Wirtschaftsgeschichte* (Jena, 1927), ch. i, indispensable for economic development in general; and H. I. Bloom, *The Economic Activities of the Jews of Amsterdam in the Seventeenth and Eighteenth Centuries* (Williamsport, Pa., 1937), a careful monograph. R. Murris, *La Hollande et les Hollandais au 17e et au 18e siècles vus par les Français* (Paris, 1925), holds the Dutch up to the critical view of their Gallic neighbor. H. de Peyster, *Les troubles de la Hollande à la veille de la Révolution française* (Paris, 1905), is useful for the political ferment.

War and Peace

The handbooks on diplomacy and the standard bibliographical guides give detailed information concerning collections of documents, texts of treaties, instructions to ambassadors and their correspondence, etc., as well as the titles of older studies now largely outmoded in interpretation but still valuable for their factual data. The two volumes of Préclin and Tapié are particularly rich in such data. The rivalry between Great Britain and France is treated briefly in E. Malcom-Smith, *British Diplomacy in the 18th Century, 1700-1789* (London, 1937), chs. vi and vii, and Sir Richard Lodge, *Great Britain and Prussia in the Eighteenth Century* (Oxford, 1923), chs. v and vi; and at greater length in the *Cambridge History of the British Empire,* 8 vols., ed. by J. H. Rose and others (Cambridge, 1939-1940), I, ch. xxiii, and the *Cambridge History of British Foreign Policy,* 3 vols., ed. by Sir A. W. Ward and . . . G. P. Gooch (Cambridge, 1922-1923), I, Introduction and ch. i, all of which rely heavily on English sources. The American aspects of the diplomacy concerning the revolt of the thirteen colonies are treated briefly in the well-informed textbook, T. A. Bailey, *A Diplomatic History of the American People* (New York, 1940), which also corrects the interpretation of E. S. Corwin, *French Policy and the American Alliance of 1778* (Princeton, 1916). The studies of L. Gottschalk, *Lafayette Comes to America, Lafayette Joins the American Army, Lafayette and the Close of the American Revolution,* and *Lafayette between the American and the French Revolution* (Chicago, 1935, 1937, 1942, and 1950, respectively), throw new light on French-American relations. There are also F. Monaghan, *John Jay* (New York, 1935); E. Kite, *Beaumarchais and the War of American Independence,* 2 vols. (New York, 1918); and the suggestive

J. J. Meng, *The Comte de Vergennes: European Phases of His American Diplomacy* (Washington, 1932). The struggle is treated in A. Bourget, *Etudes sur la politique étrangère du duc de Choiseul* (Paris, 1907); L. Blart, *Les rapports de la France et de l'Espagne après le pacte de famille* (Paris, 1915), chs. iii, iv, and vi; V. L. Brown, "Anglo-Spanish Relations in America in the Closing Years of the Colonial Era, 1763-1774," in *Hispanic-American Review*, V (1922), 325-483; and the searching R. Konetzke, *Die Politik des Grafen Aranda* (Berlin, 1929). P. W. Bamford, *Forests and French Sea Power, 1660-1789* (Toronto, 1956), is a pioneering monograph.

On the first partition, the brief account in S. Konalov, *Russo-Polish Relations: an Historical Survey* (London, 1945); fuller treatment in R. H. Lord, *The Second Partition of Poland* (Cambridge, Mass., 1915), Introduction, with its pro-Catherine interpretation; the work of C. V. Easum already cited, chs. xvii-xviii; W. F. Reddaway, "The First Partition," in the *Cambridge History of Poland* already cited. See also J. Rutkowski, "Les bases économiques des partages de l'ancienne Pologne," in *Revue d'histoire moderne* (July, 1932); and the standard biography, G. Küntzel, *Fürst Kaunitz-Rittberg als Staatsmann* (Frankfort, 1923). The progressive decline in French influence in eastern and northern Europe and the ascendancy of Russia are treated in meticulous detail in E. Amburger, *Russland und Schweden, 1762-1772* (Berlin, 1934); and L. Jacobsohn, *Russland und Frankreich in den ersten Regierungsjahren der Kaiserin Catherinas II., 1762-1772* (Berlin, 1929).

For the Prussian-Austrian duel both Easum, *op. cit.*, ch. xxi, and G. B. Volz, "Friedrich der Grosse und der Bayrische Erbfolgkrieg," in *Forschungen zur Brandenburgischen und Preussischen Geschichte,* XLIV (1932), 264-301, treat with freshness the Bavarian succession, which is the theme of the older H. W. Temperley, *Frederick the Great and Kaiser Joseph: an Episode of War and Diplomacy in the Eighteenth Century* (London, 1915), as well as of G. Grosjean, *La politique rhénane de Vergennes* (Paris, 1925). The *Politische Correspondenz Friedrichs des Grossen,* ed. by G. B. Volz (Munich, 1935-1939), XLIV-XLVI, supplement the three older studies of G. Ritter von Arneth, *Joseph II und Katharina von Russland. Ihr Briefwechsel* (Vienna, 1869); the same editor's *Joseph II und Leopold von Toskana. Ihr Briefwechsel von 1781 bis 1790,* 2 vols. (Vienna, 1872); and A. Beer, ed., *Joseph II, Leopold und Kaunitz. Ihr Briefwechsel* (Vienna, 1873), on the Austro-Russian understanding. On Potemkin, there is the brief T. Adamczyk, *Fürst G. A. Potemkin* (Emsdetten, 1936). For the Belgian and Dutch views on the Scheldt controversy there are Pirenne, VI, and Blok,

V. For the Triple Alliance of 1788, P. Bailleu, "Der Ursprung des deutschen Fürstenbundes," *Historische Zeitschrift*, XLI (1878), and "Graf Hertzberg," *ibid.*, XLII (1879), are still valuable, as are the recollections of the two leading British statesmen, G. Smyth, ed., *Memoirs and Correspondence of Sir Robert Murray Keith, 1762-1792*, 2 vols. (London, 1849), and the Third Earl of Malmesbury, ed., *Diaries and Correspondence of James Harris, First Earl of Malmesbury*, 4 vols. (London, 1845).

INDEX

THE RISE OF MODERN EUROPE

Edited by WILLIAM L. LANGER

Harvard University

The above list of titles indicates the scope of this history. The publishers will be glad to answer inquiries as to the publication date of any given volume.